Rabindranath 1
Selected Essa

One of India's most cherished Renaissance figures, **Rabindranath Tagore** (1861-1941) was a poet, short-story writer, novelist, dramatist, essayist, painter and composer. One of the foremost minds of his time, he was also widely-acclaimed as a social, political and religious thinker, an innovator in education and a champion of the 'One World' idea. His most famous work, *Gitanjali*, was awarded the Nobel Prize for literature in 1913 and his works have been instrumental in the shaping of modern Indian literature.

Rabindranath Tagore
Selected Essays

RUPA

Published by
Rupa Publications India Pvt. Ltd. 2004
7/16, Ansari Road, Daryaganj
New Delhi 110002

Sales centres:
Allahabad Bengaluru Chennai
Hyderabad Jaipur Kathmandu
Kolkata Mumbai

ISBN: 978-81-291-0391-8

10 9 8 7 6

Typeset in Classical Garamond by Mindways Design, New Delhi

Printed at Rekha Printers Pvt. Ltd., New Delhi

Contents

CREATIVE UNITY

The Poet's Religion

I

Civility is beauty of behaviour. It requires for its perfection patience, self control, and an environment of leisure. For genuine courtesy is a creation, like pictures, like music. It is a harmonious blending of voice, gesture and movement, words and action, in which generosity of conduct is expressed. It reveals the man himself and has no ulterior purpose.

Our needs are always in a hurry. They rush and hustle, they are rude and unceremonious; they have no surplus of leisure, no patience for anything else but fulfillment of purpose. We frequently see in our country at the present day men utilising empty kerosene cans for carrying water. These cans are emblems of discourtesy; they are curt and abrupt, they have not the least shame for their unmanonerliness, they do not care to be ever so slightly more than useful.

The instruments of our necessity assert that we must have food, shelter, clothes, comforts and convenience. And yet men spend an immense amount of their time and resources in contradicting this assertion, to prove that they are not a mere living catalogue of endless wants; that there is in them an ideal of perfection, a sense of unity, which is a harmony between parts and a harmony with surroundings.

The quality of the infinite is not the magnitude of extension, it is in the *advaitam*, the mystery of Unity. Fact occupy endless time and space; but the truth comprehending them all has no dimension; it is One. Wherever our heart touches the One, in the small or the big, it finds the touch of the infinite.

I was speaking to some one of the joy we have in our personality. I said it was because we were made conscious by it of a spirit of unity within ourselves. He answered that he had no such feeling of joy about himself, but I was sure he exaggerated. In all probability he had been suffering from some break of harmony between his surroundings and the spirit of unity within him, proving all the more strongly its truth. The meaning of health comes home to us with painful force when disease disturbs it; since health expresses the unity of the vital functions and is accordingly joyful. Life's tragedies occur, not to demonstrate their own reality, but to reveal that eternal principle of joy in life, to which they gave a rude shaking. It is the object of this Oneness in us to realize its infinity by perfect union of love with others. All obstacles to this union create misery, giving rise to the baser passions that are expressions of finitude, of that separateness which is negative and *maya*.

The joy of unity within ourselves, seeking expression, becomes creative; whereas our desire for the fulfilment of our needs is constructive. The water vessel, taken as a vessel only raises the question, 'Why does it exist at all?' Through its fitness of construction, it offers the apology for its existence. But where it is a work of beauty it has no question to answer; it has nothing to do, but to be. It reveals in its form a unity to which all that seems various in it is so related that, in a mysterious manner, it strikes sympathetic chords to the music of unity in our own being.

What is the truth of this world? It is not in the masses of substance, not in the number of things, but in their relatedness, which neither can be counted, nor measured, nor abstracted. It is not in the materials which are many, but in the expression which is one. All our knowledge of things is knowing them in their relation to the Universe, in that relation which is truth. A drop of water is not a particular assortment of elements; it is the miracle of a harmonious mutuality, in which the two reveal the One. No amount of analysis can reveal to us this mystery of unity. Matter is an abstraction; we shall never be able to realize what it is, for our world of reality does not acknowledge it. Even the giant forces of the world, centripetal and centrifugal, are kept out of our recognition. They are the day-labourers not admitted into the audience-hall of creation. But light and sound come to us in their gay dresses as troubadours singing serenades before the windows of the senses. What is constantly before us, claiming our attention, is not the kitchen, but the feast; not the anatomy of the world, but its countenance. There is the dancing ring of seasons; the elusive play of lights and shadows, of wind and water; the many coloured wings of erratic life flitting between birth and death. The importance of these does not lie in their existence as mere facts, but in their language of harmony, the mother-tongue of our own soul, through which they are communicated to us.

We grow out of touch with this great truth, we forget to accept its invitation and its hospitality, when in quest of external success our works become unspiritual and unexpressive. This is what Wordsworth complained of when he said:

The world is to much with us; late and soon,
Getting and spending, we lay waste our powers.
Little we see in Nature that is ours.

But it is not because the world has grown too familiar to us; on the contrary, it is because we do not see it in its aspect of unity, because we are driven to distraction by our pursuit of the fragmentary.

Materials as materials are savage; they are solitary; they are ready to hurt one another. They are like our individual impulses seeking the unlimited freedom of willfulness. Left to themselves they are destructive. But directly an ideal of unity raises its banner in their center, it brings these rebellious forces under its away and creation is revealed—the creation which is peace, which is the unity of perfect relationship. Our greed for eating is in itself ugly and selfish, it has no sense of decorum; but when brought under the ideal of social fellowship, it is regulated and made ornamental; it is changed into a daily festivity of life. In human nature sexual passion is fiercely individual and destructive, but dominated by the ideal of love, it has been made to flower into a perfection of beauty, becoming in its best expression symbolical of the spiritual truth in man which is his kinship of love with the Infinite. Thus we find it is the One which expresses itself in creation; and the Many, by giving up opposition, make the revelation of unity perfect.

II

I remember, when I was a child, that a row of coconut trees by our garden wall, with their branches beckoning the rising sun on the horizon, gave me a companionship as living as I was myself. I know it was my imagination which transmuted the world around me into my own world—the imagination which seeks unity, which deals with it. But we have to consider that this companionship was true; that the universe in which I was born had in it an element profoundly akin to my own imaginative mind, one which wakens in all children's natures the Creator, whose pleasure is in interweaving the web of creation with His own patterns of many-coloured stands. It is something akin to us, and therefore harmonious to our imagination. When we find some strings vibrating in unison with others, we know that this sympathy carries in it an eternal reality. The fact that the world stirs our imagination in sympathy tells us that this creative imagination is a common truth both in us and in the heart of existence. Wordsworth says:

I'd rather be
A pagan suckled in a creed outworn;
So might I, standing on this pleasant lea,
Have glimpses that would make me less forlorn;
Have sight of Proteus rising from the sea,
Or hear old Triton blow his wreathed horn.

In this passage the poet says we are less forlorn in a world which we meet with our imagination. That can only be possible if through our imagination is revealed, behind all appearances, the reality which gives the touch of companionship, that is to say, something which has an affinity to us. An immense amount of our activity is engaged in making images, not for serving any useful purpose or formulating rational propositions, but for giving varied responses to the varied touches of this reality. In this image-making the child creates his own world in answer to the world in which he finds himself. The child in us finds glimpses of his eternal playmate from behind the veil of things, as Proteus rising from the sea, or Triton blowing his wreathed horn. And the playmate is the Reality, that makes it possible for the child to find delight in activities which do not inform or bring assistance but merely express. There is an image-making joy in the infinite, which inspires in us our joy in imagining. The rhythm of cosmic notion produces in our mind the emotion which is creative.

A poet has said about his destiny as a dreamer, about the worthlessness of his dreams and yet their permanence:

I hang 'mid men my heedless head,
And my fruit is dreams, as theirs is bread:

> The godly men and the sun-hazed sleeper,
> Time shall reap; but after the reaper
> The world shall glean to me, me the sleeper.

The dreams persists; it is more real than even bread which has substance and use. The painted canvas is durable and substantial; it has for its production and transport to market a whole array of machines and factories. But the picture which no factory can produce is a dream, *maya,* and yet it, not the canvas, has the meaning of ultimate reality.

A poet describes Autumn:

> I saw old Autumn in the misty morn
> Stand shadowless like Silence, listening
> To silence, for no lonely bird would sing
> Into his hollow ear from woods forlorn.

Of April another poet sings:

> April, April,
> Laugh thy girlish laughter;
> Then the moment after
> Weep thy girlish tears!
> April, that mine ears
> Like a lover greetest,
> If I tell thee, sweetest,
> All my hopes and fears.

> April, April,
> Laugh thy golden laughter.
> But the moment after
> Weep thy golden tears!

This Autumn, this April,—are they nothing but phantasy?
Let us suppose that the Man from the Moon comes to the earth and listens to some music in a gramophone. He seeks

for the origin of the delight produced in his mind. The facts before him are a cabinet made of wood and a revolving disc producing sound; but the one thing which is neither seen nor can be explained is the truth of the music, which his personality must immediately acknowledge as a personal message. It is neither in the wood, nor in the disc, nor in the sound of the notes. If the Man from the Moon be a poet, as can reasonably be supposed, he will write about a fairy imprisoned in that box, who sits spinning fabrics of songs expressing her cry for a far-away magic casement opening on the foam of some perilous sea, in a fairyland. It will not be literally, but essentially true. The facts of the gramophone make us aware of the laws of sound, but the music gives us personal companionship. The bare facts about April are alternate sunshine and showers; but the subtle blending of shadows and lights, of murmurs and movements, in April, gives us not mere shocks of sensation, but unity of joy as does music. Therefore when a poet sees the vision of a girl in April, even a downright materialist is in sympathy with him. But we know that the same individual would be menacingly angry if the law of heredity or a geometrical problem were described as a girl or a rose—or even as a cat or a camel. For these intellectual abstractions have no magical touch for our lute-strings of imagination. They are no dreams, as are the harmony of bird-songs, rain-washed leaving glistening in the sun, and pale clouds floating in the blue.

The ultimate truth of our personality is that we are no mere biologists or geometricians; 'we are the dreamers of dreams, we are the music-makers.' This dreaming or music-making is not a function of the lotus-eaters, it is the creative impulse which makes songs not only with words and tunes, lines and colours, but with stones and metals, with ideas and men:

With wonderful deathless ditties
We build up the world's great cities,

And out of a fabulous story
We fashion an empire's glory.

I have been told by a scholar friend of mine that by
constant practice in logic he has weakened his natural instinct
of faith. The reason is, faith is the spectator in us which finds
the meaning of the drama from the unity of the performance;
but logic lures us into the greenroom where there is stage craft
but no drama at all; and then this logic nods its head and
wearily talks about disillusionment. But the greenroom, dealing
with its fragments, looks foolish when questioned, or wears
the sneering smile of Mephistopheles; for its does not have
the secret of unity, which is somewhere else. It is for faith
to answer, 'Unity comes to us from the One, and the One
in ourselves opens the door and receives it with joy.' The
function of poetry and the arts is to remind us that the
greenroom is the grayest of illusions, and the reality is the
drama presented before us, all its paint and tinsel, masks and
pageantry, made one in art. The ropes and wheels perish, the
stage is changed; but the dream which is drama remains true,
for there remains the eternal Dreamer.

III

Poetry and the arts cherish in them the profound faith of man
in the unity of his being with all existence, the final truth of
which is the truth of personality. It is a religion directly
apprehended, and not a system of metaphysics to be analysed
and argued. We know in our personal experience what our
creations are and we instinctively know through it what
creation around us means.

When Keats said in his "Ode to a Grecian Urn":

Thou, silent form dost tease us out of thought,
As doth eternity, ...

he felt the ineffable which is in all forms of
perfection, the mystery of the One, which takes us
beyond all thought into the immediate touch of
Infinite. This is the mystery which is for a poet to
realise and to reveal. It comes out in Keats' poems
with struggling gleams through consciousness of
suffering and despair:

Spite off despondence, of the inhuman dearth
Of noble natures, of the gloomy days,
Of all the unhealthy and o'er-darken'd ways
Made for our searching: yes, in spite of all,
Some shape of beauty moves away the pall
From our dark spirits.

In this there is a suggestion that truth reveals itself in
beauty. For if beauty were mere accident, a rent in the eternal
fabric of things, then it would hurt, would be defeated by the
antagonism of facts. Beauty is no phantasy, it has the everlasting
meaning of reality. The facts that cause despondence and
gloom are mere mist, and when through the mist beauty
breaks out in momentary gleams, we realize that Peace is true
and not conflict, Love is true and not hatred; and Truth is
the One, not the disjointed multitude. We realize that Creation
is the perpetual harmony between the infinite ideal of
perfection and the eternal continuity of its realization; that
so long as there is no absolute separation between the positive
ideal and the material obstacle to its attainment, we need not
be afraid of suffering and loss. This is the poet's religion.

Those who are habituated to the rigid framework of
sectarian creeds will find such a religion as this too indefinite
and elastic. No doubt it is so, but only because its ambition
is not to shackle the Infinite and tame it for domestic use;
but rather to help our consciousness to emancipate itself from
materialism. It is as indefinite as the morning, and yet as

luminous; it calls our thoughts, feelings, and actions into freedom, and feeds them with light. In the poet's religion we find no doctrine or injunction, but rather the attitude of our entire being towards a truth which is ever to be revealed in its own endless creation.

In dogmatic religion all questions are definitely answered, all doubts are finally laid to rest. But the poet's religion is fluid, like the atmosphere round the earth where lights and shadows play hide-and-seek, and the wind like a shepherd boy plays upon its reeds among flocks of clouds. It never undertakes to lead anybody anywhere to any solid conclusion; yet it reveals endless spheres of light, because it has no walls round itself. It acknowledges the facts of evil; it openly admits 'the weariness, the fever and the fret' in the world 'where men sit and hear each other groan'; yet it remembers that in spite of all there is the song of the nightingale, and 'haply the Queen Moon is on her throne,' and there is:

> White hawthorn, and the pastoral eglantine,
> Fast-fading violets covered up in leaves;
> And mid-day's eldest child,
> The coming musk-rose, full of dewy wine,
> The murmurous haunt of flies on summer eves.

But all this has not the definiteness of an answer; it has only the music that teases us out of thought as it fills our being.

Let me read a translation from an Eastern poet to show how this idea comes out in a poem in Bengali:

In the morning I awoke at the flutter of thy boat-sails, Lady of my Voyage, and I left the shore to follow the beckoning waves.

I asked thee, 'Does the dream-harvest ripen in the island beyond the blue?'

The silence of thy smile fell on my question like the silence of sunlight on waves.

The day passed on through storm and through calm,
The perplexed winds changed their course, time after time, and the sea moaned.

I asked thee, 'Does thy sleep-tower stand somewhere beyond the dying embers of the day's funeral pyre?'

No answer came from thee, only thine eyes smiled like the edge of a sunset cloud.

It is night. They figure grows dim in the dark.

Thy wind-blown hair flits on my cheek and thrills my sadness with its scent.

My hands grope to touch the hem of thy robe, and I ask thee—'Is there thy garden of death beyond the stars, Lady of my Voyage, where thy silence blossoms into songs?'

Thy smile shines in the heart of the hush like the star-mist of midnight.

IV

In Shelley we clearly see the growth of his religion through periods of vagueness and doubt, struggle and searching. But he did at length come to a positive utterance of his faith, though he died young. Its final expression is in his 'Hymn to Intellectual Beauty'. By the title of the poem the poet evidently means a beauty that is not merely a passive quality of particular things, but a spirit that manifests itself through the apparent antagonism of the unintellectual life. This hymn rang out of his heart when he came to the end of his pilgrimage and stood face to face with the Divinity, glimpses of which had already filled his soul with restlessness. All his experiences of beauty had ever teased him with the question as to what was its truth. Some-where he sings of a nosegay which he makes of violets, daisies, tender bluebells and—

That tall flower that wets
Like a child, half in tenderness and mirth,

Its mother's face with heaven-collected tears.

He ends by saying:

> And then, elate and gay,
> I hastened to the spot whence I had come,
> That I might there present it!—Oh! To whom?

This question, even though not answered, carries a significance. A creation of beauty suggests a fulfilment, which is the fulfilment of love. We have heard some poets scoff at it in bitterness and despair; but it is like a sick child beating its own mother—it is a sickness of faith, which hurts truth, but proves it by its very pain and anger. And the faith itself is this, that beauty is the self-offering of the One of the other One.

In the first part of his 'Hymn to Intellectual Beauty' Shelley dwells on the inconstancy and evanescence of the manifestation of beauty, which imparts to it an appearance of frailty and unreality:

> Like hues and harmonies of evening,
> Like clouds in starling widely spread,
> Like memory of music fled.

This he says, rouses in our mind the question:

> Why aught should fail and fade that once is
>   shown,
> Why fear and dream and death and birth
> Cast on the daylight of this earth
> Such gloom,—why man has such a scope
> For love and hate, despondency and hope?

The poet's own answer to this question is:

> Man were immortal, and omnipotent,
> Didst thou, unknown and awful as thou art,

Keep with thy glorious train firm state within his
heart.

This very elusiveness of beauty suggests the vision of
immortality and of omnipotence, and stimulates the effort in
man to realize it in some idea of permanence. The highest
reality has actively to be achieved. The gain of truth is not
in the end; it reveals itself through the endless length of
achievement. But what is there to guide us in our voyage of
realization? Men have ever been struggling for direction:

Therefore the names of Demon, Ghost and
    Heaven
Remain the records of their vain endeavour,
Frail spells,—whose uttered charm might not avail
    to sever,
From all we hear and all we see,
Doubt, chance and mutability.

The prevalent rites and practices of piety, according to this
poet, are like magic spells—they only prove men's desperate
endeavour and not their success. He knows that the end we
seek has its own direct calls to us, its own light to guide us
to itself. And truth's call is the call of beauty. Of this he says:

The light alone,—like mist o'er mountain driven,
Or music by the night wind sent,
Thro' strings of some still instrument,
Or moonlight on a midnight stream
Gives grace and truth to life's unquiet dream.

About this revelation of truth which calls us on, and yet
which is everywhere, a village singer of Bengal sings:

My master's flute sounds in everything,
    drawing me out of my house of everywhere.
While I listen to it I know that every step I take

is in my master's house.
For he is the sea, he is the river that leads to the
   sea,
and he is the landing place.

Religion, in Shelley, grew with his life; it was not given
to him in fixed and ready-made doctrines; he rebelled against
them. He had the creative mind which could only approach
Truth through its joy in creative effort. For true creation is
realization of truth through the translation of it into our own
symbols.

V

For man, the best opportunity for such a realization has been
in men's Society. It is a collective creation of his, through
which his social being tries to find itself in its truth and beauty.
Had that Society merely manifested its usefulness, it would
be inarticulate like a dark star. But, unless it degenerates, it
ever suggests in its concerted movements a living truth as its
soul, which has personality. In this large life of social
communion man feels the mystery of Unity, as he does in
music. From the sense of that Unity, men came to the sense
of their God. And therefore every religion began with its
tribal God.

   The one question before all others that has to be answered
by our civilizations is not what they have and in what quantity,
but what they express and how. In a society, the production
and circulation of materials, the amassing and spending of
money, may go on, as in the interminable prolonging of a
straight line, if its people forget to follow some spiritual
design of life which curbs them and transforms them into an
organic whole. For growth is not that enlargement which is
merely adding to the dimensions of incompleteness. Growth
is the movement of a whole towards a yet fuller wholeness.

Living things start with this wholeness from the beginning of their career. A child has its own perfection as a child; it would be ugly if it appeared as an unfinished man. Life is a continual process of synthesis, and not of additions. Our activities of production and enjoyment of wealth attain that spirit of wholeness when they are blended with a creative ideal. Otherwise they have the insane aspect of the eternally unfinished; they become like locomotive engines which have railway lines but no stations; which rush on towards a collision of uncontrolled forces or to a sudden breakdown of the overstrained machinery.

Through creation man expresses his truth; through that expression he gains back his truth in its fullness. Human society is for the best expression of man, and that expression, according to its perfection, leads him to the full realization of the divine in humanity. When that expression is obscure, then his faith in the Infinite that is within him becomes weak; then his aspiration cannot go beyond the idea of success. His faith in the Infinite is creative; his desire for success is constructive; one is his home, and the other is his office. With the overwhelming growth of necessity, civilization becomes a gigantic office to which the home is a mere appendix. The predominance of the pursuit of success gives to society the character of what we call *Shudra* in India. In fighting a battle, the *Kshatriya,* the noble knight,, followed his honour for his ideal, which was greater than victory itself; but the mercenary *Shudra* has success for his object. The name *Shudra* symbolizes a man who has no margin round him beyond his bare utility. The word denotes a classification which includes all naked machines that have lost their completeness of humanity, be their work manual or intellectual. They are like walking stomachs of brains, and we feel, in pity, urged to call on God and cry, 'Cover them up for mercys' sake with some veil of beauty and life!'

When Shelley in his view of the world realized the Spirit of Beauty, which is the vision of the Infinite, he thus uttered his faith:

> Never joy illumed my brow
> Unlinked with hope that thou wouldst free
> This world from its dark slavery;
> That thou,—O awful Loveliness,—
> Wouldst give whate'er these words cannot express.

This was his faith in the Infinite. It led his aspiration towards the region of freedom and perfection which was beyond the immediate and above the successful. This faith in God, this faith in the reality of the ideal of perfection, has built up all that is great in the human world. To keep indefinitely walking on, along a zigzag course of change, is negative and barren. A mere procession of notes does not make music; it is only when we have in the heart of the march of sounds some musical idea that it creates song. Our faith in the infinite reality of Perfection is that musical idea, and there is that one great creative force in our civilization. When it wakens not, then our faith in money, in material power, takes its place; it fights and destroys, and in brilliant fireworks of star-mimicry suddenly exhausts itself and dies in ashes and smoke.

VI

Men of great faith have always called us to wake up to great expectations, and the prudent have always laughed at them and said that these did not belong to reality. But the poet in man knows that reality is a creation, and human reality has to be called forth from its obscure depth by man's faith which is creative. There was a day when the human reality was the brutal reality. That was the only capital we had with which to begin our career. But age after age there has come to us the call of faith, which said against all the evidence of fact:

'You are more than you appear to be, more than your circumstances seem to warrant. You are to attain the impossible, you are immortal.' The unbelievers had laughed and tried to kill the faith. But faith grew stronger with the strength of martyrdom and at her bidding higher realities have been created over the strata of the lower. Has not a new age come to-day, borne by thunder-clouds, ushered in by a universal agony of suffering? Are we not waiting to-day for a great call of faith, which will say to us: 'Come out of your present limitations. You are to attain the impossible, you are immortal'? The nations who are not prepared to accept it, who have all their trust in their present machines of system, and have no thought or space to spare to welcome the sudden guest who comes as the messenger of emancipation, are bound to court defeat whatever may be their present wealth and power.

This great world, where it is a creation, an expression of the infinite—where its morning sings of joy to the newly awakened life, and its evening stars sing to the traveler, weary and worn, of the triumph of life in a new birth across death,— has its call for us. The call has ever roused the creator in man, and urged him to reveal the truth, to reveal the Infinite in himself. It is ever claiming from us, in our own creations, co-operation with God, reminding us of our divine nature, which finds itself in freedom of spirit. Our society exists to remind us, through its various voices, that the ultimate truth in man is not in his intellect or his possessions; it is in his illumination of mind, in his extension of sympathy across all barriers of caste and colour; in his recognition of the world, not merely as a storehouse of power, but as a habitation of man's spirit, with its eternal music of beauty and its inner light of the divine presence.

The Creative Ideal

In an old Sanskrit book there is a verse which describes the essential elements of a picture. The first in order is *Viúpa-bhédáh*—'separateness of forms.' Forms are many, forms are different, each of them having its limits. But if this were absolute, if all forms remained obstinately separate, then there would be a fearful loneliness of multitude. But the varied forms, in their very separateness, must carry something which indicates the paradox of their ultimate unity, otherwise there would be no creation.

So in the same verse, after the enumeration of separateness comes that of *Pramanani*—proportions. Proportions indicate relationship, the principle of mutual accommodation. A leg dismembered from the body has the fullest licence to make a caricature of itself. But, as a member of the body, it has its responsibility to the living unity which rules the body; it must behave properly, it must keep its proportion. If, by some monstrous chance of physiological profiteering, it could outgrow by yards its fellow-stalker, then we know what a picture it would offer to the spectator and what embarrassment to the body itself. Any attempt to overcome the law of proportion altogether and to assert absolute separateness is rebellion; it means either running the gauntlet of the rest, or remaining segregated.

The same Sanskrit word *Pramanani*, which in a book of aesthetics means proportions, in a book of logic means the proofs by which the truth of a proposition is ascertained. All proofs of truth are credentials of relationship. Individual facts have to produce such passports to show that they are not expatriated, that they are not a break in the unity of the whole. The logical relationship present in an intellectual proposition, and the aesthetic relationship indicated in the proportions of a work of art, both agree in one thing. They affirm that truth consists, not in facts, but in harmony of facts. Of this fundamental note of reality it is that the poet has said, 'beauty is truth, truth beauty.'

Proportions, which prove relativity, form the outward language of creative ideals. A crowd of men is desultory, but in a march of soldiers every man keeps his proportion of time and space and relative movement, which makes him one with the whole vast army. But this is not all. The creation of an army has, for its inner principle, one single ideas of the General. According to the nature of that ruling idea, a production is either a work of art or a mere construction. All the materials and regulations of a joint-stock company have the unity of an inner motive. But the expression of this unity itself is not the end; it ever indicates an ulterior purpose. On the other hands, the revelation of a work of art is a fulfillment in itself.

The consciousness of personality, which is the consciousness of unity in ourselves, becomes prominently distinct when coloured by joy or sorrow, or some other emotion. It is like the sky, which is visible because it is blue, and which takes different aspect with the change of colours. In the creation of art, therefore, the energy of an emotional ideal is necessary; as its unity is not like that of a crystal, passive and inert, but actively expressive. Take, for example, the following verse:

Oh, fly not Pleasure, pleasant-hearted Pleasure,
Fold me thy wings, I prithee, yet and stay.

>For my heart no measure
>Knows, nor other treasure
>To buy a garland for my love to-day.
>
>And thou too, Sorrow, tender-hearted Sorrow,
>Thou grey-eyed mourner, fly not yet away.
>For I fain would borrow
>Thy sad weeds to-morrow,
>To make a mourning for love's yesterday.

The words in this quotation, merely showing the metre, would have no appeal to us; with all its perfection and its proportion, rhyme and cadence, it would only be a construction. But when it is the outer body of an inner idea it assumes a personality. The idea flows through the rhythm, permeates the words and throbs in their rise and fall. On the other hand, the mere idea of the above-quoted poem, stated in unrhythmic prose, would represent only a fact, inertly static, which would not bear repetition. But the emotional idea, incarnated in a rhythmic form, acquires the dynamic quality needed for those things which take part in the world's eternal pageantry.

Take the following doggerel:

Thirty days hath September,
April, June, and November.

The metre is there, and it simulates the movement of life. But it finds no synchronous response in the metre of our heart-beats; it has not in its centre the living idea which creates for itself an indivisible unity. It is like a bag which is convenient, and not like a body which is inevitable.

This truth, implicit in our own works of art, gives us the clue to the mystey of creation. We find that the endless rhythms of the world are not merely constructive; they strike our own heart-strings and produce music.

Therefore it is we feel that this world is a creation; that in its centre there is a living idea which reveals itself in an eternal symphony, played on innumerable instruments, all keeping perfect time. We know that this great world-verse, that runs from sky to sky, is not made for the mere enumeration of facts—it is not "Thirty days hath September"—it has its direct revelation in our delight. That delight gives us the key to the truth of existence; it is personality acting upon personalities through incessant manifestations. The solicitor does not sing to his client, but the bridegroom sings to his bride. And when our soul is stirred by the song, we know it claims no fees from us; but it brings the tribute of love and a call from the bridegroom.

It may be said that in pictorial and other arts there are some designs that are purely decorative and apparently have no living and inner ideal to express. But this cannot be true. These decorations carry the emotional motive of the artist, which says: 'I find joy in my creation; it is good.' All the language of joy is beauty. It is necessary to note, however, that joy is not pleasure, and beauty not mere prettiness. Joy is the outcome of detachment from self and lives in freedom of spirit. Beauty is that profound expression of reality which satisfies our hearts without any other allurements but its own ultimate value. When in some pure moments of ecstasy we realize this in the world around us, we see the world, not as merely existing, but as decorated in its form, sounds, colours and lines; we feel in our hearts that there is One who through all things proclaims: 'I have joy in my creation.'

That is why the Sanskrit verse has given us for the essential elements of a picture, not only the manifoldness of forms and the unity of their proportions, but also *bhāvah*, the emotional idea.

It is needless to say that upon a mere expression of emotion—even the best expression of it—no criterion of art can rest. The following poem is described by the poet as 'An earnest Suit to his unkind Mistress':

> And wilt thou leave me thus?
> Say nay, say nay, for shame!
> To save thee from the blame
> Of all my grief and grame.
> And wilt thou leave me thus?
>   Say nay! Say nay!

I am sure the poet would not be offended if I expressed my doubts about the earnestness of his appeal, or the truth of his avowed necessity. He is responsible for the lyric and not for the sentiment, which is mere material. The fire assumes different colours according to the fuel used; but we do not discuss the fuel, only the flames. A lyric is indefinably more than the sentiment expressed in it, as a rose is more than its substance. Let us take a poem in which the earnestness of sentiment is truer and deeper than the one I have quoted above:

> The sun,
> Closing his benediction,
> Sinks, and the darkening air
> Thrills with the sense of the triumphing night,—
> Night with her train of stars
> And her great gift of sleep.
> So be my passing!
> My task accomplished and the long day done,
> My wages taken, and in my heart
> Some late lark singing,
> Let me be gathered to the quiet West,
> The sundown splendid and serene,
> Death.

The sentiment expressed in this poem is a subject for a psychologist. But for a poem the subject is completely merged in its poetry, like carbon in a living plant which the lover of plants ignores, leaving it for a charcoal-burner to seek.

This is why, when some storm of feeling sweeps across the country, art is under a disadvantage. In such an atmosphere the boisterous passion breaks through the cordon of harmony and thrusts itself forward as the subject, which with its bulk and pressure dethrones the unity of creation. For a similar reason most of the hymns used in churches suffer from lack of poetry. For in them the deliberate subject, assuming the first importance, benumbs or kills the poem. Most patriotic poems have the same deficiency. They are like hill streams born of sudden showers, which are more proud of their rocky beds than of their water currents; in them the athletic and arrogant subject takes it for granted that the poem is there to give it occasion to display its powers. The subject is the material wealth for the sake of which poetry should never be tempted to barter her soul, even though the temptation should come in the name and shape of public good or some usefulness. Between the artist and his art must be that perfect detachment which is the pure medium of love. He must never make use of this love except for its own perfect expression.

In everyday life our personality moves in a narrow circle of immediate self-interest. And therefore our feelings and events, within that short range, become prominent subjects for ourselves. In their vehement self-assertion they ignore their unity with the All. They rise up like obstructions and obscure their own background. But art gives our personality the disinterested freedom of the eternal, there to find it in its true perspective. To see our own home in flames is not to see fire in its verity. But the fire in the stars is the fire in the heart of the Infinite; there, it is the script of creation.

Matthew Arnold, in his poem addressed to a nightingale, sings:

Hark! Ah, the nightingale—
The tawny-throated!
Hark, from that moonlit cedar what a burst!
What triumph! hark!—what pain!

But pain, when met within the boundaries of limited reality, repels and hurts; it is discordant with the narrow scope of life. But the pain of some great martyrdom has the detachment of eternity. It appears in all its majesty, harmonious in the context of everlasting life; like the thunder-flash in the stormy sky, not on the laboratory wire. Pain on that scale has its harmony in great love; for by hurting love it reveals the infinity of love in all its truth and beauty. On the other hand, the pain involved in business insolvency is discordant; it kills and consumes till nothing remains but ashes.

The poet sings again:

How thick the bursts come crowding through the
    leaves!
Eternal Passion!
Eternal Pain!

And the truth of pain in eternity has been sung by those Vedic poets who had said, 'From joy has come forth all creation.' They say:

Sa tapas tapatvá sarvam asrajata yadidam kincha.
(God from the heat of his pain created all that there is.)

The sacrifice, which is in the heart of creation, is both joy and pain at the same moment. Of this sings a village mystic in Bengal:

My eyes drown in the darkness of joy,
My heart, like a lotus, closes its petals in the
rapture of the dark night.

That song speaks of a joy which is deep like the blue sea, endless like the blue sky; which has the magnificence of the night, and in its limitless darkness enfolds the radiant worlds in the awfulness of peace; it is the unfathomed joy in which all sufferings are made one.

A poet of mediaeval India tells us about his source of inspiration in a poem containing a question and an answer:

Where were your songs, my bird, when you spent
    your nights in the nest?
Was not all your pleasure stored therein?
What makes you lose your heart to the sky, the
    sky that is limitless?

The bird answers:

I have my pleasure while I rested within bounds.
    When I soared into the limitless, I found my
    songs!

To detach the individual idea from its confinement of everyday facts and to give its soaring wings the freedom of the universal: this is the function of poetry. The ambition of Macbeth, the jealousy of Othello, would be at best sensational in police court proceedings; but in Shakespeare's dramas they are carried among the flaming constellations where creation throbs with Eternal passion, Eternal Pain.

The Religion of the Forest

I

We stand before this great world. The truth of our life depends upon our attitude of mind towards it—an attitude which is formed by our habit of dealing with it according to the special circumstance of our surroundings and our temperaments. It guides our attempts to establish relations with the universe either by conquest or by union, either through the cultivation of power or through that of sympathy. And thus, in our realization of the truth of existence, we put our emphasis either upon the principle of dualism or upon the principle of unity.

The Indian sages have held in the Upanishads that the emancipation of our soul lies in its realizing the ultimate truth of unity. They said:

> *Ishāvāsyam idam sarvam yat kinch jagatyām jagat.*
> *Yéna tyakténa bhunjithā mā gradha kasyasvit dhanam.*

(Know all that moves in this moving world as enveloped by God; and find enjoyment through renunciation, not through greed of possession.)

The meaning of this is, that, when we know the multiplicity of things as the final truth, we try to augment ourselves by the external possession of them; but, when we know the Infinite Soul as the final truth, then through our union with it we realize the joy of our soul. Therefore it has been said of those who have attained their fulfillment,—'*sarvam evá vishanti*' (they enter into all things). Their perfect relation with this world is the relation of union.

This ideal of perfection preached by the forest-dwellers of ancient India runs through the heart of our classical literature and still dominates our mind. The legends related in our epics cluster under the forest shade bearing all through their narrative the message of the forest-dwellers. Our two greatest classical dramas find their background in scenes of the forest hermitage, which are permeated by the association of these sages.

The history of the Northmen of Europe is resonant with the music of the sea. That sea is not merely topographical in its significance, but represents certain ideals of life which still guide the history and inspire the creations of that race. In the sea, nature presented herself to those men in her aspect of a danger, a barrier which seemed to be at constant war with the land and its children. The sea was the challenge of untamed nature to the indomitable human soul. And man did not flinch; he fought and won, and the spirit of fight continued in him. This fight he still maintains; it is the fight against disease and poverty, tyranny of matter and of man.

This refers to a people who live by the sea, and ride on it as on a wild, champing horse, catching it by its mane and making it render service from shore to shore. They find delight in turning by force the antagonism of circumstances into obedience. Truth appears to them in her aspect of dualism, the perpetual conflict of good and evil, which has no reconciliation, which can only end in victory or defeat.

But in the level tracts of Northern India men found no barrier between their lives and the grand life that permeates the universe. The forest entered into a close living relationship with their work and leisure, with their daily necessities and contemplations. They could not think of other surroundings as separate or inimical. So the view of the truth, which these men found, did not make manifest the difference, but rather the unity of all things. They uttered their in these words: *Yadidam kincha sarvam prâna éjati nihsratam* (All that is vibrates with life, having come out from life). When we know this world as alien to us, then its mechanical aspect takes prominence in our mind; and then we set up our machines and our methods to deal with it and make as much profit as our knowledge of its mechanism allows us to do. This view of things does not play us false, for the machine has its place in this world. And not only this material universe, but human beings also, may be used as machines and made to yield powerful results. This aspect of truth cannot be ignored; it has to be known and mastered. Europe has done so and has reaped a rich harvest.

The view of this world which India has taken is summed up in one compound Sanskrit word, *Sacchidānanda*. The meaning is that Reality, which is essentially one, has three phases. The first is *sat;* it is the simple fact that things are, the fact which relates us to all things through the relationship of common existence. The second is *chit;* it is the fact that we know, which relates us to all things through the relationship of knowledge. The third is *ānanda:* it is the fact that we enjoy, which unites us with all things through the relationship of love.

According to the true Indian view, our consciousness of the world, merely as the sum total of things that exist, and as governed by laws, is imperfect. But it is perfect when our consciousness realises all things as spiritually one with it, and therefore capable of giving us joy. For us the highest purpose of this world is not merely living in it, knowing it and making use of it, but realising our own selves in it through expansion of sympathy; not alienating ourselves from it and dominating it, but comprehending and uniting it with ourselves in perfect union.

II

When Vikramaditya became king, Ujjayini a great capital, and Kâlidâsa its poet, the age of India's forest retreats had passed. Then we had taken our stand in the midst of the great concourse of humanity. The Chinese and the Hun, the Scythian and the Persian, the Greek and the Roman, had crowded round us. But, even in that age of pomp and prosperity, the love and reverence with which its poet sang about the hermitage shows what was the dominant ideal that occupied the mind of India; what was the one current of memory that continually flowed through her life.

In Kâlidâsa's drama, *Shakuntalā*, the hermitage, which dominates the play, overshadowing the king's palace, has the same idea running through it—the recognition of the kinship of man with conscious and unconscious creation alike.

A poet of a later age, while describing a hermitage in his *Kādambari*, tells us of the posture of salutation in the flowering lianas as they bow to the wind; of the sacrifice offered by the trees scattering their blossoms; of the grove resounding with the lessons chanted by the neophytes, and the verses repeated by the parrots, learnt by constantly hearing them; of the wild-fowl enjoying *vaishva-deva-bali-pinda* (the food offered to the divinity which is in all creatures); of the ducks coming up from the lake for their portion of the grass seed spread in the cottage yards to dry; and of the deer caressing with their tongues the young hermit boys. It is again the same story. The hermitage shines out, in all our ancient literature, as the place where the chasm between man and the rest of creation has been bridged.

In the Western dramas, human characters drown our attention in the vortex of their passions. Nature occasionally peeps out, but she is almost always a trespasser, who has to offer excuses, or bow apologetically and depart. But in all our dramas which still retain their fame, such as *Mrit-Shakatikâ, Shakuntalā, Uttara-Rāmacharita,* Nature stands on her own right, proving that she has her great function, to impart the peace of the eternal to human emotions.

The fury of passion in two of Shakespeare's youthful poems is exhibited in conspicuous isolation. It is snatched away, naked, from the context of the All; it has not the green earth or the blue sky around it; it is there ready to bring to our view the raging fever which is in man's desires, and not the balm of health and repose which encircles it in the universe.

Ritusamhāra is clearly a work of Kâlidâsa's immaturity. The youthful love-song in it does not reach the sublime reticence which is in *Shakuntalā* and *Kumāra-Sambhava.* But the tune of the these voluptuous outbreaks is set to the varied harmony of Nature's symphony. The moonbeams of the summer evening, resonant with the flow of fountains, acknowledge it as a part of its own melody. In its rhythm sways the Kadamaba forest, glistening in the first cool rain of the season; and the south breezes, carrying the scent of the mango blossoms, temper it with their murmur.

In the third canto of *Kumāra-Sambhava,* Madana, the God Eros, enters the forest sanctuary to set free a sudden flood of desire amid the serenity of the ascetics' meditation. But the boisterous outbreak of passion so caused was shown against a background of universal life. The divine love-thrills of Sati and Shiva found their response in the world-wide immensity of youth, in which animals and trees have their life-throbs.

Not only its third canto but the whole of the *Kumāra-Sambhava* poem is painted upon a limitless canvas. It tells of the eternal wedding of love, its wooing and sacrifice, and its fulfilment, for which the gods wait in suspense. Its inner idea is deep and of all time. It answers the one question that humanity asks through all its endeavours: 'How is the birth of the hero to be brought about, the brave one who can defy and vanquish the evil demon laying waste heaven's own kingdom?'

It becomes evident that such a problem had become acute in Kâlidâsa's time, when the old simplicity of Hindu life had broken up. The Hindu kings, forgetful of their duties, had become self-seeking epicureans, and India was being repeatedly devastated by the Scythians. What answer, then, does the poem give to the question it raises? Its message is that the cause of weakness lies in the inner life of the soul. It is in some break of harmony with the Good, some dissociation from the True. In the commencement of the poem we find that the God Shiva, the Good, had remained for long lost in the self-centred solitude of his asceticism, detached from the world of reality. And then Paradise was lost. But *Kumāra-Sambhava* is the poem of Paradise Regained. How was it regained? When Sati, the Spirit, through humiliation, suffering, and penance, won the Heart of Shiva, the Spirit of Goodness. And thus, from the union of the freedom of the real with the restraint of the Good, was born the heroism that released Paradise from the demon of Lawlessness.

Viewed from without, India, in the time of Kâlidâsa, appeared to have reached the zenith of civilization excelling as she did in luxury, literature and the arts. But from the poems of Kâlidâsa it is evident that this very magnificence of wealth and enjoyment worked against the ideal that sprang and flowed forth from the sacred solitude of the forest. These poems contain the voice of warnings against the gorgeous unreality of that age, which, like a Himalayan avalanche, was slowly gliding down to an abyss of catastrophe. And from his seat beside all the glories of Vikramaditya's throne the poet's heart yearns for the purity and simplicity of India's past age of spiritual striving. And it was this yearning which impelled him to go back to the annals of the ancient Kings of Raghu's line for the narrative poem, in which he traced the history of the rise and fall of the ideal that should guide the rulers of men.

King Dilipa, with Queen Sudakshinâ, has entered upon the life of the forest. The great monarch is busy tending the cattle of the hermitage. Thus the poem opens, amid scenes of simplicity and self-denial. But it ends in the palace of magnificence, in the extravagance of self-enjoyment. With a calm restraint of language the poet tells us of the kingly glory crowned with purity. He begins his poem as the day begins, in the serenity of sunrise. But lavish are the colours in which he describes the end, as of the evening, eloquent for a time with the sumptuous splendour of sunset, but overtaken at last by the devouring darkness which sweeps away all its brilliance into night.

In this beginning and this ending of his poem there lies hidden that message of the forest which found its voice in the poet's words. There runs through the narrative the idea that the future glowed gloriously ahead only when there was in the atmosphere the calm of self-control, of purity and renunciation. When downfall had become imminent, the hungry fires of desire, aflame at a hundred different points, dazzled the eyes of all beholders.

Kâlidâsa in almost all his works represented the unbounded impetuousness of kingly splendour on the one side and the serene strength of regulated desires on the other. Even in the minor drama of *Mālavikāgnimitra* we find the same thing in a different manner. It must never be thought that, in this play, the poet's deliberate object was to pander to his royal patron by inviting him to a literary orgy of lust and passion. The very introductory verse indicates the object towards which this play is directed. The poet begins the drama with the prayer, *Sanmārgâlókayan vyapanayatu sa nastāmasi vritimishah* (Let God, to illumine for us the path of truth, sweep away our passions, bred of darkness). This is the God Shiva, in whose nature Parvati, the eternal Woman, is ever commingled in an ascetic purity of love. The unified being of Shiva and Parvati is the perfect symbol of the eternal in the wedded love of man and woman. When the poet opens his drama with an invocation of this Spirit of the Divine Union it is evident that it contains in it the message with which he greets his kingly audience. The whole drama goes to show the ugliness of the treachery and cruelty inherent in unchecked self-indulgence. In the play the conflict of ideals is between the King and the Queen, between Agnimitra and Dhârini, and the significance of the contrast lies hidden in the very names of the hero and the heroine. Though the name Agnimitra is historical, yet it symbolizes in the poet's mind the destructive force of uncontrolled desire—just as did the name Agnivarna in *Raghuvamsha*. Agnimitra, 'the friend of the fire,' the reckless person who in his love-making is playing with fire, not knowing that all the time it is scorching him black. And what a great name is Dhârini, signifying the fortitude and forbearance that comes from majesty of soul! What an association it carries of the infinite dignity of love, purified by a self-abnegation that rises far above all insult and baseness of betrayal!

In *Shakuntalā* this conflict of ideals has been shown, all through the drama, by the contrast of the pompous heartlessness of the king's court and the natural purity of the forest hermitage. The drama opens with a hunting scene, where the king is in pursuit of an antelope. The cruelty of the chase appears like a menace symbolising the spirit of the king's life clashing against the spirit of the forest retreat, which is *sharanyam sarva-bhètānām* (where all creatures find their protection of love). And the pleading of the forest-dwellers with the king to spare the life of the deer, helplessly innocent and beautiful, is the pleading that rises from the heart of the whole drama. 'Never, oh, never is the arrow meant to pierce the tender body of a deer, even as the fire is not for the burning of flowers.'

In the *Râmâyana*, Râma and his companions, in their banishment, had to traverse forest after forest; they had to live in leaf-thatched huts, to sleep on the bare ground. But as their hearts felt their kinship with woodland, hill, and stream, they were not in exile amidst these. Poets, brought up in an atmosphere of different ideals, would have taken this opportunity of depicting in dismal colours the hardship of the forest-life in order to bring out the martyrdom of Râmachandra with all the emphasis of a strong contrast. But, in the *Râmâyana*, we are led to realize the greatness of the hero, not in a fierce struggle with Nature, but in sympathy with it. Sitâ, the daughter-in-law of a great kingly house, goes along the forest paths. We read:

"She asks Râma about the flowering trees, and shrubs and creepers which she has not seen before. At her request Lakshmana gathers and brings her plants of all kinds, exuberant with flowers, and it delights her heart to see the forest rivers, variegated with their streams and sandy banks, resounding with the call of heron and duck.

'When Râma first took his abode in the Chitrakuta peak, that delightful Chitrakuta, by the Mâlyavati river, with its easy slopes for landing, he forgot all the pain of leaving his home in the capital at the sight of those woodlands, alive with beast and bird.'

Having lived on that hill for long, Râma, who was *giri-vana-priya* (lover of the mountain and the forest), said one day to Sitâ:

'When I look upon the beauties of this hill, the loss of my kingdom troubles me no longer, nor does the separation from friends cause me any pang.'

Thus passed Râmachandra's exile, now in woodland, now in hermitage. The love which Râma and Sitâ bore to each other united them, not only to each other, but to the universe of life. That is why, when Sitâ was taken away, the loss seemed to be so great to the forest itself.

III

Strangely enough, in Shakespeare's dramas, like those of Kâlidâsa, we find a secret vein of complaint against the artificial life of the king's court—the life of ungrateful treachery and falsehood. And almost everywhere, in his dramas, foreign scenes have been introduced in connection with some working of the life of unscrupulous ambition. It is perfectly obvious in *Timon of Athens*—but there Nature offers no message or balm to the injured soul of man. In *Cymbeline* the mountainous forest and the cave appear in their aspect of obstruction to life's opportunities. These only seem tolerable in comparison with the vicissitudes of fortune in the artificial court life. In *As you Like It* the forest of Arden is didactic in its lessons. It does not bring peace, but preaches, when it says:

> Hath not old custom made this life more sweet
> Than that of painted pomp? Are not these woods
> More free from peril than the envious court?

In the *Tempest,* through Prospero's treatment of Ariel and Caliban we realize man's struggle with Nature and his longing to sever connection with her. In *Macbeth,* as a prelude to a bloody crime of treachery and treason, we are introduced to a scene of barren heath where the three witches appear as personifications of Nature's malignant forces; and in *King Lear* it is the fury of a father's love turned into curses by the ingratitude born of the unnatural life of the court that finds its symbol in the storm on the heath. The tragic intensity of *Hamlet* and *Othello* is unrelieved by any touch of Nature's eternity. Except in a passing glimpse of a moonlight night in the love scene in the *Merchant of Venice,* Nature has not been allowed in other dramas of this series, including *Romeo and Juliet* and *Antony and Cleopatra,* to contribute her own music to the music of man's love. In *The Winter's Tale* the cruelty of a king's suspicion stands bare in its relentlessness, and Nature cowers before it, offering no consolation.

I hope it is needless for me to say that these observations are not intended to minimize Shakespeare's great power as a dramatic poet, but to show in his works the gulf between Nature and human nature owing to the tradition of his race and time. It cannot be said that beauty of nature is ignored in his writings; only he fails to recognize in them the truth of the interpenetration of human life with the cosmic life of the world. We observe a completely different attitude of mind in the later English poets like Wordsworth and Shelley, which can be attributed in the main to the great mental change in Europe, at that particular period, through the influence of the newly discovered philosophy of India which stirred the soul of Germany and aroused the attention of other Western countries.

In Milton's *Paradise Lost,* the very subject—Man dwelling in the garden of Paradise—seems to afford a special opportunity for bringing out the true greatness of man's relationship with Nature. But though the poet has described to us the beauties of the garden, though he has shown to us the animals living there in amity and peace among themselves, there is no reality of kinship between them and man. They were created for man's enjoyment; man was their lord and master. We find no trace of the love between the first man and woman gradually surpassing themselves and overflowing the rest of creation, such as we find in the love scene in *Kumâra-Sambhava* and *Shakuntala.* In the seclusion of the bower, where the first man and woman rested in the garden of Paradise—

Bird, beast, insect or worm
Dust enter none, such was their awe of man.

Not that India denied the superiority of man, but the test of that superiority lay, according to her, in the comprehensiveness of sympathy, not in the aloofness of absolute distinction.

IV

India holds sacred, and counts as places of pilgrimage, all spots which display a special beauty or splendour of nature. These had no original attraction on account of any special fitness for cultivation or settlement. Here man is free, not to look upon Nature as a source of supply of his necessities, but to realise his soul beyond himself. The Himalayas of India are sacred and the Vindhya Hills. Her majestic rivers are sacred. Lake Mânasa and the confluence of the Ganges and the Jamuna are sacred. India has saturated with her love and worship the great Nature with which her children are surrounded, whose light fills their eyes with gladness, and whose water cleanses them, whose food gives them life, and from whose majestic mystery comes forth the constant revelation of the infinite in music, scent, and colour, which brings its awakening to the soul of man. India gains the world through worship, through spiritual communion; and the idea of freedom to which she aspired was based upon the realisation of her spiritual unity.

When, in my recent voyage to Europe, our ship left Aden and sailed along the sea which lay between the two continents, we passed by the red and barren rocks of Arabia on our right side and the gleaming sands of Egypt on our left. They seemed to me like two giant brothers exchanging with each other burning glances of hatred, kept apart by the tearful entreaty of the sea from whose womb they had their birth.

There was an immense stretch of silence on the left shore as well as on the right, but the two shores spoke to me of the two different historical dramas enacted. The civilization which found its growth in Egypt was continued across long centuries, elaborately rich with sentiments and expressions of life, with pictures, sculptures, temples, and ceremonials. This was a country whose guardian-spirit was a noble river, which spread the festivities of life on its banks across the heart of the land. There man never raised the barrier of alienation between himself and the rest of the world.

On the opposite shore of the Red Sea the civilization which grew up in the inhospitable soil of Arabia had a contrary character to that of Egypt. There man felt himself isolated in his hostile and bare surroundings. His idea of God became that of a jealous God. His mind naturally dwelt upon the principle of separateness. It roused in him the spirit of fight, and this spirit was a force that drove him far and wide. These two civilizations represented two fundamental divisions of human nature. The one contained in it the spirit of conquest and the other the spirit of harmony. And both of these have their truth and purpose in human existence.

The characters of two eminent sages have been described in our mythology. One was Vashishtha and another Vishvâmitra. Both of them were great, but they represented two different types of wisdom; and there was conflict between them. Vishvâmitra sought to achieve power and was proud of it; Vashishtha was rudely smitten by that power. But his hurt and his loss could not touch the illumination of his soul; for he rose above them and could forgive. Râmachandra, the great hero of our epic, had his initiation to the spiritual life from Vashishtha, the life of inner peace and perfection. But he had his initiation to war from Vishvâmitra, who called him to kill the demons and gave him weapons that were irresistible.

Those two sages symbolize in themselves the two guiding spirits of civilization. Can it be true that they shall never be reconciled? If so, can ever the age of peace and co-operation dawn upon the human world? Creation is the harmony of contrary forces—the forces of attraction and repulsion. When they join hands, all the fire and fight are changed into the smile of flowers and the songs of birds. When there is only one of them triumphant and the other defeated, then either there is the death of cold rigidity or that of suicidal explosion.

Humanity, for ages, has been busy with the one great creation of spiritual life. Its best wisdom, its discipline, its literature and art, all the teaching and self-sacrifice of its noblest teachers, have been for this. But the harmony of contrary forces, which give their rhythm to all creation, has not yet been perfected by man in his civilization, and the Creator in him is baffled over and over again. He comes back to his work, however, and makes himself busy, building his world in the midst of desolation and ruins. His history is the history of his aspiration interrupted and renewed. And one truth of which he must be reminded, therefore, is that the power which accomplishes the miracle of creation, by bringing conflicting forces into the harmony of the One, is no passion, but a love which accepts the bonds of self-control from the joy of its own immensity—a love whose sacrifice is the manifestation of its endless wealth within itself.

East and West

It is not always a profound interest in man that carries travelers nowadays to distant lands. More often it is the facility for rapid movement. For lack of time and for the sake of convenience we generalise and crush our human facts into the packages within the steel trucks that hold our travellers' reports.

Our knowledge of our own countrymen and our feelings about them have slowly and unconsciously grown out of innumerable facts which are full of contradictions and subject to incessant change. They have the elusive mystery and fluidity of life. We cannot define to ourselves what we are as a whole, because we know too much; because our knowledge is more than knowledge. It is an immediate consciousness of personality, and evaluation of which carries some emotion, joy or sorrow, shame or exaltation. But in a foreign land we try to find our compensation for the meagerness of our data by the compactness of the generalisation which our imperfect sympathy itself helps us to form. When a stranger from the West travels in the Eastern world he takes the facts that displease him and readily makes use of them for his rigid conclusions, fixed upon the unchallengeable authority of his personal experience. It is like a man who has his own boat for crossing his village steam, but, on being compelled to wade across some strange watercourse, draws angry comparisons as he goes from every patch of mud and every pebble which his feet encounter.

Our mind has faculties which are universal, but its habits are insular. There are men who become impatient and angry at the least discomfort when their habits are incommoded. In their idea of the next world they probably conjure up the ghosts of their slippers and dressing-gowns, and expect the latchkey that opens their lodging-house door on earth to fit their front door in the other world. As travelers they are a failure; for they have grown too accustomed to their mental easy-chairs, and in their intellectual nature love home comforts, which are of local make, more than the realities of life, which, like earth itself, are full of ups and downs, yet are one in their rounded completeness.

The modern age has brought the geography of the earth near to us, but made it difficult for us to come into touch with man. We go to strange lands and observe; we do not live there. We hardly meet men: but only specimens of knowledge. We are in haste to seek for general types and overlook individuals.

When we fall into the habit of neglecting to use the understanding that comes of sympathy in our travels, our knowledge of foreign people grows insensitive, and therefore easily becomes both unjust and cruel in its character, and also selfish and contemptuous in its application. Such has, too often, been the case with regard to the meeting of Western people in our days with others for whom they do not recognise any obligation of kinship.

It has been admitted that the dealings between different races of men are not merely between individuals; that our mutual understanding is either aided, or else obstructed, by the general emanations forming the social atmosphere. These emanations are our collective ideas and collective feelings, generated according to special historical circumstances.

For instance, the caste-idea is a collective idea in India. When we approach an Indian who is under the influence of this collective idea, he is no longer a pure individual with his conscience fully awake to the judging of the value of a human being. He is more or less a passive medium for giving expression to the sentiment of a whole community.

It is evident that the caste-idea is not creative; it is merely institutional. It adjusts human beings according to some mechanical arrangement. It emphasizes the negative side of the individual—his separateness. It hurts the complete truth in man.

In the West, also, the people have a certain collective idea that obscures their humanity. Let me try to explain what I feel about it.

II

Lately I went to visit some battlefields of France which had been devastated by war. The awful calm of desolation, which still bore wrinkles of pain—death-struggles stiffened into ugly ridges—brought before my mind the vision of a huge demon, which had no shape, no meaning, yet had two arms that could strike and break and tear, a gaping mouth that could devour, and bulging brains that could conspire and plan. It was a purpose, which had a living body, but no complete humanity to temper it. Because it was passion—belonging to life, and yet not having the wholeness of life—it was the most terrible of life's enemies.

Something of the same sense of oppression in a different degree, the same desolation in a different aspect, is produced in my mind when I realise the effect of the West upon Eastern life—the West which, in its relation to us, is all plan and purpose incarnate, without any superfluous humanity.

I feel the contrast very strongly in Japan. In that country the old world presents itself with some ideal of perfection, in which man has his varied opportunities of self-revelation in art, in ceremonial, in religious faith, and in customs expressing the poetry of social relationship. There one feels that deep delight of hospitality which life offers to life. And side by side, in the same soil, stands the modern world, which is stupendously big and powerful, but inhospitable. It has no simple-hearted welcome for man. It is living; yet the incompleteness of life's ideal within it cannot but hurt humanity.

The wriggling tentacles of a cold-blooded utilitarianism, with which the West has grasped all the easily yielding succulent portions of the East, are causing pain and indignation throughout the Eastern countries. The West comes to us, not with the imagination and sympathy that create and unite, but with a shock of passion—passion for power and wealth. This passion is a mere force, which has in it the principle of separation, of conflict.

I have been fortunate in coming into close touch with individual men and women of the Western countries, and have felt with them their sorrows and shared their aspirations. I have known that they seek the same God, who is my God— even those who deny Him. I feel certain that, if the great light of culture be extinct in Europe, our horizon in the East will mourn in darkness. It does not hurt my pride to acknowledge that, in the present age, Western humanity has received its mission to be the teacher of the world; that her science, through the mastery of laws of nature, is to liberate human souls from the dark dungeon of matter. For this very reason I have realised all the more strongly, on the other hand, that the dominant collective idea in the Western countries is not creative. It is ready to enslave or kill individuals, to drug a great people with soul-killing poison, darkening their whole future with the black mist of stupefaction, and emasculating entire races of men to the utmost degree of helplessness. It is wholly wanting in spiritual power to blend and harmonize; it lacks the sense of the great personality of man.

The most significant fact of modern days is this, that the West has met the East. Such a momentous meeting of humanity, in order to be fruitful, must have in its heart some great emotional idea, generous and creative. There can be no doubt that God's choice has fallen upon the knights-errant of the West for the service of the present age; arms and armour have been given to them; but have they yet realized in their hearts the single-minded loyalty to their cause which can resist all temptations of bribery from the devil? The world to-day is offered to the West. She will destroy it, if she does not use it for a great creation of man. The materials for such a creation are in the hands of science; but the creative genius is in Man's spiritual ideal.

III

When I was young a stranger from Europe came to Bengal. He chose his lodging among the people of the country, shared with them their frugal diet, and freely offered them his service. He found employment in the houses of the rich, teaching them French and German, and the money thus earned he spent to help poor students in buying books. This meant for him hours of walking in the mid-day heat of a tropical summer; for intent upon exercising the utmost economy, he refused to hire conveyances. He was pitiless in his exaction from himself of his resources, in money, time, and strength, to the point of privation; and all this for the sake of a people who were obscure, to whom he was not born, yet whom he dearly loved. He did not come to us with a professional mission of teaching sectarian creeds; he had not in his nature the least trace of that self-sufficiency of goodness, which humiliates by gifts the victims of its insolent benevolence. Though he did

not know our language, he took every occasion to frequent
our meetings and ceremonies; yet he was always afraid of
intrusion, and tenderly anxious lest he might offend us by his
ignorance of our customs. At last, under the continual strain
of work in an alien climate and surroundings, his health broke
down. He died, and was cremated at our burning-ground,
according to his express desire.

The attitude of his mind, the manner of his living, the
object of his life, his modesty, his unstinted self-sacrifice for
a people who had not even the power to give publicity to any
benefaction bestowed upon them, were so utterly unlike
anything we were accustomed to associate with the Europeans
in India, that it gave rise in our mind to a feeling of love
bordering upon awe.

We all have a realm, a private paradise, in our mind,
where dwell deathless memories of persons who brought
some divine light to our life's experience, who may not be
known to others, and whose names have no place in the pages
of history. Let me confess to you that this man lives as one
of those immortals in the paradise of my individual life.

He came from Sweden, his name was Hammargren. What
was most remarkable in the event of his coming to us in
Bengal was the fact that in his own country he had chanced
to read some works of my great countryman, Ram Mohan
Roy, and felt an immense veneration for his genius and his
character. Ram Mohan Roy lived in the beginning of the last
century, and it is no exaggeration when I describe him as one
of the immortal personalities of modern time. This young
Swede had the unusual gift of a farsighted intellect and
sympathy, which enabled him even from his distance of space
and time, and in spite of racial differences, to realize the
greatness of Ram Mohan Roy. It moved him so deeply that
he resolved to go to the country which produced this great
man, and offer her his service. He was poor, and he had to

wait some time in England before he could earn his passage money to India. There he came at last, and in reckless generosity of love utterly spent himself to the last breath of his life, away from home and kindred and all the inheritances of his motherland. His stay among us was too short to produce any outward result. He failed even to achieve during his life what he had in his mind, which was to found by the help of his scanty earnings a library as a memorial to Ram Mohan Roy, and thus to leave behind him a visible symbol of his devotion. But what I prize most in this European youth, who left no record of his life behind him, is not the memory of any service of goodwill, but the precious gift of respect which he offered to a people who are fallen upon evil times, and whom it is so easy to ignore or to humiliate. For the first time in the modern days this obscure individual from Sweden brought to our country the chivalrous courtesy of the West, a greeting of human fellowship.

The coincidence came to me with a great and delightful surprise when the Nobel Prize was offered to me from Sweden. As a recognition of individual merit it was of great value to me, no doubt; but it was the acknowledgement of the East as a collaborator with the Western continents, in contributing its riches to the common stock of civilization, which had the chief significance for the present age. It meant joining hands in comradeship by the two great hemispheres of the human world across the sea.

IV

To-day the real East remains unexplored. The blindness of contempt is more hopeless than the blindness of ignorance; for contempt kills the light which ignorance merely leaves unignited. The East is waiting to be understood by the Western races, in order not only to be able to give what is true in her, but also to be confident of her own mission.

In Indian history, the meeting of the Mussulman and the Hindu produced Akbar, the object of whose dream was the unification of hearts and ideals. It had all the glowing enthusiasm of a religion, and it produced an immediate and a vast result even in his own lifetime.

But the fact still remains that the Western mind, after centuries of contact with the East, has not evolved the enthusiasm of a chivalrous ideal which can bring this age to its fulfilment. It is everywhere raising thorny hedges of exclusion and offering human sacrifices to national self-seeking. It has intensified the mutual feelings of envy among Western races themselves, as they fight over their spoils and display a carnivorous pride in their snarling rows of teeth.

We must again guard our minds from any encroaching distrust of the individuals of a nation. The active love of humanity and the spirit of martyrdom for the cause of justice and truth which I have met with in the Western countries have been a great lesson and inspiration to me. I have no doubt in my mind that the West owes its true greatness, not so much to its marvellous training of intellect, as to its spirit of service devoted to the welfare of man. Therefore I speak with a personal feeling of pain and sadness about the collective power which is guiding the helm of Western civilization. It is a passion, not an ideal. The more success it has brought to Europe, the more costly it will prove to her at last, when the accounts have to be rendered. And the signs are unmistakable, that the accounts have been called for. The time has come when Europe must know that the forcible parasitism which she has been practising upon the two large Continents of the world—the two most unwieldy whales of humanity—must be causing to her moral nature a gradual atrophy and degeneration.

As an example, let me quote the following extract from the concluding chapter of *From the Cape to Cairo,* by Messrs.

Grogan and Sharp, two writers who have the power to inculcate their doctrines by precept and example. In their reference to the African they are candid, as when they say, 'We have stolen his land. Now we must steal his limbs.' These two sentences, carefully articulated, with a smack of enjoyment, have been more clearly explained in the following statement, where some sense of that decency which is the attenuated ghost of a buried conscience, prompts the writers to use the phrase 'compulsory labour' in place of the honest word 'slavery'; just as the modern politician adroitly avoids the word 'injunction' and uses the word 'mandate.' 'Compulsory labour in some form,' they say, 'is the corollary of our occupation of the country.' And they add: 'It is pathetic, but it is history,' implying thereby that moral sentiments have no serious effect in the history of human beings.

Elsewhere they write: 'Either we must give up the country commercially, or we must make the African work. And mere abuse of those who point out the impasse cannot change the facts. We must decide, and soon. Or rather the white man of South Africa will decide.' The authors also confess that they have seen too much of the world 'to have any lingering belief that Western civilization benefits native races.'

The logic is simple—the logic of egoism. But the argument is simplified by lopping off the greater part of the premise. For these writers seem to hold that the only important question for the white men of South Africa is, how indefinitely to grow fat on ostrich feathers and diamond mines, and dance jazz dances over the misery and degradation of a whole race of fellow-beings of a different colour from their own. Possibly they believe that moral laws have a special domesticated breed of comfortable concessions for the service of the people in power. Possibly they ignore the fact that commercial and political cannibalism, profitably practised upon foreign races, creeps back nearer home; that the cultivation of unwholesome appetites has its final reckoning with the stomach which has been made to serve it. For, after all, man is a spiritual being, and not a mere living money-bag jumping from profit to profit, and breaking the backbone of human races in its financial leapfrog.

Such, however, has been the condition of things for more than a century; and to-day, trying to read the future by the light of the European conflagration, we are asking ourselves everywhere in the East: 'Is this frightfully overgrown power really great? It can bruise us from without, but can it add to our wealth of spirit? It can sign peace treaties, but can it give peace?'

It was about two thousand years ago that all-powerful Rome in one of its eastern provinces executed on a cross a simple teacher of an obscure tribe of fishermen. On that day the Roman governor felt no falling off of his appetite or sleep. On that day there was, on the one hand, the agony, the humiliation, the death; on the other, the pomp of pride and festivity in the Governor's palace.

And to-day? To whom, then, shall we bow the head?

Kasmai devaya havisha vidhema?
(To which God shall we offer oblation?)

We know of an instance in our own history of India, when a great personality, both in his life and voice, struck the keynote of the solemn music of the soul—love for all creatures. And that music crossed seas, mountains, and deserts. Races belonging to different climates, habits, and languages were drawn together, not in the clash of arms, not in the conflict of exploitation, but in harmony of life, in amity and peace. That was creation.

When we think of it, we see at once what the confusion of thought was to which the Western poet, dwelling upon the difference between East and West, referred when he said,

'Never the twain shall meet.' It is true that they are not yet showing any real sign of meeting. But the reason is because the West has not sent out its humanity to meet the man in the East, but only its machine. Therefore the poet's line has to be changed into something like this:

Man is man, machine is machine,
And never the twain shall wed.

You must know that red tape can never be a common human bond; that official sealing-wax can never provide means of mutual attachment; that it is a painful ordeal for human beings to have to receive favours from animated pigeon-holes, and condescensions from printed circulars that give notice but never speak. The presence of the Western people in the East is a human fact. If we are to gain anything from them, it must not be a mere sum-total of legal codes and systems of civil and military service. Man is a great deal more to man than that. We have our human birthright to claim direct help from the man of the West, if he has anything great to give us. It must come to us, not through mere facts in a juxtaposition, but through the spontaneous sacrifice made by those who have the gift, and therefore the responsibility.

Earnestly I ask the poet of the Western world to realise and sing to you with all the great power of music which he has, that the East and the West are ever in search of each other, and that they must meet not merely in the fullness of physical strength, but in fullness of truth; that the right hand, which wields the sword, has the need of the left, which holds the shield of safety.

The East has its seat in the vast plains watched over by the snow-peaked mountains and fertilised by rivers carrying mighty volumes of water to the sea. There, under the blaze of a tropical sun, the physical life has bedimmed the light of its vigour and lessened its claims. There man has had the repose of mind which has ever tried to set itself in harmony with the inner notes of existence. In the silence of sunrise and sunset, and on star-crowded nights, he has sat face to face with the Infinite, waiting for the revelation that opens up the heart of all that there is. He has said, in a rapture of realization:

'Hearken to me, ye children of the Immortal, who dwell in the Kingdom of Heaven. I have known, from beyond darkness, the Supreme Person, shining with the radiance of the sun.'

The man from the East, with his faith in the eternal, who in his soul had met the touch of the Supreme Person—did he never come to you in the West and speak to you of the Kingdom of Heaven? Did he not unite the East and the West in truth, in the unity of one spiritual bond between all children of the Immortal, in the realization of one great Personality in all human persons?

Yes, the East did once meet the West profoundly in the growth of her life. Such union became possible, because the East came to the West with the ideal that is creative, and not with the passion that destroys moral bonds. The mystic consciousness of the infinite, which she brought with her, was greatly needed by the man of the West to give him his balance.

On the other hand, the East must find her own balance in Science—the magnificent gift that the West can bring to her. Truth has its nest as well as its sky. That nest is definite in structure, accurate in law of construction; and though it has to be changed and rebuilt over and over again, the need of it is never-ending and its laws are eternal. For some centuries the East has neglected the nest-building of truth. She has not been attentive to learn its secret. Trying to cross the trackless infinite, the East has relied solely upon her wings. She has spurned the earth, till, buffeted by storms, her wings are hurt and she is tired, sorely needing help. But has she then to be told that the messenger of the sky and the builder of the nest shall never meet?

The Modern Age

I

Wherever man meets man in a living relationship, the meeting finds its natural expression in works of art, the signatures of beauty, in which the mingling of the personal touch leaves its memorial.

On the other hand, a relationship of pure utility humiliates man—it ignores the rights and needs of his deeper nature; it feels no compunction in maltreating and killing things of beauty that can never be restored.

Some years ago, when I set out from Calcutta on my voyage to Japan, the first thing that shocked me, with a sense of personal injury, was the ruthless intrusion of the factories for making gunny-bags on both banks of the Ganges. The blow it gave to me was owing to the precious memory of the days of my boyhood, when the scenery of this river was the only great thing near my birthplace reminding me of the existence of a world which had its direct communication with our innermost spirit.

Calcutta is an upstart town with no depth of sentiment in her face and in her manners. It may truly be said about her genesis:—In the beginning there was the spirit of the Shop, which uttered through its megaphone, 'Let there be the Office!' and there was Calcutta. She brought with her no dower of distinction, no majesty of noble or romantic origin;

she never gathered around her any great historical associations, any annals of brave sufferings, or memory of mighty deeds. The only thing which gave her the sacred baptism of beauty was the river. I was fortunate enough to be born before the smoke-belching iron dragon had devoured the greater part of the life of its banks; when the landing-stairs descending into its waters, caressed by its tides, appeared to me like the loving arms of the villages clinging to it; when Calcutta, with her up-tilted nose and stony stare, had not completely disowned her foster-mother, rural Bengal, and had not surrendered body and soul to her wealthy paramour, the spirit of the ledger, bound in dead leather.

But as an instance of the contrast of the different ideal of a different age, incarnated in the form of a town, the memory of my last visit to Benares comes to my mind. What impressed me most deeply, while I was there, was the mother-call of the river Ganges, ever filling the atmosphere with an 'unheard melody,' attracting the whole population to its bosom every hour of the day. I am proud of the fact that India has felt a most profound love for this river, which nourishes civilization on its banks, guiding its course from the silence of the hills to the sea with its myriad voices of solitude. The love of this river, which has become one with the love of the best in man, has given rise to this town as an expression of reverence. This is to show that there are sentiments in us which are creative, which do not clamour for gain, but overflow in gifts, in spontaneous generosity of self-sacrifice.

But our minds will nevermore cease to be haunted by the perturbed spirit of the question, 'What about gunny-bags?' I admit they are indispensable, and am willing to allow them a place in society, if my opponent will only admit that even gunny-bags should have their limits, and will acknowledge the importance of leisure to man, with space for joy and worship, and a home of wholesale privacy, with associations of chaste love and mutual service. If this concession to humanity be denied or curtailed, and if profit and production are allowed to run amuck, they will play havoc with our love of beauty, of truth of justice, and also with our love for our fellow-beings. So it comes about that the peasant cultivators of jute, who live on the brink of everlasting famine, are combined against, and driven to lower the price of their labours to the point of blank despair, by those who earn more than cent per cent profit and wallow in the infamy of their wealth. The facts that man is brave and kind, that he is social and generous and self-sacrificing, have some aspect of the complete in them; but the fact that he is a manufacturer of gunny-bags is too ridiculously small to claim the right of reducing his higher nature to insignificance. The fragmentariness of utility should never forget its subordinate position in human affairs. It must not be permitted to occupy more than its legitimate place and power in society, nor to have the liberty to desecrate the poetry of life, to deaden our sensitiveness to ideals, bragging of its own coarseness as a sign of virility. The pity is that when in the centre of our activities we acknowledge, by some proud name, the supremacy of wanton destructiveness, or production not less wanton, we shut out all the lights of our souls, and in that darkness our conscience and our consciousness of shame are hidden, and our love of freedom is killed.

I do not for a moment mean to imply that in any particular period of history men were free from the disturbance of their lower passions. Selfishness ever had its share in government and trade. Yet there was a struggle to maintain a balance of forces in society; and our passions cherished no delusions about their own rank and value. They contrived no clever devices to hoodwink our moral nature. For in those days our intellect was not tempted to put its weight into the balance on the side of over-greed.

But in recent centuries a devastating change has come over our mentality with regard to the acquisition of money. Whereas in former ages men treated it with condescension, even with disrespect, now they bend their knees to it. That it should be allowed a sufficiently large place in society, there can be no question; but it becomes an outrage when it occupies those seats which are specially reserved for the immortals, by bribing us, tampering with our moral pride, recruiting the best strength of society in a traitor's campaign against human ideals, thus disguising, with the help of pomp and pageantry, its true insignificance. Such a state of things has come to pass because, with the help of science, the possibilities of profit have suddenly become immoderate. The whole of the human world, throughout its length and breadth, has felt the gravitational pull of a giant planet of greed, with concentric rings of innumerable satellites, causing in our society a marked deviation from the moral orbit. In former times the intellectual and spiritual powers of this earth upheld their dignity of independence and were not giddily rocked on the tides of the money market. But, as in the last fatal stages of disease, this fatal influence of money has got into our brain and affected our heart. Like a usurper, it has occupied the throne of high social ideals, using every means, by menace and threat, to seize upon the right, and, tempted by opportunity, presuming to judge it. It has not only science for its ally, but other forces also that have some semblance of religion, such as nation-worship and the idealising of organised selfishness. Its methods are far-reaching and sure. Like the claws of a tiger's paw, they are softly sheathed. Its massacres are invisible, because they are fundamental, attacking the very roots of life. Its plunder is ruthless behind a scientific system of screens, which have the formal appearance of being open and responsible to inquiries. By whitewashing its stains it keeps its respectability unblemished. It makes a liberal use of falsehood in diplomacy, only feeling embarrassed when its evidence is disclosed by others of the trade. An unscrupulous system of propaganda paves the way for widespread misrepresentation. It works up the crowd psychology through regulated hypnotic doses at repeated intervals, administered in bottles with moral labels upon them of soothing colours. In fact, man has been able to make his pursuit of power easier to-day by his art of mitigating the obstructive forces that come from the higher region of his humanity. Within his cult of powers and his idolatry of money he has, in a great measure, reverted to his primitive barbarism, a barbarism whose path is lit up by the lurid light of intellect. For barbarism is the simplicity of a superficial life. It may be bewildering in its surface adornments and complexities, but it lacks the ideal to impart to it the depth of moral responsibility.

II

Society suffers from a profound feeling of unhappiness, not so much when it is in material poverty as when its members are deprsived of a large part of their humanity. This unhappiness goes on smouldering in the subconscious mind of the community till its life is reduced to ashes or a sudden combustion is produced. The repressed personality of man generates an inflammable moral gas deadly in its explosive force.

We have seen in the late war, and also in some of the still more recent events of history, how human individuals freed from moral and spiritual bonds find a boisterous joy in a debauchery of destruction. There is generated a disinterested passion of ravage. Through such catastrophe we can realize what formidable forces of annihilation are kept in check in our communities by bonds of social ideas; nay, made into multitudinous manifestations of beauty and fruitfulness. Thus we know that evils are, like meteors, stray fragments of life, which need the attraction of some great ideal in order to be assimilated with the wholesomeness of creation. The evil forces are literally outlaws; they only need the control and cadence of spiritual laws to change them into good. The true goodness is not the negation of badness, it is in the mastery of it. Goodness is the miracle which turns the tumult of chaos into a dance of beauty.

In modern society the ideal of wholeness has lost its force. Therefore its different sections have become detached and resolved into their elemental character of forces. Labour is a force; so also is Capital; so are the Government and the People; so are Man and Woman. It is said that when the forces lying latent in even a handful of dust are liberated from their bond of unity, they can lift the buildings of a whole neighbourhood to the height of a mountain. Such disfranchised forces, irresponsible free-booters, may be useful to us for certain purposes, but human habitations standing secure on their foundations are better for us. To own the secret of utilising these forces is a proud fact for us, but the power of self-control and the self-dedication of love are truer subjects for the exultation of mankind. The genii of the Arabian Nights may have in their magic their lure and fascination for us. But the consciousness, of God is of another order, infinitely more precious in imparting to our minds ideas of the spiritual power of creation. Yet these genii are abroad everywhere; and even now, after the late war, their devotees are getting ready to play further tricks upon humanity by suddenly spiriting it away to some hill-top of desolation.

III

We know that when, at first, any large body of people in their history became aware of their unity, they expressed it in some popular symbol of divinity. For they felt that their combination was not an arithmetical ones; its truth was deeper than the truth of number. They felt that their community was not a mere agglutination but a creation, having upon it the living touch of the infinite Person. The realization of this truth having been an end in itself, a fulfilment, it gave meaning to self-sacrifice, to the acceptance even of death.

But our modern education is producing a habit of mind which is ever weakening in us the spiritual apprehension of truth—the truth of a person as the ultimate reality of existence. Science has its proper sphere in a analysing this world as a construction, just as grammar has its legitimate office in analysing the syntax of a poem. But the world, as a creation, is not a mere construction; it too is more than a syntax. It is a poem, which we are apt to forget when grammar takes exclusive hold of our minds.

Upon the loss of this sense of a universal personality, which is religion, the reign of the machine and of method has been firmly established, and man, humanly speaking, has been made a homeless tramp. As nomads, ravenous and restless, the men from the West have come to us. They have exploited our Eastern humanity for sheer gain of power. This modern meeting of men has not yet received the blessing of God. For it has kept us apart, though railway lines are laid far and wide, and ships are plying from shore to shore to bring us together.

It has been said in the Upanishads:

Yastu sarvāni bhutāni ātmānyevānupashyati
Sarva bhuteshu chātmānam na tato vijugupsate

(He who sees all things in *ātmā*, in the infinite spirit, and the infinite spirit in all beings, remains no longer unrevealed.)

In the modern civilization, for which an enormous number of men are used as materials, and human relationships have in a large measure become utilitarian, man is imperfectly revealed. For man's revelation does not lie in the fact that he is a power, but that he is a spirit. The prevalence of the theory which realizes the power of the machine in the universe, and organises men into machines, is like the eruption of Etna, tremendous in its force, in its outburst of fire and fume; but its creeping lava covers up human shelters made by the ages, and its ashes smother life.

IV

The terribly efficient method of repressing personality in the individuals and the races who have failed to resist it has, in the present scientific age, spread all over the world; and in consequence there have appeared signs of a universal disruption which seems not far off. Faced with the possibility of such a disaster, which is sure to affect the successful peoples of the world in their intemperate prosperity, the great Powers of the West are seeking peace, not by curbing their greed, or by giving up the exclusive advantages which they have unjustly acquired, but by concentrating their forces for mutual security.

But can powers find their equilibrium in themselves? Power has to be made secure not only against power, but also against weakness; for there lies the peril of its losing balance. The weak are as great a danger for the strong as quicksands for an elephant. They do not assist progress because they do not resist; they only drag down. The people who grow accustomed to wield absolute power over others are apt to forget that by so doing they generate an unseen force which some day rends that power into pieces. The dumb fury of the downtrodden finds its awful support from the universal law of moral balance. The air which is so thin and unsubstantial gives birth to storms that nothing can resist. This has been proved in history over and over again, and stormy forces arising from the revolt of insulted humanity are openly gathering in the air at the present time.

Yet in the psychology of the strong the lesson is despised and no count taken of the terribleness of the weak. This is the latent ignorance that, like an unsuspected worm, burrows under the bulk of the prosperous. Have we never read of the castle of power, securely buttressed on all sides, in a moment dissolving in air at the explosion caused by the weak and outraged besiegers? Politicians calculate upon the number of mailed hands that are kept on the sword-hilts: they do not possess the third eye to see the great invisible hand that clasps in silence the hand of the helpless and waits its time. The strong form their league by a combination of powers, driving the weak to form their own league alone with their God. I know I am crying in the wilderness when I raise the voice of warning; and while the West is busy with its organization of a machine-made peace, it will still continue to nourish by its iniquities the underground forces of earthquake in the Eastern Continent. The West seems unconscious that Science, by providing it with more and more power, is tempting it to suicide and encouraging it to accept the challenge of the disarmed; it does not know that the challenge comes from a higher source.

Two prophecies about the world's salvation are cherished in the hearts of the two great religions of the world. They represent the highest expectation of man, thereby indicating his faith in a truth which he instinctively considers as ultimate— the truth of love. These prophecies have not for their vision the fettering of the world and reducing it to tameness by means of a close-linked power forged in the factory of a political steel trust. One of the religions has for its meditation the image of the Buddha who is to come, Maitreya, the Buddha of love; and he is to bring peace. The other religion waits for the coming of Christ. For Christ preached peace when he preached love, when he preached the oneness of the Father with the brothers who are many. And this was the truth of peace. Christ never held that peace was the best policy. For policy is not truth. The calculation of self-interest can never successfully fight the irrational force of passion—the passion which is perversion of love, and which can only be set right by the truth of love. So long as the powers build a league on the foundation of their desire for safety, secure enjoyment of gains, consolidation of past injustice, and putting off the reparation of wrongs, while their fingers still wriggle for greed and reek of blood, rifts will appear in their union; and in future their conflicts will take greater force and magnitude. It is political and commercial egoism which is the evil harbinger of war. By different combinations it changes its shape and dimensions, but not its nature. This egoism is still held sacred, and made a religion; and such a religion, by a mere change of temple, and by new committees of priests, will never save mankind. We must know that, as, through science and commerce, the realization of the unity of the material world gives us power, so the realization of the great spiritual Unity of Man alone can give us peace.

The Nation

The people are living beings. They have their distinct personalities. But nations are organizations of power, and therefore their inner aspects and outward expressions are everywhere monotonously the same. Their differences are merely differences in degree of efficiency. In the modern world the fight is going on between the living spirit of the people and the methods of nation-organizing. It is like the struggle that began in Central Asia between cultivated areas of man's habitation and the continually encroaching desert sands, till the human region of life and beauty was choked out of existence. When the spread of higher ideals of humanity is not held to be important, the hardening method of national efficiency gains a certain strength; and for some limited period of time, at least, it proudly asserts itself as the fittest to survive. But it is the survival of that part of man which is the least living. And this is the reason why dead monotony is the sign of the spread of the Nation. The modern towns, which present the physiognomy due to this dominance of the Nation, are everywhere the same, from San Francisco to London, from London to Tokyo. They show no faces, but merely masks.

The peoples, being personalities, must have their self-expression, and this leads to their distinctive creations. These creations are literature, art, social symbols and ceremonials. They are like different dishes at one common feast. They add richness to our enjoyment and understanding of truth. They are making the world of man fertile of life and variedly beautiful.

But the nations do not create, they merely produce and destroy. Organisations for production are necessary. Even organisations for destruction may be so. But when, actuated by greed and hatred, they crowd away into a corner the living man who creates, then the harmony is lost, and the people's history runs at a break-neck speed towards some fatal catastrophe.

Humanity, where it is living, is guided by inner ideals; but where it is a dead organisation it be comes impervious to them. Its building process is only an external process, and in its response to the moral guidance it has to pass through obstacles that are gross and non-plastic.

Man as a person has his individuality, which is the field where his spirit has its freedom to express itself and to grow. The professional man carries a rigid crust around him which has very little variation and hardly any elasticity. This professionalism is the region where men specialise their knowledge and organise their power, mercilessly elbowing each other in their struggle to come to the front. Professionalism is necessary, without doubt; but it must not be allowed to exceed its healthy limits, to assume complete mastery over the personal man, making him narrow and hard, exclusively intent upon pursuit of success at the cost of his faith in ideals.

In ancient India professions were kept within limits by social regulation. They were considered primarily as social necessities, and in the second place as the means of livelihood for individuals. Thus man, being free from the constant urging unbounded competition, could have leisure to cultivate his nature in its completeness.

The Cult of the National is the professionalism of the people. This cult is becoming their greatest danger, because it is bringing them enormous success, making them impatient of the claims of higher ideals. The greater the amount of success, the stronger are the conflicts of interest and jealousy and hatred which are aroused in men's minds, thereby making it more and more necessary for other peoples, who are still living, to stiffen into nations. With the growth of nationalism, man has become the greatest menace to man. Therefore the continual presence of panic goads that very nationalism into ever-increasing menace.

Crowd psychology is a blind force. Like steam and other physical forces, it can be utilized for creating a tremendous amount of power. And therefore rulers of men, who, out of greed and fear, are bent upon turning their peoples into machines of power, try to train this crowd psychology for their special purposes. They hold it to be their duty to foster in the popular mind universal panic, unreasoning pride in their own race, and hatred of others. Newspapers, school-books, and even religious services are made use of for this object; and those who have the courage to express their disapprobation of this blind and impious cult are either punished in the law-courts, or are socially ostracized. The individual thinks, even when he feels; but the same individual, where he feels with the crowd, does not reason at all. His moral sense becomes blurred. This suppression of higher humanity in crowd minds is productive of enormous strength. For the crowd mind is essentially primitive; its forces are elemental. Therefore the Nation is for ever watching to take advantage of this enormous power of darkness.

The people's instinct of self-preservation has been made dominant at particular times of crisis. Then, for the time being, the consciousness of its solidarity becomes aggressively wide-awake. But in the Nation this hyper-consciousness is kept alive for all time by artificial means. A man has to act the part of a policeman when he finds his house invaded by burglars. But if that remains his normal condition, then his consciousness of his household becomes acute and over-wrought, making him fly at every stranger passing near his house. This intensity of self-consciousness is nothing of which a man should feel proud; certainly it is not healthful. In like manner, incessant self-consciousness in a nation is highly injurious for the people. It serves its immediate purpose, but at the cost of the eternal in man.

When a whole body of men train themselves for a particular narrow purpose, it becomes a common interest with them to keep up that purpose and preach absolute loyalty to it. Nationalism is the training of a whole people for a narrow ideal; and when it gets hold of their minds it is sure to lead them to moral degeneracy and intellectual blindness. We cannot but hold firm the faith that this Age of Nationalism, of gigantic vanity and selfishness, is only a passing phase in civilization, and those who are making permanent arrangements for accommodating this temporary mood of history will be unable to fit themselves for the coming age, when the true spirit of freedom will have sway.

With the unchecked growth of Nationalism the moral foundation of man's civilisation is unconsciously undergoing a change. The ideal of the social man is unselfishness, but the ideal of the Nation, like that of the professional man, is, selfishness. This is why selfishness in the individual is condemned while in the nation it is extolled, which leads to hopeless moral blindness, confusing the religion of the people with the religion of the nation. Therefore, to take an example, we find men more and more convinced of the superior claims of Christianity, merely because Christian nations are in possession of the greater part of the world. It is like supporting a robber's religion by quoting the amount of his stolen property. Nations celebrate their successful massacre of men in their churches. They forget that *Thugs* also ascribed their success in manslaughter to the favour of their goddess. But in the case of the latter their goddess frankly represented the principle of destruction. It was the criminal tribe's own murderous instinct deified—the instinct, not of one individual, but of the whole community, and therefore held sacred. In the same manner, in modern churches, selfishness, hatred and vanity in their collective aspect of national instincts do not scruple to share the homage paid to God.

Of course, pursuit of self-interest need not be wholly selfish; it can even be in harmony with the interest of all. Therefore, ideally speaking, the nationalism, which stands for the expression of the collective self-interest of a people, need not be ashamed of itself it is maintains its true limitations. But what we see in practice is, that every nation which has prospered has done so through its career of aggressive selfishness either in commercial adventures or in foreign possessions, or in both. And this material prosperity not only feeds continually the selfish instincts of the people, but impresses men's minds with the lesson that, for a nation, selfishness is a necessity and therefore a virtue. It is the emphasis laid in Europe upon the idea of the Nation's constant increase of power, which is becoming the greatest danger to man, both in its direct activity and its power of infection.

We must admit that evils there are in human nature, in spite of our faith in moral laws and our training in self-control. But they carry on their foreheads their own brand of infamy, their very success adding to their monstrosity. All through man's history there will be some who suffer, and others who cause suffering. The conquest of evil will never be a fully accomplished fact, but a continuous process like the process of burning in a flame.

In former ages, when some particular people became turbulent and tried to rob others of their human rights, they sometimes, achieved success and sometimes failed. And it amounted to nothing more than that. But when this idea of the Nation, which has met with universal acceptance in the present day, tries to pass off the cult of collective selfishness as a moral duty, simply because that selfishness is gigantic in stature, it not only commits depredation, but attacks the very vitals of humanity. It unconsciously generates in people's minds an attitude of defiance against moral law. For men are taught by repeated devices the lesson that the Nation is greater than the people, while yet it scatters to the wind the moral law that the people have held sacred.

It has been said that a disease becomes most acutely critical when the brain is affected. For it is the brain that is constantly directing the siege against all disease forces. The spirit of national selfishness is that brain disease of a people which shows itself in red eyes and clenched fists, in violence of talk and movements, all the while shattering its natural restorative powers. But the power of self-sacrifice, together with the moral faculty of sympathy and cooperation, is the guiding spirit of social vitality. Its function is to maintain a beneficent relation of harmony with its surroundings. But when it begins to ignore the moral law which is universal and uses it only within the bounds of its own narrow sphere, then its strength becomes like the strength of madness which ends in self-destruction.

What is worse, this aberration of a people, decked with the showy title of 'patriotism', proudly walks abroad, passing itself off as a highly moral influence. Thus it has spread its inflammatory contagion all over the world, proclaiming its fever flush to be the best sign of health. It is causing in the hearts of peoples, naturally inoffensive, a feeling of envy at not having their temperature as high as that of their delirious neighbours and not being able to cause as much mischief, but merely having to suffer from it.

I have often been asked by my Western friends how to cope with this evil, which has attained such sinister strength and vast dimensions. In fact, I have often been blamed for merely giving warning, and offering no alternative. When we suffer as a result of a particular system, we believe that some other system would bring us better luck. We are apt to forget that all systems produce evil sooner or later, when the psychology which is at the root of them is wrong. The system which is national to-day may assume the shape of the international tomorrow; but so long as men have not forsaken their idolatry of primitive instincts and collective passions, the new system will only become a new instrument of suffering. And because we are training to confound efficient system with moral goodness itself, every ruined system makes us more and more distrustful of moral law.

Therefore I do not put my faith in any new institution, but in the individuals all over the world who think clearly, feel nobly, and act rightly, thus becoming the channels of moral truth. Our moral ideals do not work with chisels and hammers. Like trees, they spread their roots in the soil and their branches in the sky, without consulting any architect for their plans.

An Eastern University

In the midst of much that is discouraging in the present state of the world, there is one symptom of vital promise. Asia is awakening. This great event, if it be but directed along the right lines, is full of hope, not only for Asia herself, but for the whole world.

On the other hand, it has to be admitted that the relationship of the West with the East, growing more and more complex and widespread for over two centuries, far from attaining its true fulfillment, has given rise to a universal spirit of conflict. The consequent strain and unrest have profoundly disturbed Asia, and antipathetic forces have been accumulating for years in the depth of the Eastern mind.

The meeting of the East and the West has remained incomplete, because the occasions of it have not been disinterested. The political and commercial adventures carried on by Western races—very often by force and against the interest and wishes of the countries they have dealt with—have created a moral alienation, which is deeply injurious to both parties. The perils threatened by this unnatural relationship have long been contemptuously ignored by the West. But the blind confidence of the strong in their apparent invincibility has often led them, from their dream of security, into terrible surprises of history.

It is not the fear of danger or loss to one people or another, however, which is most important. The demoralising influence of the constant estrangement between the two hemispheres, which affects the baser passions of man,—pride, greed and hypocrisy on the one hand; fear, suspiciousness and flattery on the other,—has been developing, and threatens us with a world-wide spiritual disaster.

The time has come when we must use all our wisdom to understand the situation, and to control it, with a stronger trust in moral guidance than in any array of physical forces.

In the beginning of man's history his first social object was to form a community, to grow into a people. At that early period, individuals were gathered together within geographical enclosures. But in the present age, with its facility of communication, geographical barriers have almost lost their reality, and the great federation of men, which is waiting either to find its true scope or to break asunder in a final catastrophe, is not a meeting of individuals, but of various human races. Now the problem before us is of one single country, which is this earth, where the races as individuals must find both their freedom of self-expression and their bond of federation. Mankind must realise a unity, wider in range, deeper in sentiment, stronger in power than ever before. Now that the problem is large, we have to solve it on a bigger scale, to realise the God in man by a larger faith and to build the temple of our faith on a sure and world-wide basis.

The first step towards realisation is to create opportunities for revealing the different peoples to one another. This can never be done in those fields where the exploiting utilitarian spirit is supreme. We must find some meeting-ground, where there can be no question of conflicting interests. One of such places is the University, where we can work together in a common pursuit of truth, share together our common heritage, and realise that artists in all parts of the world have created forms of beauty, scientists discovered secrets of the universe, philosophers solved the problems of existence, saints made the truth of the spiritual world organic in their own lives, not merely for some particular race to which they belonged, but for all mankind. When the science of meteorology knows the earth's atmosphere as continuously one, affecting the different parts of the world differently, but in a harmony of adjustments, it knows and attains truth. And so, too, we must know that the great mind of man is one, working through the many differences which are needed to ensure the full result of its fundamental unity. When we understand this truth in a disinterested spirit, it teaches us to respect all the differences in man that are real, yet remain conscious of our oneness; and to know that perfection of unity is not in uniformity, but in harmony.

This is the problem of the present age. The East, for its own sake and for the sake of the world, must not remain unrevealed. The deepest source of all calamities in history is misunderstanding. For where we do not understand, we can never be just.

Being strongly impressed with the need and the responsibility, which every individual to-day must realise according to his power, I have formed the nucleus of an International University in India, as one of the best means of promoting mutual understanding between the East and the West. This Institution, according to the plan I have in mind, will invite students from the West to study the different systems of Indian philosophy, literature, art and music in their proper environment, encouraging them to carry on research work in collaboration with the scholars already engaged in this task.

India has her renaissance. She is preparing to make her contribution to the world of the future. In the past she produced her great culture, and in the present age she has an equally important contribution to make to the culture of the New World which is emerging from the wreckage of the Old. This is a momentous period of her history pregnant with precious possibilities, when any disinterested offer of co-operation from any part of the West will have an immense moral value, the memory of which will become brighter as the regeneration of the East grows in vigour and creative power.

The Western Universities give their students an opportunity to learn what all the European peoples have contributed to their Western culture. Thus the intellectual mind of the West has been luminously revealed to the world. What is needed to complete this illumination is for the East to collect its own scattered lamps and offer them to the enlightenment of the world.

There was a time when the great countries of Asia had, each of them, to nurture its own civilisation apart in comparative seclusion. Now has come the age of co-ordination and co-operation. The seedlings that were reared within narrow plots must now be transplanted into the open fields. They must pass the test of the world-market, if their maximum value is to be obtained.

But before Asia is in a position to co-operate with the culture of Europe, she must base her own structure on a synthesis of all the different cultures which she has. When, taking her stand on such a culture, she turns toward the West, she will take, with a confident sense of mental freedom, her own view of truth, from her own vantage-ground, and open a new vista of thought to the world. Otherwise, she will allow her priceless inheritance to crumble into dust, and, trying to replace it clumsily with feeble imitations of the West, make herself superfluous, cheap and ludicrous. If she thus loses her individuality and her specific power to exist, will it in the least help the rest of the world? Will not her terrible bankruptcy involve also the Western mind? If the whole world grows at last into an exaggerated West, then such an illimitable parody of the modern age will die, crushed beneath its own absurdity.

In this belief, it is my desire to extend by degrees the scope of this University on simple lines, until it comprehends the whole range of Eastern cultures—the Aryan, Semitic, Mongolian and others. Its object will be to reveal the Eastern mind to the world.

Of one thing I felt certain during my travels in Europe, that a genuine interest has been roused there in the philosophy and the arts of the East, from which the Western mind seeks fresh inspiration of truth and beauty. Once the East had her reputation of fabulous wealth, and the seekers were attracted from across the sea. Since then, the shrine of wealth has changed its site. But the East is famed also for her storage of wisdom, harvested by her patriarchs from long successive ages of spiritual endeavour. And when, as now, in the midst of the pursuit of power and wealth, there rises the cry of privation from the famished spirit of man, an opportunity is offered to the East, to offer her store to those who need it.

Once upon a time we were in possession of such a thing as our own mind in India. It was living. It thought, it felt, it expressed itself. It was receptive as well as productive. That this mind could be of any use in the process, or in the end, of our education was overlooked by our modern educational dispensation. We are provided with buildings and books and other magnificent burdens calculated to suppress our mind. The latter was treated like a library-shelf solidly made of wood, to be loaded with leather-bound volumes of second-hand information. In consequence, it has lost its own colour and characters, and has borrowed polish from the carpenter's shop. All this has cost us money, and also our finer ideas, while our intellectual vacancy has been crammed with what is described in official reports as Education. In fact, we have bought our spectacles at the expense of our eyesight.

In India our goddess of learning is *Saraswati*. My audience in the West, I am sure, will be glad to know that her complexion is white. But the signal fact is that she is living and she is a woman, and her seat is on a lotus-flower. The symbolic meaning of this is, that she dwells in the centre of life and the heart of all existence, which opens itself in beauty to the light of heaven.

The Western education which we have chanced to know is impersonal. Its complexion is also white, but it is the whiteness of the white-washed classroom walls. It dwells in the cold-storage compartments of lessons and the ice-packed minds of the schoolmasters. The effect which it had on my mind when, as a boy, I was compelled to go to school, I have described elsewhere. My feeling was very much the same as a tree might have, which was not allowed to live its full life, but was cut down to be made into packing-cases.

The introduction of this education was not a part of the solemn marriage ceremony which was to unite the minds of the East and West in mutual understanding. It represented an artificial method of training specially calculated to produce the carriers of the white man's burden. This want of ideals still clings to our education system, though our Universities have latterly burdened their syllabus with a greater number of subjects than before. But it is only like adding to the bags of wheat the bullock carries to market; it does not make the bullock any better off.

Mind, when long deprived of it natural food of truth and freedom of growth, develops an unnatural craving for success; and our students have fallen victims to the mania for success in examinations. Success consists in obtaining the largest number of marks with the strictest economy of knowledge. It is a deliberate cultivation of disloyalty to truth, of intellectual dishonesty, of a foolish imposition by which the mind is encouraged to rob itself. But as we are by means of it made to forget the existence of mind, we are supremely happy at the result. We pass examinations, and shrivel up into clerks, lawyers and police inspectors, and we die young.

Universities should never be made into mechanical organisations for collecting and distributing knowledge. Through them the people should offer their intellectual hospitality, their wealth of mind to others, and earn their proud right in return to receive gifts from the rest of the world. But in the whole length and breadth of India there is not a single University established in the modern time where a foreign or an Indian student can properly be acquainted with the best products of the Indian mind. For that we have to cross the sea, and knock at the doors of France and Germany. Educational institutions in our country are India's alms-bowl of knowledge; they lower our intellectual self-respect; they encourage us to make a foolish display of decorations composed of borrowed feathers.

This it was that led me to found a school in Bengal, in face of many difficulties and discouragements, and in spite of my own vocation as a poet, who finds this true inspiration only when he forgets that he is a schoolmaster. It is my hope that in this school a nucleus has been formed, round which an indigenous University of our own land will find its natural growth—a University which will help India's mind to concentrate and to be fully conscious of itself; free to seek the truth and make this truth its own wherever found, to judge by its own standard, give expression to its own creative genius, and offer its wisdom to the guests who come from other parts of the world.

Man's intellect has a natural pride in is own aristocracy, which is the pride of its culture. Culture only acknowledges the excellence whose criticism is in its inner perfection, not in any external success. When this pride succumbs to some compulsion of necessity or lure of material advantage, it brings humiliation to the intellectual man. Modern India, through her very education, has been made to suffer this humiliation. Once she herself provided her children with a culture which was the product of her own ages of thought and creation. But it has been thrust aside, and we are made to tread the mill of passing examinations, not for learning anything, but for notifying that we are qualified for employments under organisations conducted in English. Our educated community is not a cultured community, but a community of qualified candidates. Meanwhile the proportion of possible employments to the number of claimants has gradually been growing narrower, and the consequent disaffection has been widespread. At last the very authorities who are responsible for this are blaming their victims. Such is the perversity of human nature. It bears its worst grudge against those it has injured.

It is as if some tribe which had the primitive habit of decorating its tribal members with birds' plumages were some day to hold these very birds guilty of the crime of being extinct. There are belated attempts on the part of our governors to read us pious homilies about disinterested love of learning, while the old machinery goes on working, whose product is not education but certificates. It is good to remind the fettered bird that its wings are for soaring; but it is better to cut the chain which is holding it to its perch. The most pathetic feature of the tragedy is that the bird itself has learnt to use its chain for its ornament, simply because the chain jingles in fairly respectable English.

In the Bengali language there is a modern maxim which can be translated, 'He who learns to read and write rides in a carriage and pair.' In English there is a similar proverb, 'Knowledge is power.' It is an offer of a prospective bribe to the student, a promise of an ulterior reward which is more important than knowledge itself. Temptations, held before us as inducements to be good or to pursue uncongenial paths, are most often flimsy lies or half-truths, such as the oft-quoted maxim of respectable piety, 'Honesty is the best policy,' at which politicians all over the world seem to laugh in their sleeves. But unfortunately, education conducted under a special providence of purposefulness, of eating the fruit of knowledge from the wrong end, *does* lead one to that special paradise on earth, the daily rides in one's own carriage and pair. And the West, I have heard from authentic sources, is aspiring in its education after that special cultivation of worldliness.

Where society is comparatively simple and obstructions are not too numerous, we can clearly see how the life-process guides education in its vital purpose. The system of folk-education, which is indigenous to India, but is dying out, was one with the people's life. It flowed naturally through the social channels and made its way everywhere. It is a system of widespread irrigation of culture. Its teachers, specially trained men, are in constant requisition, and find crowded meetings in our villages, where they repeat the best thoughts and express the ideals of the land in the most effective form. The mode of instruction includes the recitation of epics, expounding of the scriptures, reading from the Puranas, which are the classical records of old history, performance of plays founded upon the early myths and legends, dramatic narration of the lives of ancient heroes, and the singing in chorus of songs from the old religious literature. Evidently, according to this system, the best function of education is to enable us to realise that to live as a man is great, requiring profound philosophy for its ideal, poetry for its expression, and heroism in its conduct. Owing to this vital method of culture the common people of India, though technically illiterate, have been made conscious of the sanctity of social relationships, entailing constant sacrifice and self-control, urged and supported by ideals collectively expressed in one word, *Dharma*.

Such a system of education my sound too simple for the complexities of modern life. But the fundamental principle of social life in its different stages of development remains the same; and in no circumstance can the truth be ignored that all human complexities must harmonise in organic unity with life, failing which there will be endless conflict. Most things in the civilised world occupy more than their legitimate space. Much of their burden is needless. By bearing this burden civilised man may be showing great strength, but he displays little skill. To the gods, viewing this from on high, it must seem like the flounderings of a giant who has got out of his depth and knows not how to swim.

The main source of all forms of voluntary slavery is the desire of gain. It is difficult to fight against this when modern civilisation is tainted with such a universal contamination of avarice. I have realised it myself in the little boys of my own school. For the first few years there is no trouble. But as soon as the upper class is reached, their worldly wisdom—the malady of the aged—begins to assert itself. They rebelliously insist that they must no longer learn, but rather pass examinations. Professions in the modern age are more numerous and lucrative than ever before. They need specialisation of training and knowledge, tempting education to yield its spiritual freedom to the claims of utilitarian ambitions. But man's deeper nature is hurt; his smothered life seeks to be liberated from the suffocating folds and sensual ties of prosperity. And this is why we find almost everywhere in the world a growing dissatisfaction with the prevalent system of teaching, which betrays the encroachment of senility and worldly prudence over pure intellect.

In India, also, a vague feeling of discontent has given rise to numerous attempts at establishing national schools and colleges, but, unfortunately, our very education has been successful in depriving us of our real initiative and our courage of thought. The training we get in our schools has the constant implication in it that it is not for us to produce but to borrow. And we are casting about to borrow our educational plans from European institutions. The trampled plants of Indian corn are dreaming of recouping their harvest from the neighbouring wheat fields. To change the figure, we forget that, for proficiency in walking, it is better to train the muscles of our own legs than to strut upon wooden ones of foreign make, although they clatter and cause more surprise at our skill in using them than if they were living and real.

But when we go to borrow help from a foreign neighbourhood we are apt to overlook the real source of help behind all that is external and apparent. Had the deep-water fishes happened to produce a scientist who chose the jumping of a monkey for his research work, I am sure he would give most of the credit to the branches of the trees and very little to the monkey itself. In a foreign University we see the branching wildernesses of its buildings, furniture, regulations, and syllabus, but the monkey, which is a difficult creature to catch and more difficult to manufacture, we are likely to treat as a mere accident of minor importance. It is convenient for us to overlook the fact that among the Europeans the living spirit of the University is widely spread in their society, their parliament, their literature, and the numerous activities of their corporate life. In all these functions they are in perpetual touch with the great personality of the land which is creative and heroic in its constant acts of self-expression and self-sacrifice. They have their thoughts published in their books as well as through the medium of living men who think those thoughts, and who criticise, compare and disseminate them. Some at least of the drawbacks of their academic education are redeemed by the living energy of the intellectual personality pervading their social organism. It is like the stagnant reservoir of water which finds its purification in the showers of rain to which it keeps itself open. But, to our misfortune, we have in India all the furniture of the European University except the human teacher. We have, instead, mere purveyors of book-lore in whom the paper god of the bookshop has been made vocal.

A most important truth, which we are apt to forget, is that a teacher can never truly teach unless he is still learning himself. A lamp can never light another lamp unless it continues to burn its own flame. The teacher who has come to the end of his subject, who has no living traffic with his knowledge, but merely repeats his lessons to his students, can only load their minds; he cannot quicken them. Truth not only must inform but inspire. If the inspiration dies out, and the information only accumulates, then truth loses its infinity. The greater part of our learning in the schools has been wasted because, for most of our teachers, their subjects are like dead specimens of once living things, with which they have a learned acquaintance, but no communication of life and love.

The educational institution, therefore, which I have in mind has primarily for its object the constant pursuit of truth, from which the imparting of truth naturally follows. It must not be a dead cage in which living minds are fed with food artificially prepared. It should be an open house, in which students and teachers are at one. They must live their complete life together, dominated by a common aspiration for truth and a need of sharing all the delights of culture. In former days the great master-craftsmen had students in their workshops where they co-operated in shaping things to perfection. That was the place where knowledge could become living—that knowledge which not only has its substance and law, but its atmosphere subtly informed by a creative art, in which the man who explores truth expresses something which is human in him—his enthusiasm, his courage, his sacrifice, his honesty, and his skill. In merely academical teaching we find subjects, but not the man who pursues the subjects; therefore the vital part of education remains incomplete.

For our Universities we must claim, not labelled packages of truth and authorised agents to distribute them, but truth in its living association with her lovers and seekers and discoverers. Also we must know that the concentration of the mind-forces scattered throughout the country is the most important mission of a University, which, like the nucleus of a living cell, should be the centre of the intellectual life of the people.

The bringing about of an intellectual unity in India is, I am told, difficult to the verge of impossibility owing to the fact that India has so many different languages. Such a statement is as unreasonable as to say that man, because he has a diversity of limbs, should find it impossible to realise life's unity in himself, and that only an earthworm composed of a tail and nothing else could truly know that it had a body.

Let us admit that India is not like any one of the great countries of Europe, which has its own separate language; but is rather like Europe herself, branching out into different peoples with many different languages. And yet Europe has a common civilisation, with an intellectual unity which is not based upon uniformity of language. It is true that in the earlier stages of her culture the whole of Europe had Latin for her learned tongue. That was in her intellectual budding time, when all her petals of self-expression were closed in one point. But the perfection of her mental unfolding was not represented by the singularity of her literary vehicle. When the grate European countries found their individual languages, then only the true federation of cultures became possible in the West, and the very differences of the channels made the commerce of ideas in Europe so richly copious and so variedly active. We can well imagine what the loss to European civilisation would be if France, Italy and Germany, and England herself, had not through their separate agencies contributed to the common coffer their individual earnings.

There was a time with us when India had her common language of culture in Sanskrit. But, for the complete commerce of her thought, she required that all her vernaculars should attain their perfect powers, through which her different peoples might manifest their idiosyncrasies; and this could never be done through a foreign tongue.

In the United States, in Canada and other British Colonies, the language of the people is English. It has a great literature which had its birth and growth in the history of the British Islands. But when this language, with all its products and acquisitions, matured by ages on its own mother soil, is carried into foreign lands, which have their own separate history and their own life-growth, it must constantly hamper the indigenous growth of culture and destroy individuality of judgement and the perfect freedom of self-expression. The inherited wealth of the English language, with all its splendour, becomes an impediment when taken into different surroundings, just as when lungs are given to the whale in the sea. If such is the case even with races whose grandmother-tongue naturally continues to be their own mother-tongue, one can imagine what sterility it means for a people which accepts, for its vehicle of culture, an altogether foreign language. A language is not like an umbrella or an overcoat, that can be borrowed by unconscious or deliberate mistake; it is like the living skin itself. If the body of a draught-horse enters into the skin of a race-horse, it will be safe to wager that such an anomaly will never win a race, and will fail even to drag a cart. Have we not watched some modern Japanese artists imitating European art? The imitation may sometimes produce clever results; but such cleverness has only the perfection of artificial flowers which never bear fruit.

All great countries have their vital centres for intellectual life, where a high standard of learning is maintained, where the minds of the people are naturally attracted, where they find their genial atmosphere, in which to prove their worth and to contribute their share to the country's culture. Thus they kindle, on the common altar of the land, that great sacrificial fire which can radiate the sacred light of wisdom abroad.

Athens was such a centre in Greece, Rome in Italy; and Paris is such today in France. Benares has been and still continues to be the centre of our Sanskrit culture. But Sanskrit learning does not exhaust all the elements of culture that exist in modern India.

If we were to take for granted, what some people maintain, that Western culture is the only source of light for our mind, then it would be like depending for daybreak upon some star, which is the sun of a far distant sphere. The star may give us light, but not the day; it may give us direction in our voyage of exploration, but it can never open the full view of truth before our eyes. In fact, we can never use this cold starlight for stirring the sap in our branches, and giving colour and bloom to our life. This is the reason why European education has become for India mere school lessons and no culture; a box of matches, good for the small uses of illumination, but not the light of morning, in which the use and beauty, and all the subtle mysteries of life are blended in one.

Let me say clearly that I have no distrust of any culture because of its foreign character. On the contrary, I believe that the shock of such extraneous forces is necessary for the vitality of our intellectual nature. It is admitted that much of the spirit of Christianity runs counter, not only to the classical culture of Europe, but to the European temperament altogether. And yet this alien movement of ideas, constantly running against the natural mental current of Europe, has been a most important factor in strengthening and enriching her civilisation, on account of the sharp antagonism of its intellectual direction. In fact, the European vernaculars first woke up to life and fruitful vigour when they felt the impact of this foreign thought-power with all its oriental forms and affinities. The same thing is happening in India. The European culture has come to us, not only with its knowledge, but with its velocity.

Then, again, let us admit that modern Science is Europe's great gift to humanity for all time to come. We, in India, must claim it from her hands, and gratefully accept it in order to be saved from the curse of futility by lagging behind. We shall fail to reap the harvest of the present age if we delay.

What I object to is the artificial arrangement by which foreign education tends to occupy all the space of out national mind, and thus kills, or hampers, the great opportunity for the creation of a new thought-power by a new combination of truths. It is this which makes me urge that all the elements in our own culture have to be strengthened, not to resist the Western culture, but truly to accept and assimilate it; to use it for our sustenance, not as our burden; to get mastery over this culture, and not to live on its outskirts as the hewers of texts and drawers of book-learning.

The main river in Indian culture has flowed in four streams,—the Vedic, the Puranic, the Buddhist, and the Jain. It has its source in the heights of the Indian consciousness. But a river, belonging to a country, is not fed by its own waters alone. The Tibetan Brahmaputra is a tributary to the Indian Ganges. Contributions have similarly found their way to India's original culture. The Muhammadan, for example, has repeatedly come into India's original culture. The Muhammadan, for example, has repeatedly come into India from outside, laden with his own stores of knowledge and feeling and his wonderful religious democracy, bringing freshet after freshet to swell the current. To our music, our architecture, our pictorial art, our literature, the Muhammadans have made their permanent and precious contribution. Those who have studied the lives and writings of our medieval saints, and all the great religious movements that sprang up in the time of the Muhammadan rule, know how deep is our debt to this foreign current that has so intimately mingled with our life.

So, in our centre of Indian learning, we must provide for the co-ordinate study of all these different cultures,—the Vedic, the Puranic, the Buddhist, the Jain, the Islamic, the Sikh and the Zoroastrian. The Chinese, Japanese, and Tibetan will also have to be added; for, in the past, India did not remain isolated within her own boundaries. Therefore, in order to learn what she was, in her relation to the whole continent of Asia, these cultures too must be studied. Side by side with them must finally be placed the Western culture. For only then shall we be able to assimilate this last contribution to our common stock. A river flowing within banks is truly our own, and it can contain its due tributaries; but our relations with a flood can only prove disastrous.

There are some who are exclusively modern, who believe that the past is the bankrupt time, leaving no assets for us, but only a legacy of debts. They refuse to believe that the army which is marching forward can be fed from the rear. It is well to remind such persons that the great ages of renaissance in history were those when man suddenly discovered the seeds of thought in the granary of the past.

The unfortunate people who have lost the harvest of their past have lost their present age. They have missed their seed for cultivation, and go begging for their bare livelihood. We must not imagine that we are one of these disinherited peoples of the world. The time has come for us to break open the treasure-trove of our ancestors, and use it for our commerce of life. Let us, with its help, make our future our own, and not continue our existence as the eternal rag-pickers in other people's dustbins. So far I have dwelt only upon the intellectual aspect of Education. For, even in the West, it is the intellectual training which receives almost exclusive emphasis. The Western universities have not yet truly recognized that fulness of life. And a large part of man can never find its expression in the mere language of words. It must therefore seek for its other languages,—lines and colours, sounds and movements. Through our mastery of these we not only make our whole nature articulate, but also understand man in all his attempts to reveal his innermost being in every age and clime. The great use of Education is not merely to collect facts, but to know man and to make oneself known to man. It is the duty of every human being to master, at least to some extent, not only the language of intellect, but also that personality which is the language of Art. It is a great world of reality for man,— vast and profound,—this growing world of his own creative nature. This is the world of Art. To be brought up in ignorance of it is to be deprived of the knowledge and use of that great inheritance of humanity, which has been growing and waiting for every one of us from the beginning of our history. It is to remain deaf to the eternal voice of Man, that speaks to all men the messages that are beyond speech. From the educational point of view we know Europe where it is scientific, or at best literary. So our notion of its modern culture is limited within the boundary lines of grammar and the laboratory. We almost completely ignore the aesthetic life of man, leaving it uncultivated, allowing weeds to grow there. Our newspapers are prolific, our meeting-places are vociferous; and in them we wear to shreds the things we have borrowed from our English teachers. We make the air dismal and damp with the tears of our grievances. But where are our arts, which, like the outbreak of spring flowers, are the spontaneous overflow of our deeper nature and spiritual magnificence?

Through this great deficiency of our modern education, we are condemned to carry to the end a dead load of dumb wisdom. Like miserable outcasts, we are deprived of our place in the festival of culture, and wait at the outer court, where the colours are not for us, nor the forms of delight, nor the songs. Ours is the education of a prison-house, with hard labour and with a drab dress cut to the limits of minimum decency and necessity. We are made to forget that the perfection of colour and form and expression belongs to the perfection of vitality,—that the joy of life is only the other side of the strength of life. The timber merchant may think that the flowers and foliage are mere frivolous decorations of a tree; but if these are suppressed, he will know to his cost that the timber too will fail.

During the Moghal period, music and art in India found a great impetus from the rulers, because their whole life— not merely their official life—was lived in this land; and it is the wholeness of life from which originates Art. But our English teachers are birds of passage; they cackle to us, but do not sing,—their true heart is not in the land of their exile.

Construction of life, owing to this narrowness of culture, must no longer be encouraged. In the centre of Indian culture which I am proposing, music and art must have their prominent seats of honour, and not be given merely a tolerant nod of recognition. The different systems of music and different schools of art which lie scattered in the different ages and provinces of India, and in the different strata of society, and also those belonging to the other great countries of Asia, which had communication with India, have to be brought there together and studied.

I have already hinted that Education should not be dragged out of its native element, the life-current of the people.

Economic life covers the whole width of the fundamental basis of society, because its necessities are the simplest and the most universal. Educational institutions, in order to obtain their fulness of truth, must have close association with this economic life. The highest mission of education is to help us to realise the inner principle of the unity of all knowledge and all the activities of our social and spiritual being. Society in its early stage was held together by its economic co-operation, when all its members felt in unison a natural interest in their right to live. Civilisation could never been started at all if such was not the case. And civilisation will fall to pieces if it never again realises the spirit of mutual help and the common sharing of benefits in the elemental necessaries of life. The idea of such economic co-operation should be made the basis of our University. It must not only instruct, but live; not only think, but produce.

Our ancient *tapovanas*, or forest schools, which were our natural universities, were not shut off from the daily life of the people. Masters and students gathered fruit and fuel, and took their cattle out to graze, supporting themselves by the work of their own hands. Spiritual education was a part of the spiritual life itself, which comprehended all life. Out centre of culture should not only be the centre of the intellectual life of India, but the centre of her economic life also. I must co-operate with the villages round it, cultivate land, breed cattle, spin cloths, press oil from oil from oil-seeds; it must produce all the necessaries, devising the best means, using the best materials, and calling science to its aid. Its very existence should depend upon the success of its industrial activities carried out on the co-operative principle, which will unite the teachers and students and villagers of the neighbourhood in a living and active bond of necessity. This will give us also a practical industrial training, whose motive force is not the greed of profit.

Before I conclude my paper, a delicate question remains to be considered. What must be the religious ideal that is to rule our centre of Indian culture? The one abiding ideal in the religious life of India has been *mukti*, the deliverance of man's soul from the grip of self, its communion with the Infinite Soul through its union in *ânanda* with the universe. This religion of spiritual harmony is not a theological doctrine to be taught, as a subject in the class, for half an hour each day. It is the spiritual truth and beauty of our attitude towards our surroundings, our conscious relationship with the Infinite, and the lasting power of the Eternal in the passing moments of our life. Such a religious ideal can only be made possible by making provision for students to live in intimate touch with nature, daily to grow in an atmosphere of service offered to all creatures, tending trees, feeding birds and animals, learning to feel the immense mystery of the soil and mater and air.

Along with this, there should be some common sharing of life with the tillers of the soil and the humble workers in the neighbouring villages; studying their crafts, inviting them to the feasts, joining them in works of co-operation for communal welfare; and in our intercourse we should be guided, not by moral maxims or the condescension of social superiority, but by natural sympathy of life for life, and by the sheer necessity of love's sacrifice for its own sake. In such an atmosphere students would learn to understand that humanity is a divine harp of many strings, waiting for its one grand music. Those who realise this unity are made ready for the pilgrimage through the night of suffering, and along the path of sacrifice, to the great meeting of Man in the future, for which the call comes to us across the darkness.

Life, in such a centre, should be simple and clean. We should never believe that simplicity of life might make us unsuited to the requirements of the society of our time. It is the simplicity of the tuning-fork, which is needed all the more because of the intricacy of strings in the instrument. In the morning of our career our nature needs the pure and the perfect note of a spiritual ideal in order to fit us for the complications of our later years.

In other words, this institution should be a perpetual creation by the co-operative enthusiasm of teachers and students, growing with the growth of their soul; a world in itself, self-sustaining, independent, rich with ever-renewing life radiating life across space and time, attracting and maintaining round it a planetary system of dependent bodies. Its aim should lie in imparting life-breath to the complete man, who is intellectual as well as economic, bound by social bonds, but aspiring towards spiritual freedom and final perfection.

SĀDHĀNA

The Relation of the Individual
to the Universe

The civilization of ancient Greece was nurtured within city walls. In fact, all the modern civilizations have their cradles of brick and mortar.

These walls leave their mark deep in the minds of men. They set up a principle of 'divide and rule' in our mental outlook, which begets in us a habit of securing all our conquests by fortifying them and separating them from one another. We divide nation and nation, knowledge and knowledge, man and nature. It breeds in us a strong suspicion of whatever is beyond the barriers we have built, and everything has to fight hard for its entrance into our recognition.

When the first Aryan invaders appeared in India it was a vast land of forests, and the new-comers rapidly took advantage of them. These forests afforded them shelter from the fierce heat of the sun and the ravages of tropical storms, pastures for cattle, fuel for sacrificial fire, and materials for building cottages. And the different Aryan clans with their patriarchal heads settled in the different forest tracts which had some special advantage of natural protection, and food and water in plenty.

Thus in India it was in the forests that our civilization had its birth, and it took a distinct character from this origin and environment. It was surrounded by the vast life of nature, was fed and clothed by her, and had the closest and most constant intercourse with her varying aspects.

Such a life, it may be thought, tends to have the effect of dulling human intelligence and dwarfing the incentives to progress by lowering the standards of existence. But in ancient India we find that the circumstances of forest life did not overcome man's mind, and did not enfeeble the current of his energies, but only gave to it a particular direction. Having been in constant contact with the living growth of nature, his mind was free from the desire to extend his dominion by erecting boundary walls around his acquisitions. His aim was not to acquire but to realise, to enlarge his consciousness by growing with and growing into his surroundings. He felt that truth is all-comprehensive, that there is no such thing as absolute isolation in existence, and the only way of attaining truth is through the interpenetration of our being into all objects. To realise this great harmony between manŌs spirit and the spirit of the world was the endeavour of the forest-dwelling sages of ancient India.

In later days there came a time when these primeval forests gave way to cultivated fields, and wealthy cities sprang up on all sides. Mighty kingdoms were established, which had communications with all the great powers of the world. But even in the heyday of its material prosperity the heart of India ever looked back with adoration upon the early ideal of strenuous self-realization, and the dignity of the simple life of the forest hermitage, and drew its best inspiration from the wisdom stored there.

The west seems to take a pride in thinking that it is subduing nature; as if we are living in a hostile world where we have to wrest everything we want from an unwilling and alien arrangement of things. This sentiment is the product of the city-wall habit and training of mind. For in the city life man naturally directs the concentrated light of his mental vision upon his own life and works, and this creates an artificial dissociation between himself and the Universal Nature within whose bosom he lies.

But in India the point of view was different; it included the world with the man as one great truth. India put all her emphasis on the harmony that exists between the individual and the universal. She felt we could have no communication whatever with our surroundings if they were absolutely foreign to us. Man's complaint against nature is that he has to acquire most of his necessaries by his own efforts. Yes, but his efforts are not in vain; he is reaping success every day, and that shows there is a rational connection between him and nature, for we never can make anything our own except that which is truly related to us.

We can look upon a road from two different points of view. One regards it as dividing us from the object of our desire; in that case we count every step of our journey over it as something attained by force in the face of obstruction. The other sees it as the road which leads us to our destination; and as such it is part of our goal. It is already the beginning of our attainment, and by journeying over it we can only gain that which in itself it offers to us. This last point of view is that of India with regard to nature. For her, the great fact is that we are in harmony with nature; that man can think because his thoughts are in harmony with things; that he can use the forces of nature for his own purpose only because his power is in harmony with the power which is universal, and that in the long run his purpose never can knock against the purpose which works through nature.

In the west the prevalent feeling is that nature belongs exclusively to inanimate things and to beasts, that there is a sudden unaccountable break where human-nature begins. According to it, everything that is low in the scale of beings is merely nature, and whatever has the stamp of perfection on it, intellectual or moral, is human-nature. It is like dividing the bud and the blossom into two separate categories, and putting their grace to the credit of two different and antithetical principles. But the Indian mind never has any hesitation in acknowledging its kinship with nature, its unbroken relation with all.

The fundamental unity of creation was not simply a philosophical speculation for India; it was her life-object to realise this great harmony in feeling and in action. With meditation and service, with a regulation of her life, she cultivated her consciousness in such a way that everything had a spiritual meaning to her. The earth, water and light, fruits and flowers, to her were not merely physical phenomena to be turned to use and then left aside. They were necessary to her in the attainment of her ideal of perfection, as every note is necessary to the completeness of the symphony. India intuitively felt that the essential fact of this world has a vital meaning for us; we have to be fully alive to it and establish a conscious relation with it, not merely impelled by scientific curiosity or greed of material advantage, but realising it in the spirit of sympathy, with a large feeling of joy and peace.

The man of science knows, in one aspect, that the world is not merely what it appears to be to our senses; he knows that earth and water are really the play of forces that manifest themselves to us as earth and water—how, we can but partially apprehend. Likewise the man who has his spiritual eyes open knows that the ultimate truth about earth and water lies in our apprehension of the eternal will which works in time and takes shape in the forces we realise under those aspects. This is not mere knowledge, as science is, but it is a perception of the soul by the soul. This does not lead us to power, as knowledge does, but it gives us joy, which is the product of the union of kindred things. The man whose acquaintance with the world does not lead him deeper than science leads him, will never understand what it is that the man with the spiritual vision finds in these natural phenomena. The water does not merely cleanse his limbs, but it purifies his heart; for it touches his soul. The earth does not merely hold his body, but it gladdens his mind; for its contact is more than a physical contact—it is a living presence. When a man does not realise his kinship with the world, he lives in a prison-house whose walls are alien to him. When he meets the eternal spirit in all objects, then is he emancipated for then he discovers the fullest significance of the world into which he is born; then he finds himself in perfect truth, and his harmony with the all is established. In India men are enjoined to be fully awake to the fact that they are in the closest relation to things around them, body and soul, and that they are to hail the morning sun, the flowing water, the fruitful earth, as the manifestation of the same living truth which holds them in its embrace. Thus the text of our everyday meditation is the Gayatri, a verse which is considered to be the epitome of all the Vedas. By its help we try to realise the essential unity of the world with the conscious soul of man; we learn to perceive the unity held together by the one Eternal Spirit, whose power creates the earth, the sky, and the stars, and at the same time irradiates our minds with the light of a consciousness that moves and exists in unbroken continuity with the outer world.

It is not true that India has tried to ignore differences of value in different things, for she knows that would make life impossible. The sense of the superiority of man in the scale of creation has not been absent from her mind. But she has had her own idea as to that in which his superiority really consists. It is not in the power of possession but in the power of union. Therefore India chose her places of pilgrimage wherever there was in nature some special grandeur or beauty, so that her mind could come out of its world of narrow necessities and realise its place in the infinite. This was the reason why in India a whole people who once were meat-eaters gave up taking animal food to cultivate the sentiment of universal sympathy for life, an event unique in the history of mankind.

India knew that when by physical and mental barriers we violently detach ourselves from the inexhaustible life of nature; when we become merely man, not man-in-the-universe, we create bewildering problems, and having shut off the source of their solution, we try all kinds of artificial methods each of which brings its own crop of interminable difficulties. When man leaves his resting-place in universal nature, when he walks on the single rope of humanity, ·it means either a dance or a fall for him, he has ceaselessly to strain every nerve and muscle to keep his balance at each step, and then, in the intervals of his weariness, he fulminates against Providence and feels a secret pride and satisfaction in thinking that he has been unfairly dealt with by the whole scheme of things.

But this cannot go on for ever. Man must realise the wholeness of his existence, his place in the infinite; he must know that hard as he may strive he can never create his honey within the cells of his hive, for the perennial supply of his life food is outside their walls. He must know that when man shuts himself out from the vitalising and purifying touch of the infinite, and falls back upon himself for his sustenance and his healing, then he goads himself into madness, tears himself into shreds, and eats his own substance. Deprived of the background of the whole, his poverty loses its one great quality, which is simplicity, and becomes squalid and shamefaced. His wealth is no longer magnanimous; it grows merely extravagant. His appetites do not minister to his life, keeping to the limits of their purpose; they become an end in themselves and set fire to his life and play the fiddle in the lurid light of the conflagration. Then it is that in our self-expression we try to startle and not to attract; in art we strive for originality and lose sight of truth which is old and yet ever new; in literature we miss the complete view of man which is simple and yet great. Man appears instead as a psychological problem, or as the embodiment of a passion that is intense because abnormal, being exhibited in the glare of a fiercely emphatic artificial light. When man's consciousness is restricted only to the immediate vicinity of his human self, the deeper roots of his nature do not find their permanent soil, his spirit is ever on the brink of starvation, and in the place of healthful strength he substitutes rounds of stimulation. Then it is that man misses his inner perspective and measures his greatness by its bulk and not by its vital link with the infinite, judges his activity by its movement and not by the repose of perfection—the repose which is in the starry heavens, in the ever-flowing rhythmic dance of creation.

The first invasion of India has its exact parallel in the invasion of America by the European settlers. They also were confronted with primeval forests and a fierce struggle with aboriginal races. But this struggle between man and man, and man and nature lasted till the very end; they never came to any terms. In India the forests which were the habitation of barbarians became the sanctuary of sages, but in America these great living cathedrals of nature had no deeper significance to man. They brought wealth and power to him, and perhaps at times they ministered to his enjoyment of beauty, and inspired a solitary poet. They never acquired a sacred association in the hearts of men as the site of some great spiritual reconcilement where man's soul had its meeting-place with the soul of the world.

I do not for a moment wish to suggest that things should have been otherwise. It would be an utter waste of opportunities if history were to repeat itself exactly in the same manner in every place. It is best for the commerce of the spirit that people differently situated should bring their different produces into the market of humanity, each of which is complementary and necessary to the others. All that I wish to say is that India at the outset of her career met with a special combination of circumstances which was not lost upon her. She had, according to her opportunities, thought and pondered, striven and suffered, dived into the depths of existence, and achieved something which surely cannot be without its value to people whose evolution in history took a different way altogether. Man for his perfect growth requires all the living elements that constitute his complex life; that is why his food has to be cultivated in different fields and brought from different sources.

Civilization is a kind of mould that each nation is busy making for itself to shape its men and women according to its best ideal. All its institutions, its legislature, its standard of approbation and condemnation, its conscious and unconscious teachings tend toward that object. The modern civilization of the west, by all its organised efforts, is trying to turn out men perfect in physical, intellectual, and moral efficiency. There the vast energies of the nations are employed in extending man's power over his surroundings, and people are combining and straining every faculty to possess and to turn to account all that they can lay their hands upon, to overcome every obstacle on their path of conquest. They are ever disciplining themselves to fight nature and other races; their armaments are getting more and more stupendous every day; their machines, their appliances, their organisations go on multiplying at an amazing rate. This is a splendid achievement, no doubt, and a wonderful manifestation of man's masterfulness, which knows no obstacle and has for its object the supremacy of himself over everything else.

The ancient civilization of India had its own ideal of perfection towards which its efforts were directed. Its aim was not attaining power, and it neglected to cultivate to the utmost its capacities, and to organize men for defensive and offensive purposes, for co-operation in the acquisition of wealth and for military and political ascendancy. The ideal that India tried to realise led her best men to the isolation of a contemplative life, and the treasures that she gained for mankind by penetrating into the mysteries of reality cost her dear in the sphere of worldly success. Yet, this also was a sublime achievement,—it was a supreme manifestation of that human aspiration which knows no limit, and which has for its object nothing less than the realization of the Infinite.

There were the virtuous, the wise, the courageous; there were the statesmen, kings and emperors of India; but whom amongst all these classes did she look up to and choose to be the representative of men?

They were the rishis. What were the rishis? *They who having attained the supreme soul in knowledge were filled with wisdom, and having found him in union with the soul were in perfect harmony with the inner self; they having realised him in the heart were free from all selfish desires, and having experienced him in all the activities of the world, had attained calmness. The rishis were they who having reached the supreme God from all sides had found abiding peace, had become united with all, had entered into the life of the Universe.*[1]

Thus the state of realising our relationship with all, of entering into everything through union with God, was considered in India to be the ultimate end and fulfilment of humanity.

Man can destroy and plunder, earn and accumulate, invent and discover, but he is great because his soul comprehends

---

1. Samprāpyainam rishayo jñānatriptāh
   Kritātmānō vītarāgāh praçantāh
   tē sarvagam sarvatah prāpya dhīrāh
   Yuktātmānah sarvamēvāviçanti.

all. It is dire destruction for him when he envelopes his soul in a dead shell of callous habits, and when a blind fury of works whirls round him like an eddying dust storm, shutting out the horizon. That indeed kills the very spirit of his being, which is the spirit of comprehension. Essentially man is not a slave either of himself or of the world; but he is a lover. His freedom and fulfilment is in love, which is another name for perfect comprehension. By this power of comprehension, this permeation of his being, he is united with the all-pervading Spirit, who is also the breath of his soul. Where a man tries to raise himself to eminence by pushing and jostling all others, to achieve a distinction by which he prides himself to be more than everybody else, there he is alienated from that Spirit. This is why the Upanishads describe those who have attained the goal of human life as 'peaceful'[2] and as 'at-one-with-God,'[3] meaning that they are in perfect harmony with man and nature, and therefore in undisturbed union with God.

We have a glimpse of the same truth in the teachings of Jesus when he says, 'It is easier for a camel to pass through the eye of a needle than for a rich man to enter the kingdom of Heaven'—which implies that whatever we treasure for ourselves separates us from others; our possessions are our limitations. He who is bent upon accumulating riches is unable, with his ego continually bulging, to pass through the gates of comprehension of the spiritual world, which is the world of perfect harmony; he is shut up within the narrow walls of his limited acquisitions.

Hence the spirit of the teachings of the Upanishads is: In order to find him you must embrace all. In the pursuit of wealth you really give up everything to gain a few things, and that is not the way to attain him who is completeness.

---

2. Praçantāh.
3. Yuktāmānah.

Some modern philosophers of Europe, who are directly or indirectly indebted to the Upanishads, far from realising their debt, maintain that the Brahma of India is a mere abstraction, a negation of all that is in the world. In a word, that the Infinite Being is to be found nowhere except in metaphysics. It may be, that such a doctrine has been and still is prevalent with a section of our countrymen. But this is certainly not in accord with the pervading spirit of the Indian mind. Instead, it is the practice of realising and affirming the presence of the infinite in all things which has been its constant inspiration.

We are enjoined to see *whatever there is in the world as being enveloped by God.*[4]

I bow to God over and over again who is in fire and in water, who permeates the whole world, who is in the annual crops as well as in the perennial trees.[5]

Can this be God abstracted from the world? Instead, it signifies not merely seeing him in all things, but saluting him, in all the objects of the world. The attitude of the God-conscious man of the Upanishad towards the universe is one of a deep feeling of adoration. His object of worship is present everywhere. It is the one living truth that makes all realities true. This truth is not only of knowledge but of devotion. 'Namonamah,'—we bow to him everywhere, and over and over again. It is recognized in the outburst of the Rishi, who addresses the whole world in a sudden ecstasy of joy: *Listen to me, ye sons of the immortal spirit, ye who live in the heavenly abode, I have known the Supreme Person whose light shines forth from beyond the darkness.*[6] Do we

---

4. Içāvāsyamidam sarvam yat kiñcha jagatyāñ jagat.
5. Yo dēvō'gnau y'ōpsu yō viçvambhuvanamāvieça ya ōshadhishu yō vanaspatishu tasmai dēvāya namōnamah.
6. Criṇvantu viçve amritasya putrā ā ye divya dhāmāni tasthuh vedāhametam purusham mahāntam āditya varnam tamasah parastāt.

not find the overwhelming delight of a direct and positive experience where there is not the least trace of vagueness or passivity?

Buddha, who developed the practical side of the teaching of the Upanishads, preached the same message when he said, *With everything, whether it is above or below, remote or near, visible or invisible, thou shalt preserve a relation of unlimited love without any animosity or without a desire to kill. To live in such a consciousness while standing or walking, sitting or lying down till you are asleep, is Brahma vihāra, or, in other words, is living and moving and having your joy in the spirit of Brahma.*

What is that spirit? The Upanishad says, *The being who is in his essence the light and life of all, who is world-conscious, is Brahma.*[7] To feel all, to be conscious of everything, is his spirit. We are immersed in his consciousness body and soul. It is through his consciousness that the sun attracts the earth; it is through his consciousness that the light-waves are being transmitted from planet to planet.

Not only in space, but *this light and life, this all-feeling being is in our souls.*[8] He is all-conscious in space, or the world of extension; and he is all-conscious in soul, or the world of intension.

Thus to attain our world-consciousness, we have to unite our feeling with this all-pervasive infinite feeling. In fact, the only true human progress is coincident with this widening of the range of feeling. All our poetry, philosophy, science, art, and religion are serving to extend the scope of our consciousness towards higher and larger spheres. Man does

---

7. Yaçchāyamasminnākāçē tējōmayō'mritamayah purushah sarvānubhūh.
8. Yaçchāyamasminnātmani tējōmayō'mritamayah purushah sarvānubhūh.

not acquire rights through occupation of larger space, nor through external conduct, but his rights extend only so far as he is real, and his reality is measured by the scope of his consciousness. We have, however, to pay a price for this attainment of the freedom of consciousness. What is the price? It is to give oneŌs self away. Our soul can realise itself truly only by denying itself. The Upanishad says, *Thou shalt gain by giving away*,[9] *Thou shalt not covet*.[10]

In the Gita we are advised to work disinterestedly, abandoning all lust for the result. Many outsiders conclude from this teaching that the conception of the world as something unreal lies at the root of the so-called disinterestedness preached in India. But the reverse is the truth.

The man who aims at his own aggrandizement underrates everything else. Compared with himself the rest of the world is unreal. Thus in order to be fully conscious of the reality of all, man has to be free himself from the bonds of personal desires. This discipline we have to go through to prepare ourselves for our social duties—for sharing the burdens of our fellow-beings. Every endeavour to attain a larger life requires of man 'to gain by giving away, and not to be greedy.' And thus to expand gradually the consciousness of one's unity with all is the striving of humanity.

The Infinite in India was not a thin nonentity, void of all content. The Rishis of India asserted emphatically, 'To know him in this life is to be true; not to know him in this life is the desolation of death.'[11] How to know him then? 'By realising

---

9. Tyaktēna bhuñjīthāh.
10. Mā gridhah.
11. Iha chēt avēdit atha satyamasti, nachēt iha avēdit mahat´ vinashtih.

him in each and all.'[12] Not only in nature, but in the family, in society, and in the state, the more we realise the World-conscious in all, the better for us. Failing to realise this, we turn our faces to destruction.

It fills me with great joy and a high hope for the future of humanity when I realise that there was a time in the remote past when our poet-prophets stood under the lavish sunshine of an Indian sky and greeted the world with the glad recognition of kindred. It was not an anthropomorphic hallucination. It was not seeing man reflected everywhere in grotesquely exaggerated images, and witnessing the human drama acted on a gigantic scale in nature's arena of flitting lights and shadows. On the contrary, it meant crossing the limiting barriers of the individual, to become more than man, to become one with the All. It was not a mere play of the imagination, but it was the liberation of consciousness from all the mystifications and exaggerations of the self. These ancient seers felt in the serene depth of their mind that the same energy, which vibrates and passes into the endless forms of the world, manifests itself in our inner being as consciousness; and there is no break in unity. For these seers there was no gap in their luminous vision of perfection. They never acknowledged even death itself as creating a chasm in the field of reality. They said, *His reflection is death as well as immortality*.[13] They did not recognize any essential opposition between life and death, and they said with absolute assurance, 'It is life that is death.[14] They saluted with the same serenity of gladness 'life in its aspect of appearing and in its aspect of departure'—*That which is past is hidden in life, and*

---

12. Bhūtēshu bhūtēshu vichintya.
13. Yasya chhāyāmritam yasya mrityuh.
14. Prāṇo mrityuh.

that which is to come.[15] They knew that mere appearance and disappearance are on the surface like waves on the sea, but life which is permanent knows no decay or diminution. *Everything has sprung from immortal life and is vibrating with life,*[16] for *life is immense.*[17] This is the noble heritage from our forefathers waiting to be claimed by us as our own, this ideal of the supreme freedom of consciousness. It is not merely intellectual or emotional, it has an ethical basis, and it must be translated into action. In the Upanishad it is said, *The supreme being is all-pervading, therefore he is the innate good in all.*[18] To be truly united in knowledge, love, and service with all beings, and thus to realise one's self in the all-pervading God is the essence of goodness, and this is the keynote of the teachings of the Upanishads: *Life is immense!*[19]

---

15. Namō astu āyatē namō astu parāyatē. Prāṇē ha bhūtam bhavyañ cha.
16. Yadidan kinñcha praṇa ejati nihsritam.
17. Prāṇo virāt.
18. Sarvavyāpī sa bhagavān tasmāt sarvagatah çivah.
19. Prāṇo virāt.

The Problem of Evil

The question why there is evil in existence is the same as why there is imperfection, or, in other words, why there is creation at all. We must take it for granted that it could not be otherwise; that creation must be imperfect, must be gradual, and that it is futile to ask the question, Why are we?

But this is the real question we ought to ask: Is this imperfection the final truth, is evil absolute and ultimate? The river has its boundaries, its banks, but is a river all banks? or are the banks the final facts about the river? Do not these obstructions themselves give its water an onward motion? The towing rope binds a boat, but is the bondage its meaning? Does it not at the same time draw the boat forward?

The current of the world has its boundaries, otherwise it could have no existence, but its purpose is not shown in the boundaries which restrain it, but in its movement, which is towards perfection. The wonder is not that there should be obstacles and sufferings in this world, but that there should be law and order, beauty and joy, goodness and love. The idea of God that man has in his being is the wonder of all wonders. He has felt in the depths of his life that what appears as imperfect is the manifestation of the perfect; just as a man who has an ear for music realises the perfection of a song, while in fact he is only listening to a succession of notes. Man has found out the great paradox that what is limited is not imprisoned within its limits; it is ever moving, and therewith shedding its finitude every moment. In fact, imperfection is not a negation of perfectness; finitude is not contradictory to infinity: they are but completeness manifested in parts, infinite revealed within bounds.

Pain, which is the feeling of our finiteness, is not a fixture in our life. It is not an end in self, as joy is. To meet with it is to know that it has no part in the true permanence of creation. It is what error is in our intellectual life. To go through the history of the development of science is to go through the maze of mistakes it made current at different times. Yet no one really believes that science is the one perfect mode of disseminating mistakes. The progressive ascertainment of truth is the important thing to remember in the history of science, not its innumerable mistakes. Error, by its nature, cannot be stationary; it cannot remain with truth; like a tramp, it must quit its lodging as soon as it fails to pay its score to the full.

As in intellectual error, so in evil of any other form, its essence is impermanence, for it cannot accord with the whole. Every moment it is being corrected by the totality of things and keeps changing its aspect. We exaggerate its importance by imagining it as at a standstill. Could we collect the statistics of the immense amount of death and putrefaction happening every moment in this earth, they would appal us. But evil is ever moving; with all its incalculable immensity it does not effectually clog the current of our life; and we find that the earth, water, and air remain sweet and pure for living beings. All such statistics consist of our attempts to represent statically what is in motion; and in the process things assume a weight in our mind which they have not in reality. For this reason a man, who by his profession is concerned with any particular aspect of life, is apt to magnify its proportions; in laying undue stress upon facts he loses his hold upon truth. A detective may have the opportunity of studying crimes in detail, but he loses his sense of their relative place in the whole social economy. When science collects facts to illustrate the struggle for existence that is going on in the animal kingdom, it raises a picture in our minds of 'nature red in tooth and claw.' But in these mental pictures we give a fixity to colours and forms which are really evanescent. It is like calculating the weight of the air on each square inch of our body to prove that it must be crushingly heavy for us. With every weight, however, there is an adjustment, and we lightly bear our burden. With the struggle for existence in nature there is reciprocity. There is the love for children and for comrades; there is the sacrifice of self, which springs from love; and this love is the positive element in life.

If we kept the search-light of our observation turned upon the fact of death, the world would appear to us like a huge charnel-house; but in the world of life the thought of death has, we find, the least possible hold upon our minds. Not because it is the least apparent, but because it is the negative aspect of life; just as, in spite of the fact that we shut our eyelids every second, it is the openings of the eyes that count. Life as a whole never takes death seriously. It laughs, dances and plays, it builds, hoards and loves in death's face. Only when we detach one individual fact of death do we see its blankness and become dismayed. We lose sight of the wholeness of a life of which death is part. It is like looking at a piece of cloth through a microscope. It appears like a net; we gaze at the big holes and shiver in imagination. But the truth is, death is not the ultimate reality. It looks black, as the sky looks blue; but it does not blacken existence, just as the sky does not leave its stain upon the wings of the bird.

When we watch a child trying to walk, we see its countless failures; its successes are but few. If we had to limit our observation within a narrow space of time, the sight would be cruel. But we find that in spite of its repeated failures there is an impetus of joy in the child which sustains it in its seemingly impossible task. We see it does not think of its falls so much as of its power to keep its balance though for only a moment. Like these accidents in a child's attempts to walk, we meet with sufferings in various forms in our life every day, showing the imperfections in our knowledge and our available power, and in the application of our will. But if these revealed our weakness to us only, we should die of utter depression. When we select for observation a limited area of our activities, our individual failures and miseries loom large in our minds; but our life leads us instinctively to take a wider view. It gives us an ideal of perfection which ever carries us beyond our present limitations. Within us we have a hope which always walks in front of our present narrow experiences; it is the undying faith in the infinite in us; it will never accept any of our disabilities as a permanent fact; it sets no limit to its own scope; it dares to assert that man has oneness with God; and its wild dreams become true every day.

We see the truth when we set our mind towards the infinite. The ideal of truth is not in the narrow present, not in our immediate sensations, but in the consciousness of the whole which gives us a taste of what we *should* have in what we *do* have. Consciously or unconsciously we have in our life this feeling of Truth which is ever larger than its appearance; for our life is facing the infinite, and it is in movement. Its aspiration is therefore infinitely more than its achievement, and as it goes on it finds that no realization of truth ever leaves it stranded on the desert of finality, but carries it to a region beyond. Evil cannot altogether arrest the course of life on the highway and rob it of its possessions. For the evil has to pass on, it has to grow into good; it cannot stand and give battle to the All. If the least evil could stop anywhere indefinitely, it would sink deep and cut into the very roots of existence. As it is, man does not really believe in evil, just as he cannot believe that violin strings have been purposely made to create the exquisite torture of discordant notes, though by the aid of statistics is can be mathematically proved that the probability of discord is far greater than that of harmony, and for one who can play the violin there are thousands who cannot. The potentiality of perfection outweighs actual contradictions. No doubt there have been people who asserted existence to be an absolute evil, but man can never take them seriously. Their pessimism is a mere pose, either intellectual or sentimental, but life itself is optimistic: it wants to go on. Pessimism is a form of mental dipsomania, it disdains healthy nourishment, indulges in the strong drink of denunciation, and creates an artificial dejection which thirsts for a stronger draught. If existence were an evil, it would wait for no philosopher to prove it. It is like convicting a man of suicide, while all the time he stands before you in the flesh. Existence itself is here to prove that it cannot be an evil.

An imperfection which is not all imperfection, but which has perfection for its ideal, must go through a perpetual realization. Thus, it is the function of our intellect to realise the truth through untruths, and knowledge is nothing but the continually burning up of error to set free the light of truth. Our will, our character, has to attain perfection by continually overcoming evils, either inside or outside us, or both; our physical life is consuming bodily materials every moment to maintain the life fire; and our moral life too has its fuel to burn. This life process is going on—we know it, we have felt it; and we have a faith which no individual instances to the contrary can shake, that the direction of humanity is from evil to good. For we feel that good is the positive element in man's nature, and in every age and every clime what man values most is his ideal of goodness. We have known the good, we have loved it, and we have paid our highest reverence to men who have shown in their lives what goodness is.

The question will be asked, What is goodness; what does our moral nature mean? My answer is, that when a man begins to have an extended vision of his true self, when he realises that he is much more than at present he seems to be, he begins to get conscious of his moral nature. Then he grows aware of that which he is yet to be, and the state not yet experienced by him becomes more real than that under his direct experience. Necessarily, his perspective of life changes, and his will takes the place of his wishes. For will is the supreme wish of the larger life, the life whose greater portion is out of our present reach, whose objects are not for the most part before our sight. Then comes the conflict of our lesser man with our greater man, of our wishes with our will, of the desire for things affecting our senses with the purpose that is within our heart. Then we begin to distinguish between what we immediately desire and what is good. For good is that which is desirable for our greater self. Thus the sense of goodness comes out of a truer view of our life, which is the connected view of the wholeness of the field of life, and which takes into account not only what is present before us but what is not, and perhaps never humanly can be. Man, who is provident, feels for that life of his which is not yet existent, feels much more for that than for the life that is with him; therefore he is ready to sacrifice his present inclination for the unrealised future. In this he becomes great, for he realises truth. Even to be efficiently selfish a man has to recognize this truth, and has to curb his immediate impulses—in other words, has to be moral. For our moral faculty is the faculty by which we know that life is not made up of fragments, purposeless and discontinuous. This moral sense of man not only gives him the power to see that the self has a continuity in time, but it also enables him to see that he is not true when he is only restricted to his own self. He is more in truth than he is in fact. He truly belongs to individuals who are not included in his own individuality, and whom he is never even likely to know. As he has a feeling for his future self which is outside his present consciousness, so he has a feeling for his greater self which is outside the limits of his personality. There is no man who has not this feeling to some extent, who has never sacrificed his selfish desire for the sake of some other person, who has never felt a pleasure in undergoing some loss or trouble because it pleased somebody else. It is a truth that man is not a detached being, that he has a universal aspect; and when he recognizes this, he becomes great. Even the most evilly-disposed selfishness has to recognize this when he seeks the power to do evil; for it cannot ignore truth and yet be strong. So in order to claim the aid of truth, selfishness has to be unselfish to some extent. A band of robbers must be moral in order to hold together as a band; they may rob the whole world but not each other. To make an immoral intention successful, some of its weapons must be moral. In fact, very often it is our very moral strength which gives us most effectively the power to do evil, to exploit other individuals for our own benefit, to rob other people of their just rights. The life of an animal is unmoral, for it is aware only of an immediate present; the life of a man can be immoral, but that only means that it must have a moral basis. What is immoral is imperfectly moral just as what is false is true to a small extent, or it cannot be false. Not to see is to be blind, but to see wrongly is to see only in an imperfect manner. Man's selfishness is a beginning to see some connection, some purpose in life; and to act in accordance with its dictates requires self-restraint and regulation of conduct. A selfish man willingly undergoes troubles for the sake of the self, he suffers hardship and privation without a murmur, simply because he knows that what is pain and trouble, looked at from the point of view of a short space of time, is just the opposite when seen in a larger perspective. Thus what is a loss to the smaller man is a gain to the greater, and *vice versa*.

To the man who lives for an idea, for his country, for the good of humanity, life has an extented meaning, and to that extent pain becomes important to him. To live the life of goodness is to live the life of all. Pleasure is for one's own self, but goodness is concerned with the happiness of all humanity and for all time. From the point of view of the good, pleasure and pain appear in a different meaning; so much so, that pleasure may be shunned, and pain be courted in its place, and death itself be made welcome as giving a higher value to life. From these higher standpoints of a man's life, the standpoints of the good, pleasure and pain lose their absolute value. Martyrs prove it in history, and we prove it every day in our life in our little martyrdoms. When we take a pitcherful of water from the sea it has its weight, but when we take a dip into the sea itself a thousand pitchersful of water flow above our head, and we do not feel their weight. We have to carry the pitcher of self with our strength; and so, while on the plane of selfishness pleasure and pain have their full weight, on the moral plane they are so much lightened that the man who has reached it appears to us almost super-human in his patience under crushing trials, and his forbearance in the face of malignant persecution.

To live in perfect goodness is to realise one's life in the infinite. This is the most comprehensive view of life which we can have by our inherent power of the moral vision of the wholeness of life. And the teaching of Buddha is to cultivate this moral power to the highest extent, to know that our field of activities is not bound to the plane of our narrow self. This is the vision of the heavenly kingdom of Christ. When we attain to that universal life, which is the moral life, we become free from bonds of pleasure and pain, and the place vacated by our self becomes filled with an unspeakable joy which springs from measureless love. In this state the soul's activity is all the more heightened, only its motive power is not from desires, but in its own joy. This is the *Karmayoga* of the Gita, the way to become one with the infinite activity by the exercise of the activity of disinterested goodness.

When Buddha meditated upon the way of releasing mankind from the grip of misery he came to this truth: that when man attains his highest end by merging the individual in the universal, he becomes free from the thraldom of pain. Let us consider this point more fully.

A student of mine once related to me his adventure in a storm, and complained that all the time he was troubled with the feeling that this great commotion in nature behaved to him as if he were no more than a mere handful of dust. That he was a distinct personality with a will of his own had not the least influence upon what was happening.

I said, 'If consideration for our individuality could sway nature from her path, then it would be the individuals who would suffer most.'

But he persisted in his doubt, saying that there was this fact which could not be ignored—the feeling that I am. The 'I' in us seeks for a relation which is individual to it.

I replied that the relation of the 'I' is with something which is 'not-I.' So we must have a medium which is common to both, and we must be absolutely certain that it is the same to the 'I' as it is to the 'not-I'.

This is what needs repeating here. We have to keep in mind that our individuality by its nature is impelled to seek for the universal. Our body can only die if it tries to eat its own substance, and our eye loses the meaning of its function if it can only see itself.

Just as we find that the stronger the imagination the less is it merely imaginary and the more is it in harmony with truth, so we see the more vigorous our individuality the more does it widen towards the universal. For the greatness of a personality is not in itself but in its content, which is universal, just as the depth of a lake is judged not by the size of its cavity but by the depth of its water.

So, if it is a truth that the yearning of our nature is for reality, and that our personality cannot be happy with a fantastic universe of its own creation, then it is clearly best for it that our will can only deal with things by following their law, and cannot do with them just as it pleases. This unyielding sureness of reality sometimes crosses our will, and very often leads us to disaster, just as the firmness of the earth invariably hurts the falling child who is learning to walk. Nevertheless it is the same firmness that hurts him which makes his walking possible. Once, while passing under a bridge, the mast of my boat got stuck in one of its girders. If only for a moment the mast would have bent an inch or two, or the bridge raised its back like a yawning cat, or the river given in, it would have been all right with me. But they took no notice of my helplessness. That is the very reason why I could make use of the river, and sail upon it with the help of the mast, and that is why, when its current was inconvenient, I could rely upon the bridge. Things are what they are, and we have to know them if we would deal with them, and knowledge of them is possible because our wish is not their law. This knowledge is a joy to us, for the knowledge is one of the channels of our relation with the things outside us; it is making them our own, and thus widening the limit of our self.

At every step we have to take into account others than ourselves. For only in death are we alone. A poet is a true poet when he can make his personal idea joyful to all men, which he could not do if he had not a medium common to all his audience. This common language has its own law which the poet must discover and follow, by doing which he becomes true and attains poetical immortality.

We see then that man's individuality is not his highest truth; there is that in him which is universal. If he were made to live in a world where his own self was the only factor to consider, then that would be the worst prison imaginable to him, for man's deepest joy is in growing greater and greater by more and more union with the all. This, as we have seen, would be an impossibility if there were no law common to all. Only by discovering the law and following it, do we become great, do we realise the universal; while, so long as our individual desires are at conflict with the universal law, we suffer pain and are futile.

There was a time when we prayed for special concessions, we expected that the laws of nature should be held in abeyance for our own convenience. But now we know better. We know that law cannot be set aside, and in this knowledge we have become strong. For this law is not something apart from us; it is our own. The universal power which is manifested in the universal law is one with our own power. It will thwart us where we are small, where we are against the current of things; but it will help us where we are great, where we are in unison with the all. Thus, through the help of science, as we come to know more of the laws of nature, we gain in power; we tend to attain a universal body. Our organ of sight, our organ of locomotion, our physical strength becomes world-wide; steam and electricity become our nerve and muscle. Thus we find that, just as throughout our bodily organization there is a principle of relation by virtue of which we can call the entire body our own, and can use it as such, so all through the universe there is that principle of uninterrupted relation by virtue of which we can call the whole world our extended body and use it accordingly. And in this age of science it is our endeavour fully to establish our claim to our world-self. We know all our poverty and sufferings are owing to our inability to realise this legitimate claim of ours. Really, there is no limit to our powers, for we are not outside the universal power which is the expression of universal law. We are on our way, to overcome disease and death, to conquer pain and poverty; for through scientific knowledge we are ever on our way to realise the universal in its physical aspect. And as we make progress we find pain, disease, and poverty of power are not absolute, but that it is only the want of adjustment of our individual self to our universal self which gives rise to them.

It is the same with our spiritual life. When the individual man in us chafes against the lawful rule of the universal man we become morally small, and we must suffer. In such a condition our successes are our greatest failures, and the very fulfilment of our desires leaves us poorer. We hanker after special gains for ourselves, we want to enjoy privileges which none else can share with us. But everything that is absolutely special must keep up a perpetual warfare with what is general. In such a state of civil war man always lives behind barricades, and in any civilization which is selfish our homes are not real homes, but artificial barriers around us. Yet we complain that we are not happy, as if there were something inherent in the nature of things to make us miserable. The universal spirit is waiting to crown us with happiness, but our individual spirit would not accept it. It is our life of the self that causes conflicts and complications everywhere, upsets the normal balance of society and gives rise to miseries of all kinds. It brings things to such a pass that to maintain order we have to create artificial coercions and organized forms of tyranny, and tolerate infernal institutions is our midst, whereby at every moment humanity is humiliated.

We have seen that in order to be powerful we have to submit to the laws of the universal forces, and to realise in practice that they are our own. So, in order to be happy, we have to submit our individual will to the sovereignty of the universal will, and to feel in truth that it is our own will. When we reach that state wherein the adjustment of the finite in us to the infinite is made perfect, then pain itself becomes a valuable asset. It becomes a measuring rod with which to gauge the true value of our joy.

The most important lesson that man can learn from his life is not that there *is* pain in this world, but that it depends upon him to turn it into good account, that it is possible for him to transmute it into joy. That lesson has not been lost altogether to us, and there is no man living who would willingly be deprived of his right to suffer pain, for that is his right to be a man. One day the wife of a poor labourer complained bitterly to me that her eldest boy was going to be sent away to a rich relative's house for part of the year. It was the implied kind intention of trying to relieve her of her trouble that gave her the shock, for a mother's trouble is a mother's own by her inalienable right of love, and she was not going to surrender it to any dictates of expediency. Man's freedom is never in being saved troubles, but it is the freedom to take trouble for his own good, to make the trouble an element in his joy. It can be made so only when we realise that our individual self is not the highest meaning of our being, that in us we have the world-man who is immortal, who is not afraid of death or sufferings, and who looks upon pain as only the other side of joy. He who has realised this knows that it is pain which is our true wealth as imperfect beings, and has made us great and worthy to take our seat with the perfect. He knows that we are not beggars; that it is the hard coin which must be paid for everything valuable in this life, for our power, our wisdom, our love; that in pain is symbolised the infinite possibility of perfection, the eternal unfolding of joy; and the man who loses all pleasure in accepting pain sinks down and down to the lowest depth of penury and degradation. It is only when we invoke the aid of pain for our self-gratification that she becomes evil and takes her vengeance for the insult done to her by hurling us into misery. For she is the vestal virgin consecrated to the service of the immortal perfection, and when she takes her true place before the altar of the infinite she casts off her dark veil and bares her face to the beholder as a revelation of supreme joy.

The Problem of Self

At one pole of my being I am one with stocks and stones. There I have to acknowledge the rule of universal law. That is where the foundation of my existence lies, deep down below. Its strength lies in its being held firm in the clasp of the comprehensive world, and in the fullness of its community with all things.

But at the other pole of my being I am separate from all. There I have broken through the cordon of equality and stand alone as an individual. I am absolutely unique, I am I, I am incomparable. The whole weight of the universe cannot crush out this individuality of mine. I maintain it in spite of the tremendous gravitation of all things. It is small in appearance but great in reality. For it holds its own against the forces that would rob it of its distinction and make it one with the dust.

This is the superstructure of the self which rises from the indeterminate depth and darkness of its foundation into the open, proud of its isolation, proud of having given shape to a single individual idea of the architect's which has no duplicate in the whole universe. If this individuality be demolished then though no material be lost, not an atom destroyed the creative joy which was crystallised therein is gone. We are absolutely bankrupt if we are deprived of this speciality, this individuality, which is the only thing we can call our own; and which, if lost, is also a loss to the whole world. It is most valuable because it is not universal. And therefore only through it can we gain the universe more truly than if we were lying within its breast unconscious of our distinctiveness. The universal is ever seeking its consummation in the unique. And the desire we have to keep our uniqueness intact is really the desire of the universe acting in us. It is our joy of the infinite in us that gives us our joy in ourselves.

That this separateness of self is considered by man as his most precious possession is proved by the sufferings he undergoes and the sins he commits for its sake. But the consciousness of separation has come from the eating of the fruit of knowledge. It has led man to shame and crime and death; yet it is dearer to him than any paradise where the self lies, securely slumbering in perfect innocence in the womb of mother nature.

It is a constant striving and suffering for us to maintain the separateness of this self of ours. And in fact it is this suffering which measures its value. One side of the value is sacrifice, which represents how much the cost has been. The other side of it is the attainment, which represents how much has been gained. If the self meant nothing to us but pain and sacrifice, it could have no value for us, and on no account would we willingly undergo such sacrifice. In such case there could be no doubt at all that the highest object of humanity would be the annihilation of self.

But if there is a corresponding gain, if it does not end in a void but in a fullness, then it is clear that its negative qualities, its very sufferings and sacrifices, make it all the more precious. That it is so has been proved by those who have realised the positive significance of self, and have accepted its responsibilities with eagerness and undergone sacrifices without flinching.

With the foregoing introduction it will be easy for me to answer the question once asked by one of my audience as to whether the annihilation of self was not been held by India as the supreme goal of humanity?

In the first place we must keep in mind the fact that man is never literal in the expression of his ideas, except in matters most trivial. Very often man's words are not a language at all, but merely a local gesture of the dumb. They may indicate, but do not express his thoughts. The more vital his thoughts the more have his words to be explained by the context of his life. Those who seek to know his meaning by the aid of the dictionary only technically reach the house, for they are stopped by the outside wall and find no entrance to the hall. This is the reason why the teachings of our greater prophets give rise to endless disputations when we try to understand them by following their words and not by realising them in our own lives. The men who are cursed with the gift of the literal mind are the unfortunate ones who are always busy with the nets and neglect the fishing.

It is not only in Buddhism and the Indian religion but in Christianity too, that the ideal of selflessness is preached with all fervour. In the last the symbol of death has been used for expressing the idea of man's deliverance from the life which is not true. This is the same as Nirvāna, the symbol of the extinction of the lamp.

In the typical thought of India it is held that the true deliverance of man is the deliverance from *avidyā,* from ignorance. It is not in destroying anything that is positive and real, for that cannot be possible, but that which is negative, which obstructs our vision of truth. When this obstruction, which is ignorance, is removed, then only is the eye lid drawn up which is no loss to the eye.

It is our ignorance which makes us think that our self, as self, is real, that it has its complete meaning in itself. When we take that wrong view of self then we try to live in such a manner as to make self the ultimate object of our life. Then are we doomed to disappointment like the man who tries to reach his destination by firmly clutching the dust of the road. Our self has no means of holding us, for its own nature is to pass on; and by clinging to this thread of self which is passing through the loom of life we cannot make it serve the purpose of the cloth into which it is being woven. When a man, with elaborate care, arranges for an enjoyment of the self, he lights a fire but has no dough to make his bread with; the fire flares up and consumes itself to extinction, like an unnatural beast that eats its own progeny and dies.

In an unknown language the words are tyrannically prominent. They stop us but say nothing. To be rescued from this fetter of words we must rid ourselves of the *avidyā*, our ignorance, and then our mind will find its freedom in the inner idea. But it could be foolish to say that our ignorance of the language can be dispelled only by the destruction of the words. No, when the perfect knowledge comes, every word remains in its place, only they do not bind us to themselves, but let us pass through them and lead us to the idea which is emancipation.

Thus it is only *avidyā* which makes the self our fetter by making us think that it is an end in itself, and by preventing our seeing that it contains the idea that transcends its limits. That is why the wise man comes and says, 'Set yourselves free from the *avidyā*; know your true soul and be saved from the grasp of the self which imprisons you.'

We gain our freedom when we attain our truest nature. The man who is an artist finds his artistic freedom when he finds his ideal of art. Then is he freed from laborious attempts at imitation, from the goadings of popular approbation. It is the function of religion not to destroy our nature but to fulfil it.

The Sanskrit word *dharma* which is usually translated into English as religion has a deeper meaning in our language. *Dharma* is the innermost nature, the essence, the implicit truth, of all things. *Dharma* is the ultimate purpose that is working in our self. When any wrong is done we say that *dharma* is violated, meaning that the lie has been given to our true nature.

But this *dharma,* which is the truth in us, is not apparent, because it is inherent. So much so, that it has been held that sinfulness is the nature of man, and only by the special grace of God can a particular person be saved. This is like saying that the nature of the seed is to remain enfolded within its shell, and it is only by some special miracle that it can be grown into a tree. But do we not know that the *appearance* of the seed contradicts its true nature. When you submit it to chemical analysis you may find in it carbon and protein and a good many other things, but not the idea of a branching tree. Only when the tree begins to take shape do you come to see its *dharma,* and then you can affirm without doubt that the seed which has been wasted and allowed to rot in the grounds has been thwarted in its *dharma,* in the fulfilment of its true nature. In the history of humanity we have known the living seed in us to sprout. We have seen the great purpose in us taking shape in the lives of our greatest men, and have felt certain that though there are numerous individual lives that seem ineffectual, still it is not their *dharma* to remain barren; but it is for them to burst their cover and transform themselves into a vigorous spiritual shoot, growing up into the air and light, and branching out in all directions.

The freedom of the seed is in the attainment of its *dharma,* its nature and destiny of becoming a tree; it is the non-accomplishment which is its prison. The sacrifice by which a thing attains its fulfilment is not a sacrifice which ends in death; it is the casting-off of bonds which wins freedom.

When we know the highest ideal of freedom which a man has, we know his *dharma,* the essence of his nature, the real meaning of his self. At first sight it seems that man counts that as freedom by which he gets unbounded opportunities of self-gratification and self-aggrandizement. But surely this is not borne out by history. Our revelatory men have always been those who have lived the life of self-sacrifice. The higher nature in man always seeks for something which transcends itself and yet is its deepest truth; which claims all its sacrifice, yet makes this sacrifice its own recompense. This is man's *dharma,* man's religion, and man's self is the vessel which is to carry this sacrifice to the altar.

We can look at our self in its two different aspects. The self which displays itself, and the self which transcends itself and thereby reveals its own meaning. To display itself it tries to be big, to stand upon the pedestal of its accumulations, and to retain everything to itself. To reveal itself it gives up everything it has, thus becoming perfect like a flower that has blossomed out from the bud, pouring from its chalice of beauty all its sweetness.

The lamp contains its oil, which it holds securely in its close grasp and guards from the least loss. Thus is it separate from all other objects around it and is miserly. But when lighted it finds its meaning at once; its relation with all things far and near is established, and it freely sacrifices its fund of oil to feed the flame.

Such a lamp is our self. So long as it hoards its possessions it keeps itself dark, its conduct contradicts its true purpose. When it finds illumination it forgets itself in a moment, holds the light high, and serves it with everything it has; for therein is its revelation. This revelation is the freedom which Buddha preached. He asked the lamp to give up its oil. But purposeless giving up is a still darker poverty which he never could have meant. The lamp must give up its oil to the light and thus set free the purpose it has in its hoarding. This is emancipation. The path Buddha pointed out was not merely the practice of self-abnegation, but the widening of love. And therein lies the true meaning of Buddha's preaching.

When we find that the state of *Nirvāna* preached by Buddha is through love, then we know for certain that *Nirvāna* is the highest culmination of love. For love is an end unto itself. Everything else raises the question 'Why?' in our mind, and we require a reason for it. But when we say, 'I love,' then there is no room for the 'why'; it is the final answer in itself.

Doubtless, even selfishness impels one to give away. But the selfish man does it on compulsion. That is like plucking fruit when it is unripe; you have to tear it from the tree and bruise the branch. But when a man loves, giving becomes a matter of joy to him, like the tree's surrender of the ripe fruit. All our belongings assume a weight by the ceaseless gravitation of our selfish desires; we cannot easily cast them away from us. They seem to belong to our very nature, stick to us as a second skin, and we bleed as we detach them. But when we are possessed by love, its force acts in the opposite direction. The things that closely adhered to us lose their adhesion and weight, and we find that they are not of us. Far from being a loss to give them away, we find in that the fulfilment of our nature.

Thus we find in perfect love the freedom of our self. That only which is done for love is done freely, however much pain it may cause. Therefore working for love is freedom in action. This is the meaning of the teaching of disinterested work in the Gītā.

The Gītā says action we must have, for only in action do we manifest our nature. But this manifestation is not perfect so long as our action is not free. In fact, our nature is obscured by work done by the compulsion of want or fear. The mother reveals herself in the service of her children, so our true freedom is not the freedom *from* action but freedom *in* action, which can only be attained in the work of love.

God's manifestation is in his work of creation, and it is said in the Upanishad, *Knowledge, power, and action are of his nature,*[1] they are not imposed upon him from outside. Therefore his work is his freedom, and in his creation he realises himself. The same thing is said elsewhere in other words: *From joy does spring all this creation, by joy is it maintained, towards joy does it progress, and into joy does it enter.*[2] This means that God's creation has not its source in any necessity; it comes from his fullness of joy; it is his love that creates, therefore in creation is his own revealment.

The artist who has a joy in the fullness of his artistic idea objectifies its and thus gains it more fully by holding it afar. It is joy which detaches ourselves from us, and then gives it form in creations of love in order to make it more perfectly our own. Hence there must be this separation, not a separation of repulsion but a separation of love. Repulsion has only the one element, the element of severance. But love has two, the element of severance, which is only an appearance, and the element of union which is the ultimate truth. Just as when the father tosses his child up from his arms it has the appearance of rejection but its truth is quite the reverse.

So we must know that the meaning of our self is not to be found in its separateness from God and others, but in the ceaseless realization of *yoga,* of union; not on the side of the canvas where it is blank, but on the side where the picture is being painted.

This is the reason why the separateness of our self has been described by our philosophers as *māyā,* as an illusion, because it has no intrinsic reality of its own. It looks perilous; it raises its isolation to a giddy height and casts a black shadow

---

1. 'Svābhāvikī jnāna bala kriyācha.'
2. Ānandādhyēva khalvimāni bhūtāni jāyantē, ānandēna jātāni jīvanti, ānandamprayantyabhisamvicanti.

upon the fair face of existence; from the outside it has an
aspect of a sudden disruption, rebellious and destructive; it
is proud, domineering and wayward, it is ready to rob the
world of all its wealth to gratify its craving of a moment; to
pluck with a reckless, cruel hand all the plumes from the
divine bird of beauty to deck its ugliness for a day; indeed
man's legend has it that it bears the black mark of disobedience
stamped on its forehead for ever; but still all this is *māyā*,
envelopment of *avidyā* it is the mist, it is not the sun; it is
the black smoke that presages the fire of love.

Imagine some savage who, in his ignorance, thinks that
it is the paper of the banknote that has the magic, by virtue
of which the possessor of it gets all he wants. He piles up
the papers, hides them, handles them in all sorts of absurd
ways, and then at last, wearied by his efforts, comes to the
sad conclusion that they are absolutely worthless, only fit to
be thrown into the fire. But the wise man knows that the
paper of the banknote is all *māyā*, and until it is given up
to the bank it is futile. It is only *avidyā*, our ignorance, that
makes us believe that the separateness of our self like the
paper of the banknote is precious in itself, and by acting on
this belief our self is rendered valueless. It is only when the
avidyā is removed that this very self comes to us with a wealth
which is priceless. For *He manifests Himself in deathless
forms which His joy assumes.*[3] These forms are separate from
Him, and the value that these forms have is only what his
joy has imparted to them. When we transfer back these forms
into that original joy, which is love, then we cash them in the
bank and we find their truth.

When pure necessity drives man to his work it takes an
accidental and contingent character, it becomes a mere makeshift
arrangement; it is deserted and left in ruins when necessity

---

3. Ānandarūpamamritam yadvibhāti.

changes its course. But when his work is the outcome of joy, the forms that it takes have the elements of immortality. The immortal in man imparts to it its own quality of permanence. Our self, as a form of God's joy, is deathless. For his joy is *amritam*, eternal. This it is in us which makes us sceptical of death, even when the fact of death cannot be doubted. In reconcilement of this contradiction in us we come to the truth that in the dualism of death and life there is a harmony. We know that the life of a soul, which is finite in its expression and infinite in its principle, must go through the portals of death in its journey to realise the infinite. It is death which is monistic, it has no life in it. But life is dualistic; it has an appearance as well as truth; and death is that appearance, that *māyā*, which is an inseparable companion to life. Our self to live must go through a continual change and growth of form, which may be termed a continual death and a continual life going on at the same time. It is really courting death when we refuse to accept death; when we wish to give the form of the self some fixed changelessness; when the self feels no impulse which urges it to grow out of itself; when it treats its limits as final and acts accordingly. Then comes our teacher's call to die to this death; not a call to annihilation but so eternal life. It is the extinction of the lamp in the morning light; not the abolition of the sun. It is really asking us consciously to give effect to the innermost wish that we have in the depths of our nature.

We have a dual set of desires in our being, which it should be our endeavour to bring into a harmony. In the region of our physical nature we have one set of which we are conscious always. We wish to enjoy our food and drink, we hanker after bodily pleasure and comfort. These desires are self-centred; they are solely concerned with their respective impulses. The wishes of our palate often run counter to what our stomach can allow.

But we have another set, which is the desire of our physical system as a whole, of which we are usually unconscious. It is the wish for health. This is always doing its work, mending and repairing, making new adjustments in cases of accident, and skilfully restoring the balance wherever disturbed. It has no concern with the fulfilment of our immediate bodily desires, but it goes beyond the present time. It is the principle of our physical wholeness, it links our life with its past and its future and maintains the unity of its parts. He who is wise knows it, and makes his other physical wishes harmonise with it.

We have a greater body which is the social body. Society is an organism, of which we as parts have our individual wishes. We want our own pleasure and licence. We want to pay less and gain more than anybody else. This causes scramblings and fights. But there is that other wish in us which does its work in the depths of the social being. It is the wish for the welfare of the society. It transcends the limits of the present and the personal. It is on the side of the infinite.

He who is wise tries to harmonise the wishes that seek for self-gratification with the wish for the social good, and only thus can he realise his higher self.

In its finite aspect the self is conscious of its separateness, and there it is ruthless in its attempt to have more distinction than all others. But in its infinite aspect its wish is to gain that harmony which leads to its perfection and not its mere aggrandizement.

The emancipation of our physical nature is in attaining health, of our social being in attaining goodness, and of our self in attaining love. This last is what Buddha describes as extinction—the extinction of selfishness. This is the function of love, and it does not lead to darkness but to illumination. This is the attainment of *bodhi,* or the true awakening; it is the revealing in us of the infinite joy by the light of love.

The passage of our self is through its selfhood, which is independent, to its attainment of soul, which is harmonious. This harmony can never be reached through compulsion. So our will, in the history of its growth, must come through independence and rebellion to the ultimate completion. We must have the possibility of the negative form of freedom, which is licence, before we can attain the positive freedom, which is love.

This negative freedom, the freedom of self-will, can turn its back upon its highest realization, but it cannot cut itself away from it altogether, for then it will lose its own meaning. Our self-will has freedom up to a certain extent; it can know what it is to break away from the path, but it cannot continue in that direction indefinitely. For we are finite on our negative side. We must come to an end in our evil doing, in our career of discord. For evil is not infinite, and discord cannot be an end in itself. Our will has freedom in order that it may find out that its true course is towards goodness and love. For goodness and love are infinite, and only in the infinite is the perfect realization of freedom possible. So our will can be free not towards the limitations of our self, not where it is *māyā* and negation, but towards the unlimited, where is truth and love. Our freedom cannot go against its own principle of freedom and yet be free; it cannot commit suicide and yet live. We cannot say that we should have infinite freedom to fetter ourselves, for the fettering ends the freedom.

So in the freedom of our will, we have the same dualism of appearance and truth—our self-will is only the appearance of freedom and love is the truth. When we try to make this appearance independent of truth, then our attempt brings misery and proves its own futility in the end. Everything has this dualism of *māyā* and *satyam*, appearance and truth. Words are *māyā* where they are merely sounds and finite, they are *satyam* where they are ideas and infinite. Our self is *māyā* where it is merely individual and finite, where it considers its separateness as absolute; it is *satyam* where it recognizes its essence in the universal and infinite, in the supreme self, in *paramātman*. This is what Christ means when he says, 'Before Abraham was I am.' This is the eternal *I am* that speaks through the *I am* that is in me. The individual *I am* attains its perfect end when it realises its freedom of harmony in the infinite *I am*. Then is its *mukti*, its deliverance from the thraldom of *māyā*, of appearance which springs from *avidyā*, from ignorance; its emancipation in *çāntam çivam advaitam*, in the perfect repose in truth, in the perfect activity in goodness, and in the perfect union in love.

Not only in our self but also in nature is there this separateness from God, which has been described as *māyā* by our philosophers, because the separateness does not exist by itself, it does not limit God's infinity from outside. It is his own will that has imposed limits to itself, just as the chess-player restricts his will with regard to the moving of the chessmen. The player willingly enters into definite relations with each particular piece and realises the joy of his power by these very restrictions. It is not that he cannot move the chessmen just as he pleases, but if he does so then there can be no play. If God assumes his role of omnipotence, then his creation is at an end and his power loses all its meaning. For power to be a power must act within limits. God's water must be water, his earth can never be other than earth. The law that has made them water and earth is his own law by which he has separated the play from the player, for therein the joy of the player consists.

As by the limits of law nature is separated from God, so it is the limits of its egoism which separates the self from him. He has willingly set limits to his will, and has given us mastery over the little world of our own. It is like a father's settling upon his son some allowance within the limit of which he is free to do what he likes. Though it remains a portion of the father's own property, yet he frees it from the operation of his own will. The reason of it is that the will, which is love's will and therefore free, can have its joy only in a union with another free will. The tyrant who must have slaves looks upon them as instruments of his purpose. It is the consciousness of his own necessity which makes him crush the will out of them to make his self-interest absolutely secure. This self-interest cannot brook the least freedom in others, because it is not itself free. The tyrant is really dependent on his slaves, and therefore he tries to make them completely useful by making them subservient to his own will. But a lover must have two wills for the realization of his love, because the consummation of love is in harmony, the harmony between freedom and freedom. So God's love from which our self has taken form has made it separate from God; and it is God's love which again establishes a reconciliation and unites God with our self through the separation. That is why our self has to go through endless renewals. For in its career of separateness it cannot go on for ever. Separateness is the finitude where it finds its barriers to come back again and again to its infinite source. Our self has ceaselessly to cast off its age, repeatedly shed its limits in oblivion and death, in order to realise its immortal youth. Its personality must merge in the universal time after time, in fact pass through it every moment, ever to refresh its individual life. It must follow the eternal rhythm and touch the fundamental unity at every step, and thus maintain its separation balanced in beauty and strength.

The play of life and death we see everywhere—this transmutation of the old into the new. The day comes to us every morning, naked and white, fresh as a flower. But we know it is old. It is age itself. It is that very ancient day which took up the newborn earth in its arms, covered it with its white mantle of light, and sent it forth on its pilgrimage among the stars.

Yet its feet are untired and its eyes undimmed. It carries the golden amulet of ageless eternity, at whose touch all wrinkles vanish from the forehead of creation. In the very core of the world's heart stands immortal youth. Death and decay cast over its face momentary shadows and pass on; they leave no marks of their steps—and truth remains fresh and young.

This old, old day of our earth is born again and again every morning. It comes back to the original refrain of its music. If its march were the march of an infinite straight line, if it had not the awful pause of its plunge in the abysmal darkness and its repeated rebirth in the life of the endless beginning, then it would gradually soil and bury truth with its dust and spread ceaseless aching over the earth under its heavy tread. Then every moment would leave its load of weariness behind, and decrepitude would reign supreme on its throne of eternal dirt.

But every morning the day is reborn among the newly-blossomed flowers with the same message retold and the same assurance renewed that death eternally dies, that the waves of turmoil are on the surface, and that the sea of tranquillity is fathomless. The curtain of night is drawn aside and truth emerges without a speck of dust on its garment, without a furrow of age on its lineaments.

We see that he who is before everything else is the same to-day. Every note of the song of creation comes fresh from his voice. The universe is not a mere echo, reverberating from sky to sky, like a homeless wanderer—the echo of an old song sung once for all in the dim beginning of things and then left orphaned. Every moment it comes from the heart of the master, it is breathed in his breath.

And that is the reason why it overspreads the sky like a thought taking shape in a poem, and never has to break into pieces with the burden of its own accumulating weight. Hence the surprise of endless variations, the advent of the unaccountable, the ceaseless procession of individuals, each of whom is without a parallel in creation. As at the first so to the last, the beginning never ends—the world is ever old and ever new.

It is for our self to know that it must be born anew every moment of its life. It must break through all illusions that encase it in their crust to make it appear old, burdening it with death.

For life is immortal youthfulness, and it hates age that tries to clog its movements—age that belongs not to life in truth, but follows it as the shadow follows the lamp.

Our life, like a river, strikes its banks not to find itself closed in by them, but to realise anew every moment that it has its unending opening towards the sea. It is as a poem that strikes its metre at every step not to be silenced by its rigid regulations, but to give expression every moment to the inner freedom of its harmony.

The boundary walls of our individuality thrust us back within our limits, on the one hand, and thus lead us, on the other, to the unlimited. Only when we try to make these limits infinite are we launched into an impossible contradiction and court miserable failure.

This is the cause which leads to the great revolutions in human history. Whenever the part, spurning the whole, tries to run a separate course of its own, the great pull of the all gives it a violent wrench, stops it suddenly, and brings it to the dust. Whenever the individual tries to dam the ever-flowing current of the world-force and imprison it within the area of his particular use, it brings on disaster. However powerful a king may be, he cannot raise his standard of rebellion against the infinite source of strength, which is unity, and yet remain powerful.

It has been said, *By unrighteousness men prosper, gain what they desire, and triumph over their enemies, but at the end they are cut off at the root and suffer extinction.*[4] Our roots must go deep down into the universal if we would attain the greatness of personality.

It is the end of our self to seek that union. It must bend its head low in love and meekness and take its stand where great and small all meet. It has to gain by its loss and rise by its surrender. His games would be a horror to the child if he could not come back to his mother, and our pride of personality will be a curse to us if we cannot give it up in love. We must know that it is only the revelation of the Infinite which is endlessly new and eternally beautiful in us and gives the only meaning to our self.

---

4. Adharmēnaidhatē tāvat tatō bhadrāni pacyati tatah sapatnān jayati samūlastu vinaçyati.

Realization in Love

We come now to the eternal problem of the coexistence of the infinite and the finite, of the supreme being and our soul. There is the sublime paradox that lies at the root of existence. We never can go round it, because we never can stand outside the problem and weigh it against any other possible alternative. But the problem exists in logic only; in reality it does not offer us any difficulty at all. Logically speaking, the distance between two points, however near, may be said to be infinite, because it is infinitely divisible. But we *do* cross the infinite at every step, and meet the eternal in every second. Therefore some of our philosophers say there is no such thing as finitude; it is but a *māya,* an illusion. The real is the infinite, and it is only *māya,* the unreality, which causes the appearance of the finite. But the word *māya* is a mere name, it is no explanation. It is merely saying that with truth there is this appearance which is the opposite of truth; but how they come to exist at one and the same time is incomprehensible.

We have what we call in Sanskrit *dvandva,* a series of opposites in creation; such as, positive pole and the negative, the centripetal force and the centrifugal, attraction and repulsion. These are also mere names, they are no explanations. They are only different ways of asserting that the world in its essence is a reconciliation of pairs of opposing forces. These forces, like the left and the the right hands of the creator, are acting in absolute harmony, yet acting from opposite directions.

There is a bond of harmony between our two eyes, which makes them act in unison. Likewise there is an unbreakable continuity of relation in the physical world between heat and cold, light and darkness, motion and rest, as between the bass and treble notes of a piano. That is why these opposites do not bring confusion in the universe, but harmony. If creation were but a chaos, we should have to imagine the two opposing principles as trying to get the better of each other. But the universe is not under martial law, arbitrary and provisional. Here we find no force which can run amok, or go on indefinitely in its wild road, like an exiled outlaw, breaking all harmony with its surroundings; each force, on the contrary, has to come back in a curved line to its equilibrium. Waves rise, each to its individual height in a seeming attitude of unrelenting competition, but only up to a certain point; and thus we know of the great repose of the sea to which they are all related, and to which they must all return in a rhythm which is marvellously beautiful.

In fact, these undulations and vibrations, these risings and fallings, are not due to the erratic contortions of disparate bodies, they are a rhythmic dance. Rhythm never can be born of the haphazard struggle of combat. Its underlying principle must be unity, not opposition.

This principle of unity is the mystery of all mysteries. The existence of a duality at once raises a question in our minds, and we seek its solution in the One. When at last we find a relation between these two, and thereby see them as one in essence, we feel that we have come to the truth. And then we give utterance to this most startling of all paradoxes, that the One appears as many, that the appearance is the opposite of truth and yet is inseparably related to it.

Curiously enough, there are men who lose that feeling of mystery, which is at the root of all our delights, when they discover the uniformity of law among the diversity of nature. As if gravitation is not more of a mystery than the fall of an apple, as if the evolution from one scale of being to the other is not something which is even more shy of explanation than a succession of creations. The trouble is that we very often stop at such a law as if it were the final end of our search, and then we find that it does not even begin to emancipate our spirit. It only gives satisfaction to our intellect, and as it does not appeal to our whole being it only deadens in us the sense of the infinite.

A great poem, when analysed, is a set of detached sounds. The reader who finds out the meaning, which is the inner medium that connects these outer sounds, discovers a perfect law all through, which is never violated in the least; the law of the evolution of ideas, the law of the music and the form.

But law in itself is a limit. It only shows that whatever is can never be otherwise. When a man is exclusively occupied with the search for the links of causality, his mind succumbs to the tyranny of law in escaping from the tyranny of facts. In learning a language, when from mere words we reach the laws of words we have gained a great deal. But if we stop at that point, and only concern ourselves with the marvels of the formation of a language, seeking the hidden reason of all its apparent caprices, we do not reach the end—for grammar is not literature, prosody is not a poem.

When we come to literature we find that though it conforms to rules of grammar it is yet a thing of joy, it is freedom itself. The beauty of a poem is bound by strict laws, yet it transcends them. The laws are its wings, they do not keep it weighed down, they carry it to freedom. Its form is in law but its spirit is in beauty. Law is the first step towards freedom, and beauty is the complete liberation which stands on the pedestal of law.

Beauty harmonises in itself the limit and the beyond, the law and the liberty.

In the world-poem, the discovery of the law of its rhythms, the measurement of its expansion and contraction, movement and pause, the pursuit of its evolution of forms and characters, are true achievements of the mind; but we cannot stop there. It is like a railway station; but the station platform is not our home. Only he has attained the final truth who knows that the whole world is a creation of joy.

This leads me to think how mysterious the relation of the human heart with nature must be. In the outer world of activity nature has one aspect, but in our hearts, in the inner world, it presents an altogether different picture.

Take an instance—the flower of a plant. However fine and dainty it may look, it is pressed to do a great service, and its colours and forms are all suited to its work. It must bring forth the fruits, or the continuity of plant life will be broken and the earth will be turned into a desert ere long. The colour and the smell of the flower are all for some purpose therefore; no sooner is it fertilised by the bee, and the time of its fruition arrives, than it sheds its exquisite petals and a cruel economy compels it to give up its sweet perfume. It has no time to flaunt its finery, for it is busy beyond measure. Viewed from without, necessity seems to be the only factor in nature for which everything works and moves. There the bud develops into the flower, the flower into the fruit, the fruit into the seed, the seed into a new plant again, and so forth, the chain of activity running on unbroken. Should there crop up any disturbance or impediment, no excuse would be accepted, and the unfortunate thing thus choked in its movement would at once be labelled as rejected, and be bound to die and disappear post-haste. In the great office of nature there are innumerable departments with endless work going on, and the fine flower that you behold there, gaudily attired and scented like a dandy, is by no means what it appears to be, but rather, is like a labourer toiling in sun and shower, who has to submit a clear account of his work and has and no breathing space to enjoy himself in playful frolic.

But when this same flower enters the heart of men its aspect of busy practicality is gone, and it becomes the very emblem of leisure and repose. The same object that is the embodiment of endless activity without is the perfect expression of beauty and peace within.

Science here warns us that we are mistaken, that the purpose of a flower is nothing but what is outwardly manifested, and that the relation of beauty and sweetness which we think it bears to us is all our own making, gratuitous and imaginary.

But our heart replies that we are not in the least mistaken. In the sphere of nature the flower carries with it a certificate which recommends it as having immense capacity for doing useful work, but it brings an altogether different letter of introduction when it knocks at the door of our hearts. Beauty becomes its only qualification. At one place it comes as a slave, and at another as a free thing. How, then, should we give credit to its first recommendation and disbelieve the second one? That the flower has got its being in the unbroken chain of causation is true beyond doubt; but that is an outer truth. The inner truth is: *Verily from the everlasting joy do all objects have their birth.*[1]

A flower, therefore, has not its only function in nature, but has another great function to exercise in the mind of man. And what is that function? In nature its work is that of a servant who has to make his appearance at appointed times, but in the heart of man it comes like a messenger from the King. In the Rāmāyana, when Sītā, forcibly separated

---

1. Ānandādhyāva khalvimāni bhūtāni jāyantā.

from her husband, was bewailing her evil fate in Ravana's golden palace, she was met by a messenger who brought with him a ring of her beloved Rāmchandra himself. The very sight of it convinced Sītā of the truth of the tidings he bore. She was at once reassured that he came indeed from her beloved one, who had not forgotten her and was at hand to rescue her.

Such a messenger is a flower from our great lover. Surrounded with the pomp and pageantry of worldliness, which may be likened to Ravana's golden city, we still live in exile, while the insolent spirit of worldly prosperity tempts us with allurements and claims us as its bride. In the meantime the flower comes across with a message from the other shore, and whispers in our ears, 'I am come. He has sent me. I am a messenger of the beautiful, the one whose soul is the bliss of love. This island of isolation has been bridged over by him, and he has not forgotten thee, and will rescue thee even now. He will draw thee unto him and make thee his own. This illusion will not hold thee in thraldom for ever.'

If we happen to be awake then, we question him: 'How are we to know that thou art come from him indeed?' The messenger says, 'Look! I have this ring from him. How lovely are its hues and charms!'

Ah, doubtless it is his—indeed, it is our wedding ring. Now all else passes into oblivion, only this sweet symbol of the touch of the eternal love fills us with a deep longing. We realise that the palace of gold where we are has nothing to do with us—our deliverance is outside it—and there our love has its fruition and our life its fulfilment.

What to the bee in nature is merely colour and scent, and the marks or spots which show the right track to the honey, is to the human heart beauty and untrammelled by necessity. They bring a love-letter to the heart written in many-coloured inks.

I was telling you, therefore, that however busy our active nature outwardly may be, she has a secret chamber within the heart where she comes and goes freely, without any design whatsoever. There the fire of her workshop is transformed into lamps of a festival, the noise of her factory is heard like music. The iron chain of cause and effect sounds heavily outside in nature, but in the human heart its unalloyed delight seems to sound, as it were, like the golden strings of a harp.

It indeed seems to be wonderful that nature has these two aspects at one and the same time, and so antithetical—one being of thraldom and the other of freedom. In the same form, sound, colour, and taste two contrary notes are heard, one of necessity and the other of joy. Outwardly nature is busy and restless, inwardly she is all silence and peace. She has toil on one side and leisure on the other. You see her bondage only when you see her from without, but within her heart is a limitless beauty.

Our seer says, 'From joy are born all creatures, by joy they are sustained, towards joy they progress, and into joy they enter.'

Not that he ignores law, or that his contemplation of this infinite joy is born of the intoxication produced by an indulgence in abstract thought. He fully recognises the inexorable laws of nature, and says, 'Fire burns for fear of him (*i.e.* by his law); the sun shines by fear of him; and for fear of him the wind, the clouds, and death perform their offices.' It is a reign of iron rule, ready to punish the least transgression. Yet the poet chants the glad song, 'From joy are born all creatures, by joy they are sustained, towards joy they progress, and into joy they enter.'

The immortal being manifests himself in joy-form.[2] His manifestation in creation is out of his fulness of joy. It is the

2. Ānandarūpamamritam yad vibhāti.

nature of this abounding joy to realise itself in form which is law. The joy, which is without form, must create, must translate itself into forms. The joy of the singer is expressed in the form of a song, that of the poet in the form of a poem. Man in his rôle of a creator is ever creating forms, and they come out of his abounding joy.

This joy, whose other name is love, must by in very nature have duality for its realization. When the singer has his inspiration he makes himself into two; he has within him his other self as the hearer, and the outside audience is merely an extension of this other self of his. The lover seeks his own other self in his beloved. It is the joy that creates this separation, in order to realise through obstacles the union.

The *amritam*, the immortal bliss, has made himself into two. Our soul is the loved one, it is his other self. We are separate; but if this separation were absolute, then there would have been absolute misery and unmitigated evil in this world. Then from untruth we never could reach truth, and from sin we never could hope to attain purity of heart; then all opposites would ever remain opposite, and we could never find a medium through which our differences could ever tend to meet. Then we could have no language, no understanding, no blending of hearts, no co-operation in life. But on the contrary, we find that the separateness of objects is in a fluid state. Their individualities are ever changing, they are meeting and merging into each other, till science itself is turning into metaphysics, matter losing its boundaries, and the definition of life becoming more and more indefinite.

Yes, our individual soul has been separated from the supreme soul, but this has not been from alienation but from the fulness of love. It is for that reason that untruths, sufferings, and evils are not at a standstill; the human soul can defy them, can overcome them, nay, can altogether transform them into new power and beauty.

The singer is translating his song into singing, joy into forms, and the hearer has to translate back the singing into the original joy; then the communion between the singer and the hearer is complete. The infinite joy is manifesting itself in manifold forms, taking upon itself the bondage of law, and we fulfil our destiny when we go back from forms to joy, from law to the love, when we untie the knot of the finite and hark back to the infinite.

The human soul is on its journey from the law to love, from discipline to liberation, from the moral plane to the spiritual. Buddha preached the discipline of self-restraint and moral life; it is a complete acceptance of law. But this bondage of law cannot be an end by itself; by mastering it thoroughly we acquire the means of getting beyond it. It is going back to Brahma, to the infinite love, which is manifesting itself through the finite forms of law. Buddha names it *Brahma-vihāra*, the joy of living in Brahma. He who wants to reach this stage, according to Buddha, 'shall deceive none, entertain no hatred for anybody, and never wish to injure through anger. He shall have measureless love for all creatures, even as a mother has for her only child, whom she protects with her own life. Up above, below, and all around him he shall extend his love, which is without bounds and obstacles, and which is free from all cruelty and antagonism. While standing, sitting, walking, lying down, till he falls asleep, he shall keep his mind active in this exercise of universal goodwill.'

Want of love is a degree of callousness; for love is the perfection of consciousness. We do not love because we do not comprehend, or rather we do not comprehend because we do not love. For love is the ultimate meaning of everything around us. It is not a mere sentiment; it is truth; it is the joy that is at the root of all creation. It is the white light of pure consciousness that emanates from Brahma. So, to be one with this *sarvānubhūh*, this all-feeling being who is in the external sky, as well as in our inner soul, we must attain to that summit of consciousness, which is love: *Who could have breathed or moved if the sky were not filled with joy, with love?*[3] It is through the heightening of our consciousness into love, and extending it all over the world, that we can attain *Brahma-vihāra,* communion with this infinite joy.

Love spontaneously gives itself in endless gifts. But these gifts lose their fullest significance if through them we do not reach that love, which is the giver. To do that, we must have love in our own heart. He who has no love in him values the gifts of his lover only according to their usefulness. But utility is temporary and partial. It can never occupy our whole being; what is useful only touches us at the point where we have some want. When the want is satisfied, utility becomes a burden if it still persists. On the other hand, a mere token is of permanent worth to us when we have love in our heart. For it is not for any special use. It is an end in itself; it is for our whole being and therefore can never tire us.

The question is, In what manner do we accept this world, which is a perfect gift of joy? Have we been able to receive it in our heart where we keep enshrined things that are of deathless value to us? We are frantically busy making use of the forces of the universe to gain more and more power; we feed and we clothe ourselves from its stores, we scramble for its riches, and it becomes for us a field of fierce competition. But were we born for this, to extend our proprietary rights over this world and make of it a marketable commodity? When our whole mind is bent only upon making use of this world it loses for us its true value. We make it cheap by our sordid desires; and thus to the end of our days we only try to feed upon it and miss its truth, just like the greedy child who tears leaves from a precious book and tries to swallow them.

---

3. Ko hyēvānyāt kah prānyāt yadēsha ākāça ānandō na syāt.

In the lands where cannibalism is prevalent man looks upon man as his food. In such a country civilization can never thrive, for there man loses his higher value and is made common indeed. But there are other kinds of cannibalism, perhaps not so gross, but not less heinous, for which one need not travel far. In countries higher in the scale of civilization we find sometimes man looked upon as a mere body, and he is bought and sold in the market by the price of his flesh only. And sometimes he gets his sole value from being useful; he is made into a machine, and is traded upon by the man of money to acquire for him more money. Thus our lust, our greed, our love of comfort result in cheapening man to his lowest value. It is self-deception on a large scale. Our desires blind us to the *truth* that there is in man, and this is the greatest wrong done by ourselves to our own soul. It deadens our consciousness, and is but a gradual method of spiritual suicide. It produces ugly sores in the body of civilization, gives rise to its hovels and brothels, its vindictive penal codes, its cruel prison systems, its organised method of exploiting foreign races to the extent of permanently injuring them by depriving them of the discipline of self-government and means of self-defence.

Of course man is useful to man, because his body is a marvellous machine and his mind an organ of wonderful efficiency. But he is a spirit as well, and this spirit is truly known only by love. When we define a man by the market value of the service we can expect of him, we know him imperfectly. With this limited knowledge of him it becomes easy for us to be unjust to him and to entertain feelings of triumphant self-congratulation when, on account of some cruel advantage on our side, we can get out of him much more than we have paid for. But when we know him as a spirit we know him as our own. We at once feel that cruelty to him is cruelty to ourselves, to make him small is stealing from our own humanity, and in seeking to make use of him solely for personal profit we merely gain in money or comfort what we pay for in truth.

One day I was out in a boat on the Ganges. It was a beautiful evening in autumn. The sun had just set; the silence of the sky was full to the brim with ineffable peace and beauty. The vast expanse of water was without a ripple, mirroring all the changing shades of the sunset glow. Miles and miles of a desolate sandbank lay like a huge amphibious reptile of some antediluvian age, with its scales glistening in shining colours. As our boat was silently gliding by the precipitous river-bank, riddled with the nest-holes of a colony of birds, suddenly a big fish leapt up to the surface of the water and then disappeared, displaying on its vanishing figure all the colours of the evening sky. It drew aside for a moment the many-coloured screen behind which there was a silent world full of the joy of life. It came up from the depths of its mysterious dwelling with a beautiful dancing motion and added its own music to the silent symphony of the dying day. I felt as if I had a friendly greeting from an alien world in its own language, and it touched my heart with a flash of gladness. Then suddenly the man at the helm exclaimed with a distinct note of regret, 'Ah, what a big fish!' It at once brought before his vision the picture of the fish caught and made ready for his supper. He could only look at the fish through his desire, and thus missed the whole truth of its existence. But man is not entirely an animal. He aspires to a spiritual vision, which is the vision of the whole truth. This gives him the highest delight, because it reveals to him the deepest harmony that exists between him and his surroundings. It is our desires that limit the scope of our self-realization, hinder our extension of consciousness, and give rise to sin, which is the innermost barrier that keeps us apart from our God, setting up disunion and the arrogance of exclusiveness.

For sin is not one mere action, but it is an attitude of life which takes for granted that our goal is finite, that our self is the ultimate truth, and that we are not all essentially one but exist each for his own separate individual existence.

So I repeat we never can have a true view of man unless we have a love for him. Civilization must be judged and prized, not by the amount of power it has developed, but by how much it has evolved and given expression to, by its laws and institutions, the love of humanity. The first question and the last which it has to answer is, Whether and how far it recognises man more as a spirit than as a machine? Whenever some ancient civilization fell into decay and died, it was owing to causes which produced callousness of heart and led to the cheapening of man's worth; when either the state or some powerful group of men began to look upon the people as a mere instrument of their power; when, by compelling weaker races to slavery and trying to keep them down by every means, man struck at the foundation of his greatness, his own love of freedom and fair-play. Civilization can never sustain itself upon cannibalism of any form. For that by which alone man is true can only be nourished by love and justice.

As with man, so with this universe. When we look at the world through the veil of our desires we make it small and narrow, and fail to perceive its full truth. Of course it is obvious that the world serves us and fulfils our needs, but our relation to it does not end there. We are bound to it with a deeper and truer bond than that of necessity. Our soul is drawn to it; our love of life is really our wish to continue our relation with this great world. This relation is one of love. We are glad that we are in it; we are attached to it with numberless threads, which extend from this earth to the stars. Man foolishly tries to prove his superiority by imagining his radical separateness from what he calls his physical world, which, in his blind fanaticism, he sometimes goes to the extent of ignoring altogether, holding it as his direst enemy. Yet the more his knowledge progresses, the more it becomes difficult for man to establish this separateness, and all the imaginary boundaries he had set up around himself vanish one after another. Every time we lose some of our badges of absolute distinction by which we conferred upon our humanity the right to hold itself apart from its surroundings, it gives us a shock of humiliation. But we have to submit to this. If we set up our pride on the path of our self-realization to create divisions and disunion, then it must sooner or later come under the wheels of truth and be ground to dust. No, we are not burdened with some monstrous superiority, unmeaning in its singular abruptness. It would be utterly degrading for us to live in a world immeasurably less than ourselves in the quality of soul, just as it would be repulsive and degrading to be surrounded and served by a host of slaves, day and night, from birth to the moment of death. On the contrary, this world is our compeer, nay, we are one with it.

Through our progress in science the wholeness of the world and our oneness with it is becoming clearer to our mind. When this perception of the perfection of unity is not merely intellectual, when it opens out our whole being into a luminous consciousness of the all, then it becomes a radiant joy, an overspreading love. Our spirit finds its larger self in the whole world, and is filled with an absolute certainty that it is immortal. It dies a hundred times in its enclosures of self; for separateness is doomed to die, it cannot be made eternal. But it never can die where it is one with the all, for there is its truth, its joy. When a man feels the rhythmic throb of the soul-life of the whole world in his own soul, then is he free. Then he enters into the secret courting that goes on between this beautiful world-bride, view with the veil of the many-coloured finiteness and the *paramatmam,* the bridegroom, in his spotless white. Then he knows that he is the partaker in this gorgeous love festival, and he is the honoured guest at the feast of immortality. Then he understands the meaning of the seer-poet who sings, 'From love the world is born, by love it is sustained, towards love it moves, and into love it enters.'

In love all the contradictions of existence merge themselves and are lost. Only in love are unity and duality not at variance. Love must be one and two at the same time.

Only love is motion and rest in one. Our heart ever changes its place till it finds love, and then it has its rest. But this rest itself is an intense form of activity where utter quiescence and unceasing energy meet at the same point in love.

In love, loss and gain are harmonised. In its balance-sheet, credit and debit accounts are in the same column, and gifts are added to gains. In this wonderful festival of creation, this great ceremony of self-sacrifice of God, the lover constantly gives himself up to gain himself in love. Indeed, love is what brings together and inseparably connects both the act of abandoning and that of receiving.

In love at one of its poles you find the personal, and at the other the impersonal. At one you have the positive assertion—Here I am; at the other the equally strong denial—I am not. Without this ego what is love? And again, with only this ego how can love be possible?

Bondage and liberation are not antagonistic in love. For love is most free and at the same time most bound. If God were absolutely free there would be no creation. The infinite being has assumed unto himself the mystery of finitude. And in him who is love the finite and the infinite are made one.

Similarly, when we talk about the relative values of freedom and non-freedom, it becomes a mere play of words. It is not that we desire freedom alone, we want thraldom as well. It is the high function of love to welcome all limitations and to transcend them. For nothing is more independent than love, and where else, again, shall we find so much of dependence? In love, thraldom is as glorious as freedom.

The *Vaishnava* religion has boldly declared that God has bound himself to man, and in that consists the greatest glory of human existence. In the spell of the wonderful rhythm of the finite he fetters himself at every step, and thus gives his love out in music in his most perfect lyrics of beauty. Beauty is his wooing of our heart; it can have no other purpose. It tells us everywhere that the display of power is not the ultimate meaning of creation; wherever there is a bit of colour, a note of song, a grace of form, there comes the call for our love. Hunger compels us to obey its behests, but hunger is not the last word for a man. There have been men who have deliberately defied its commands to show that the human soul is not to be led by the pressure of wants and threat of pain. In fact, to live the life of man we have to resist its demands every day, the least of us as well as the greatest. But, on the other hand, there is a beauty in the world, which never insults our freedom, never raises even its little finger to make us acknowledge its sovereignty. We can absolutely ignore it and suffer no penalty in consequence. It is a call to us, but not a command. It seeks for love in us, and love can never be had by compulsion. Compulsion is not indeed the final appeal to man, but joy is. And joy is everywhere; it is in the earth's green covering of grass; in the blue serenity of the sky; in the reckless exuberance of spring; in the severe abstinence of grey winter; in the living flesh that animates our bodily frame; in the perfect poise of the human figure, noble and upright; in living; in the exercise of all our powers; in the acquisition of knowledge; in fighting evils; in dying for gains we never can share. Joy is there everywhere; it is superfluous, unnecessary; nay, it very often contradicts the most peremptory behests of necessity. It exists to show that the bonds of law can only be explained by love; they are like body and soul. Joy is the realization of the truth of oneness, the oneness of our soul with the world and of the world-soul with the supreme lover.

MAN

Lecture II

Supreme Man

The scientist solves the mystery of a piece of iron and says that it is nothing but the constant movements of electric particles of a special rhythm. The intervals between them in such a system are, in proportion to their size, immense. If our unaided eyes could see what has been discovered by scientific vision, then, like the individuals in human society, we should have seen the particles as distinct and separate. However distinct these may be, a force,—for let us call it a force—is working among them. It is a relating force,—the community force of the piece of iron. When we see the piece of iron, we do not see the multitude of electrons, we see the mass. In fact, the visible appearance of the iron is a symbol; it is not what it ultimately is. To take an analogy we are given a ten-rupee note. He knows it truly who at sight recognizes the piece of paper as a symbol of unity that represents ten separate silver coins.

We see the piece of iron to be iron, and yet it is only a physical symbol revealing the mysterious spirit of relationship which cannot be seen by the bodily eye. Likewise, the distinctions of time and place between individual men are very great, and yet there is a large and deep unity encompassing all men. This unity, imperceptible by the senses, is not that of a numerical aggregate, for it transcends all aggregates.

Those who have in them the great capacity of feeling within themselves the one Spirit in all men, are the people to whom we give the name *Mahaâtmaâ* or Great Soul. It is they who can lay down their lives for the good of all men. It is they who can address the comprehensive spirit within and without them and say:

तदेतत् प्रेयः पुत्रात् प्रेयो वित्तात् प्रयोऽन्यस्मात् सर्वस्मादन्तरतरं
यदयमात्मा

He is dearer than a son, dearer than wealth, dearer than all else is this spirit who is in our inmost heart.

The scientist condemns such statements. He says that we attribute humanity to God in calling Him our Beloved. I reply that it is not *attributing,* but *realizing* humanity. It is by developing the sense of the dignity of his human truth that man has attained to his God. The human mind cannot therefore protest against the attribution of humanity to his God, and it would not be at all true if he did so. Man does not arrtibute lighthood to the vibrations of ether, he feels and uses the vibrations themselves as light and is not deceived in such use.

There is the ultimate world entity even beyond the immediate entity of man, as we have the stellar sphere beyond the solar system. But it is primarily the solar system of which the earth is a part, it is solar heat that is the life of the earth, and it is the solar connection that governs the earth's movements and its day and night. We have knowledge of the stellar sphere, but it is the solar system we fully comprehend with our body and our mind. Similarly, the greatness which is supremely cosmical is for us an object of knowledge, but the greatness which is human is a matter for the fulfilment of all our body, mind and character.

But even the impersonal world with regard to which we can trace no distinctions of good and evil, beautiful and ugly, about which nothing more can be said beyond the fact that it exists, is bounded by human knowledge. And therefore by knowing it we become aware of the extension of our own consciousness and we are glad. The world we know or hope to know sometimes through scientific experience is itself a human world. *Man* alone perceives this world in the form of *his* thought within the scaffoldings of *his* Understanding and Reason. It is possible to conceive of a mind which perceives a world that is beyond the range of our mathematical measurements and does not exist in the space which *we* know. But how shall we call extra-human the world whose fundamental truths are found by man in conformity with the innate principles of his thought? That is why a modern scientist describes the universe as the creation of mathematical mind. But even this mathematical mind is not beyond the bounds of the human mind. If it were, then we could not have at all known the scientific theory of the world, like the dogs and cats who can never reach it.

The true character of Him who is the Qualified Reality, *Sagunna Brahma,* is defined in our scriptures as *Sarvendriyagunnābhaāsam.* All the qualities which belong to the external and internal faculties of man have their suggestion in Him. The very meaning of this is that the ultimate Truth for us is *human* Truth, and that is why this world we know is necessarily a *human* world. Even if there be any other world beside this, it is non-existent for us, not only for to-day, but for ever.

We give the name Love to that relation of one soul to another which is the deepest and truest. Our actual acquaintance with the physical world is through sense perception, but our true comprehension of the spiritual world is through love. In the love of his parents, man begins his acquaintance with the spiritual world from the very moment of his birth. Here we find immeasurable mystery,—the contact of the indescribable. The question may arise, wherein lies the basis of the truth of parenthood. It must be in Him, who is पितृतमः पितृणाम् who contains the perfection of the fatherhood of all fathers. We can understand the characteristics of this earth to which we are born by scrutinizing it from outside, but the mystery of parenthood we can comprehend only in the depth of our own spirit, and it is there in this depth that we realize the Supreme Father. This Supreme Father does not dwell in any particular heaven, nor is he to be found in the history of any particular time or country. He has not expressed Himself once and for good in any particular individual but extends His love over the past and future of humainty and pervades the whole world of man.

We hear of the God of man:

यद् यद् विभूतिमत् सत्त्वं श्रीमद् ऊर्जितमेव वा
तत्तदेवोवगच्छ त्वं मम तेजोंशसम्भवम्।

Whatever has splendour, has beauty and excellence, is born of an aspect of my own divine energy.

In the universe there are many things great and small. So far as bare existence is concerned, they all have the same worth. From the point of view of mere actuality, there is no distinction for better or worse between the lotus and the clod of earth. But man has in his mind a standard of value, which does not judge by need, nor by the measurement of size or degree. In man, there is the sense of perfection transcending all quantitative standards—a consciousness of the inmost satisfaction. This is what he means by excellence, and yet we find no unanimity of opinion about this excellence. How then can we say that this excellence is based upon an impersonal and eternal truth which is in the universal man.

We know all scienticfic truths have passed through innumerable errors. In fact, the errors are many, the truth is one. The errors are personal, the truth belongs to the all. The astronomer wants to study the planet with his telescope, but he has many obstacles to overcome. In our sky there are the dust of the earth, the enveloping atmosphere, the veils of vapour and many kinds of disturbances all around. Defects are possible in the instrument, and the mind which observes is clouded by its predispositions. Pure truth can be attained only when all the obstacles—internal and external—have been overcome.

It is easy to admit that the realization of pure truth is the manifestation of the universal mind, but it is possible to doubt whether in aesthetic experience, we realize the universal mind. How can there be an absolute standard of beauty when our sense of joy in it often varies with the country, time and the individual? And yet, when we look at human history over a large period, we find that the minds of all artists of all times tend to agree in their judgement of the merit of artistic beauty. It has to be admitted that it is not absolutely every man that finds complete joy in an artistic creation. Many have minds blind to beauty: their personal preferences do not agree with universal appreciation. There are also among men many who are naturally impervious to science. Their conceptions of the world are confusingly irrelevant and antagonistic, because their minds are prejudiced, for the prejudice of one does not agree with that of another. Yet they are so inordinately vain of the truth of their own particular wrong view that they are prepared to go to any lengths in support of their doctrine. Similarly, there is no lack of persons in the world with naturally deficient taste. In their case also, differences of opinion become dangerous. We cannot question the universal perfection of knowledge simply because there are different levels of born stupidity, of every variety, from the lowest to the highest. It is the same with regard to the ideal of beauty.

Bertrand Russell has expressed in some writing of his, that Beethoven's symphonies cannot be regarded as creations of the Universal Mind, for they are personal to him. Russell means that a symphony is not like a mathematical truth, which is an object to all minds and has the mind of the individual as merely the occasion of its formualtion. But if it has to be admitted that everyone ought to appreciate it when with proper training the opposition of ignorance and unaccustomedness have been dispelled, then it must also be admitted that the appreciation of the best composer is to be fully met with in the mind of Man and is impeded only in some particular men as listeners.

The intellect is indispensable for the preservation of life, but there are many instances of worldly success in spite of an imperfect sense of beauty. The sense of beauty has no sanction of vital urgency, nor does licence in this sphere carry with it its own necessary punishment. And yet a stupendous amount of effort is being applied to the task of creating beauty although in the maintenance of life it serves no purpose: only its influence is for transforming our inner being.

In the *Upanissads* we again and again find mention of this attainment through being. From these we understand that man is one in spirit with the Supreme Object of his strivings.

नाविरतो दुश्चरितान् नाशान्तो नासमाहितः।
नाशान्तमानसो वापि प्रज्ञानेनैनमाप्नुयात्॥

It is said that He cannot be reached through mere knowledge. He has to be relaized through the perfection of being, by refraining from evil conduct, by achieving a steadfast mind through the control of the passions. In other words, this realization is the attainment of one's own eternal truth.

I have stated before that we must remove all impurities and disturbances of the environment and all individual idiosyncrasies if we want to see physical truth in its purity. This applies even more to spiritual truths. It is when we attribute to spiritual truth the perversions arising out of our lower nature that our mistakes become most dangerous. We can understand how much more ruinous than mistakes in knowledge are our mistakes in being when we find that the very forces which we have brought under our control through science become our medium of the hatred and avarice of man and extend the sphere of his self-destruction from one end of the earth to the other. It is for this reason that perversion of the nature of some particular individual or group in the name of the community or religion incites man's will to evil far more than scientific mistakes or conflicts of material interest. The communal god thus becomes the receptacle of hatred, vanity, snobbishness and stupidity. Insulted Godhead degrades man and keeps him in constant fear of his own fellows. This calamity strikes at the very root of power and fortune in our country.

There are instances of this in other countries as well. The traditional Christians express their contempt for the degradation and cruelty in the characters of the traditional gods and modes of worship of some Indian communities. On account of habit they cannot, however, see that their own conception of God is equally possessed by the evil genius of man. The community whose sacred books condemn to eternal hell a child that has died before its baptism, has attributed to God a degree of cruelty that is perhaps unparalleled anywhere else. In fact, the conception of eternal hell, for any sin however heinous, is the most potent invention of human cruelty. Herein lies the explanation of the anti-scientific and anti-religious persecution practised in mediaeval Europe in order to preserve intact the faith in scriptural religion. Even to-day that conception of hell pervades with horror the prisons of civilized man, where there is no principle of reformation, but only the ferocity of punishment.

It is with the development of humanity that the realization of God gradually grows free of prejudice, at any rate, it ought to be so. The reason that it is not always so is due to the fact that we take anything and everything connected with religion to be eternal. It does not follow from our reverence for the eternal ideal of religion, that we must accept any particular religious dogma as also eternal. If we were fanatically to assert that every scientific opinion is eternally true, because there is eternal truth as the foundation of physical science, then we should have to assert, even to-day, that the sun is revolving round the earth. It is this mistake we generally make with regard to religion. The community gives the name of religion to its own traditional opinion, and thus strikes at Religion itself. The conflict, the cruelty, the unreasoning and unintelligent superstition, which then emerge, are without parallel in any other sphere of human life.

Mistakes in science, or in our code of conduct, arise from our inability to comprehend the wholeness of truth. In spiritual life we realize the wholeness of our being when it is conscious of a centre in a great and eternal meaning.

The earth revolves round its own axis and yet it circles round the sun along its vast orbit. Whatever happens in human society also exhibits these two tendencies. On the one hand, the paraphernalia of wealth and power are accumulated through the urge of the individual ego, and yet on the other, under the inspiration of the Universal Man, men unite with one another in their activity and their joy and make sacrifices for one another's sake.

Some years ago there was a report published in the London *Times*, which I came to know through the *Nation* of America. The British air force was destroying from the air a Mahsud village in Afghanistan. One of the bombing planes was damaged and came down. An Afghan girl led the airmen into a neighbouring cave, and to protect them, a Malik remained on guard at the entrance of the cave. Forty men with brandished knives rushed forward to attack them, but the Malik dissuaded them. All this time, bombs were dropping from above and people were crowding in to take shelter in the cave. Some Maliks of the neighbourhood and a Mollah proposed to help the Britishers and some of the women offered to feed them. After some time they at last disguised the airmen as Mahsuds and brought them out to a safe place.

In this incident, we find the two aspects of human nature revealed in their extremest forms. In the bombing from aeroplanes we have an instance of the wonderful development of human power—the vast expanse of his mailed fist from earth to heaven. But to forgive and protect the enemy engaged in dealing death reveals another aspect of man. The natural instinct to kill enemies is the prompting of man's animal nature: but he transcended it and uttered the strange command: Forgive your enemies.

Our scriptures lay down that at the time of battle a charioteer must not attack the man who is not in a chariot but on the ground. Nor must he kill one who is impotent, or a supplicant, nor one who is seated or has his hair untied, nor one who humbly offers to submit. Nor yet must he kill one who is asleep or unprotected, naked or unarmed, a spectator or a non-combatant, or engaged in fighting another. He must remember the teachings of virtue and refrain from killing one whose weapons are broken, one who is afflicted with sorrow, one who is wounded or frightened.

We have heard Man say 'Do not sin against those that sin against you'. Whether or not the individual conforms in his conduct to this law he does not laugh it away as the ravings of a lunatic. In human life, we only occasionally find conformity to this principle and generally we find its opposite. In other words, its truth is hardly seen in a mere count of heads, and yet its truth is acknowledged. Where lies the basis of the aspect of man which realizes it? Let us see what answers have been given by man to this question.

यस्यात्मा विरतः पापात् कल्याणे च निवेशितः।
तेन सर्वमिदं बुद्धं प्रकृतिर्विकृतिश्च या॥

He whose spirit refrains from evil and attends to the good
has comprehended the *sarvam,* the totality. He therefore
knows what is natural to him and what is an aberration.

Man comprehends his nature only when he abstains from
evil and works for the good of all. This means that only the
great among men understand human nature. How do they
know it?

With a transparent heart, they comprehend the totality.
The true and the good are in the totality. It is when man
refrains from the sin which belongs to his nature as limited
by the ego that he knows his own spiritual wholeness—it is
then that he understands his own nature. His nature does not
concern the individual alone : it concerns Him of Whom the
Gita says, पूरूणः नृष 'He is the humanity in Men'.

All that we have said so far about the good and evil is
not from the point of view of the preservation of society. The
code based on the solid foundation of praise and blame, which
society promulgates through commands and precepts for its
own preservation, gives but a secondary importance to the
eternal principle of Truth : the preservation of the traditional
society is its primary object. We are therfore told that it is
harmful to introduce into society the Religion of Truth in all
its purity. It is often said that there is a great deal of stupidity
in the common man. To keep him away from evil, he must
therefore, if need be, be kept engaged with delusions, frightened
or comforted with false fears or hopes, in short, treated as
.ternally a child or a brute. It is with society as with religious
communities. The opinions and customs prevalent at some
previous time are loath to give up their rights even at a later
age. In the insect-world, we find some harmless insects that
adopt the disguise of terrible ones and thus secure themselves.

It is the same with social laws. They try to make themselves powerful and permanent by disguising themselves as eternal truths. On the one hand, they have the external show of piety, and on the other, the terrors of torture in the after-life, various strict and sometimes unjust means of social punishment, compelling blind conformity to needless conventions under the threat of a made-to-order Hell. The Andamans, the Devil Islands of France, and the Lipari Isles of Italy, are the symbols of this very attitude in the field of politics. The inner truth about them is that the pure law of Truth and man-made laws do not move with the same rhythm. Those who revere the True, the Good, the Human as the ultimate goals of man have throughout the ages fought against this attitude.

It is not the object of this lecture to estimate the value of the good as conformity to society or the State. I want to discuss the basis of man's acceptance of the Truth, to discuss wherein Truth lies. In the many fields of interest in society and the State, we find at every step contradiction of the Truth in daily conduct, and yet man has given to it the highest place in his self-knowledge, called it his *dharma* which means his ultimate nature. In spite of the many differences of opinion with regard to the ideal of the good that different countries, times, and individuals have, all men have honoured the reality of the good. What I have discussed are the implications of this fact with regard to the nature of the Religion of Man. The conflict of "It is" and "It ought to be" has raged from the very beginnings of human history. In discussing the reason of this conflict, I have said that in the mind of man, there is, on the one hand, the Universal Man, and on the other, the animal man limited by his self-seeking. It is the attempts at harmonizing the two that reveal themselves in different forms according to different religious systems. Otherwise, only advantage and disadvantage, the pleasant and the unpleasant, could have prevailed in the law of life. There could have been no significance at all of sin and virtue, of good and evil.

The question has been asked about the truth, in the Universal Mind, of the pain and pleasure one feels in his individual mind. If we think about it, we find that the pleasure and pain within the limits of the ego are transformed at the borders of the spirit. The man who dedicates his life for Truth, for the sake of his country and for the good of man, who thinks of himself against a vast background of ideals, finds that personal happiness and misery have changed their meaning for him. Such a man gives up his happiness with ease, and by accepting pain, he transcends it. In the life of self-interest he feels the burden so light that his patience when faced with the bitterest suffering and his forgiveness in spite of the heaviest insults seem to us to be superhuman.

Discords become too evident when the tuning of the instrument is going on, but they are not a part of the music itself. Discords jar on us, and if they did not, we should not progress on our quest after harmony. That is why we give the name *Rudra* or Terrible to the Infinite—He draws us towards freedom along the path of the pain of disharmony.

The *Upaniṣad* declares:

एषास्य परमागतिरेषास्य परमा सम्पत्
एषोऽस्य परमो लोक एषोऽस्य परम आनन्दः।

Here we have the dualism of He and this, the individual man and the other One who is within him and beyond him. It is said that *He* is the ultimate aim of *this,* its richest possession, its final rest and supreme joy. In other words, it is in Him that *this* has its perfection.

He is not a mere abstraction. He is an immediate object of the most intimate awareness, just as much as the self which I call my own. When my devotion yearns after Him and in Him I find my joy, it is my self-consciousness that is enlarged, deepened, and extended to the Truth beyond the limits of my narrow existence. It is *Eṣṣaḥḥ,* this great He who challenges man to strike after perfection through endeavours to struggle from the unreal to the real, from darkness towards the light, from death towards immortality.

This challenge never allowed man to stop anywhere; it made of him an eternal wayfarer. Tired and worn out, those who abandon the road and build themselves a permanent house have in fact built their own mausoleums. Animals have their lairs, but man has taken to the road. Those who are great among men are the road-builders and the path-finders. The lure of the call of the infinite in him has brought man out on the way in quest of the unattained. Empires rose and fell by the roadside of his journey, riches were amassed and then lost beneath the dust. Man built many an image to give form to his desire and again smashed them to pieces, like childhood's toys when childhood is over. He tried again and again to construct the magic key and open with it nature's teasure-house and again he discarded them all and started anew to search out the secret path leading to its depths. Age follows age in human history, and man continues in his ceaseless search not for the satisfaction of his material needs, but in order to strive with all his might for the revelation of the Universal Man in the world of men, to rescue his own inmost truth from the crude obstacles set up by himself. That is the Truth which is greater than all his accumulated wealth, greater than all his achievements, greater than all his traditional beliefs and knows no death nor decay. Man's mistakes and failures have been many, leaving their ruins on the way along which he came. The strain of his sorrow and suffering has been infinite, but they mark his strong perseverance to shatter the bonds of his imprisoned ideals. Who could have, even for a moment, endured all this struggle, if it did not have an eternal significance in an inspiration which ever urges him to realize a greater unity in wisdom and love with him who can lead his heart and mind into the truth of all things. Who among men can seek for comfort and where for him is rest? The only goal of human life is to offer freedom and be free, the freedom that guides it to the life which is worth while.

PERSONALITY

What is Art?

We are face to face with this great world and our relations to it are manifold. One of these is the necessity we have to live, to till the soil, to gather food, to clothe ourselves, to get materials from nature. We are always making things that will satisfy our need, and we come in touch with Nature in our efforts to meet these needs. Thus we are always in touch with this great world through hunger and thirst and all our physical needs.

Then we have our mind; and mind seeks its own food. Mind has its necessity also. It must find out reason in things. It is faced with a multiplicity of facts, and is bewildered when it cannot find one unifying principle which simplifies the heterogeneity of things. Man's constitution is such that he must not only find facts, but also some laws which will lighten the burden of mere number and quantity.

There is yet another man in me, not the physical, but the personal man; which has its likes and dislikes, and wants to find something to fulfil its needs of love. This personal man is found in the region where we are free from all necessity,— above the needs, both of body and mind,—above the expedient and useful. It is the highest in man,—this personal man. And it has personal relations of its own with the great world, and comes to it for something to satisfy personality.

The world of science is not a world of reality, it is an abstract world of force. We can use it by the help of our intellect but cannot realize it by the help of our personality. It is like a swarm of mechanics who though producing things for ourselves as personal beings, are mere shadows to us.

But there is another world which is real to us. We see it, feel it; we deal with it with all our emotions. Its mystery is endless because we cannot analyse it or measure it. We can but say, "Here you are.'

This is the world from which Science turns away, and in which Art takes its place. And if we can answer the question as to what art is, we shall know what this world is with which art has such intimate relationship.

It is not an important question as it stands. For Art, like life itself, has grown by its own impulse, and man has taken his pleasure in it without definitely knowing what it is. And we could safely leave it there, in the subsoil of consciousness, where things that are of life are nourished in the dark.

But we live in an age when our world is turned inside out and when whatever lies at the bottom is dragged to the surface. Our very process of living, which is an unconscious process, we must bring under the scrutiny of our knowledge,— even though to know is to kill our object of research and to make it a museum specimen.

The question has been asked, 'What is Art?" and answers have been given by various persons. Such discussions introduce elements of conscious purpose into the region where both our faculties of creation and enjoyment have been spontaneous and half-conscious. They aim at supplying us with very definite standards by which to guide our judgement of art productions. Therefore we have heard judges in the modern time giving verdict, according to some special rules of their own making, for the dethronement of immortals whose supremacy has been unchallenged for centuries.

This meteorological disturbance in the atmosphere of art criticism, whose origin is in the West, has crossed over to our own shores in Bengal bringing mist and clouds in its wake where there was a clear sky. We have begun to ask ourselves whether creations of art should not be judged either according to their fitness to be universally understood, or their philosophical interpretation of life, or their usefulness for solving the problems of the day, or their giving expression to something which is peculiar to the genius of the people to which the artist belongs. Therefore when men are seriously engaged in fixing the standard of value in art by something which is not inherent in it,—or, in other words, when the excellence of the river is going to be judged by the point of view of a canal, we cannot leave the question to its fate, but must take our part in the deliberations.

Should we begin with a definition? But definition of a thing which has a life growth is really limiting one's own vision in order to be able to see clearly. And clearness is not necessarily the only, or the most important, aspect of a truth. A bull's-eye lantern view is a clear view, but not a complete view. If we are to know a wheel in motion, we need not mind if all its spokes cannot be counted. When not merely the accuracy of shape, but velocity of motion, is important, we have to be content with a somewhat imperfect definition of the wheel. Living things have far-reaching relationships with their surroundings, some of which are invisible and go deep down into the soil. In our zeal for definition we may lop off branches and roots of a tree to turn it into a log, which is easier to roll about from classroom to classroom, and therefore suitable for a text-book. But because it allows a nakedly clear view of itself, it cannot be said that a log gives a truer view of a tree as a whole.

Therefore I shall not define Art, but question myself about the reason of its existence, and try to find out whether it owes its origin to some social purpose, or to the need of catering for our aesthetic enjoyment, or whether it has come out of some impulse of expression, which is the impulse of our being itself.

A fight has been going on for a long time round the saying, 'Art for Art's sake,' which seems to have fallen into disrepute among a section of Western critics. It is a sign of the recurrence of the ascetic ideal of the puritanism age, when enjoyment as an end in itself was held to be sinful. But all puritanism is a reaction. It does not represent truth in its normal aspect. When enjoyment loses its direct touch with life, growing fastidious and fantastic in its world of elaborate conventions, then comes the call for renunciation which rejects happiness itself as a snare. I am not going into the history of your modern art, which I am not at all competent to discuss; yet I can assert, as a general truth, that when a man tries to thwart himself in his desire for delight, converting it merely into his desire to know, or to do good, then the cause must be that his power of feeling delight has lost its natural bloom and healthiness.

The rhetoricians in old India had no hesitation in saying, that enjoyment is the soul of literature,—the enjoyment which is disinterested. But the word 'enjoyment' has to be used with caution. When analysed, its spectrum shows an endless series of rays of different colours and intensity throughout its different worlds of stars. The art world contains elements which are distinctly its own and which emit lights that have their special range and property. It is our duty to distinguish them and arrive at their origin and growth.

The most important distinction between the animal and man is this, that the animal is very nearly bound within the limits of its necessities, the greater part of its activities being necessary for its self-preservation and the preservation of race. Like a retail shopkeeper, it has no large profit from its trade of life; the bulk of its earnings must be spent in paying back the interest to its bank. Most of its resources are employed in the mere endeavour to live. But man, in life's commerce, is a big merchant. He earns a great deal more than he is absolutely compelled to spend. Therefore there is a vast excess of wealth in man's life, which gives him the freedom to be useless and irresponsible to a great measure. There are large outlying tracts, surrounding his necessities, where he has objects that are ends in themselves.

The animals must have knowledge, so that their knowledge can be employed for useful purposes of their life. But there they stop. They must know their surroundings in order to be able to take their shelter and seek their food, some properties of things in order to build their dwellings, some signs of the different seasons to be able to get ready to adapt themselves to the changes. Man also must know because he must live. But man has a surplus where he can proudly assert that knowledge is for the sake of knowledge. There he has the pure enjoyment of his knowledge, because there knowledge is freedom. Upon this fund of surplus his science and philosophy thrive.

Then again, there is a certain amount of altruism in the animal. It is the altruism of parenthood, the altruism of the herd and the hive. This altruism is absolutely necessary for race preservation. But in man there is a great deal more than this. Though he also has to be good, because goodness is necessary for his race, yet he goes far beyond that. His goodness is not a small pittance, barely sufficient for a hand-to-mouth moral existence. He can amply afford to say that goodness is for the sake of goodness. And upon this wealth of goodness,—where honesty is not valued for being the best policy, but because it can afford to go against all policies,— man's ethics are founded.

The idea of 'Art for Art's sake' also has its origin in this region of the superfluous. Let us, therefore, try to ascertain what activity it is, whose exuberance leads to the production of Art.

For man, as well as for animals, it is necessary to give expression to feelings of pleasure and displeasure, fear, anger and love. In animals, these emotional expressions have gone little beyond their bounds of usefulness. But in man, though they still have roots in their original purposes, they have spread their branches far and wide in the infinite sky high above their soil. Man has a fund of emotional energy which is not all occupied with his self-preservation. This surplus seeks its outlet in the creation of Art, for man's civilization is built upon his surplus.

A warrior is not merely content with fighting which is needful, but, by the aid of music and decorations, he must give expression to the heightened consciousness of the warrior in him, which is not only unnecessary, but in some cases suicidal. The man who has a strong religious feeling not only worships his deity with all care, but his religious personality craves, for its expression, the splendour of the temple, the rich ceremonials of worship.

When a feeling is aroused in our hearts which is far in excess of the amount that can be completely absorbed by the object which has produced it, it comes back to us and makes us conscious of ourselves by its return waves. When we are in poverty, all our attention is fixed outside us,— upon the objects which we must acquire for our need. But when our wealth greatly surpasses our needs, its light is reflected back upon us, and we have the exultation of feeling that we are rich persons. This is the reason why, of all creatures, only man knows himself, because his impulse of knowledge comes back to him in its excess. He feels his personality more intensely than other creatures, because his power of feeling is more than can be exhausted by his objects. This efflux of the consciousness of his personality requires an outlet of expression. Therefore, in Art, man reveals himself and not his objects. His objects have their place in books of information and science, where he has completely to conceal himself.

I know I shall not be allowed to pass unchallenged when I use the word 'personality,' which has such an amplitude of meaning. These loose words can be made to fit ideas which have not only different dimensions, but shapes also. They are like raincoats, hanging in the hall, which can be taken away by absent-minded individuals who have no claim upon them.

Man as a knower, is not fully himself,—his mere information does not reveal him. But, as a person, he is the organic man, who has the inherent power to select things from his surroundings in order to make them his own. He has his forces of attraction and repulsion by which he not merely piles up things outside him, but creates himself. The principal creative forces, which transmute things into our living structure, are emotional forces. A man, where he is religious, is a person, but not where he is a mere theologian. His feeling for the divine is creative. But his mere knowledge of the divine cannot be formed into his own essence because of this lack of the emotional fire.

Let us here consider what are the contents of this personality and how it is related to the outer world. This world appears to us as an individual, and not merely as a bundle of invisible forces. For this, as everybody knows, it is greatly indebted to our senses and our mind. This apparent world is man's world. It has taken its special features of shape, colour and movement from the peculiar range and qualities of our perception. It is what our sense limits have specially acquired and built for us and walled up. Not only the physical and chemical forces, but man's perceptual forces, are its potent factors,—because it is man's world, and not an abstract world of physics or metaphysics.

This world, which takes its form in the mould of man's perception, still remains only as the partial world of his senses and mind. It is like a guest and not like a kinsman. It becomes completely our own when it comes within the range of our emotions. With our love and hatred, pleasure and pain, fear and wonder, continually working upon it, this world becomes a part of our personality. It grows with our growth, it changes with our changes. We are great or small, according to the magnitude and littleness of this assimilation, according to the quality of its sum total. If this world were taken away, our personality would lose all its content.

Our emotions are the gastric juices which transform this world of appearance into the more intimate world of sentiments. On the other hand, this outer world has its own juices, having their various qualities which excite our emotional activities. This is called in our Sanskrit rhetoric *rasa*, which signifies outer juices having their response in the inner juices of our emotions. And a poem, according to it, is a sentence or sentences containing juices, which stimulate the juices of emotion. It brings to us ideas, vitalized by feelings, ready to be made into the life-stuff of our nature.

Bare information on facts is not literature, because it gives us merely the facts which are independent of ourselves. Repetition of the facts that the sun is round, water is liquid, fire is hot, would be intolerable. But a description of the beauty of the sunrise has its eternal interest for us,—because there, it is not the fact of the sunrise, but its relation to ourselves, which is the object of perennial interest.

It is said in the Upanishad, that 'Wealth is dear to us, not because we desire the fact of the wealth itself, but because we desire ourselves.' This means that we feel ourselves in our wealth,—and therefore we love it. The things which arouse our emotions arouse our own self-feeling. It is like our touch upon the harp-string: if it is too feeble, then we are merely aware of the touch, but if it is strong, then our touch comes back to us in tunes and our consciousness is intensified.

There is the world of science, from which the elements of personality have been carefully removed. We must not touch it with our feelings. But there is also the vast world, which is personal to us. We must not merely know it, and then put it aside, but we must feel it,—because, by feeling it, we feel ourselves.

But how can we express our personality, which we only know by feeling? A scientist can make known what he has learned by analysis and experiment. But what an artist has to say, he cannot express by merely informing and explaining. The plainest language is needed when I have to say what I know about a rose, but to say what I feel about a rose is different. There it has nothing to do with facts, or with laws,—it deals with taste, which can be realized only by tasting. Therefore the Sanskrit rhetoricians say, in poetry we have to use words which have got the proper taste,—which do not merely talk, but conjure up pictures and sing. For pictures and songs are not merely facts,—they are personal facts. They are not only themselves; but ourselves also. They defy analysis and they have immediate access to our hearts.

It has to be conceded, that man cannot help revealing his personality, also, in the world of use. But there self-expression is not his primary object. In everyday life, when we are mostly moved by our habits, we are economical in our expression; for then our soul-consciousness is at its low level,—it has just volume enough to glide on in accustomed grooves. But when our heart is fully awakened in love, or in other great emotions, or personality is in its floodtide. Then it feels the longing to express itself for the very sake of expression. Then comes Art, and we forget the claims of necessity, the thrift of usefulness,— the spires of our temples try to kiss the stars and the notes of our music to fathom the depth of the ineffable.

Man's energies, running on two parallel lines,—that of utility and of self-expression—tend to meet and mingle. By constant human associations sentiments gather around our things of use and invite the help of art to reveal themselves,— as we see the warrior's pride and love revealed in the ornamental sword-blade, and the comradeship of festive gatherings in the wine goblet.

The lawyer's office, as a rule, is not a thing of beauty, and the reason is obvious. But in a city where men are proud of their citizenship, public buildings must in their structure express this love for the city. When the British capital was removed from Calcutta of Delhi, there was discussion about the style of architecture which should be followed in the new buildings. Some advocated the Indian style of the Moghal period,—the style which was the joint production of the Moghal and the Indian genius. The fact that they lost sight of was that all true art has its origin in sentiment. Moghal Delhi and Moghal Agra show their human personality in their buildings. Moghal emperors were men, they were not mere administrators. They lived and died in India, they loved and fought. The memorials of their reigns do not persist in the ruins of factories and offices, but in immortal works of art,—not only in great buildings, but in pictures and music and workmanship in stone and metal, in cotton and wool fabrics. But the British government in India is not personal. It is official and therefore an abstraction. It has nothing to express in the true language of art. For law, efficiency and exploitation cannot sing themselves into epic stones. Lord Lytton, who unfortunately was gifted with more imagination than was necessary for an Indian Viceroy, tried to copy one of the state functions of the Moghals,—the Durbar ceremony. But state ceremonials are works of art. They naturally spring from the reciprocity of personal relationship between the people and their monarch. When they are copies, they show all the signs of the spurious.

How utility and sentiment take different lines in their expression can be seen in the dress of a man compared with that of a woman. A man's dress, as a rule, shuns all that is unnecessary and merely decorative. But a woman has naturally selected the decorative, not only in her dress, but in her manners. She has to be picturesque and musical to make manifest what she truly is,—because, in her position in the world, woman is more concrete and personal than man. She is not to be judged merely by her usefulness, but by her delightfulness. Therefore she takes infinite care in expressing, not her profession, but her personality.

The principal object of art, also, being the expression of personality, and not of that which is abstract and analytical, it necessarily uses the language of picture and music. This has led to a confusion in our thought that the object of art is the production of beauty; whereas beauty in art has been the mere instrument and not its complete and ultimate significance.

As a consequence of this, we have often heard it argued whether manner, rather than matter, is the essential element in art. Such arguments become endless, like pouring water into a vessel whose bottom has been taken away. These discussions owe their origin to the idea that beauty is the object of art, and, because mere matter cannot have the property of beauty, it becomes a question whether manner is not the principal factor in art.

But the truth is, analytical treatment will not help us in discovering what is the vital point in art. For the true principle of art is the principle of unity. When we want to know the food-value of certain of our diets, we find in their component parts; but its taste-value is in its unity, which cannot be analysed. Matter, taken by itself, is an abstraction which can be dealt with by science; while manner, which is merely manner, is an abstraction which comes under the laws of rhetoric. But when they are indissolubly one, then they find their harmonics in our personality, which is an organic complex of matter and manner, thoughts and things, motives and actions.

Therefore we find all abstract ideas are out of place in true art, where, in order to gain admission, they must come under the disguise of personification. This is the reason why poetry tries to select words that have vital qualities,—words that are not for mere information, but have become naturalized in our hearts and have not been worn out of their shapes by too constant use in the market. For instance, the English word 'consciousness' has not yet outgrown the cocoon stage of its scholastic inertia, therefore it is seldom used in poetry; whereas its Indian synonym 'chetana' is a vital word and is of constant poetical use. On the other hand the English word 'feeling' is fluid with life, but its Bengali synonym 'anubhuti' is refused in poetry, because it merely has a meaning and no flavour. And likewise there are some truths, coming from science and philosophy, which have acquired life's colour and taste, and some which have not. Until they have done this, they are, for art, like uncooked vegetables, unfit to be served at a feast. History, so long as it copies science and deals with abstractions, remains outside the domain of literature. But, as a narrative of facts, it takes its place by the side of the epic poem. For narration of historical facts imparts to the time to which they belong a taste of personality. Those periods become human to us, we feel their living heart-beats.

The world and the personal man are face to face, like friends who question one another and exchange their inner secrets. The world asks the inner man,—'Friend, have you seen me? Do you love me?—not as one who provides you with foods and fruits, not as one whose laws you have found out, but as one who is personal, individual?'

The artist's answer is, 'Yes, I have seen you, I have loved and known you,—not that I have any need of you, not that I have taken you and used your laws for my own purposes of power. I know the forces that act and drive and lead to power, but it is not that. I see you, where you are what I am.'

But how do you know that the artist has known, has seen, has come face to face with this Personality?

When I first meet any one who is not yet my friend, I observe all the numberless unessential things which attract the attention at first sight: and in the wilderness of that diversity of facts the friend who is to be my friend is lost.

When our steamer reached the coast of Japan, one of our passengers, a Japanese, was coming back home from Rangoon; we on the other hand were reaching that shore for the first time in our life. There was a great difference in our outlook. We noted every little peculiarity, and innumerable small things occupied our attention. But the Japanese passenger dived at once into the personality, the soul of the land, where his own soul found satisfaction. *He* saw fewer things, *we* saw more things; but what he saw was the soul of Japan. It could not be gauged by any quantity or number, but by something invisible and deep. It could not be said, that because we saw those innumerable things, we saw Japan better, but rather the reverse.

If you ask me to draw some particular tree and I am no artist, I try to copy every detail, lest I should otherwise lose the peculiarity of the tree, forgetting that the peculiarity is not the personality. But when the true artist comes, he overlooks all details and gets into the essential characterization.

Our rational man also seeks to simplify things into their inner principle; to get rid of the details; to get to the heart of things where things are One. But the difference is this,— the scientist seeks an impersonal principle of unification, which can be applied to all things. For instance he destroys the human body which is personal in order to find out physiology, which is impersonal and general.

But the artist finds out the unique, the individual, which yet is in the heart of the universal. When he looks on a tree, he looks on that tree as unique, not as the botanist who generalizes and classifies. It is the function of the artist to particularize that one tree. How does he do it? Not through the peculiarity which is the discord of the unique, but through the personality which is harmony. Therefore he has to find out the inner concordance of that one thing with its outer surroundings of all things.

The greatness and beauty of Oriental art, especially in Japan and China, consist in this, that there the artists have seen this soul of things and they believe in it. The West may believe in the soul of Man, but she does not really believe that the universe has a soul. Yet this is the belief of the East, and the whole mental contribution of the East to mankind is filled with this idea. So, we, in the East need not go into details and emphasize them; for the most important thing is this universal soul, for which the Eastern sages have sat in meditation, and Eastern artists have joined them in artistic realization.

Because we have faith in this universal soul, we in the East know that Truth, Power, Beauty, lie in Simplicity,—where it is transparent, where things do not obstruct the inner vision. Therefore, all our sages have tried to make their lives simple and pure, because thus they have the realization of a positive Truth, which, though invisible, is more real than the gross and the numerous.

When we say that art only deals with those truths that are personal, we do not exclude philosophical ideas which are apparently abstract. They are quite common in our Indian literature, because they have been woven with the fibres of our personal nature. I give here an instance which will make my point clear. The following is a translation of an Indian poem written by a woman poet of mediaeval India,—its subject is Life.

> I salute the Life which is like a sprouting seed,
>   With its one arm upraised in the air, and the other
>   down in the soil;

The Life which is one in its outer form and its inner
sap;
The Life that ever appears, yet ever eludes.
The Life that comes I salute, and the Life that goes;
I salute the Life that is revealed and that is hidden;
I salute the Life in suspense, standing still like a
mountain,
And the Life of the surging sea of fire;
The Life that is tender like a lotus, and hard like a
thunderbolt.
I salute the Life which is of the mind, with its one
side in the dark and the other in the light.
I salute the Life in the house and the Life abroad in
the unknown,
The Life full of joy and the Life weary with its pains,
The Life eternally moving, rocking the world into
stillness,
The Life deep and silent, breaking out into roaring
waves.

This idea of life is not a mere logical deduction; it is as
real to the poetess as the air to the bird who feels it at every
beat of its wings. Woman has realized the mystery of life in
her child more intimately than man has done. This woman's
nature in the poet has felt the deep stir of life in all the world.
She has known it to be infinite,—not through any reasoning
process, but through the illumination of her feeling. Therefore
the same idea, which is a mere abstraction to one whose sense
of the reality is limited, becomes luminously real to another
whose sensibility has a wider range. We have often heard the
Indian mind described by Western critics as metaphysical,
because it is ready to soar in the infinite. But it has to be noted
that the infinite is not a mere matter of philosophical
speculation to India; it is as real to her as the sunlight. She

must see it, feel it, make use of it in her life. Therefore it has come out so profusely in her symbolism of worship, in her literature. The poet of the Upanishad has said that the slightest movement of life would be impossible if the sky were not filled with infinite joy. This universal presence was as much of reality to him as the earth under his feet, nay, even more. The realization of this has broken out in a song of an Indian poet who was born in the fifteenth century:

There fall the rhythmic beat of life and death:

> Rapture wells forth, and all space is radiant with light.
> There the unstruck music is sounded; it is the love music of three worlds.
> There millions of lamps of sun and moon are burning;
> There the drum beats and the lover swings in play,
> There love songs resound, and light rains in showers.

In India, the greater part of our literature is religious, because God with us is not a distant God; He belongs to our homes, as well as to our temples. We feel His nearness to us in all the human relationship of love and affection, and in our festivities He is the chief guest whom we honour. In seasons of flowers and fruits, in the coming of the rain, in the fulness of the autumn, we see the hem of His mantle and hear His footsteps. We worship Him in all the true objects of our worship and love Him wherever our love is true. In the woman who is good we feel Him, in the man who is true we know Him, in our children He is born again and again, the Eternal Child. Therefore religious songs are our love songs, and our domestic occurrences, such as the birth of a son, or the coming of the daughter from her husband's house to her parents and her departure again, are woven in our literature as a drama whose counterpart is in the divine.

It is thus that the domain of literature has extended into the region which seems hidden in the depth of mystery and made it human and speaking. It is growing, keeping pace with the conquest made by the human personality in the realm of truth. It is growing, not only into history, science and philosophy, but, with our expanding sympathy, into our social consciousness. The classical literature of the ancient time was only peopled by saints and kings and heroes. It threw no light upon men who loved and suffered in obscurity. But as the illumination of man's personality throws its light upon a wider space, penetrating into hidden corners, the world of art also crosses its frontiers and extends its boundaries into unexplored regions. Thus art is signalizing man's conquest of the world by its symbols of beauty, springing up in spots which were barren of all voice and colours. It is supplying man with his banners, under which he marches to fight against the inane and the inert, proving his living claims far and wide in God's creation. Even the spirit of the desert has owned its kinship with him, and the lonely pyramids are there as memorials of the meeting of Nature's silence with the silence of the human spirit. The darkness of the caves has yielded its stillness to man's soul, and in exchange has secretly been crowned with the wreath of art. Bells are ringing in temples, in villages and populous towns to proclaim that the infinite is not a mere emptiness to man. This encroachment of man's personality has no limit, and even the markets and factories of the present age, even the schools where children of man are imprisoned and jails where are the criminals, will be mellowed with the touch of art, and lose their distinction of rigid discordance with life. For the one effort of man's personality is to transform everything with which he has any true concern into the human. And art is like the spread of vegetation, to show how far man has reclaimed the desert for his own.

We have said before that where there is an element of the superfluous in our heart's relationship with the world, Art has its birth. In other words, where our personality feels its wealth it breaks out in display. What we devour for ourselves is totally spent. What overflows our need becomes articulate. The stage of pure utility is like the state of heat which is dark. When it surpasses itself, it becomes white heat and then it is expressive.

Take, for instance, our delight in eating. It is soon exhausted, it gives no indication of the infinite. Therefore, though in its extensiveness it is more universal than any other passion, it is rejected by art. It is like an immigrant coming to these Atlantic shores, who can show no cash balance in his favour.

In our life we have one side which is finite, where we exhaust ourselves at every step, and we have another side, where our aspiration, enjoyment and sacrifice are infinite. This infinite side of man must have its revealments in some symbols which have the elements of immortality. There it naturally seeks perfection. Therefore it refuses all that is flimsy and feeble and incongruous. It builds for its dwelling a paradise, where only those materials are used that have transcended the earth's mortality.

For men are the children of light. Whenever they fully realize themselves they feel their immortality. And, as they feel it, they extend their realm of the immortal into every region of human life.

This building of man's true world—the living world of truth and beauty—is the function of Art.

Man is true, where he feels his infinity, where he is divine, and the divine is the creator in him. Therefore with the attainment of his truth he creates. For he can truly live in his own creation and make out of God's world his own world. This is indeed his own heaven, the heaven of ideas shaped into perfect forms, with which he surrounds himself; where his children are born, where they learn how to live and to die, how to love and to fight, where they know that the real is not that which is merely seen and wealth is not that which is stored. If man could only listen to the voice that rises from the heart of his own creation, he would hear the same message that came from the Indian sage of the ancient time:

'Hearken to me, ye children of the Immortal, dwellers of the heavenly worlds, I have known the Supreme Person who comes as light from the dark beyond.'

Yes, it is that Supreme Person, who has made himself known to man and made this universe so deeply personal to him. Therefore, in India, our places of pilgrimage are there, where in the confluence of the river and the sea, in the eternal snow of the mountain peak, in the lonely seashore, some aspect of the infinite is revealed which has its great voice for our heart, and there man has left in his images and temples, in his carvings of stone, these words,—'Hearken to me, I have known the Supreme Person.' In the mere substance and law of this world we do not meet the person, but where the sky is blue, and the grass is green, where the flower has its beauty and fruit its taste, where there is not only perpetuation of race, but joy of living and love of fellow-creatures, sympathy and self-sacrifice, there is revealed to us the Person who is infinite. There, not merely are facts pelted down upon our heads, but we feel the bond of the personal relationship binding our hearts with this world through all time. And this is Reality, which is truth made our own,—truth that has its eternal relation with the Supreme Person. This world, whose soul seems to be aching for expression in its endless rhythm of lines and colours, music and movements, hints and whispers, and all the suggestion of the inexpressible, finds its harmony in the ceaseless longing of the human heart to make the Person manifest in its own creations.

The desire for the manifestation of this Person makes us lavish with all our resources. When we accumulate wealth, we have to account for every penny; we reason accurately and we act with care. But when we set about to express our wealthiness, we seem to lose sight of all lines of limit. In fact, none of us has wealth enough fully to express what we mean by wealthiness. When we try to save our life from an enemy's attack, we are cautious in our movements. But when we feel impelled to express our personal bravery, we willingly take risks and go to the length of losing our lives. We are careful of expenditure in our everyday life, but on festive occasions, when we express our joy, we are thriftless even to the extent of going beyond our means. For when we are intensely conscious of our own personality, we are apt to ignore the tyranny of facts. We are temperate in our dealings with the man with whom our relation is the relationship of prudence. But we feel we have not got enough for those whom we love. The poet says of the beloved:

'It seems to me that I have gazed at your beauty from the beginning of my existence, that I have kept you in my arms for countless ages, yet it has not been enough for me.'

He says, 'Stones would melt in tenderness, if touched by the breeze of your mantle.'

He feels that his 'eyes long to fly like birds to see his beloved.'

Judged from the standpoint of reason these are exaggerations, but from that of the heart, freed from limits of facts, they are true.

It is not the same in God's creation. There, forces and matters are alike mere facts—they have their strict accounts kept and they can be accurately weighed and measured. Only beauty is not a mere fact; it cannot be accounted for, it cannot be surveyed and mapped. It is an expression. Facts are like wine-cups that carry it, they are hidden by it, it overflows them. It is infinite in its suggestions, it is extravagant in its words. It is personal, therefore, beyond science. It sings as does the poet, 'It seems to me that I have gazed at you from the beginning of my existence, that I have kept you in my arms for countless ages, yet it has not been enough for me.'

So we find that our world of expression does not accurately coincide with the world of facts, because personality surpasses facts on every side. It is conscious of its infinity and creates from its abundance; and because, in art, things are challenged from the standpoint of the immortal Person, those which are important in our customary life of facts become unreal when placed on the pedestal of art. A newspaper account of some domestic incident in the life of a commercial magnate may create agitation in Society, yet would lose all its significance if placed by the side of great works of art. We can well imagine how it would hide its face in shame, if by some cruel accident it found itself in the neighbourhood of Keats's 'Ode on a Grecian Urn.'

Yet the very same incident, if treated deeply, divested of its conventional superficiality, might have a better claim in art than the negotiation for raising a big loan for China, or the defeat of British diplomacy in Turkey. A mere household event of a husband's jealousy of his wife, as depicted in one of Shakespeare's tragedies, has greater value in the realm of art than the code of caste regulations in Manu's scripture or the law prohibiting inhabitants of one part of the world from receiving human treatment in another. For when facts are looked upon as mere facts, having their chain of consequences in the world of facts, they are rejected by art.

When, however, such laws and regulations as I have mentioned are viewed in their application to some human individual, in all their injustice, insult and pain, then they are seen in their complete truth and they become subjects for art. The disposition of a great battle may be a great fact, but it is useless for the purpose of art. But what that battle has caused to a single individual soldier, separated from his loved ones and maimed for his life, has a vital value for art which deals with reality.

Man's social world is like some nebulous system of stars, consisting largely of a mist of abstractions, with such names as society, state, nation, commerce, politics and war. In their dense amorphousness man is hidden and truth is blurred. The one vague idea of war covers from our sight a multitude of miseries, and obscures our sense of reality. The idea of the nation is responsible for crimes that would be appalling, if the mist could be removed for a moment. The idea of society has created forms of slavery without number, which we tolerate simply because it has deadened our consciousness of the reality of the personal man. In the name of religion deeds have been done that would exhaust all the resources of hell itself for punishment, because with its creeds and dogmas it has applied an extensive plaster of anaesthetic over a large surface of feeling humanity. Everywhere in man's world the Supreme Person is suffering from the killing of the human reality by the imposition of the abstract. In our schools the idea of the class hides the reality of the school children;—they become students and not individuals. Therefore it does not hurt us to see children's lives crushed, in their classes, like flowers pressed between book leaves. In government, the bureaucracy deals with generalizations and not with men. And therefore it costs it nothing to indulge in wholesale cruelties. Once we accept as truth such a scientific maxim as 'Survival of the Fittest' it immediately transforms the whole world of human personality into a monotonous desert of abstraction, where things become dreadfully simple because robbed of their mystery of life.

In these large tracts of nebulousness Art is creating its stars—stars that are definite in their forms but infinite in their personality. Art is calling us the 'children of the immortal,' and proclaiming our right to dwell in the heavenly worlds.

What is it in man that asserts its immortality in spite of the obvious fact of death? It is not his physical body or his mental organization. It is that deeper unity, that ultimate mystery in him, which, from the centre of his world, radiates towards its circumference; which is in his body, yet transcends his body; which is in his mind, yet grows beyond his mind; which through the things belonging to him, expresses something that is not in them; which, while occupying his present, overflows its banks of the past and the future. It is the personality of man, conscious of its inexhaustible abundance; it has the paradox in it that it is more than itself; it is more than as it is seen, as it is known, as it is used. And this consciousness of the infinite, in the personal man, ever strives to make its expressions immortal and to make the whole world its own. In Art the person in us is sending its answers to the Supreme Person, who reveals Himself to us in a world of endless beauty across the lightless world of facts.

The World of Personality

The night is like a dark child just born of her mother day.
Million of stars crowding round its cradle watch it,
standing still, afraid lest it should wake up.'

I am ready to go on in this strain, but I am interrupted
by Science laughing at me. She takes objection to my statement
that stars are standing still.

But if it is a mistake, then apology is not due from me
but from those stars themselves. It is quite evident that they
are standing still. It is a fact that is impossible to argue away.

But science *will* argue, it is her habit. She says, 'When you
think that stars are still, that only proves that you are too far
from them.'

I have my answer ready, that when you say that stars are
rushing about, it only proves that you are too near them.

Science is astonished at my temerity.

But I obstinately hold my ground and say that if Science
has the liberty to take the side of the near and fall foul of
the distant, she cannot blame me when I take the opposite
side and question the veracity of the near.

Science is emphatically sure that the near view is the most
reliable view.

But I doubt whether she is consistent in her opinions. For
when I was sure that the earth was flat under my feet, she
corrected me by saying that the near view was not the correct
view, that to get at the complete truth it is necessary to see
it from a distance.

I am willing to agree with her. For do we not know that a too near view of ourselves is the egotistical view, which is the flat and the detached view—but that when we see ourselves in others, we find that the truth about us is round and continuous?"

But if Science has faith at all in the wholesomeness of distance then she must give up her superstition about the restlessness of the stars. We the children of the earth attend our night school to have a glimpse of the world as a whole. Our great teacher knows that the complete view of the universe is as much too awful for our sight as that of the midday sun. We must see it through a smoked glass. Kind Nature has held before our eyes the smoked glass of the night and of the distance. And what do we see through it? We see that the world of stars is still. For we see these stars in their relation to each other, and they appear to us like chains of diamonds hanging on the neck of some god of silence. But Astronomy like a curious child plucks out an individual star from that chain and then we find it rolling about.

The difficulty is to decide whom to trust. The evidence of the world of stars is simple. You have but to raise your eyes and see their face and you believe them. They do not set before you elaborate arguments, and to my mind, that is the surest test of reliability. They do not break their hearts if you refuse to believe them. But when some one of these stars singly comes down from the platform of the universe and slyly whispers its information into the ears of mathematics, we find the whole story different.

Therefore let us boldly declare that both facts are equally true about the stars. Let us say that they are unmoved in the plane of the distant and they are moving in the plane of the near. The stars in their one relation to me are truly still and in their other relation are truly moving. The distant and the near are the keepers of two different sets of facts, but they both belong to one truth which is their master. Therefore when we take the side of the one to revile the other, we hurt the truth which comprehends them both.

About this truth the Indian sage of Ishopanishad says: 'It moves. It moves not. It is distant. It is near.'

The meaning is, that when we follow truth in its parts which are near, we see truth moving. When we know truth as a whole, which is looking at it from a distance, it remains still. As we follow a book in its chapters the book moves, but when we have known the whole book, then we find it standing still, holding all the chapters in their interrelations.

There is a point where in the mystery of existence contradictions meet; where movement is not all movement and stillness is not all stillness; where the idea and the form, the within and the without, are united; where infinite becomes finite, without losing its infinity. If this meeting is dissolved, then things become unreal.

When I see a rose leaf through a microscope, I see it in a more extended space than it usually occupies for me. The more I extend the space the more vague it becomes. So that in the pure infinite it is neither rose leaf nor anything at all. It only becomes a rose leaf where the infinite reaches finitude at a particular point. When we disturb that point towards the small or the great, the rose leaf begins to assume unreality.

It is the same with regard to time. If by some magic I could remain in my normal plane of time while enhancing its quickness with regard to the rose leaf, condensing, let us say, a month into a minute, then it would rush through its point of first appearance to that of its final disappearance with such a speed that I would hardly be able to see it. One can be sure that there are things in this world which are known by other creatures, but which, since their time is not synchronous with ours, are nothing to us. The phenomenon which a dog perceives as a smell does not keep its time with that of our nerves, therefore it falls outside our world.

Let me give an instance. We have heard of prodigies in mathematics who can do difficult sums in an incredibly short time. With regard to mathematical calculations their minds are acting in a different plane of time, not only from ours, but also from their own in other spheres of life. As if the mathematical part of their minds were living in a comet, while the other parts were the inhabitants of this earth. Therefore the process through which their minds rush to their results is not only invisible to us, it is not even seen by themselves.

It is a well-known fact that our dreams often flow in a measure of time different from that of our waking consciousness. The fifty minutes of our sundial of dreamland may be represented by five minutes of our clock. If from the vantage of our wakeful time we could watch these dreams, they would rush past us like an express train. Or if from the window of our swift-flying dreams we could watch the slower world of our waking consciousness, it would seem receding away from us at a great speed. In fact if the thoughts that move in other minds than our own were open to us, our perception of them would be different from theirs, owing to our difference of mental time. If we could adjust our focus of time according to our whims, we should see the waterfall standing still and the pine forest running fast like the waterfall of a green Niagara.

So that it is almost a truism to say that the world is what we perceive it to be. We imagine that our mind is a mirror, that it is more or less accurately reflecting what is happening outside us. On the contrary, our mind itself is the principal element of creation. The world, while I am perceiving it, is being incessantly created for myself in time and space.

The variety of creation is due to the mind seeing different phenomena in different foci of time and space. When it sees stars in a space which may be metaphorically termed as dense then they are close to each other and motionless. When it sees planets, it sees them in much less density of sky and then they appear far apart and moving. If we could have the sight to see the molecules of a piece of iron in a greatly different space, they could be seen in movement. But because we see things in various adjustments of time and space therefore iron is iron, water is water, and clouds are clouds for us.

It is a well-known psychological fact that by adjustment of our mental attitude things seem to change their properties, and objects that were pleasurable become painful to us and *vice versa*. Under a certain state of exultation of mind mortification of the flesh has been resorted to by men to give them pleasure. Instances of extreme martyrdom seem to us superhuman because the mental attitude under the influence of which they become possible, even desirable, has not been experienced by us. In India, cases of firewalking have been observed by many, though they have not been scientifically investigated. There may be differences of opinion about the degree of efficacy of faith cure, which shows the influence of mind upon matter, but its truth has been accepted and acted upon by men from the early dawn of history. The methods of our moral training have been based upon the fact that by changing our mental focus, our perspective, the whole world is changed and becomes in certain respects a different creation with things of changed value. Therefore what is valuable to a man when he is bad becomes worse than valueless when he is good.

Walt Whitman shows in his poems a great dexterity in changing his position of mind and thus changing his world with him from that of other people, rearranging the meaning of things in different proportions and forms. Such mobility of mind plays havoc with things whose foundations lie fixed in convention. Therefore he says in one of his poems:

I hear that it was charged against me that I sought to
destroy institutions;
But really I am neither for nor against institutions;
(What indeed have I in common with them—
Or what with the destruction of them?)
Only I will establish in thee Manhattan, and in every
city of these States, inland and seaboard,
And in the fields and woods, and above every keel,
little or large, that dents the water,
Without edifices, or rules, or trustees or any argument,
This institution of dear love of comrades.

Institutions which are so squarely built, so solid and thick,
become like vapour in this poet's world. It is like a world of
Röntgen rays, for which some of the solid things of the world
have no existence whatever. On the other hand, love of
comrades, which is a fluid thing in the ordinary world, which
seems like clouds that pass and repass the sky without leaving
a trace of a track, is to the poet's world more stable than all
institutions. Here he sees things in a time in which the
mountains pass away like shadows, but the rain-clouds with
their seeming transitoriness are eternal. He perceives in his
world that this love of comrades, like clouds that require no
solid foundation, is stable and true, is established without
edifices, rules, trustees or arguments.

When the mind of a person like Walt Whitman moves in
a time different from that of others, his world does not
necessarily come to ruin through dislocation, because there
in the centre of his world dwells his own personality. All the
facts and shapes of this world are related to this central
creative power, therefore they become interrelated
spontaneously. His world may be like a comet among stars,
different in its movement from others, but it has its own
consistency because of the central personal force. It may be

a bold world or even a mad world, with an immense orbit swept by its eccentric tail, yet a world it is.

But with Science it is different. For she tries to do away altogether with that central personality, in relation to which the world is a world. Science sets up an impersonal and unalterable standard of space and time which is not the standard of creation. Therefore at its fatal touch the reality of the world is so hopelessly disturbed that it vanishes in an abstraction where things become nothing at all. For the world is not atoms and molecules or radio-activity or other forces, the diamond is not carbon, and light is not vibrations of ether. You can never come to the reality of creation by contemplating it from the point of view of destruction. Not only the world but God Himself is divested of reality by Science, which subjects Him to analysis in the laboratory of reason outside our personal relationship, and then describes the result as unknown and unknowable. It is a mere tautology to say that God is unknowable, when we leave altogether out of account the person who can and who does know Him. It is the same thing as saying that food is uneatable when the eater is absent. Our dry moralists also play the same tricks with us in order to wean away our hearts from their desired objects. Instead of creating for us a world in which moral ideals find their natural places in beauty, they begin to wreck the world that we have built ourselves, however imperfectly. They put moral maxims in the place of human personality and give us the view of things in their dissolution to prove that behind their appearances they are hideous deceptions. But when you deprive truth of its appearance, it loses the best part of its reality. For appearance is a personal relationship; it is for me. Of this appearance, which seems to be of the surface, but which carries the message of the inner spirit, your poet has said:

Beginning my studies, the first step pleased me so
much,
The mere fact, consciousness—these forms—the power
of motion,
The least insect or animal—the senses—eyesight—
love;
The first step, I say, aw'd me and pleased me so much,
I have hardly gone, and hardly wished to go, any
farther,
But stop and loiter all the time, and sing it in ecstatic
songs.

Our scientific world is our world of reasoning. It has its
greatness and uses and attractions. We are ready to pay the
homage due to it. But when it claims to have discovered the
real world for us and laughs at the worlds of all simple-
minded men, then we must say it is like a general grown
intoxicated with the power, usurping the throne of his king.
For the reality of the world belongs to the personality of man
and not to reasoning, which, useful and great though it be,
is not the man himself.

If we could fully know what a piece of music was in
Beethoven's mind we could ourselves become so many
Beethovens. But because we cannot grasp its mystery we may
altogether distrust the element of Beethoven's personality in
his Sonata—though we are fully aware that its true value lies
in its power of touching the depth of our own personality.
But it is simpler to keep observation of the facts when that
sonata is played upon the piano. We can count the black and
white keys of the key-board, measure the relative lengths of
the strings, the strength, velocity and order to sequence in
the movements of fingers, and triumphantly assert that this
is Beethoven's Sonata. Not only so, we can predict the accurate
production of the same sonata wherever and whenever our

experiment is repeated according to those observations. By constantly dealing with the sonata from this point of view we may forget that both in its origin and object dwells the personality of man, and however accurate and orderly may be the facts of the interactions of the fingers and strings they do not comprehend the ultimate reality of the music.

A game is a game where there is a player to play it. Of course, there is a law of the game which it is of use to us to analyse and to master. But if it be asserted that in this law is its reality, then we cannot accept it. For the game is what it is to the players. The game changes its aspects according to the personality of its players: for some its end is the lust of gain, in others that of applause; some find in it the means for whiling away time and some the means for satisfying their social instinct, and there are others who approach it in the spirit of disinterested curiosity to study its secrets. Yet all through its manifold aspects law remains the same. For the nature of Reality is the variedness of its unity. And the world is like this game to us—it is the same and yet not the same to us all.

Science deals with this element of sameness, the law of perspective and colour combination, and not with the pictures—the pictures which are the creations of a personality and which appeal to the personality of those who see them. Science does this by eliminating from its field of research the personality of creation and fixing its attention only upon the medium of creation.

What is this medium? It is the medium of finitude which the infinite Being sets before him for the purpose of his self-expression. It is the medium which represents his self-imposed limitations—the law of space and time, of form and movement. This law is Reason, which is universal—Reason which guides the endless rhythm of the creative idea, perpetually manifesting itself in its ever-changing forms.

Our individual minds are the strings which catch the rhythmic vibrations of this universal mind and respond in music of space and time. The quality and number and pitch of our mind strings differ and their tuning has not yet come to its perfection, but their law is the law of the universal mind, which is the instrument of finitude upon which the Eternal Player plays his dance music of creation.

Because of the mind instruments which we possess we also have found our place as creators. We create not only art and social organizations, but our inner nature and outer surroundings, the truth of which depends upon their harmony with the laws of the universal mind. Of course, our creations are mere variations upon God's great theme of the universe. When we produce discords, they either have to end in a harmony or in silence. Our freedom as a creator finds its highest joy in contributing its own voice to the concert of the world-music.

Science is apprehensive of the poet's sanity. She refuses to accept the paradox of the infinite assuming finitude.

I have nothing to say in my defence except that this paradox is much older than I am. It is the paradox which lies at the root of existence. It is as mysterious yet as simple as the fact that I am aware of this wall, which is a miracle that can never be explained.

Let me go back to the sage of Ishopanishad and hear what he says about the contradiction of the infinite and the finite. He says:

'They enter the region of the dark who are solely occupied with the knowledge of the finite, and they into a still greater darkness who are solely occupied with the knowledge of the infinite.'

Those who pursue the knowledge of finite for its own sake cannot find truth. For it is a dead wall obstructing the beyond. This knowledge merely accumulates but does not illuminate. It is like a lamp without its light, a violin without its music. You cannot know a book by measuring and weighing and counting its pages, by analysing its paper. An inquisitive mouse may gnaw through the wooden frame of a piano, may cut all its strings to pieces, and yet travel farther and farther away from the music. This is the pursuit of the finite for its own sake.

But according to the Upanishad the sole pursuit of the infinite leads to a deeper darkness. For the absolute infinite is emptiness. The finite is something. It may be a mere cheque-book with no account in the bank. But the absolute infinite has no cash and not even a cheque-book. Profound may be the mental darkness of the primitive man who lives in the conviction that each individual apple falls to the ground according to some individual caprice, but it is nothing compared to the blindness of him who lives in the mediation of the law of gravitation which has no apple or anything else that falls.

Therefore Ishopanishad in the following verse says:

'He who knows that the knowledge of the finite and the infinite is combined in one, crosses death by the help of the knowledge of the finite and achieves immortality by the help of the knowledge of the infinite.'

The infinite and the finite are one as song and singing are one. The singing is incomplete; by a continual process of death it gives up the song which is complete. The absolute infinite is like a music which is devoid of all definite tunes and therefore meaningless.

The absolute eternal is timelessness, and that has no meaning at all,—it is merely a world. The reality of the eternal is there, where it contains all times in itself.

Therefore Upanishad says: 'They enter the region of darkness who pursue the transitory. But they enter the region of still greater darkness who pursue the eternal. He who knows the transitory and the eternal combined together crosses the steps of death by the help of the transitory and reaches immortality by the help of the eternal.'

We have seen that forms of things and their changes have no absolute reality at all. Their truth dwells in our personality, and only there is it real and not abstract. We have seen that a mountain and a waterfall would become something else, or nothing at all to us, if our movement of mind changed in time and space.

We have also seen that this relational world of ours is not arbitrary. It is individual, yet it is universal. My world is mine, its element is my mind, yet it is not wholly unlike your world. Therefore it is not in my own individual personality that this reality is contained, but in an infinite personality.

When in its place we substitute law, then the whole world crumbles into abstractions; then it is elements and force, ions and electrons; it loses its appearance, its touch and taste; the world drama with its language of beauty is hushed, the music is silent, the stage mechanism becomes a ghost of itself in the dark, an unimaginable shadow of nothing, standing before no spectator.

In this connection I quote once again your poet-seer, Walt Whitman:

When I heard the learned astronomer,
When the proofs, the figures, were ranged in columns before me,
When I was shown the charts and diagrams, to add, divide and measure them,
When I sitting heard the astronomer where he lectured with much applause in the lecture room,
How soon unaccountably I became tired and sick,
Till rising and gliding out I wandered off by myself,
In the mystical moist night air, and from time to time,
Looked up in perfect silence at the stars.

The prosody of the stars can be explained in the classroom by diagrams, but the poetry of the stars is in the silent meeting of soul with soul, at the confluence of the light and the dark, where the infinite, prints its kiss on the forehead of the finite, where we can hear the music of the Great I Am pealing from the grand organ of creation through its countless reeds in endless harmony. It is perfectly evident that the world is movement. (The Sanskrit word for the world means 'the moving one.') All its forms are transitory, but that is merely its negative side. All through its changes it has a chain of relationship which is eternal. In a story-book the sentences run on, but the positive element of the book is the relation of the sentences in the story. This relation reveals a will of personality in its author which establishes its harmony with the personality of the reader. If the book were a collection of disjointed words of no movement and meaning, then we should be justified in saying that it was a product of chance, and in that case it would have no response from the personality of the reader. In like manner the world through all its changes is not to us a mere runaway evasion, and because of its movements it reveals to us something which is eternal.

For revealment of idea, form is absolutely necessary. But the idea which is infinite cannot be expressed in forms which are absolutely finite. Therefore forms must always move and change, they must necessarily die to reveal the deathless. The expression as expression must be definite, which it can only be in its form; but at the same time, as the expression of the infinite, it must be indefinite, which it can only be in its movement. Therefore when the world takes its shape it always transcends its shape; it carelessly runs out of itself to say that its meaning is more than what it can contain.

The moralist sadly shakes his head and says that this world is vanity. But that vanity is not vacuity—truth is in that vainness itself. If the world remained still and became final, then it would be a prison-house of orphaned facts which had lost their freedom of truth, the truth that is infinite. Therefore what the modern thinker says is true in this sense, that in movement lies the meaning of all things—because the meaning does not entirely rest in the things themselves but in that which is indicated by their outgrowing of their limits. This is what Ishopanishad means when it says that neither the transitory nor the eternal has any meaning separately. When they are known in harmony with each other, only then through help of that harmony we cross the transitory and realize the immortal.

Because this world is the world of infinite personality it is the object of our life to establish a perfect and personal relationship with it, is the teaching of Ishopanishad. Therefore it begins with the following verse:

'Know that all that moves in this moving world is held by the infinity of God; and enjoy by that which he renounces. Desire not after other possessions.'

That is to say, we have to know that these world movements are not mere blind movements, they are related to the will of a Supreme Person. A mere knowledge of truth is imperfect because impersonal. But enjoyment is personal and the God of my enjoyment moves; he is active; he is giving himself. In this act of giving the infinite has taken the aspect of the finite, and therefore become real, so that I can have my joy in him.

In our crucible of reason the world of appearance vanishes and we call it illusion. This is the negative view. But our enjoyment is positive. A flower is nothing when we analyse it, but it is positively a flower when we enjoy it. This joy is real because it is personal. And perfect truth is only perfectly known by our personality.

And therefore Upanishad has said: 'Mind comes back baffled and words also. But he who realizes the joy of Brahma fears nothing.'

The following is the translation of another verse in which Ishopanishad deals with the passive and the active aspects of the infinite:

'He who is without a stain, without a body, and therefore without bodily injury or bodily organs of strength, without mixture and without any touch of evil, enters into everywhere. He who is the poet, the ruler of mind, the all-becoming, the self-born, dispenses perfect fulfillment to the endless years.'

Brahma, in his negative qualities, is quiescent. Brahma, in his positive qualities, acts upon all time. He is the poet, he uses mind as his instrument, he reveals himself in limits, the revelation which comes out of his abundance of joy and not from any outside necessity. Therefore it is he who can fulfil our needs through endless years by giving himself.

From this we find our ideal. Perpetual giving up is the truth of life. The perfection of this is our life's perfection. We are to make this life our poem in all its expressions; it must be fully suggestive of our soul which is infinite, not merely of our possessions which have no meaning in themselves. The consciousness of the infinite in us proves itself by our joy in giving ourselves out of our abundance. And then our work is the process of our renunciation, it is one with our life. It is like the flowing of the river, which is the river itself.

Let us live, Let us have the true joy of life, which is the joy of the poet in pouring himself out in his poem. Let us express our infinite in everything round us, in works we do, in things we use, in men with whom we deal, in the enjoyment of the world with which we are surrounded. Let our soul permeate our surroundings and create itself in all things, and show its fulness by fulfilling needs of all times. This life of ours has been filled with the gifts of the divine giver. The stars have sung to it, it has been blessed with the daily blessing of the morning light, the fruits have been sweet to it, and the earth has spread its carpet of grass so that it may have its rest. And let it like an instrument fully break out in music of its soul in response to the touch of the infinite soul.

And this is why the poet of the Ishopanishad says:

'Doing work in this world thou shouldst wish to live a hundred years. Thus it is with thee and not otherwise. Let not the work of man cling to him.'

Only by living life fully can you outgrow it. When the fruit has served its full term, drawing its juice from the branch as it dances with the wind and matures in the sun, then it feels in its core the call of the beyond and becomes ready for its career of a wider life. But the wisdom of living is in that which gives you the power to give it up. For death is the gate of immortality. Therefore it is said, Do your work, but let not your work cling to you. For the work expresses your life so long as it flows with it, but when it clings, then it impedes, and shows, not the life, but itself. Then like the sands carried by the stream it chokes the soul-current. Activity of limbs is in the nature of physical life; but when limbs move in convulsion, then the movements are not in harmony with life, but become a disease, like works that cling to man and kill his soul.

No, we must not slay our souls. We must not forget that life is here to express the eternal in us. If we smother our consciousness of the infinite either by slothfulness or by passionate pursuit of things that have no freedom of greatness in them, then like the fruit whose seed has become dead we go back into the primal gloom of the realm of the unformed. Life is perpetual creation; it has its truth when it outgrows itself in the infinite. But when it stops and accumulates and turns back to itself, when it has lost its outlook upon the beyond, then it must die. Then it is dismissed from the world of growth and with all its heaps of belongings crumbles into the dust of dissolution. Of them Ishopanishad has said: 'Those who slay their souls pass from hence to the gloom of the sunless world.'

The question, 'What is this soul,' has thus been answered by the Ishopanishad:

'It is one, and though unmoving is swifter than mind; organs of sense cannot reach it; while standing it progresses beyond others that run; in it the life inspiration maintains the fluid forces of life.'

The mind has its limitations, the sense organs are severally occupied with things that are before them, but there is a spirit of oneness in us which goes beyond the thoughts of its mind, the movements of its bodily organs, which carries whole eternity in its present moment, while through its presence the life inspiration ever urges the life forces onward. Because we are conscious of this One in us which is more than all its belongings, which outlives the death of its moments, we cannot believe that it can die. Because it is one, because it is more than its parts, because it is continual survival, perpetual overflow, we feel it beyond all boundaries of death.

This consciousness of oneness beyond all boundaries is the consciousness of soul. And of this soul Ishopanishad has said: 'It moves. It moves not. It is in the distant. It is in the near. It is within all. It is outside all.'

This is to know the soul across the boundaries of the near and the distant, of the within and the without. I have known this wonder of wonders, this one in myself which is the centre of all reality for me. But I cannot stop here. I cannot say that it exceeds all boundaries, and yet is bounded by myself. Therefore Ishopanishad says:

'He who sees all things in the soul and the soul in all things is nevermore hidden.'

We are hidden in ourselves, like a truth hidden in isolated facts. When we know that this One in us is One in all, then our truth is revealed.

But this knowledge of the unity of soul must not be an abstraction. It is not that negative kind of universalism which belongs neither to one nor to another. It is not an abstract soul, but it is my own soul which I must realize in others. I must know that if my soul were singularly mine, then it could not be true; at the same time if it were not intimately mine, it would not be real.

Through the help of logic we never could have arrived at the truth that the soul which is the unifying principle in me finds its perfection in its unity in others. We have known it through the joy of this truth. Our delight is in realizing ourselves outside us. When I love, in other words, when I feel I am truer in some one else than myself, then I am glad, for the One in me realizes its truth of unity by uniting with others, and there is its joy.

Therefore the spirit of One in God must have the many for the realization of the unity. And God is giving himself in love to all. Ishopanishad says: 'Thou shouldst enjoy what God is renouncing.' He is renouncing; and I have my joy when I feel that he is renouncing himself. For this joy of mine is the joy of love which comes of the renouncing of myself in him.

Where Ishopanishad teaches us to enjoy God's renunciation it says: 'Desire not after other man's possessions.'

For desire is hindrance to love. It is the movement towards the opposite direction of truth, towards the illusion that self is our final object.

Therefore the realization of our soul has its moral and its spiritual side. The moral side represents training of unselfishness, control of desire; the spiritual side represents sympathy and love. They should be taken together and never separated. The cultivation of the merely moral side of our nature leads us to the dark region of narrowness and hardness of heart, to the intolerant arrogance of goodness; and the cultivation of the merely spiritual side of nature leads us to a still darker region of revelry in intemperance of imagination.

By following the poet of Ishopanishad we have come to the meaning of all reality, where the infinite is giving himself out through finitude. Reality is the expression of personality, like a poem, like a work of art. The Supreme Being is giving himself in his world and I am making it mine, like a poem which I realize by finding myself in it. If my own personality leaves the centre of my world, then in a moment it loses all its attributes. From this I know that my world exists in relation to me, and I know that it has been given to the personal *me* by a personal being. The process of the giving can be classified and generalized by science, but not the gift. For the gift is the soul unto the soul, therefore it can only be realized by the soul in joy, not analysed by the reason in logic.

Therefore the one cry of the personal man has been to know the Supreme Person. From the beginning of his history man has been feeling the touch of personality in all creation, and trying to give it names and forms, weaving it in legends round his life and the life of his races, offering it worship and establishing relations with it through countless forms of ceremonial. This feeling of the touch of personality has given the centrifugal impulse in man's heart to break out in a ceaseless flow of reaction, in songs and pictures and poems, in images and temples and festivities. This has been the centripetal force which attracted men into groups and clans and communal organizations. And while man tills his soil and spins his cloths, mates and rears his children, toils for wealth and fights for power, he does not forget to proclaim in languages of solemn rhythm, in mysterious symbols, in structures of majestic stone, that in the heart of his world he has met the Immortal Person. In the sorrow of death, and suffering of despair, when trust has been betrayed and love desecrated, when existence becomes tasteless and unmeaning, man standing upon the ruins of his hopes stretches his hands to the heavens to feel the touch of the Person across his darkened world.

Man has also known direct communication of the person with the Person, not through the world of forms and changes, the world of extension in time and space, but in the innermost solitude of consciousness, in the region of the profound and the intense. Through this meeting he has felt the creation of a new world, a world of light and love that has no language but of music of silence.

Of this the poet has sung:

> There is an endless world, O my Brother.
> And there is a nameless Being of whom nought can
> be said.

Only he knows who has reached that region:

> It is other than all that is heard and said.
> No form, no body, no length, no breadth, is seen
> there:
> How can I tell you that which it is?

Kabir says: 'It cannot be told by the words of the mouth, it cannot be written on paper:

> It is like a dumb person who tastes a sweet thing—
> how shall it be explained?'
> No, it cannot be explained, it has to be realized;
> and when man has done, so, he sings:
> The inward and the outward has become as one sky,

The infinite and the finite are united:

> I am drunken with the sight of this All.

The poet in this has reached Reality which is ineffable, where all contradictions have been harmonized. For the ultimate reality is in the Person and not in the law and substance. And man must feel that if this universe is not the manifestation of Supreme Person, then it is a stupendous deception and a perpetual insult to him. He should know that under such enormous weight of estrangement his own personality would have been crushed out of its shape in the very beginning and have vanished in the meaninglessness of an abstraction that had not even the basis of a mind for its conception.

The poet of Ishopanishad at the end of his teachings suddenly breaks out in a verse which in the depth of its simplicity carries the lyrical silence of the wide earth gazing at the morning sun. He sings:

'In the golden vessel is hidden the face of truth. O thou Giver of Nourishment, remove the cover for our sight, for us who must know the law of truth. O thou giver of nourishment, thou who movest alone, who dost regulate the creation, who art the spirit of the lord of all creatures, collect thy rays, draw together thy light, let me behold in thee the most blessed of all forms,—the Person who is there, who is there, he is I Am.'

Then at the conclusion this poet of deathless personality thus sings of death:

'Life breath is the breath of immortality. The body ends in ashes. O my will, remember thy deeds, O my will, remember thy deeds. O God, O Fire, thou knowest all deeds. Lead us through good paths to fulfillment. Separate from us the crooked sin. To thee we offer our speech of salutation.'

Here stops the poet of Ishopanishad, who has travelled from life to death and from death to life again; who has had the boldness to see Brahma as the infinite Being and the finite Becoming at the same moment; who declares that life is through work, the work that expresses the soul; whose teaching is to realize our soul in the Supreme Being through our renunciation of self and union with all.

The profound truth to which the poet of Ishopanishad has given expression is the truth of the simple mind which is in deep love with the mystery of reality and cannot believe in the finality of that logic which by its method of decomposition brings the universe to the brink of dissolution.

Have I not known the sunshine to grow brighter and the moonlight deeper in its tenderness when my heart was filled with a sudden excess of love assuring me that this world is one with my soul? When I have sung the coming of the clouds, the pattering of rains has found its pathos in my songs. From the dawn of our history the poets and artists have been infusing the colours and music of their soul into the structure of existence. And from this I have known certainly that the earth and the sky are woven with the fibres of man's mind, which is the universal mind at the same time. If this were not true, then poetry would be false and music a delusion, and the mute world would compel man's heart into utter silence. The Great Master plays; the breath is his own, but the instrument is our mind through which he brings out his songs of creation, and therefore I know that I am not a mere stranger resting in the wayside inn of this earth on my voyage of existence, but I live in a world whose life is bound up with mine. The poet has known that the reality of this world is personal and has sung:

> The earth is His joy: His joy is the sky;
> His joy is the flashing of the sun and the moon;
> His joy is the beginning, the middle, and the end;
> His joy is eyes, darkness and light.
> Oceans and waves are His joy;
> His joy the Saraswati, the Jamuna and the Ganges.
> The Master is One: and life and death,
> Union and separation are all His plays of joy.

Woman

When male creatures indulge in their fighting propensity to kill one another Nature connives at it, because comparatively speaking, females are needful to her purpose, while males are barely necessary. Being of an economic disposition she does not specially care for the hungry broods who are quarrelsomely voracious and who yet contribute very little towards the payment of Nature's bill. Therefore in the insect world, we witness the phenomenon of the females taking it upon themselves to keep down the male population to the bare limit of necessity.

But because greatly relieved of their responsibility to Nature, the males in the human world have had the freedom of their occupation and adventures. The definition of the human being is said to be that he is the tool-making animal. This tool-making is outside of nature's scope. In fact, with our tool-making power we have been able to defy Nature. The human male, having the most part of his energies free, developed this power, and became formidable. Thus, though in the vital department of humanity woman still occupies the throne given to her by Nature, man in the mental department has created and extended his own dominion. For this great work detachment of mind and freedom of movement were necessary.

Man took advantage of his comparative freedom from physical and emotional bondage, and marched unencumbered towards his extension of life's boundaries. In this he has travelled through the perilous path of revolutions and ruins. Time after time his accumulations have been swept away and the current of progress has disappeared at its source. Though the gain has been considerable yet the waste in comparison has been still more enormous, especially when we consider that much of the wealth, when vanished, has taken away the records with it. Through this repeated experience of disasters man has discovered, though he has not fully utilized, the truth, that in all his creations the moral rhythm has to be maintained to save them from destruction; that a mere unlimited augmentation of power does not lead to real progress, and there must be balance of proportion, must be harmony of the structure with its foundation, to indicate a real growth in truth.

This ideal of stability is deeply cherished in woman's nature. She is never in love with merely going on, shooting wanton arrows of curiosity into the heart of darkness. All her forces instinctively work to bring things to some shape of fulness,—for that is the law of life. In life's movement though nothing is final yet every step has its rhythm of completeness. Even the bud has its ideal of rounded perfection, so has the flower, and also the fruit. But an unfinished building has not that ideal of wholeness in itself. Therefore if it goes on indefinitely in its growth of dimensions, it gradually grows out of its standard of stability. The masculine creations of intellectual civilization are towers of Babel, they dare to defy their foundations and therefore topple down over and over again. Thus human history is growing up over layers of ruins; it is not a continuous life growth. The present war is an illustration of this. The economic and political organizations, which merely represent mechanical power, born of intellect, are apt to forget their centres of gravity in the foundational world of life. The cumulative greed of power and possession which can have no finality of completeness in itself, which has no harmony with the ideal of moral and spiritual perfection, must at last lay a violent hand upon its own ponderousness of material.

At the present stage of history civilization is almost exclusively masculine, a civilization of power, in which woman has been thrust aside in the shade. Therefore it has lost its balance and it is moving by hopping from war to war. Its motive forces are the forces of destruction, and its ceremonials are carried through by an appalling number of human sacrifices. This one-sided civilization is crashing along a series of catastrophes at a tremendous speed because of its one-sidedness. And at last the time has arrived when woman must step in and impart her life rhythm to this reckless movement of power.

For woman's function is the passive function of the soil, which not only helps the tree to grow but keeps its growth within limits. The tree must have life's adventure and send up and spread out its branches on all sides, but all its deeper bonds of relation are hidden and held firm in the soil and this helps it to live. Our civilization must also have its passive element, broad and deep and stable. It must not be mere growth but harmony of growth. It must not be all tune but it must have its time also. This time is not a barrier, it is what the banks are to the river; they guide into permanence the current which otherwise would lose itself in the amorphousness of morass. It is rhythm, the rhythm which does not check the world's movements but leads them into truth and beauty.

Woman is endowed with the passive qualities of chastity, modesty, devotion and power of self-sacrifice in a greater measure than man is. It is the passive quality in nature which turns its monster forces into perfect creations of beauty— taming the wild elements into the delicacy to tenderness fit for the service of life. This passive quality has given woman that large and deep placidity which is so necessary for the healing and nourishing and storing of life. If life were all spending, then it would be like a rocket, going up in a flash and coming down the next moment in ashes. Life should be like a lamp where the potentiality of light is far greater in quantity than what appears as the flame. It is in the depth of passiveness in woman's nature that this potentiality of life is stored.

I have said elsewhere that in the woman of the Western world a certain restlessness is noticed which cannot be the normal aspect of her nature. For women who want something special and violent in their surroundings to keep their interests active only prove that they have lost touch with their own true world. Apparently, numbers of women as well as men in the West condemn the things that are commonplace. They are always hankering after something which is out of the common, straining their powers to produce a spurious originality that merely surprises though it may not satisfy. But such efforts are not a real sign of vitality. And they must be more injurious to women than to men, because women have the vital power more strongly in them than men have. They are the mothers of her race, and they have a real interest in the things that are around them, that are the common things of life; if they did not have that, then the race would perish.

If, by constantly using outside stimulation, they form something like a mental drug habit, become addicted to a continual dram-drinking of sensationalism, then they lose the natural high sensibility which they have, and with it the bloom of their womanhood, and their real power to sustain the human race with what it needs the most.

A man's interest in his fellow-beings becomes real when he finds in them some special gift of power of usefulness, but a woman feels interest in her fellow-beings because they are living creatures, because they are human, not because of some particular purpose which they can serve, or some power which they possess and for which she has a special admiration. And because woman has this power, she exercises such charm over our minds; her exuberance of vital interest is so attractive that it makes her speech, her laughter, her movement, everything graceful; for the note of gracefulness is in this harmony with all our surrounding interests.

Fortunately for us, our everyday world has the subtle and unobtrusive beauty of the commonplace, and we have to depend upon our own sensitive minds to realize its wonders which are invisible because spiritual. If we can pierce through the exterior, we find that the world in its commonplace aspects is a miracle.

We realize this truth intuitively through our power of love; and women, through this power, discover that the object of their love and sympathy, in spite of its ragged disguise of triviality, has infinite worth. When women have lost the power of interest in things that are common, then leisure frightens them with its emptiness, because, their natural sensibilities being deadened, there is nothing in their surroundings to occupy their attention. Therefore they keep themselves frantically busy, not in utilizing the time, but merely in filling it up. Our everyday world is like a reed, its true value is not in itself,—but those who have the power and the serenity of attention can hear the music which the Infinite plays through its very emptiness. But when women form the habit of valuing things for themselves, then they may be expected furiously to storm your mind, to decoy your soul from her love-tryst of the eternal and to make you try to smother the voice of the Infinite by the unmeaning rattle of ceaseless movement.

I do not mean to imply that domestic life is the only life for a woman. I mean that the human world is the woman's world, be it domestic or be it full of the other activities of life, which are human activities, and not merely abstract efforts to organize. Wherever there is something which is concretely personal and human, there is woman's world. The domestic world is the world where every individual finds his worth as an individual, therefore his value is not the market value, but the value of love; that is to say, the value that God in his infinite mercy has set upon all his creatures. This domestic world has been the gift of God to woman. She can extend her radiance of love beyond its boundaries on all sides, and even leave it to prove her woman's nature when the call comes to her. But this is a truth which cannot be ignored, that the moment she is born in her mother's arms, she is born in the centre of her own true world, the world of human relationship.

Woman should use her power to break through the surface and go to the centre of things, where in the mystery of life dwells an eternal source of interest. Man has not this power to such an extent. But woman has it, if she does not kill it,— and therefore she loves creatures who are not lovable for their uncommon qualities. Man has to do his duty in a world of his own where he is always creating power and wealth and organizations of different kinds. But God has sent woman to love the world, which is a world of ordinary things and events. She is not in the world of the fairy tale where the fair woman sleeps for ages till she is touched by the magic wand. In God's world women have their magic wands everywhere, which keep their hearts awake,—and these are not the golden wands of wealth nor the iron rods of power.

All our spiritual teachers have proclaimed the infinite worth of the individual. It is the rampant materialism of the present age which ruthlessly sacrifices individuals to the bloodthirsty idols of organization. When religion was materialistic, when men worshipped their gods for fear of their malevolence, or for greed of wealth and power, then the ceremonies of worship were cruel and sacrifices were claimed without number. With the growth of man's spiritual life, our worship has become the worship of love

At the present stage of civilization, when the mutilation of individuals is not only practised, but glorified, women are feeling ashamed of their own womanliness. For God, with his message of love, has sent them as guardians of individuals, and, in this their divine vocation, individuals are more to them than army and navy and parliament, shops and factories. Here they have their service in God's own temple of reality, where love is of more value than power.

But because men in their pride of power have taken to deriding things that are living and relationships that are human, a large number of women are screaming themselves hoarse to prove that they are not women, that they are true where they represent power and organization. In the present age they feel that their pride is hurt when they are taken as mere mothers of the race, as the ministers to the vital needs of its existence, and to its deeper spiritual necessity of sympathy and love.

Because men praise with pious unctuousness the idolatry of their manufactured images of abstractions, women in shame are breaking their own true god, who is waiting for his worship of self-sacrifice in love.

Changes have been going on for a long time underneath the solid crust of society on which woman's world has its foundation. Of late, with the help of science, civilization has been growing increasingly masculine, so that the full reality of the individual is more and more ignored. Organization is encroaching upon the province of personal relationship, and sentiment is giving way to law. In some societies, too much dominated by masculine ideals, infanticide prevailed, which ruthlessly kept down the female element of the population as low as possible. The same thing in another form has taken place in modern civilization. In its inordinate lust for power and wealth it has robbed woman of the most part of her world, and the home is every day being crowded out by the office. It is taking the whole world for itself, leaving hardly any room for woman. It is not merely inflicting injury but insult upon her.

But woman cannot be pushed back for good into the mere region of the decorative by man's aggressiveness of power. For she is not less necessary in civilization than man but possibly more so. In the geological history of earth the periods of gigantic cataclysms have passed when the earth had not attained that mellowness of maturity which despises all violent exhibition of force. And the civilization of competing commerce and fighting powers must also make room for that stage of perfection whose power lies deep in beauty and beneficence. Too long has ambition been at the helm of our history so that every right of the individual has had to be wrenched by force from the party in power and man has had to invoke the help of evil to attain what was good for him. But such an arrangement cannot be lasting, but must give way time after time; for the seeds of violence lie in wait in its cracks and crevices, and roots of disruption spread in the dark and cause breakdown when it is least expected.

Therefore although in the present state of history man is asserting his masculine supremacy and building his civilization with stone blocks, ignoring the living principle of growth, he cannot altogether crush woman's nature into dust or into his dead building materials. Woman's home may have been shattered, but woman is not, and cannot, herself be killed. It is not that woman is merely seeking her freedom of livelihood, struggling against man's monopoly of business, but against man's monopoly of civilization where he is breaking her heart every day and desolating her life. She must restore the lost social balance by putting the full weight of the woman into the creation of the human world. The monster car of organization is creaking and growling along life's highway, spreading misery and mutilation, for it must have speed before everything else in the world. Therefore woman must come into the bruised and maimed world of the individual; she must claim each one of them as her own, the useless and the insignificant. She must protect with her care all the beautiful flowers of sentiment from the scorching laughter of the science of proficiency. The growing impurities, born of the deprivation of its normal conditions imposed upon life by the organized power of greed, she must sweep away. The time has come when woman's responsibility has become greater than ever before, when her field of work has far transcended the domestic sphere of life. The world with its insulted individuals has sent its appeal to her. These individuals must find their true value, raise their heads once again in the sun, and renew their faith in God's love through her love.

Men have seen the absurdity of to-day's civilization, which is based upon nationalism,—that is to say, on economics and politics and its consequent militarism. Men have been losing their freedom and their humanity in order to fit themselves for vast mechanical organizations. So the next civilization, it is hoped, will be based not merely upon economical and political competition and exploitation but upon worldwide social co-operation; upon spiritual ideals of reciprocity, and not upon economic ideals of efficiency. And then women will have their true place.

Because men have been building up vast and monstrous organizations they have got into the habit of thinking that this turning-out power has something of the nature of perfection in itself. The habit is ingrained in them, and it is difficult for them to see where truth is missing in their present ideal of progress.

But woman can bring her fresh mind and all her power of sympathy to this new task of building up a spiritual civilization, if she will be conscious of her responsibilities. Of course, she can be frivolous or very narrow in her outlook, and then she will miss her great mission. And just because woman has been insulated, has been living in a sort of obscurity, behind man, I think she will have her compensation in the civilization which is waiting to come.

And these human beings who have been boastful of their power, and aggressive in their exploitation, who have lost faith in the real meaning of the teaching of their Master, that the meek shall inherit the earth, will be defeated in the next generation of life. It is the same thing that happened in the ancient days, in the prehistoric times, to those great monsters like the mammoths and dinosaurs. They have lost their inheritance of the earth. They had the gigantic muscles for mighty efforts but they had to give up to creatures who were much feebler in their muscles and who took up much less space with their dimensions. And in the future civilization and the women, the feebler creatures,—feebler at least in their outer aspects,—who are less muscular, and who have been behind hand, always left under the shadow of those huge creatures, the men,—they will have their place, and those bigger creatures will have go give way.

NATIONALISM

Nationalism in India

Our real problem in India is not political. It is social. This is a condition not only prevailing in India, but among all nations. I do not believe in an exclusive political interest. Politics in the West have dominated western ideals, and we in India are trying to imitate you. We have to remember that in Europe, where peoples had their racial unity from the beginning, and where natural resources were insufficient for the inhabitants, the civilisation has naturally taken on the character of political and commercial aggressiveness. For on the one hand they had no internal complications, and on the other they had to deal with neighbours who were strong and rapacious. To have perfect combination among themselves and a watchful attitude of animosity against others was taken as the solution of their problems. In former days they organised and plundered; in the present age the same spirit continues— and they organise and exploit the whole world.

But from the earliest beginnings of history India has had her own problem constantly before her—it is the race problem. Each nation must be conscious of its mission, and we in India must realise that we cut a poor figure when we try to be political, simply because we have not yet been finally able to accomplish what was set before us by our providence.

This problem of race unity which we have been trying to solve for so many years has likewise to be faced by you here in America. Many people in this country ask me what is happening to the caste distinctions in India. But when this question is asked me, it is usually done with a superior air. And I feel tempted to put the same question to our American critics with a slight modification: 'What have you done with the Red Indian and the Negro?' For you have not got over your attitude of caste towards them. You have used violent methods to keep aloof from other races, but until you have solved the question, here in America, you have no right to question India.

In spite of our great difficulty, however, India has done something. She has tried to make an adjustment of races, to acknowledge the real differences between them where these exist, and yet seek for some basis of unity. This basis has come through our saints, like Nanak, Kabir, Chaitanya[1] and others, preaching one God to all races of India.

In finding the solution of our problem we shall have helped to solve the world problem as well. What India has been, the whole world is now. The whole world is becoming one country through scientific facility. And the moment is arriving when you must also find a basis of unity which is not political. If India can offer to the world her solution, it will be a contribution to humanity. There is only one history— the history of man. All national histories are merely chapters in the larger one. And we are content in India to suffer for such a great cause.

Each individual has his self-love. Therefore his brute instinct leads him to fight with others in the sole pursuit of his self-interest. But man has also his higher instincts of sympathy and mutual help. The people who are lacking in this higher moral power and who therefore cannot combine in fellowship with one another must perish or live in a state of degradation. Only

------

1. Nanak (1469-1533), Kabir (1440-1518),
   Chaitanya (1485-1533.

those peoples have survived and achieved civilisation who have this spirit of co-operation strong in them. So we find that from the beginning of history men had to choose between fighting with one another and combining, between serving their own interest or the common interest of all.

In our early history, when the geographical limits of each country and also the facilities of communication were small, this problem was comparatively small in dimension. It was sufficient for men to develop their sense of unity within their area of segregation. In those days they combined among themselves and fought against others. But it was this moral spirit of combination which was the true basis of their greatness, and this fostered their art, science and religion. At that early time the most important fact that man had to take count of was the fact of the members of one particular race of men coming in close contact with one another. Those who truly grasped this fact through their higher nature made their mark in history.

The most important fact of the present age is that all the different races of men have come close together. And again we are confronted with two alternatives. The problem is whether the different groups of peoples shall go on fighting with one another or find out some true basis of reconciliation and mutual help; whether it will be interminable competition or co-operation.

I have no hesitation in saying that those who are gifted with the moral power of love and vision of spiritual unity, who have the least feeling of enmity against aliens, and the sympathetic insight to place themselves in the position of others, will be the fittest to take their permanent place in the age that is lying before us, and those who are constantly developing their instincts for fight and intolerance of aliens will be eliminated. For this is the problem before us, and we have to prove our humanity by solving it through the help of our higher nature. The gigantic organisations for hurting others and warding off their blows, for making money by dragging others back, will not help us. On the contrary, by their crushing weight, their enormous cost and their deadening effect upon living humanity, they will seriously impede our freedom in the larger life of a higher civilisation.

During the evolution of the Nation the moral culture of brotherhood was limited by geographical boundaries, because at that time those boundaries were true. Now they have become imaginary lines of tradition divested of the qualities of real obstacles. So the time has come when man's moral nature must deal with this great fact with all seriousness or perish. The first impulse of this change of circumstance has been the churning up of man's baser passions of greed and cruel hatred. If this persists indefinitely, and armaments go on exaggerating themselves to unimaginable absurdities, and machines and storehouses envelop this fair earth with their dirt and smoke and ugliness, then it will end in a conflagration of suicide. Therefore man will have to exert all his power of love and clarity of vision to make another great moral adjustment which will comprehend the whole world of men and not merely the fractional groups of nationality. The call has come to every individual in the present age to prepare himself and his surroundings for this dawn of a new era, when man shall discover his soul in the spiritual unity of all human beings.

If it is given at all to the West to struggle out of these tangles of the lower slopes to the spiritual summit of humanity then I cannot but think that it is the special mission of America to fulfil this hope of God and man. You are the country of expectation, desiring something else than what is. Europe has her subtle habits of mind and her conventions. But America, as yet, has come to no conclusions. I realise how much America is untrammelled by the traditions of the past, and I can appreciate that experimentalism is a sign of America's youth. The foundation of her glory is in the future, rather than in the past, and if one is gifted with the power of clairvoyance, one will be able to love the America that is to be.

America is destined to justify western civilisation to the East. Europe has lost faith in humanity, and has become distrustful and sickly. America, on the other hand, is not pessimistic or blasé. You know, as a people, that there is such a thing as a better and a best, and that knowledge drives you on. There are habits that are not merely passive but aggressively arrogant. They are not like mere walls, but are like hedges of stinging nettles. Europe has been cultivating these hedges of habits for long years, till they have grown round her dense and strong and high. The pride of her traditions has sent its roots deep into her heart. I do not wish to contend that it is unreasonable. But pride in every form breeds blindness at the end. Like all artificial stimulants its first effect is a heightening of consciousness, and then with the increasing dosage it muddles it and brings an exultation that is misleading. Europe has gradually grown hardened in her pride in all her outer and inner habits. She not only cannot forget that she is western, but she takes every opportunity to hurl this fact against others to humiliate them. This is why she is growing incapable of imparting to the East what is best in herself, and of accepting in a right spirit the wisdom that the East has stored for centuries.

In America national habits and traditions have not had time to spread their clutching roots round your hearts. You have constantly felt and complained of your disadvantages when you compared your nomadic restlessness with the settled traditions of Europe—the Europe which can show her picture of greatness to the best advantage because she can fix it against the background of the past. But in this present age of transition, when a new era of civilisation is sending its trumpet-call to all peoples of the world across an unlimited future, this very freedom of detachment will enable you to accept its invitation and to achieve the goal for which Europe began her journey but lost herself mid-way. For she was tempted out of her path by her pride of power and greed of possession.

Not merely your freedom from habits of mind in individuals, but also the freedom of your history from all unclean entanglements, fits you in your career of holding the banner of civilisation of the future. All the great nations of Europe have their victims in other parts of the world. This not only deadens their moral sympathy but also their intellectual sympathy, which is so necessary for the understanding of races which are different from one's own. Englishmen can never truly understand India, because their minds are not disinterested with regard to that country. If you compare England with Germany or France you will find she has produced the smallest number of scholars who have studied Indian literature and philosophy with any amount of sympathetic insight or thoroughness. This attitude of apathy and contempt is natural where the relationship is abnormal and founded upon national selfishness and pride. But your history has been disinterested, and that is why you have been able to help Japan in her lessons in western civilisation, and that is why China can look upon you with the best confidence in this, her darkest period of danger. In fact you are carrying all the responsibility of a great future because you are untrammelled by the grasping miserliness of a past. Therefore, of all countries of the earth, America has to be fully conscious of this future; her vision must not be obscured and her faith in humanity must be strong with the strength of youth.

A parallelism exists between America and India—the parallelism of welding together into one body various races.

In my country we have been seeking to find out something common to all races, which will prove their real unity. No nation looking for a mere political or commercial basis of unity will find such a solution sufficient. Men of thought and power will discover the spiritual unity, will realise it, and preach it.

India has never had a real sense of nationalism. Even though from childhood I had been taught that idolatry of the Nation is almost better than reverence for God and humanity, I believe I have outgrown that teaching, and it is my conviction that my countrymen will truly gain their India by fighting against the education which teaches them that a country is greater than the ideals of humanity.

The educated Indian at present is trying to absorb some lessons from history contrary to the lessons of our ancestors. The East, in fact, is attempting to take unto itself a history, which is not the outcome of its own living. Japan, for example, thinks she is getting powerful through adopting western methods but, after she has exhausted her inheritance, only the borrowed weapons of civilisation will remain to her. She will not have developed herself from within.

Europe has her past. Europe's strength therefore lies in her history. We in India must make up our minds that we cannot borrow other people's history, and that if we stifle our own we are committing suicide. When you borrow things that do not belong to your life, they only serve to crush your life.

And therefore I believe that it does India no good to compete with western civilisation in its own field. But we shall be more than compensated if, in spite of the insults heaped upon us, we follow our own destiny.

There are lessons which impart information or train our minds for intellectual pursuits. These are simple and can be acquired and used with advantage. But there are others which affect our deeper nature and change our direction of life.

Before we accept them and pay their value by selling our own inheritance, we must pause and think deeply. In man's history there come ages of fireworks which dazzle us by their force and movement. They laugh not only at our modest household lamps but also at the eternal stars. But let us not for that provocation be precipitate in our desire to dismiss our lamps. Let us patiently bear our present insult and realise that these fireworks have splendour but not permanence, because of the extreme explosiveness which is the cause of their power, and also of their exhaustion. They are spending a fatal quantity of energy and substance compared to their gain and production.

Anyhow, our ideals have been evolved through our own history, and even if we wished we could only make poor fireworks of them because their materials are different from yours, as is also their moral purpose. If we cherish the desire of paying our all to buy a political nationality it will be as absurd as if Switzerland had staked her existence on her ambition to build up a navy powerful enough to compete with that of England. The mistake that we make is in thinking that man's channel of greatness is only one—the one which has made itself painfully evident for the time being by its depth of insolence.

We must know for certain that there is a future before us and that future is waiting for those who are rich in moral ideals and not in mere things. And it is the privilege of man to work for fruits that are beyond his immediate reach, and to adjust his life not in slavish conformity to the examples of some present success or even to his own prudent past, limited in its aspiration, but to an infinite future bearing in its heart the ideals of our highest expectations.

We must recognise that it is providential that the West has come to India. And yet someone must show the East to the West, and convince the West that the East has her contribution to make to the history of civilisation. India is no beggar of the West. And yet even though the West may think she is, I am not for thrusting off western civilisation and becoming segregated in our independence. Let us have a deep association. If Providence wants England to be the channel of that communication, of that deeper association, I am willing to accept it with all humility. I have great faith in human nature, and I think the West will find its true mission. I speak bitterly of western civilisation when I am conscious that it is betraying its trust and thwarting its own purpose. The West must not make herself a curse to the world by using her power for her own selfish needs but, by teaching the ignorant and helping the weak, she should save herself from the worst danger that the strong is liable to incur by making the feeble acquire power enough to resist her intrusion. And also she must not make her materialism to be the final thing, but must realise that she is doing a service in freeing the spiritual being from the tyranny of matter.

I am not against one nation in particular, but against the general idea of all nations. What is the Nation?

It is the aspect of a whole people as an organised power. This organisation incessantly keeps up the insistence of the population on becoming strong and efficient. But this strenuous effort after strength and efficiency drains man's energy from his higher nature where he is self-sacrificing and creative. For thereby man's power of sacrifice is diverted from his ultimate object, which is moral, to the maintenance of this organisation, which is mechanical. Yet in this he feels all the satisfaction of moral exaltation and therefore becomes supremely dangerous to humanity. He feels relieved of the urging of his conscience when he can transfer his responsibility to this machine which is the creation of his intellect and not of his complete moral personality. By this device the people which loves freedom perpetuates slavery in a large portion of the world with the comfortable feeling of pride in having done its duty; men who are naturally just can be cruelly unjust both in their act and their thought, accompanied by a feeling that they are helping the world to receive its deserts; men who are honest can blindly go on robbing others of their human rights for self-aggrandisement, all the while abusing the deprived for not deserving better treatment. We have seen in our everyday life even small organisations of business and profession produce callousness of feeling in men who are not naturally bad, and we can well imagine what a moral havoc it is causing in a world where whole peoples are furiously organising themselves for gaining wealth and power.

Nationalism is a great menace. It is the particular thing which for years has been at the bottom of India's troubles. And inasmuch as we have been ruled and dominated by a nation that is strictly political in its attitude, we have tried to develop within ourselves, despite our inheritance form the past, a belief in our eventual political desitny.

There are different parties in India, with different ideals. Some are struggling for political independence. Others think that the time has not arrived for that, and yet believe that India should have the rights that the English colonies have. They wish to gain autonomy as far as possible.

In the beginning of the history of political agitation in India there was not the conflict between parties which there is today. At that time there was a party known as the Indian Congress;[2] they had no real programme. They had a few grievances for redress by the authorities. They wanted larger representation in the Council House, and more freedom in Municipal Government. They wanted scraps of things, but they had no constructive ideal. Therefore I was lacking in enthusiasm for their methods. It was my conviction that what India most needed was constructive work coming from within

---

2. The Indian National Congress was founded in 1885.

herself. In this work we must take all risks and go on doing the duties which by right are ours, though in the teeth of persecution, winning moral victory at every step, by our failure and suffering. We must show those who are over us that we have in ourselves the strength of moral power, the power to suffer for truth. Where we have nothing to show, we have only to beg. It would be mischievous if the gifts we wish for were granted to us at once, and I have told my countrymen, time and again, to combine for the work of creating opportunities to give vent to our spirit of self-sacrifice, and not for the purpose of begging.

The party, however, lost power because the people soon came to realise how futile was the half policy adopted by them. The party split,[3] and there arrived the Extremists, who advocated independence of action, and discarded the begging method—the easiest method of relieving one's mind from his responsibility towards his country. Their ideals were based on western history. They had no sympathy with the special problems of India. They did not recognise the patent fact that there were causes in our social organisation which made the Indian incapable of coping with the alien. What should we do if, for any reason, England was driven away? We should simply be victims for other nations. The same social weaknesses would prevail. The thing we in India have to think of is this: to remove those social customs and ideals which have generated a want of self-respect and a complete dependence on those above us—a state of affairs which has been brought about entirely by the domination in India of the caste system, and the blind and lazy habit of relying upon the authority of traditions that are incongruous anachronisms in the present age.

---

3. In 1907, at the annual session of the Indian National Congress, held at Surat.

Once again I draw your attention to the difficulties India has had to encounter and her struggle to overcome them. Her problem was the problem of the world in miniature. India is too vast in its area and too diverse in its races. It is many countries packed in one geographical receptacle. It is just the opposite of what Europe truly is; namely, one country made into many. Thus Europe in its culture and growth has had the advantage of the strength of the many as well as the strength of the one. India, on the contrary, being naturally many, yet adventitiously one, has all along suffered from the looseness of its diversity and the feebleness of its unity. A true unity is like a round globe; it rolls on, carrying its burden easily. But diversity is a many-cornered thing which has to be dragged and pushed with all force. Be it said to the credit of India that this diversity was not her own creation; she has had to accept it as a fact from the beginning of her history. In America and Australia, Europe has simplified her problem by almost exterminating the original population. Even in the present age this spirit of extermination is making itself manifest, in the inhospitable shutting out of aliens, by those who themselves were aliens in the lands they now occupy. But India tolerated difference of races from the first, and that spirit of toleration has acted all through her history.

Her caste system is the outcome of this spirit of toleration. For India has all along been trying experiments in evolving a social unity within which all the different peoples could be held together, while fully enjoying the freedom of maintaining their own differences. The tie has been as loose as possible, yet as close as the circumstances permitted. This has produced something like a United States of a social federation, whose common name is Hinduism.

India had felt that diversity of races there must be and should be, whatever may be its drawbacks, and you can never coerce nature into your narrow limits of convenience without paying one day very dearly for it. In this India was right; but what she failed to realise was that in human beings differences are not like the physical barriers of mountains, fixed for ever—they are fluid with life's flow, they are changing their courses and their shapes and volumes.

Therefore in her caste regulations India recognised differences, but not the mutability which is the law of life. In trying to avoid collisions she set up boundaries of immovable walls, thus giving to her numerous races the negative benefit of peace and order but not the positive opportunity of expansion and movement. She accepted nature where it produces diversity, but ignored it where it uses that diversity for its world-game of infinite permutations and combinations. She treated life in all truth where it is manifold, but insulted it where it is ever moving. Therefore Life departed from her social system and in its place she is worshipping with all ceremony the magnificent cage of countless compartments that she has manufactured.

The same thing happened where she tried to ward off the collisions of trade interests. She associated different trades and professions with different castes. This had the effect of allaying for good the interminable jealousy and hatred of competition—the competition which breeds cruelty and makes the atmosphere thick with lies and deception. In this also India laid all her emphasis upon the law of heredity, ignoring the law of mutation, and thus gradually reduced arts into crafts and genius into skill.

However, what western observers fail to discern is that in her caste system India in all seriousness accepted her responsibility to solve the race problem in such a manner as to avoid all friction, and yet to afford each race freedom within its boundaries. Let us admit India has not in this achieved a full measure of success. But this you must also concede: that the West, being more favourably situated as to homogeneity of races, has never given her attention to this problem, and whenever confronted with it she has tried to make it easy by ignoring it altogether. And this is the source of her anti-Asiatic agitations for depriving aliens of their right to earn their honest living on these shores. In most of your colonies you only admit them on condition of their accepting the menial positions of hewers of wood and drawers of water. Either you shut your doors against the aliens or reduce them into slavery. And this is your solution to the problem of race-conflict. Whatever may be its merits you will have to admit that it does not spring from the higher impulses of civilisation but from the lower passions of greed and hatred. You say this is human nature—and India also thought she knew human nature when she strongly barricaded her race distinctions by the fixed barriers of social gradations. But we have found out to our cost that human nature is not what it seems, but what it is in truth, which is in its infinite possibilities. And when we in our blindness insult humanity for its ragged appearance it sheds its disguise to disclose to us that we have insulted our God. The degradation which we cast upon others in our pride or self-interest degrades our own humanity—and this is the punishment which is most terrible, because we do not detect it till it is too late.

Not only in your relation with aliens but with the different sections of your own society you have not achieved harmony of reconciliation. The spirit of conflict and competition is allowed the full freedom of its reckless career. And because its genesis is the greed of wealth and power it can never come to any other end but to a violent death. In India the production of commodities was brought under the law of social adjustments. Its basis was co-operation, having for its object the perfect satisfaction of social needs. But in the West it is guided by the impulse of competition, whose end is the gain of wealth for individuals. But the individual is like the geometrical line; it is length without breadth. It has not got the depth to be able to hold anything permanently. Therefore its greed or gain can never come to finality. In its lengthening process of growth it can cross other lines and cause entanglements, but will ever go on missing the ideal of completeness in its thinness of isolation.

In all our physical appetites we recognise a limit. We know that to exceed that limit is to exceed the limit of health. But has this lust for wealth and power no bounds beyond which is death's dominion? In these national carnivals of materialism are not the western peoples spending most of their vital energy in merely producing things and neglecting the creation of ideals? And can a civilisation ignore the law of moral health and go on in its endless process of inflation by gorging upon material things? Man in his social ideals naturally tries to regulate his appetites, subordinating them to the higher purpose of his nature. But in the economic world our appetites follow no other restrictions but those of supply and demand which can be artificially fostered, affording individuals opportunities for indulgence in an endless feast of grossness. In India our social instincts imposed restrictions upon our appetites— maybe it went to the extreme of repression—but in the West the spirit of economic organisation with no moral purpose goads the people into the perpetual pursuit of wealth; but has this no wholesome limit?

The ideals that strive to take form in social institutions have two objects. One is to regulate our passions and appetites for the harmonious development of man, and the other is to help him to cultivate disinterested love for his fellow-creatures. Therefore society is the expression of those moral and spiritual aspirations of man which belong to his higher nature.

Our food is creative, it builds our body; but not so wine, which stimulates. Our social ideals create the human world, but when our mind is diverted from them to greed of power then in that state of intoxication we live in a world of abnormality where our strength is not health and our liberty is not freedom. Therefore political freedom does not give us freedom when our mind is not free. An automobile does not create freedom of movement, because it is a mere machine. When I myself am free I can use the automobile for the purpose of my freedom.

We must never forget in the present day that those people who have got their political freedom are not necessarily free; they are merely powerful. The passions which are unbridled in them are creating huge organisations of slavery in the disguise of freedom. Those who have made the gain of money their highest end are unconsciously selling their life and soul to rich persons or to the combinations that represent money. Those who are enamoured of their political power and gloat over their extension of dominion over foreign races gradually surrender their own freedom and humanity to the organisations necessary for holding other peoples in slavery. In the so-called free countries the majority of the people are not free; they are driven by the minority to a goal which is not even known to them. This becomes possible only because people do not acknowledge moral and spiritual freedom as their object. They create huge eddies with their passions, and they feel dizzily inebriated with the mere velocity of their whirling movement, taking that to be freedom. But the doom which is waiting to overtake them is as certain as death—for man's truth is moral truth and his emancipation is in the spiritual life.

The general opinion of the majority of the present-day nationalists in India is that we have come to a final completeness in our social and spiritual ideals, the task of the constructive work of society having been done several thousand years before we were born, and that now we are free to employ all our activities in the political direction. We never dream of blaming our social inadequacy as the origin of our present helplessness, for we have accepted as the creed of our nationalism that this social system has been perfected for all time to come by our ancestors, who had the superhuman vision of all eternity and supernatural power for making infinite provision for future ages. Therefore, for all our miseries and shortcomings, we hold responsible the historical surprises that burst upon us from outside. This is the reason why we think that our one task is to build a political miracle of freedom upon the quicksand of social slavery. In fact we want to dam up the true course of our own historical stream, and only borrow power from the sources of other peoples' history.

Those of us in India who have come under the delusion that mere political freedom will make us free have accepted their lessons from the West as the gospel truth and lost their faith in humanity. We must remember that whatever weakness we cherish in our society will become the source of danger in politics. The same inertia which leads us to our idolatry of dead forms in social institutions will create in our politics prison-houses with immovable walls. The narrowness of sympathy which makes it possible for us to impose upon a considerable portion of humanity the galling yoke of inferiority will assert itself in our politics in creating the tyranny of injustice.

When our nationalists talk about ideals they forget that the basis of nationalism is wanting. The very people who are upholding these ideals are themselves the most conservative in their social practice. Nationalists say, for example: look at Switzerland where, in spite of race differences, the people have solidified into a nation. Yet, remember that in Switzerland the races can mingle, they can intermarry, because they are of the same blood. In India there is no common birthright. And when we talk of western nationality we forgot that the nations there do not have that physical repulsion, one for the other, that we have between different castes. Have we an instance in the whole world where a people who are not allowed to mingle their blood shed their blood for one another except by coercion or for mercenary purposes? And can we ever hope that these moral barriers against our race amalgamation will not stand in the way of our political unity?

Then again we must give full recognition to this fact that our social restrictions are still tyrannical, so much so as to make men cowards. If a man tells me that he has heterodox ideas, but that he cannot follow them because he would be socially ostracised, I excuse him for having to live a life of untruth, in order to live at all. The social habit of mind which impels us to make the life of our fellow-being a burden to them where they differ from us even in such a thing as their choice of food, is sure to persist in our political organisation and result in creating engines of coercion to crush every rational difference which is the sign of life. And tyranny will only add to the inevitable lies and hypocrisy in our political life. Is the mere name of freedom so valuable that we should be willing to sacrifice for its sake our moral freedom?

The intemperance of our habits does not immediately show its effects when we are in the vigour of our youth. But it gradually consumes that vigour, and when the period of decline sets in then we have to settle accounts and pay off our debts, which leads us to insolvency. In the West you are still able to carry your head high, though your humanity is suffering every moment form its dipsomania of organising power. India also in the heyday of her youth could carry in her vital organs the dead weight of her social organisations stiffened to rigid perfection, but it has been fatal to her, and has produced a gradual paralysis of her living nature. And this is the reason why the educated community of India has become insensible of her social needs. They are taking the very immobility of our social structures as the sign of their perfection—and because the healthy feeling of pain is dead in the limbs of our social organism they delude themselves into thinking that it needs no ministration. Therefore they think that all their energies need their only scope in the political field. It is like a man whose legs have become shrivelled and useless, trying to delude himself that these limbs have grown still because they have attained their ultimate salvation, and all that is wrong about him is the shortness of his sticks.

So much for the social and the political regeneration of India. Now we come to her industries, and I am very often asked whether there is in India any industrial regeneration since the advent of the British government. It must be remembered that at the beginning of the British rule in India our industries were suppressed, and since then we have not met with any real help or encouragement to enable us to make a stand against the monster commercial organisations of the world. The nations have decreed that we must remain purely an agricultural people, even forgetting the use of arms for all time to come. Thus India is being turned into so many predigested morsels of food ready to be swallowed at any moment by any nation which has even the most rudimentary set of teeth in its head.

India therefore has very little outlet for her industrial originality. I personally do not believe in the unwieldy organisations of the present day. The very fact that they are ugly shows that they are in discordance with the whole creation. The vast powers of nature do not reveal their truth in hideousness, but in beauty. Beauty is the signature which the Creator stamps upon His works when He is satisfied with them. All our products that insolently ignore the laws of perfection and are unashamed in their display of ungainliness bear the perpetual weight of God's displeasure. So far as your commerce lacks the dignity of grace it is untrue. Beauty and her twin brother Truth require leisure and self-control for their growth. But the greed of gain has no time or limit to its capaciousness. Its one object is to produce and consume. It has pity neither for beautiful nature nor for living human beings. It is ruthlessly ready without a moment's hesitation to crush beauty and life out of them, moulding them into money. It is this ugly vulgarity of commerce which brought upon it the censure of contempt in our earlier days, when men had leisure to have an unclouded vision of perfection in humanity. Men in those times were rightly ashamed of the instinct of mere money-making. But in this scientific age money, by its very abnormal bulk, has won its throne. And when from its eminence of piled-up things it insults the higher instincts of man, banishing beauty and noble sentiments from its surroundings, we submit. For we in our meanness have accepted bribes from its hands and our imagination has grovelled in the dust before its immensity of flesh.

But its very unwieldiness and its endless complexities are its true signs of failure. The swimmer who is an expert does not exhibit his muscular force by violent movements, but exhibits some power which is invisible and which shows itself in perfect grace and reposefulness. The true distinction of man from animals is in his power and worth which are inner and invisible. But the present-day commercial civilisation of man is not only taking too much time and space but killing time and space. Its movements are violent; its noise is discordantly loud. It is carrying its own damnation because it is trampling into distortion the humanity upon which it stands. It is strenuously turning out money at the cost of happiness. Man is reducing himself to his minimum in order to be able to make amplest room for his organisations. He is deriding his human sentiments into shame because they are apt to stand in the way of his machines.

In our mythology we have the legend that the man who performs penances for attaining immortality has to meet with temptations sent by Indra, the Lord of the Immortals. If he is lured by them he is lost. The West has been striving for centuries after its goal of immortality. Indra has sent her the temptation to try her. It is the gorgeous temptation of wealth. She has accepted it, and her civilisation of humanity has lost its path in the wilderness of machinery.

This commercialism with its barbarity of ugly decorations is a terrible menace to all humanity, because it is setting up the ideal of power over that of perfection. It is making the cult of self-seeking exult in its naked shamelessness. Our nerves are more delicate than our muscles. Things that are the most precious in us are helpless as babes when we take away from them the careful protection which they claim from us for their very preciousness. Therefore, when the callous rudeness of power runs amuck in the broadway of humanity it scares away by its grossness the ideals which we have cherished with the martyrdom of centuries.

The temptation which is fatal for the strong is still more so for the weak. And I do not welcome it in our Indian life, even though it be sent by the Lord of the Immortals. Let our life be simple in its outer aspect and rich in its inner gain. Let our civilisation take its firm stand upon its basis of social co-operation and not upon that of economic exploitation and conflict. How to do it in the teeth of the drainage of our lifeblood by the economic dragons is the task set before the thinkers of all oriental nations who have faith in the human soul. It is a sign of laziness and impotency to accept conditions imposed upon us by others who have other ideals than ours. We should actively try to adapt the world powers to guide our history to its own perfect end.

From the above you will know that I am not an economist. I am willing to acknowledge that there is a law of demand and supply and an infatuation of man for more things than are good for him. And yet I will persist in believing that there is such a thing as the harmony of completeness in humanity, where poverty does not take away his riches, where defeat may lead him to victory, death to immortality, and where in the compensation of Eternal Justice those who are the last may yet have their insult transmuted into a golden triumph.

CRISIS IN CIVILISATION &
OTHER ESSAYS

Crisis in Civilisation

Today I complete eighty years of my life. As I look back on the vast stretch of years that lie behind me and see in clear perspective the history of my early development, I am struck by the change that has taken place both in my own attitude and in the psychology of my countrymen—a change that carries within it a cause of profound tragedy.

Our direct contact with the larger world of men was linked up with the contemporary history of the English people whom we came to know in those earlier days. It was mainly through their mighty literature that we formed our ideas with regard to these newcomers to our Indian shores. In those days the type of learning that was served out to us was neither plentiful nor diverse, nor was the spirit of scientific enquiry very much in evidence. Thus their scope being strictly limited, the educated of those days had recourse to English language and literature. Their days and nights were eloquent with the stately declamations of Burke, with Macaulay's long-rolling sentences; discussions centred upon Shakespeare's drama and Byron's poetry and above all upon the large-hearted liberalism of the nineteenth-century English politics.

At the time though tentative attempts were being made to gain our national independence, at heart we had not lost faith in the generosity of the English race. This belief was so firmly rooted in the sentiments of our leaders as to lead them to hope that the victor would of his own grace pave the path of freedom for the vanquished. This belief was based upon the fact that England at the time provided a shelter to all those who had to flee from persecution in their own country. Political martyrs who had suffered for the honour of their people were accorded unreserved welcome at the hands of the English. I was impressed by this evidence of liberal humanity in the character of the English and thus I was led to set them on the pedestal of my highest respect. This generosity in their national character had not yet been vitiated by Imperialist pride. About this time, as a boy in England, I had the opportunity of listening to the speeches of John Bright, both in and outside Parliament. The large-hearted, radical liberalism of those speeches, overflowing all narrow national bounds, had made so deep an impression on my mind that something of it lingers even today, even in these days of graceless disillusionment.

Certainly that spirit of abject dependence upon the charity of our rulers was no matter for pride. What was remarkable, however, was the wholehearted way in which we gave our recognition to human greatness even when it revealed itself in the foreigner. The best and noblest gifts of humanity cannot be the monopoly of a particular race or country; its scope may not be limited nor may it be regarded as the miser's hoard buried underground. That is why English literature which nourished our minds in the past, does even now convey its deep resonance to the recesses of our heart.

It is difficult to find a suitable Bengali equivalent for the English word 'civilisation'. That phase of civilisation with which we were familiar in this country has been called by Manu 'Sadachar' (lit. proper conduct), that is, the conduct prescribed by the tradition of the race. Narrow in themselves these time-honoured social conventions originated and held good in a circumscribed geographical area, in that strip of land, Brahmavarta by name, bound on either side by the rivers

Saraswati and Drisadvati. That is how a pharisaic formalism gradually got the upper hand of free thought and the ideal of 'proper conduct' which Manu found established in Brahmavarta steadily degenerated into socialised tyranny.

During my boyhood days the attitude of the cultured and educated section of Bengal, nurtured on English learning, was charged with a feeling of revolt against these rigid regulations of society. A perusal of what Rajnarain Bose has written describing the ways of the educated gentry of those days will amply bear out what I have said just now. In place of these set codes of conduct we accepted the ideal of 'civilisation' as represented by the English term.

In our own family this change of spirit was welcomed for the sake of its sheer rational and moral force and its influence was felt in every sphere of our life. Born in that atmosphere, which was moreover coloured by our intuitive bias for literature, I naturally set the English on the throne of my heart. Thus passed the first chapters of my life. Then came the parting of ways accompanied with a painful feeling of disillusion when I began increasingly to discover how easily those who accepted the highest truths of civilisation disowned them with impunity whenever questions of national self-interest were involved.

There came a time when perforce I had to snatch myself away from the mere appreciation of literature. As I emerged into the stark light of bare facts, the sight of the dire poverty of the Indian masses rent my heart. Rudely shaken out of my dreams, I began to realise that perhaps in no other modern state was there such hopeless dearth of the most elementary needs of existence. And yet it was this country whose resources had fed for so long the wealth and magnificence of the British people. While I was lost in the contemplation of the great world of civilisation, I could never have remotely imagined that the great ideals of humanity would end in such ruthless travesty. But today a glaring example of it stares me in the face in the utter and contemptuous indifference of a so-called civilised race to the well-being of crores of Indian people.

That mastery over the machine, by which the British have consolidated their sovereignty over their vast Empire, has been kept a sealed book, to which due access has been denied to this helpless country. And all the time before our very eyes Japan has been transforming herself into a mighty and prosperous nation. I have seen with my own eyes the admirable use to which Japan has put in her own country the fruits of this progress. I have also been privileged to witness, while in Moscow, the unsparing energy with which Russia has tried to fight disease and illiteracy, and has succeeded in steadily liquidating ignorance and poverty, wiping off the humiliation from the face of a vast continent. Her civilisation is free from all invidious distinction between one class and another, between one sect and another. The rapid and astounding progress achieved by her made me happy and jealous at the same time. One aspect of the Soviet administration which particularly pleased me was that it provided no scope for unseemly conflict of religious difference nor set one community against another by unbalanced distribution of political favours. That I consider a truly civilised administration which impartially serves the common interests of the people.

While other imperialist powers sacrifice the welfare of the subject races to their own national greed, in the USSR I found a genuine attempt being made to harmonise the interests of the various nationalities that are scattered over its vast area. I saw peoples and tribes, who, only the other day, were nomadic savages being encouraged and indeed trained, to avail themselves freely of the benefits of civilisation. Enormous sums are being spent on their education to expedite the process. When I see elsewhere some two hundred nationalities—which only a few years ago were at vastly different stages of development—marching ahead in peaceful progress and amity, and when I look about my own country and see a very highly evolved and intellectual people drifting into the disorder of barbarism, I cannot help contrasting the two systems of governments, one based on cooperation, the other on exploitation, which have made such contrary conditions possible.

I have also seen Iran, newly awakened to a sense of national self-sufficiency, attempting to fulfil her own destiny freed from the deadly griding-stones of two European powers. During my recent visit to that country I discovered to my delight that Zoroastrians who once suffered from the fanatical hatred of the major community and whose rights had been curtailed by the ruling power were now free from this age-long repression, and that civilised life had established itself in the happy land. It is significant that Iran's good fortune dates from the day when she finally disentangled herself from the meshes of European diplomacy. With all my heart I wish Iran well.

Turning to the neighbouring kingdom of Afghanistan I find that though there is much room for improvement in the field of education and social development, yet she is fortunate in that she can look forward to unending progress; for none of the European powers, boastful of their civilisation, has yet succeeded in overwhelming and crushing her possibilities.

Thus while these other countries were marching ahead, India, smothered under the dead weight of British administration, lay static in her utter helplessness. Another great and ancient civilisation for whose recent tragic history the British cannot disclaim responsibility, is China. To serve their own national profit the British first doped her people with opium and then appropriated a portion of her territory. As the world was about to forget the memory of this outrage, we were painfully surprised by another event. While Japan was quietly devouring North China, her act of wanton aggression was ignored as a minor incident by the veterans of British diplomacy. We have also witnessed from this distance how actively the British statesmen acquiesced in the destruction of the Spanish Republic.

On the other hand, we also noted with admiration how a band of valiant Englishmen laid down their lives for Spain. Even though the English had not aroused themselves sufficiently to their sense of responsibility towards China in the Far East, in their own immediate neighbourhood they did not hesitate to sacrifice themselves to the cause of freedom. Such acts of heroism reminded me over again of the true English spirit to which in those early days I had given my full faith, and made me wonder how imperialist greed could bring about so ugly a transformation in the character of so great a race.

Such is the tragic tale of the gradual loss of my faith in the claims of the European nations to civilisation. In India the misfortune of being governed by a foreign race is daily brought home to us not only in the callous neglect of such minimum necessities of life as adequate provision for food, clothing, educational and medical facilities for the people, but in an even unhappier form in the way the people have been divided among themselves. The pity of it is that the blame is laid at the door of our own society. So frightful a culmination of the history of our people would never have been possible, but for the encouragement it has received from secret influences emanating from high places.

One cannot believe that Indians are in anyway inferior to the Japanese in intellectual capacity. The most effective difference between these two eastern peoples is that whereas India lies at the mercy of the British, Japan has been spared the shadow of alien domination. We know what we have been deprived of. That which was truly best in their own civilisations the upholding of the dignity of human relationship, has no place in the British administration of this country. If in its place they have established, with baton in hand, a reign of 'law and order', in other words a policeman's rule, such mockery of civilisation can claim no respect from us. It is the mission of civilisation to bring unity among people and establish peace and harmony. But in unfortunate India the social fabric is being rent into shreds by unseemly outbursts of hooliganism daily growing in intensity, right under the very aegis of 'law and order'. In India, so long as no personal injury is inflicted upon any member of the ruling race, this barbarism seems to be assured of perpetuity, making us ashamed to live under such an administration.

And yet my good fortune has often brought me into close contact with really large-hearted Englishmen. Without the slightest hesitation I may say that the nobility of their character was without parallel—in no country or community have I come across such greatness of soul. Such examples would not allow me wholly to lose faith in the race which produced them. I had the rare blessing of having Andrews—a real Englishman, a real Christian and a true man—for a very close friend. Today in the perspective of death his unselfish and courageous magnanimity shines all the brighter. The whole of India remains indebted to him for innumerable acts of love and devotion. But personally speaking, I am especially beholden to him because he helped me to retain in my old age that feeling of respect for the English race with which in the past I was inspired by their literature and which I was about to lose completely. I count such Englishmen as Andrews not only as my personal and intimate friends but as friends of the whole human race. To have known them has been to me a treasured privilege. It is my belief that such Englishmen will save British honour from shipwreck. At any rate if I had not known them, my despair at the prospect of western civilisation would be unrelieved.

In the meanwhile the demon of barbarity has given up all pretence and has emerged with unconcealed fangs, ready to tear up humanity in an orgy of devastation. From one end of the world to the other the poisonous fumes of hatred darken the atmosphere. The spirit of violence which perhaps lay dormant in the psychology of the West, has at last roused itself and desecrates the spirit of Man.

The wheels of Fate will some day compel the English to give up their Indian empire. But what kind of India will they leave behind, what stark misery? When the stream of their centuries' administration runs dry at last, what a waste of mud and filth they will leave behind them! I had at one time believed that the springs of civilisation would issue out of the heart of Europe. But today when I am about to quit the world that faith has gone bankrupt altogether.

As I look around I see the crumbling ruins of a proud civilisation strewn like a vast heap of futility. And yet I shall not commit the grievous sin of losing faith in Man. I would rather look forward to the opening of a new chapter in his history after the cataclysm is over and the atmosphere rendered clean with the spirit of service and sacrifice. Perhaps that dawn will come from this horizon, from the East where the sun rises. A day will come when unvanquished Man will retrace his path of conquest, despite all barriers, to win back his lost human heritage.

Today we witness the perils which attend on the insolence of might; one day shall be borne out the full truth of what the sages have proclaimed:

'By unrighteousness man prospers, gains what appears desirable, conquers enemies, but perishes at the root.'

Civilisation and Progress

A Chinese author writes: "The terrible tragic aspect of the situation in China is that, while the Chinese nation is called upon to throw away its own civilisation and adopt the civilisation of modern Europe, there is not one single educated man in the whole Empire who has the remotest idea of what this modern European civilisation really is."

The word 'civilisation' being a European word, we have hardly yet taken the trouble to find out its real meaning. For over a century we have accepted it, as we may accept a gift horse, with perfect trust, never caring to count its teeth. Only very lately we have begun to wonder if we realise in its truth what the western people mean when they speak of civilisation. We ask ourselves, "Has it the same meaning as some word in our own language which denotes for us the idea of human perfection?"

Civilisation cannot merely be a growing totality of happenings that by chance have assumed a particular shape and tendency which we consider to be excellent. It must be the expression of some guiding moral force which we have evolved in our society for the object of attaining perfection. The word 'perfection' has a simple and definite meaning when applied to an inanimate thing, or even to a creature whose life has principally a biological significance. But man being complex and always on the path of transcending himself, the meaning of the word 'perfection' as applied to him, cannot be crystallised into an inflexible idea. This has made it possible for different races to have different shades of definition for this term.

The Sanskrit word *dharma* is the nearest synonym in our own language, that occurs to me, for the word civilisation. In fact, we have no other word except perhaps some newly-coined one, lifeless and devoid of atmosphere. The specific meaning of *dharma* is that principle which holds us firm together and leads us to our best welfare. The radical meaning of this word is the essential quality of a thing.

Dharma for man is the best expression of what he is in truth. He may reject *dharma* and may choose to be an animal or a machine and thereby may not injure himself, may even gain strength and wealth from an external and material point of view; yet this will be worse than death for him as a man. It has been said in our scriptures: "Through *a-dharma* (the negation of *dharma*) man prospers, gains what appears desirable, conquers enemies, but perishes at the root."

One who is merely a comfortable money-making machine does not carry in himself the perfect manifestation of man. He is like a gaudily embroidered purse which is empty. He raises a rich altar in his life to the blind and deaf image of a yawning negation and all the costly sacrifices continually offered to it are poured into the mouth of an ever hungry abyss. And according to our scriptures, even while he swells and shouts and violently gesticulates, he perishes.

The same idea has been expressed by the great Chinese sage, Lao-tze, in a different manner, when he says: "One who may die, but will not perish, has life everlasting." In this he also suggests that when a man reveals his truth he lives, and that truth itself is *dharma*. Civilisation, according to this ideal should be the expression of man's *dharma* in his corporate life.

We have for over a century been dragged by the prosperous West behind its chariot, choked by the dust, deafened by the noise, humbled by our own helplessness, and overwhelmed by the speed. We agreed to acknowledge that this chariot-drive was progress, and that progress was civilisation. If we ever ventured to ask, 'Progress towards what, and progress for whom?' it was considered to be peculiarly and ridiculously oriental to entertain such doubts about the absoluteness of progress. Of late, a voice has come to us bidding us to take count not only of the scientific perfection of the chariot but of the depth of the ditches lying across its path.

When I was a child I had the freedom to make my own toys out of trifles and create my own games from imagination. In my happiness my playmates had their full share; in fact the complete enjoyment of my games depended upon their taking part in them. One day, in this paradise of our childhood, entered a temptation from the market world of the adult. A toy bought from an English shop was given to one of our companions; it was perfect, big and wonderfully life-like. He became proud of the toy and less mindful of the game; he kept that expensive thing carefully away from us, glorying in his exclusive possession of it, feeling himself superior to his playmates whose toys were cheap. I am sure if he could have used the modern language of history he would have said that he was more civilised than ourselves to the extent of his owning that ridiculously perfect toy.

One thing he failed to realise in his excitement—a fact which at the moment seemed to him insignificant—that this temptation obscured something a great deal more perfect than his toy, the revelation of the perfect child. The toy merely expressed his wealth, but not the child's creative spirit, not the child's generous joy in his play, his open invitation to all who were his compeers to his play-world.

Once there was an occasion for me to motor down to Calcutta from a place a hundred miles away. Something wrong with the mechanism made it necessary for us to have a repeated supply of water almost every half an hour. At the first village where we were compelled to stop, we asked the help of a man to find water for us. It proved quite a task for him, but when we offered him his reward, poor though he was, he refused to accept it. In fifteen other villages the same thing happened. In a hot country where travellers constantly need water, and where the water-supply grows scanty in summer, the villagers consider it their duty to offer water to those who need it. They could easily make a business of it, following the inexorable law of demand and supply. But the ideal which they consider to be their *dharma* has become one with their life. To ask them to sell it, is like asking them to sell their life. They do not claim any personal merit for possessing it.

Lao-tze speaking about the man who is truly good says: "He quickens, but owns not. He acts, but claims not. Merit he accomplishes, but dwells not on it. Since he does not dwell on it, it will never leave him." That which is outside ourselves we can sell, but that which is one with our life we cannot. This complete assimilation of truth belongs to the paradise of perfection; it lies beyond the purgatory of self-consciousness. To have reached it proves a long process of civilisation.

To be able to take a considerable amount of trouble in order to supply water to a passing stranger and yet never to claim merit or reward for it seems absurdly and negligibly simple compared with the capacity to produce an amazing number of things per minute. A millionaire tourist, ready to corner the food market and grow rich by driving the whole world to the brink of starvation, is sure to feel too superior to notice this simple thing while rushing through our villages at sixty miles an hour. For it is not aggressive like a telegraphic pole that pokes our attention with its hugely long finger, or resounding like his own motor engine that shouts its discourtesy to the silent music of the spheres.

Yes, it is simple; but that simplicity is the product of centuries of culture; such simplicity is difficult of imitation. In a few years' time it might be possible for me to learn how to make holes in thousands of needles instantaneously by turning a wheel, but to be absolutely simple in one's hospitality to one's enemy or to a stranger requires generations of training. Simplicity takes no account of its own value, claims no wages, and therefore those who are enamoured of power do not realise that simplicity of spiritual expression is the highest product of civilisation.

A process of disintegration can kill this rare fruit of a higher life, as a whole race of birds possessing some rare beauty can be made extinct by the vulgar power of avarice which has civilised weapons. This fact was clearly proved to me when I found that the only place where a price was expected for the water given to us, was when we reached a suburb of Calcutta, where life was richer, the water-supply easier and more abundant, and where progress flowed in numerous channels in all directions. We must get to know this force of disintegration, and how it works.

Creation is the revelation of truth through the rhythm of form, its dualism consisting of the expression and the material. Of these the material must offer itself as a sacrifice in absolute loyalty to the expression. It must know that it can be no end in itself and therefore by the pressure of its voluminousness it should not carry men away from their creative activities.

In India we have a species of Sanskrit poem in which all the complex grammatical rules are deliberately illustrated. This produces continual sparks of delight in the minds of some readers, who, even in a work of art, seek some tangible proof of power, almost physical in its manifestation. This shows that by special cultivation a kind of mentality can be produced which is capable of taking delight in the mere spectacle of power, manipulating materials, forgetting that

materials have no value of their own. We see the same thing
in the modern western world where progress is measured by
the speed with which materials are multiplying. Their measure
by horse-power is one before which spirit-power has made
itself humble. Horse-power drives, spirit-power sustains. That
which drives is called the principle of progress, that which
sustains we call *dharma*; and this word *dharma* I believe
should be translated as civilisation.

We have heard from the scientist that an atom consists
of a nucleus drawing its companions round it in a rhythm of
dance and thus forms a perfect unit. A civilisation remains
healthy and strong as long as it contains in its centre some
creative ideal that binds its members in a rhythm of relationship.
It is a relationship which is beautiful and not merely utilitarian.
When this creative ideal which is *dharma* gives place to some
overmastering passion, then this civilisation bursts into
conflagration like a star that has lighted its own funeral pyre.
From its modest glow of light this civilisation flares up into
a blaze, only to end in violent extinction.

Western society, for some ages, had for its central motive
force a great spiritual ideal and not merely an impetus to
progress. It had its religious faith which was actively busy in
bringing about reconciliation among the conflicting forces of
society. What it held to be of immense value was the perfection
of human relationship, to be obtained by controlling the
egoistic instincts of man, and by giving him a philosophy of
his fundamental unity. In the course of the last two centuries,
however, the West found access to Nature's storehouse of
power, and ever since all its attention has been irresistibly
drawn in that direction. Its inner ideal of civilisation has thus
been pushed aside by the love of power.

Man's ideal has for its field of activity the whole of human
nature from its depth to its height. The light of this ideal is
gentle because diffused, its life is subdued because all-

embracing. It is serene because it is great; it is meek because it is comprehensive. But our passion is narrow; its limited field gives it an intensity of impulse. Such an aggressive force of greed has of late possessed the western mind. This has happened within a very short period, and has created a sudden deluge of things smothering all time and space over the earth. All that was human is being broken into fragments.

In trying to maintain some semblance of unity among such a chaos of fractions, organisations are established for manufacturing, in a wholesale quantity, peace, or piety, or social welfare. But such organisations can never have the character of a perfect unit. Surely they are needed as we need our drinking vessels, but more for the water than for themselves. They are more burdens by themselves and if we take pleasure in multiplying them indefinitely the result may be astoundingly clever, but unfortunately fatal to life.

I have read somewhere an observation of Plato in which he says: "An intelligent and socialised community will continue to grow only as long as it can remain a unit; beyond that point growth must cease, or the community will disintegrate and cease to be an organic being." That spirit of the unit is only maintained when its nucleus is some living sentiment of *dharma,* leading to cooperation and to a common sharing of life's gifts.

Lao-tze has said: "Not knowing the eternal causes passions to rise; and that is evil. Comforts and conveniences are pursued, things are multiplied, the eternal is obscured, the passions are roused, and the evil marches triumphant from continent to continent mutilating man. And we are asked to build triumphal arches for this march of death. Let us at least refuse to acknowledge its victory, even if we cannot retard its progress. Let us die, as your Lao-tze has said, and yet not perish.

It is said in our scriptures: "In greed is sin, in sin death." The Chinese philosopher has said: "No greater calamity than greed." These sentences carry the wisdom of ages. When greed becomes the dominant character of a people it forebodes destruction for them, and no mere organisation like the League of Nations can ever save them. To let the flood of self-seeking flow unchecked from the heart of the nation and at the same time try to build an outer dam across its path can never succeed. The deluge will burst forth with a greater force because of the resistance. Lao-tze says: "Not self-seeking, he gaineth life." Life's principle is in this and therefore in a society all the training and teachings that make for life are those that help us in our control of selfish greed.

When civilisation was living, that is to say, when most of its movements were related to an inner ideal and not to an external compulsion, then money had not the same value as it has now. Do you not realise what an immense difference that fact has made in our life, and how barbarously it has cheapened those things which are invaluable in our inheritance? We have grown so used to this calamitous change that we do not fully realise the indignity it imposes upon us.

I ask you to imagine a day, if it does ever come, when in a meeting everybody will leave his chair and stand up in awe if a man enters who has a greater number of human skulls strung in his necklace than have his fellow beings. We can have no hesitation today in admitting that this would be pure barbarism. Are there no other tokens of a similar degradation for man—are there no other forms of human skulls than those which the savages so proudly wear?

In olden times the mere hoarding of millions was never considered as wealth unless it had some crown of glory with which to proclaim its ideal greatness. In the East as well as in the West, man in order to save his inherent dignity positively despised money which represented merely a right of possession and no moral responsibility. Money-making as a profession was everywhere contemptuously treated, and men who made big profits the sole end of their life were looked down upon.

There was a time in India when our Brahmins were held in reverence, not only for their learning and purity of life, but for their utter indifference to material wealth. This only shows that our society was fully conscious that its very life depended upon its ideals, which were never to be insulted by anything that belonged to a passion for self-seeking. But because today progress is considered to be characteristic of civilisation, and because this progress goes on gathering an un-ending material extension, money has established its universal sovereignty. For in this world of ambition money is the central power-house sending impulsions in all directions.

In former days, the monarchs of men were not ashamed humbly to pay their respect to men of intellect or those who had spiritual or creative gifts. For the qualities of the higher life were the motive force of the civilisation of those times. But today men, whatever their position, never think that they are humiliating themselves when they offer their homage to men of corpulent cash, not always because they expect any benefit therefrom, but because of the bare fact of its possession. This denotes a defeat of the complete man by the material man. This huge degradation, like a slimy reptile, has spread its coils round the whole human world. Before we can rescue humanity from the bondage of its interminable tail, we must free our mind from the sacrilege of worship offered to this unholy power, this evil dragon which can never be the presiding deity of the civilisation of man.

The danger, however, is not so much from the enemy who attacks, but from the defender who may betray. It fills my heart with a great feeling of dismay when, among the present generation of young men, I see signs of their succumbing to a fascination for mere size and power. They go about seeking for civilisation amongst the wilderness of sky-scrapers, in the shrieking headlines of news-journals, and the shouting vociferation of demagogues. They leave their own great prophets who had a far-seeking vision of truth, and roam in the dusk begging for a loan of light from some glow-worm which can only hold its niggardly lantern for the purpose of crawling towards its nearest dust.

They will learn the meaning of the word civilisation, when they come back home and truly understand what that great master, Lao-tze wanted to teach when he said: "Those who have virtue attend to their obligations; those who have no virtue attend to their claims." In this saying he has expressed in a few words what I have tried to explain in this paper. Progress which is not related to an inner ideal, but to an attraction which is external, seeks to satisfy our endless claims. But civilisation, which is an ideal, gives us power and joy to fulfil our obligations.

About the stiffening of life and hardening of heart caused by the organisation of power and production, he says with profound truth:

"The grass as well as the trees, while they live, are tender, are supple; when they die they are rigid and dry. Thus the hard and the strong are the companions of death. The tender and the delicate are the companions of life. Therefore he who in arms is strong will not conquer. The strong and the great stay below. The tender and the delicate stay above."

Our sage in India says, as I have quoted before: "By the help of *a-dharma* men prosper, they find what they desire, they conquer enemies, but they perish at the root." The wealth which is not welfare grows with a rapid vigour, but it carries within itself the seed of death. This wealth has been nourished in the West by the blood of men and the harvest is ripening. The same warning was given centuries ago by your sage when he said: "Things thrive and then grow old. This is called Un-reason. Unreason soon ceases."

Your teacher has said: "To increase life is called a blessing." For, the increase of life, unlike the increase of things, never transcends the limits of life's unity. The mountain pine grows tall and great, its every inch maintains the rhythm of an inner balance, and therefore even in its seeming extravagance it has the reticent grace of self-control. The tree and its productions belong to the same vital system of cadence; the timber, leaves, flowers and fruits are one with the tree; their exuberance is not a malady of exaggeration, but a blessing. But systems which mainly are for making profits and not for supplying life's needs, encourage an obesity of ugliness in our society, obliterating the fine modulations of personality from its features. Not being one with our life, they do not conform to its rhythm.

Our living society, which should have dance in its steps, music in its voice, beauty in its limbs, which should have its metaphor in stars and flowers, maintaining its harmony with God's creation, becomes, under the tyranny of a prolific greed, like an overladen market-cart, jolting and creaking on the road that leads from things to the Nothing, tearing ugly ruts across the green life till it breaks down under the burden of its vulgarity on the wayside, reaching nowhere. For, this is called Unreason, as your teacher has said, and Unreason soon ceases.

The Religion of an Artist

I was born in 1861: That is not an important date of history, but it belongs to a great epoch in Bengal, when the currents of three movements had met in the life of our country. One of these, the religious, was introduced by a very great-hearted man of gigantic intelligence, Raja Rammohan Roy. It was revolutionary, for he tried to reopen the channel of spiritual life which had been obstructed for many years by the sands and debris of creeds that were formal and materialistic, fixed in external practices lacking spiritual significance. People who cling to an ancient past have their pride in the antiquity of their accumulations, in the sublimity of time-honoured walls around them. They grow nervous and angry when some great spirit, some lover of truth, breaks open their enclosure and floods it with the sunshine of thought and the breath of life. Ideas cause movement and all forward movements they consider to be a menace to their warehouse security.

This was happening about the time I was born. I am proud to say that my father was one of the great leaders of that movement, a movement for whose sake he suffered ostracism and braved social indignities. I was born in this atmosphere of the advent of new ideals, which at the same time were old, older than all the things of which that age was proud.

There was a second movement equally important. Bankimchandra Chatterjee, who, though much older than myself, was my contemporary and lived long enough for me to see him, was the first pioneer in the literary revolution which happened in Bengal about that time. Before his arrival our literature had been oppressed by a rigid rhetoric that choked its life and loaded it with ornaments that became its fetters. Bankimchandra was brave enough to go against the orthodoxy which believed in the security of tombstones and in that finality which can only belong to the lifeless. He lifted the dead weight of ponderous forms from our language and with a touch of his magic wand aroused our literature from her age-long sleep. A great promise and a vision of beauty she revealed to us when she awoke in the fulness of her strength and grace.

There was yet another movement started about this time called the National. It was not fully political, but it began to give voice to the mind of our people trying to assert their own personality. It was a voice of impatience at the humiliation constantly heaped upon us by people who were not oriental, and who had, especially at that time, the habit of sharply dividing the human world into the good and the bad according to the hemispheres to which they belong.

This contemptuous spirit of separatedness was perpetually hurting us and causing great damage to our own world of culture. It generated in our young men a distrust of all things that had come to them as an inheritance from their past. The old Indian pictures and other works of art were laughed at by our students in imitation of the laughter of their European schoolmasters of that age of philistinism.

Though later on our teachers themselves had changed their mind, their disciples had hardly yet fully regained confidence in the merit of our art. They have had a long period of encouragement in developing an appetite for third-rate copies of French pictures, for gaudy oleographs abjectly cheap, for the pictures that are products of mechanical accuracy of a stereotyped standard, and they still considered it to be a symptom of superior culture to be able disdainfully to refuse oriental works of creation.

The modern young men of that period nodded their heads and said that true originality lay not in the discovery of the rhythm of the essential in the heart of reality but in the full lips, tinted cheeks and bare breasts of imported pictures. The same spirit of rejection, born of utter ignorance, was cultivated in other departments of our culture. It was the result of the hypnotism exercised upon the minds of the younger generation by people who were loud of voice and strong of arm. The national movement was started to proclaim that we must not be indiscriminate in our rejection of the past. This was not a reactionary movement but a revolutionary one, because it set out with a great courage to deny and to oppose all pride in mere borrowings.

These three movements were on foot and in all three the members of my own family took active part. We were ostracised because of our heterodox opinions about religion and therefore we enjoyed the freedom of the outcast. We had to build our own world with our own thoughts and energy of mind.

I was born and brought up in an atmosphere of the confluence of three movements, all of which were revolutionary. My family had to live its own life, which led me from my young days to seek guidance for my own self-expression in my own inner standard of judgement. The medium of expression doubtless was my mother tongue. But the language which belonged to the people had to be modulated according to the urge which I as an individual had.

No poet should borrow his medium ready-made from some shop of orthodox respectability. He should not only have his own seeds but prepare his own soil. Each poet has his own distinct medium of language—not because the whole language is of his own make, but because his individual use of it, having life's magic touch, transforms it into a special vehicle of his own creation.

The races of man have poetry in their heart and it is necessary for them to give, as far as is possible, a perfect expression to their sentiments. For this they must have a medium, moving and pliant, which can freshly become their very own, age after age. All great languages have undergone and are still undergoing changes. Those languages which resist the spirit of change are doomed and will never produce great harvests of thought and literature. When forms become fixed, the spirit either weakly accepts its imprisonment within them or rebels. All revolutions consist of the fight of the within against invasion by the without.

There was a great chapter in the history of life on this earth when some irresistible inner force in man found its way out into the scheme of things, and sent forth its triumphant mutinous voice, with the cry that it was not going to be overwhelmed from outside by the huge brute beast of a body. How helpless it appeared at the moment, but has it not nearly won? In our social life also, revolution breaks out when some power concentrates itself in outside arrangements and threatens to enslave for its own purpose the power which we have within us.

When an organisation which is a machine becomes a central force, political, commercial, educational or religious, it obstructs the free flow of inner life of the people and waylays and exploits it for the augmentation of its own power. Today, such concentration of power is fast multiplying on the outside and the cry of the oppressed spirit of man is in the air which struggles to free itself from the grip of screws and bolts, of unmeaning obsessions.

Revolution must come and men must risk revilement and misunderstanding, especially from those who want to be comfortable, who put their faith in materialism, and who belong truly to the dead past and not to modern times, the past that had its age in distant antiquity when physical flesh and size predominated, and not the mind of man.

Purely physical dominance is mechanical and modern machines are merely exaggerating our bodies, lengthening and multiplying our limbs. The modern mind, in its innate childishness, delights in this enormous bodily bulk, representing an inordinate material power saying: "Let me have the big toy and no sentiment which can disturb it." It does not realise that in this we are returning to that antediluvian age which revelled in its production of gigantic physical frames, leaving no room for the freedom of the inner spirit.

All great human movements in the world are related to some great ideal. Some of you may say that such a doctrine of spirit has been in its death throes for over a century and is now moribund; that we have nothing to rely upon but external forces and material foundations. But I say, on my part, that your doctrine was obsolete long ago. It was exploded in the springtime of life, when mere size was swept off the face of the world, and was replaced by man, brought naked into the heart of creation, man with his helpless body, but with his indomitable mind and spirit.

When I began my life as a poet, the writers among our educated community took their guidance from their English text-books which poured upon them lessons that did not fully saturate their minds. I suppose it was fortunate for me that I never in my life had the kind of academic training which is considered proper for a boy of respectable family. Though I cannot say I was altogether free from the influence that ruled young minds of those days, the course of my writings was nevertheless saved from the groove of imitative forms. In my versification, vocabulary and ideas, I yielded myself to the vagaries of an untutored fancy which brought castigation upon me from critics who were learned, and uproarious laughter from the witty. My ignorance combined with my heresy turned me into a literary outlaw.

When I began my career I was ridiculously young; in fact, I was the youngest of that band who had made themselves articulate. I had neither the protective armour of mature age, nor enough English to command respect. So in my seclusion of contempt and qualified encouragement I had my freedom. Gradually I grew up in years—for which, however, I claim no credit. Steadily I cut my way through derision and occasional patronage into a recognition in which the proportion of praise and blame was very much like that of land and water on our earth.

What gave me boldness when I was young was my early acquaintance with the old Vaishnava poems of Bengal, full of the freedom of metre and courage of expression. I think I was only twelve when these poems first began to be reprinted. I surreptitiously got hold of copies from the desks of my elders. For the edification of the young I must confess that this was not right for a boy of my age. I should have been passing my examinations and not following a path that would lead to loss of marks. I must also admit that the greater part of these lyrics was erotic and not quite suited to a boy just about to reach his teens. But my imagination was fully occupied with the beauty of their forms and the music of their words; and their breath, heavily laden with voluptuousness, passed over my mind without distracting it.

My vagabondage in the path of my literary career had another reason. My father was the leader of a new religious movement, a strict monotheism based upon the teachings of the *Upanishads*. My countrymen in Bengal thought him almost as bad as a Christian, if not worse. So we were completely ostracised, which probably saved me from another disaster, that of imitating our own past.

Most of the members of my family had some gift—some were artists, some poets, some musicians and the whole atmosphere of our home was permeated with the spirit of creation. I had a deep sense almost from infancy of the beauty of Nature, an intimate feeling of companionship with the trees and the clouds, and felt in tune with the musical touch of the seasons in the air. At the same time, I had a peculiar susceptibility to human kindness. All these craved expression. The very earnestness of my emotions yearned to be true to themselves, though I was too immature to give their expression any perfection of form.

Since then I have gained a reputation in my country, but till very late a strong current of antagonism in a large section of my countrymen persisted. Some said that my poems did not spring from the national heart; some complained that they were incomprehensible; others that they were unwholesome. In fact, I have never had complete acceptance from my own people, and that too has been a blessing; for nothing is so demoralising as unqualified success.

This is the history of my career. I wish I could reveal it more clearly through the narration of my own work in my own language. I hope that will be possible some day or other. Languages are jealous. They do not give up their best treasures to those who try to deal with them through an intermediary belonging to an alien rival. We have to court them in person and dance attendance on them. Poems are not like market commodities transferable. We cannot receive the smiles and glances of our sweetheart through an attorney, however diligent and dutiful he may be.

I myself have tried to get at the wealth of beauty in the literature of the European languages, long before I gained a full right to their hospitality. When I was young I tried to approach Dante, unfortunately through an English translation.

I failed utterly, and felt it my pious duty to desist. Dante remained a closed book to me.

I also wanted to know German literature and, by reading Heine in translation, I thought I had caught a glimpse of the beauty there. Fortunately I met a missionary lady from Germany and asked her help. I worked hard for some months, but being rather quick-witted, which is not a good quality, I was not persevering. I had the dangerous facility which helps one to guess the meaning too easily. My teacher thought I had almost mastered the language, which was not true. I succeeded, however, in getting through Heine, like a man walking in sleep crossing unknown paths with ease, and I found immense pleasure.

Then I tried Goethe. But that was too ambitious. With the help of the little German I had learnt, I did go through *Faust*. I believe I found my entrance to the palace, not like one who has keys for all the doors, but as a casual visitor who is tolerated in some general guest-room, comfortable but not intimate. Properly speaking, I do not know my Goethe, and in the same way many other great luminaries are dusky to me.

This is as it should be. Man cannot reach the shrine if he does not make the pilgrimage. So, one must not hope to find anything true from my own language in translation.

In regard to music, I claim to be something of a musician myself. I have composed many songs which have defied the canons of orthodox propriety and good people are disgusted at the impudence of a man who is audacious only because he is untrained. But I persist, and God forgives me because I do not know what I do. Possibly that is the best way of doing things in the sphere of art. For I find that people blame, but also sing my songs, even if not always correctly.

Please do not think I am vain. I can judge myself objectively and can openly express admiration for my own work, because

I am modest. I do not hesitate to say that my songs have found their place in the heart of my land, along with her flowers that are never exhausted, and that the folk of the future, in days of joy or sorrow or festival, will have to sing them. This too is the work of a revolutionist.

If I feel reluctant to speak about my own view of religion, it is because I have not come to my own religion through the portals of passive acceptance of a particular creed owing to some accident of birth. I was born to a family who were pioneers in the revival in our country of a religion based upon the utterance of Indian sages in the *Upanishads*. But owing to my idiosyncrasy of temperament, it was impossible for me to accept any religious teaching on the only ground that people in my surroundings believed it to be true. I could not persuade myself to imagine that I had religion simply because everybody whom I might trust believed in its value.

My religion is essentially a poet's religion. Its touch comes to me through the same unseen and trackless channels as does the inspiration of my music. My religious life has followed the same mysterious line of growth as has my poetical life. Somehow they are wedded to each other, and though their betrothal had a long period of ceremony, it was kept secret from me. I am not, I hope, boasting when I confess to my gift of poesy, an instrument of expression delicately responsive to the breath that comes from depth of feeling. From my infancy I had the keen sensitiveness which always kept my mind tingling with consciousness of the world around me, natural and human.

I had been blessed with that sense of wonder which gives a child his right of entry into the treasure-house of mystery which is in the heart of existence. I neglected my studies because they rudely summoned me away from the world around me, which was my friend and my companion, and when I was thirteen I freed myself from the clutch of an educational system that tried to keep me imprisoned within the stone-walls of lessons.

I had a vague notion as to who or what it was that touched my heart's chords, like the infant which does not know its mother's name, or who or what she is. The feeling which I always had was a deep satisfaction of personality that flowed into my nature through living channels of communication from all sides.

It was a great thing for me that my consciousness was never dull about the facts of the surrounding world. That the cloud was the cloud, that a flower was a flower, was enough, because they directly spoke to me, because I could not be indifferent to them. I still remember the very moment, one afternoon, when coming back from school I alighted from the carriage and suddenly saw in the sky, behind the upper terrace of our house, an exuberance of deep, dark rain-clouds lavishing rich, cool shadows on the atmosphere. The marvel of it, the very generosity of its presence, gave me a joy which was freedom, the freedom we feel in the love of our dear friend.

There is an illustration I have made use of in another paper, in which I supposed that a stranger from some other planet has paid a visit to our earth and happens to hear the sound of a human voice on the gramophone. All that is obvious to him, and most seemingly active, is the revolving disk; he is unable to discover the personal truth that lies behind, and so might accept the impersonal scientific fact of the disk as final—the fact that could be touched and measured. He would wonder how it could be possible for a machine to speak to the soul. Then if in pursuing the mystery, he should suddenly come to the heart of the music through a meeting with the composer, he would at once understand the meaning of that music as a personal communication.

Mere information of facts, mere discovery of power, belongs to the outside and not to the inner soul of things.

Gladness is the one criterion of truth as we know when we have touched Truth by the music it gives, by the joy of the greeting it sends forth to the truth in us. That is the true foundation of all religions; it is not in dogma. As I have said before, it is not as ether waves that we receive light; the morning does not wait for some scientist for its introduction to us. In the same way, we touch the infinite reality immediately within us only when we perceive the pure truth of love or goodness, not through the explanation of theologians, not through the erudite discussion of ethical doctrines.

I have already confessed that my religion is a poet's religion; all that I feel about it is from vision and not from knowledge. I frankly say that I cannot satisfactorily answer questions about the problem of evil, or about what happens after death. And yet I am sure that there have come moments when my soul has touched the infinite and has become intensely conscious of it through the illumination of joy. It has been said in our *Upanishads* that our mind and our words come away baffled from the supreme Truth, but he who knows that, through the immediate joy of his own soul, is saved from all doubts and fears.

In the night we stumble over things and become acutely conscious of their individual separateness, but the day reveals the great unity which embraces them. And the man, whose inner vision is bathed in an illumination of his consciousness, at once realises the spiritual unity reigning supreme over all differences of race and his mind no longer awkwardly stumbles over individual facts of separateness in the human world, accepting them as final; he realises that peace is in the inner harmony which dwells in truth, and not in any outer adjustments; and that beauty carries an eternal assurance of our spiritual relationship to reality, which waits for its perfection in the response of our love.

II

The renowned Vedic commentator, Sāyanāchārya, says:

Jajne hutāvaśishasya odanasya
Sarvajagatkāranabhuta brahmābhedena stutih kriyate.

The food offering which is left over after the completion of sacrificial rites is praised because it is symbolical of Brahma, the original source of the universe.

According to this explanation, Brahma is boundless in his superfluity which inevitably finds its expression in the eternal world process. Here we have the doctrine of the genesis of creation, and therefore of the origin of art. Of all living creatures in the world, man has his vital and mental energy vastly in excess of his need, which urges him to work in various lines of creation for its own sake. Like Brahma himself, he takes joy in productions that are unnecessary to him, and therefore representing his extravagance and not his hand-to-mouth penury. The voice that is just enough can speak and cry to the extent needed for everyday use, but that which is abundant sings, and in it we find our joy. Art reveals man's wealth of life, which seeks its freedom in forms of perfection which are an end in themselves.

All that is inert and inanimate is limited to the bare fact of existence. Life is perpetually creative because it contains in itself that surplus which ever overflows the boundaries of the immediate time and space, restlessly pursuing its adventure of expression in the varied forms of self-realisation. Our living body has its vital organs that are important in maintaining its efficiency, but this body is not a mere convenient sac for the purpose of holding stomach, heart, lungs and brains; it is an image—its highest value is in the fact that it communicates its personality. It has colour, shape and movement, most of which belong to the superfluous, that are needed only for self-expression and not for self-preservation.

This living atmosphere of superfluity in man is dominated by his imagination, as the earth's atmosphere by the light. It helps us to integrate desultory facts in a vision of harmony and then to translate it into our activities for the very joy of its perfection, it invokes in us the Universal Man who is the seer and the doer of all times and countries. The immediate consciousness of reality in its purest form, unobscured by the shadow of self-interest, irrespective of moral or utilitarian recommendation, gives us joy as does the self-revealing personality of our own. What in common language we call beauty, which is in harmony of lines, colours, sounds, or in grouping of words or thoughts, delights us only because we cannot help admitting a truth in it that is ultimate. "Love is enough", the poet has said; it carries its own explanation, the joy of which can only be expressed in a form of art which also has that finality. Love gives evidence to something which is outside us but which intensely exists and thus stimulates the sense of our own existence. It radiantly reveals the reality of its objects, though these may lack qualities that are valuable or brilliant.

The 'I am' in me realises its own extension, its own infinity whenever it truly realises something else. Unfortunately, owing to our limitations and a thousand and one preoccupations, a great part of our world though closely surrounding us, is far away from the lamp-post of our attention: it is dim, it passes by us, a caravan of shadows, like the landscape seen in the night from the window of an illuminated railway compartment: the passenger knows that the outside world exists, that it is important, but for the time being the railway carriage for him is far more significant. If among the innumerable objects in this world there be a few that come under the full illumination of our soul and thus assume reality for us, they constantly cry to our creative mind for a permanent representation. They belong to the same domain as the desire of ours which represents the longing for the permanence of our own self.

I do not mean to say that things to which we are bound by the tie of self-interest have the inspiration of reality; on the contrary, these are eclipsed by the shadow of our own self. The servant is not more real to us than the beloved. The narrow emphasis of utility diverts our attention from the complete man to the merely useful man. The thick label of market-price obliterates the ultimate value of reality.

That fact that we exist has its truth in the fact that everything else does exist, and the 'I am' in me crosses its finitude whenever it deeply realises itself in the 'Thou art'. This crossing of the limit produces joy, the joy that we have in beauty, in love, in greatness. Self-forgetting, and in a higher degree, self-sacrifice, is our acknowledgment of this our experience of the infinite. This is the philosophy which explains our joy in all arts, the arts that in their creations intensify the sense of the unity which is the unity of truth we carry within ourselves. The personality in me is a self-conscious principle of a living unity; it at once comprehends and yet transcends all the details of facts that are individually mine, my knowledge, feeling, wish and will, my memory, my hope, my love, my activities, and all my belongings. This personality which has the sense of the 'One' in its nature, realises it in things, thoughts and facts made into units. The principle of unity which it contains is more or less perfectly satisfied in a beautiful face or a picture, a poem, a song, a character or a harmony of inter-related ideas or facts and then for it these things become intensely real, and therefore joyful. Its standard of reality, the reality that has its perfect revelation in a perfection of harmony, is hurt when there is a consciousness of discord—because discord is against the fundamental unity which is in its centre.

All other facts have come to us through the gradual course of our experience, and our knowledge of them is constantly undergoing contradictory changes through the discovery of new data. We can never be sure that we have come to know the final character of anything that there is. But such a knowledge has come to us immediately with a conviction which needs no arguments to support it. It is this, that all my activities have their sources in this personality of mine which is indefinable and yet about the truth of which I am more certain than anything in this world. Though all the direct evidence that can be weighed and measured support the fact that only my fingers are producing marks on the paper, yet no sane man ever can doubt that it is not these mechanical movements that are the true origin of my writings but some entity that can never be known, unless known through sympathy. Thus we have come to realise in our own person the two aspects of activities, one of which is the aspect of law represented in the medium, and the other the aspect of will residing in the personality.

Limitation of the unlimited is personality: God is personal where he creates. He accepts the limits of his own law and the play goes on, which is this world whose reality is in its relation to the Person. Things are distinct not in their essence but in their appearance; in other words, in their relation to one to whom they appear. This is art, the truth of which is not in substance or logic, but in expression. Abstract truth may belong to science and metaphysics, but the world of reality belongs to Art.

The world as an art is the play of the Supreme Person revelling in image making. Try to find out the ingredients of the image—they elude you, they never reveal to you the eternal secret of appearance. In your effort to capture life as expressed in living tissue, you will find carbon, nitrogen and many other things utterly unlike life, but never life itself. The appearance does not offer any commentary of itself through its material. You may call it *māyā* and pretend to disbelieve it, but the great artist, the *māyāvin,* is not hurt. For art is *māyā,* it has no other explanation but that it seems to be what it is. It never tries to conceal its evasiveness, it mocks even its own definition and plays the game of hide-and-seek through its constant flight in changes.

And thus life, which is an incessant explosion of freedom, finds its metre in a continual falling back in death. Every day is a death, every moment even. If not, there would be amorphous desert of deathlessness eternally dumb and still. So life is *māyā* as moralists love to say, it *is* and *is not.* All that we find in it is the rhythm through which it shows itself. Are rocks and minerals any better? Has not science shown us the fact that the ultimate difference between one element and another is only that of rhythm? The fundamental distinction of gold from mercury lies merely in the difference of rhythm in their respective atomic constitution, like the distinction of the king from his subject which is not in their different constituents, but in the different metres of their situation and circumstance. There you find behind the scene the Artist, the Magician of rhythm, who imparts an appearance of substance to the unsubstantial.

What is rhythm? It is the movement generated and regulated by harmonious restriction. This is the creative force in the hand of the artist. So long as words remain in uncadenced prose form, they do not give any lasting-feeling of reality. The moment they are taken and put into rhythm they vibrate into a radiance. It is the same with the rose. In the pulp of its petals you may find everything that went to make the rose, but the rose which is *māyā,* an image, is lost; its finality which has the touch of the infinite is gone. The rose appears to me to be still, but because of its metre of composition it has a lyric of movement within that stillness, which is the same as the dynamic quality of a picture that has a perfect harmony. It produces a music in our consciousness by giving it a swing of motion synchronous with its own. Had the picture consisted of a disharmonious aggregate of colours and lines, it would be deadly still.

In perfect rhythm, the art-form becomes like the stars which in their seeming stillness are never still, like a motionless flame that is nothing but movement. A great picture is always speaking, but news from a newspaper, even of some tragic happening, is still-born. Some news may be a mere commonplace in the obscurity of a journal; but give it a proper rhythm and it will never cease to shine. That is art. It has the magic wand which gives undying reality to all things it touches, and relates them to the personal being in us. We stand before its productions and say: I know you as I know myself, you are real.

A Chinese friend of mine, while travelling with me through the streets of Peking, suddenly, with great excitement, called my attention to a donkey. Ordinarily a donkey does not have any special force of truth for us, except when it kicks us or when we need its reluctant service. But in such cases, the truth is not emphasised in the donkey but in some purpose or bodily pain exterior to it. The behaviour of my Chinese friend at once reminded me of the Chinese poems in which the delightful sense of reality is so spontaneously felt and so simply expressed.

This sensitiveness to the touch of things, such abundant delight in the recognition of them, is obstructed when insistent purposes become innumerable and intricate in our society, when problems crowd in our path clamouring for attention, and life's movement is impeded with things and thoughts too difficult for a harmonious assimilation.

This has been growing evident every day in the modern age, which gives more time to the acquisition of life's equipment than to the enjoyment of it. In fact, life itself is made secondary to life's materials, even like a garden buried under the bricks gathered for the garden wall. Somehow the mania for bricks and mortar grows, the kingdom of rubbish dominates, the days of spring are made futile and the flowers never come.

Our modern mind, a hasty tourist, in its rush over the miscellaneous, ransacks cheap markets of curios which mostly are delusions. This happens because its natural sensibility for simple aspects of existence is dulled by constant preoccupations that divert it. The literature that it produces seems always to be poking her nose into out-of-the-way places for things and effects that are out of the common. She racks her resources in order to be striking. She elaborates inconstant changes in style, as in modern millinery; and the product suggests more the polish of steel than the bloom of life.

Fashions in literature that rapidly tire of themselves seldom come from the depth. They belong to the frothy rush of the surface, with its boisterous clamours for the recognition of the moment. Such literature, by its very strain, exhausts its inner development and quickly passes through outer changes like autumn leaves—produces with the help of paints and patches an up-to-dateness, shaming its own appearance of the immediately preceding date. Its expressions are often grimaces, like the cactus of the desert which lacks modesty in its distortions and peace in its thorns, in whose attitude an aggressive discourtesy bristles up, suggesting a forced pride of poverty. We often come across its analogy in some of the modern writings which are difficult to ignore because of their prickly surprises and paradoxical gesticulations. Wisdom is not rare in these works, but it is a wisdom that has lost confidence in its serene dignity, afraid of being ignored by crowds which are attracted by the extravagant and the unusual. It is sad to see wisdom struggling to seem clever, a prophet arrayed in caps and bells before an admiring multitude.

But in all great arts, literary or otherwise, man has expressed his feelings that are usual in a form that is unique and yet not abnormal. When Wordsworth described in his poem a life deserted by love, he invoked for his art the usual pathos expected by all normal minds in connection with such a subject. But the picture in which he incarnated the sentiment was unexpected and yet every sane reader acknowledges it with joy when the image is held before him of

> *...a forsaken bird's nest filled with snow*
> Mid its own bush of leafless eglantine.

On the other hand, I have read some modern writing in which the coming out of the stars in the evening is described as the sudden eruption of disease in the bloated body of darkness. The writer seems afraid to own the feeling of a cool purity in the star-sprinkled night which is usual lest he should be found out as commonplace. From the point of view of realism the image may not be wholly inappropriate and may be considered as outrageously virile in its unshrinking incivility. But this is not art; this is a jerky shriek, something like the convulsive advertisement of the modern market that exploits mob psychology against its inattention. To be tempted to create an illusion of forcefulness through an over-emphasis of abnormally is a sign of anaesthesia. It is the waning vigour of imagination which employs desperate dexterity in the present-day art for producing shocks in order to poke out into a glare the sensation of the unaccustomed. When we find that the literature of any period is laborious in the pursuit of a spurious novelty in its manner and matter, we must know that it is the symptom of old age, of anaemic sensibility which seeks to stimulate its palsied taste with the pungency of indecency and the tingling touch of intemperance. It has been explained to me that these symptoms mostly are the outcome of a reaction against the last-century literature which developed a mannerism too daintily saccharin, unmanly in the luxury of its toilet and over-delicacy of its expressions. It seemed to have reached an extreme limit of refinement which almost codified its conventions, making it easy for the timid talents to reach a comfortable level of literary respectability. This explanation may be true; but unfortunately reactions seldom have the repose of spontaneity, they often represent the obverse side of the mintage which they try to repudiate as false. A reaction against a particular mannerism is liable to produce its own mannerism in a militant fashion, using the toilet preparation of the war paint, deliberately manufactured style of primitive rudeness. Tired of the elaborately planned flowerbeds, the gardener proceeds with grim determination to set up everywhere artificial rocks, avoiding natural inspiration of rhythm in deference to a fashion of tyranny which itself is a tyranny of fashion. The same herd instinct is followed in a cult of rebellion as it was in the cult of conformity and the defiance, which is a mere counteraction of obedience, also shows obedience in a defiant fashion. Fanaticism of virility produces a brawny athleticism meant for a circus and not the natural chivalry which is modest but invincible, claiming its sovereign seat of honour in all arts.

It has often been said by its advocates that this show of the rudely loud and cheaply lurid in art has its justification in the unbiased recognition of facts as such; and according to them realism must not be shunned even if it be ragged and evil-smelling. But when it does not concern science but concerns the arts we must draw a distinction between realism and reality. In its own wide perspective of normal environment, disease is a reality which has to be acknowledged in literature. But disease in a hospital is realism fit for the use of science. It is an abstraction which, if allowed to haunt literature, may assume a startling appearance because of its unreality. Such vagrant spectres do not have a proper modulation in a normal surrounding; and they offer a false proportion in their feature because the proportion of their environment is tampered with. Such a curtailment of the essential is not art, but a trick which exploits mutilation in order to assert a false claim to reality. Unfortunately men are not rare who believe that what forcibly startles them allows them to see more than the facts which are balanced and restrained, which they have to woo and win. Very likely, owing to the lack of leisure, such persons are growing in number, and the dark cellars of sex-psychology and drug-stores of moral virulence are burgled to give them the stimulus which they wish to believe to be the stimulus of aesthetic reality.

I know a simple line sung by some primitive folk in our neighbourhood which I translate thus: "My heart is like a pebble-bed hiding a foolish stream." The psycho-analyst may classify it as an instance of repressed desire and thus at once degrade it to a mere specimen advertising a supposed fact, as it does a piece of coal suspected of having smuggled within its dark the flaming wine of the sun of a forgotten age. But it is literature; and what might have been the original stimulus that startled this thought into a song the significant fact about it is that it has taken the shape of an image, a creation of a uniquely personal and yet universal character. The facts of the repression of a desire are numerously common; but this particular expression is singularly uncommon. The listener's mind is touched not because it is a psychological fact, but because it is an individual poem, representing a personal reality, belonging to all time and place in the human world.

But this is not all. This poem no doubt owed its form to the touch of the person who produced it; but at the same time with a gesture of utter detachment, it has transcended its material—the emotional mood of the author. It has gained its freedom from any biographical bondage by taking a rhythmic perfection which is precious in its own exclusive merit. There is a poem which confesses by its title its origin in a mood of dejection. Nobody can say that to a lucid mind the feeling of despondency has anything pleasantly memorable. Yet these verses are not allowed to be forgotten, because directly a poem is fashioned, it is eternally freed from its genesis, it minimises its history and emphasises its independence. The sorrow which was solely personal in an emperor was liberated directly it took the form of verses in stone, it became a triumph of lament, an overflow of delight, hiding the black boulder of its suffering source. The same thing is true of all creation. A dewdrop is a perfect integrity that has no filial memory of its parentage.

When I use the word creation, I mean that through it some imponderable abstractions have assumed a concrete unity in its relation to us. Its substance can be analysed but not this unity which is in its self-introduction. Literature as an art offers us the mystery which is in its unity.

We read the poem:

> Never seek to tell thy love
>   Love that never told can be;
> For the gentle wind does move
>   Silently, invisibly.
> I told my love, I told my love,
>   I told all my heart;
> Trembling cold in ghastly fears
>   Ah, she did depart.
> Soon as she was gone from me
>   A traveller came by;
> Silently, invisibly,
>   He took her with a sigh.

It has its grammar, its vocabulary. When we divide them part by part and try to torture out a confession from them, the poem which is 'one' departs like the gentle wind, silently, invisibly. No one knows how it exceeds all its parts, transcends all its laws, and communicates with the person. The significance which is in unity is an eternal wonder.

As for the definite meaning of the poem, we may have our doubts. If it were told in ordinary prose, we might feel impatient and be roused to contradict it. We would certainly have asked for an explanation as to who the traveller was and why he took away love without any reasonable provocation. But in this poem we need not ask for an explanation unless we are hopelessly addicted to meaning-collection which is like the collection mania for dead butterflies. The poem as a creation, which is something more than as an idea, inevitably conquers our attention; and any meaning which we feel in its words is like the feeling in a beautiful face of a smile that is inscrutable, elusive and profoundly satisfactory.

The unity as a poem introduces itself in a rhythmic language in a gesture of character. Rhythm is not merely in some measured blending of words, but in a significant adjustment of ideas, in a music of thought produced by a subtle principle of distribution, which is not primarily logical but evidential. The meaning which the word 'character' contains is difficult to define. It is comprehended in a special grouping of aspects which gives it an irresistible impetus. The combination it represents may be uncouth, may be unfinished, discordant; yet it has a dynamic vigour in its totality which claims recognition, often against our wishes for the assent of our reason. An avalanche has a character, which even a heavier pile of snow has not; its character is in its massive movement, its incalculable possibilities.

It is for the artist to remind the world that with the truth of our expression we grow in truth. When the man-made world is less an expression of man's creative soul than a mechanical device for some purpose of power, then it hardens itself, acquiring proficiency at the cost of the subtle suggestiveness of living growth. In his creative activities man makes Nature instinct with his own life and love. But with his utilitarian energies he fights Nature, banishes her from his world, deforms and defiles her with the ugliness of his ambitions.

This world of man's own manufacture, with its discordant shrieks and swagger, impresses on him the scheme of a universe which has no touch of the person and therefore no ultimate significance. All the great civilisations that have become extinct must have come to their end through such wrong expression of humanity; through parasitism on a gigantic scale bred by wealth, by man's clinging reliance on material resources; through a scoffing spirit of denial, of negation, robbing us of our means of sustenance in the path of truth.

It is for the artist to proclaim his faith in the everlasting yes—to say: "I believe that there is an ideal hovering over and permeating the earth, an ideal of that Paradise which is not the mere outcome of fancy, but the ultimate reality in which all things dwell and move."

I believe that the vision of Paradise is to be seen in the sunlight and the green of the earth, in the beauty of the human face and the wealth of human life, even in objects that are seemingly insignificant and unprepossessing. Everywhere in this earth the spirit of Paradise is awake and sending forth its voice. It reaches our inner ear without our knowing it. It tunes our harp of life which sends our aspiration in music beyond the finite, not only in prayers and hopes, but also in temples which are flames of fire in stone, in pictures which are dreams made everlasting, in the dance which is ecstatic meditation in the still centre of movement.

The Principle of Literature

In the world of our fairy tales, the son of the Detective, the son of the Merchant and the son of the King set forth in the adventurous quest of the Princess: the Truth, represented by her, is approached from three sides by three different types of mind.

The process which one of them follows is, by analysis, to find in her the secrets of body and mind; but in this region of science, she is of no more value than any other girl—there is no difference between Princess and scullery-maid. The Detective, be he scientist or philosopher, has nothing to do with feeling, no sense even of utility, all he has is the spirit of Question.

The Princess has another aspect—that in which she is useful. She spins, weaves and embroiders. The eyes with which the Merchant's son observes her—turning her spindle, wielding her shuttle, plying her needle—have in their gaze neither feeling, nor questioning, but only calculation.

The King's son is not physiologist or psychologist, nor has he passed any examination in economics. What he has passed, methinks, is just his twenty-fourth year, and also the impassable heath of the fairy tales. He has crossed difficult paths, not for learning, nor for riches, but for the Princess herself, whose palace is not in the laboratory, nor in the market-place, but in that heart's paradise of Eternal Spring where bloom the flowers in the poet's bower of phantasy.

That which is not known by logic, which defies definition, whose value is not in any practical use, but which can only be intimately felt, finds its expression in literature, is the subject of aesthetics. No man who has the gift of enjoyment ever nags or pokes any creation of art with the questions: Why art thou here? What art thou?—He exclaims: It is enough for me that thou art thyself! This was what the King's son whispered in the ear of the Princess, and it was for the proper utterance of these very words that Shahjahan was compelled to build the Taj Mahal.

We can only define that which can be measured; that which is immeasurable, which eludes all attempts at capture, is not attainable by reason, but *by* immediate perception. The *Upanishad* says of the Infinite Being that we can reach Him not with speech, nor with the mind, but by our consciousness of delight, wherewith all fear departs from us. Our soul has her hunger for this immediateness of realisation, whereby she is enabled also to know herself. The love, the contemplation, the vision that alone can satisfy this hunger finds its place in literature, in art.

The space enclosed within walls has been appropriated by my business office, which there buys and sells, pays and charges rent, by the yard. Outside, where is the assembly of stars, undivided space is realised by me through my sense of joy in the boundless. This vastness is superfluous for the purpose of mere physical life, as is proved by the worms that burrow underground. There are in this world also human worms for whom a dearth of sky is no privation; for in them has been killed the mind that cannot live without expanding its wings outside the prison bars of necessity. It was the tyranny of the ghosts of such dead souls that frightened the poet into the prayer:

Doom me not to the futility
Of offering things of joy to the callous!

But the heart of the King's son is fresh and sensitive. He realises in the Princess that sweep of immensity which is in the sky lighted by the eternal stars; and his response to the sight of her is as befits such realisation. The others behave differently. To measure the rhythm of the heart-throbs of the King's daughter, the scientist has no compunction in improvising a tube of tin. The Merchant finds his satisfaction in the tin-can wherein he safe-keeps the cream churned by the Princess' own hand. But the King's son does not so much as dream of ordering tin armlets for the Princess—should he perchance do so it would be for him a veritable nightmare. If, when he wakes, he happens to find gold scarce, he is forthwith impelled to sally forth in search of rose buds for her.

From this can be understood why, in Sanskrit, rhetoric is called the grammar of ornament. Ornament is the symbol of the ultimate. The mother who finds the finality of her joy in her babe, translates this absolute consciousness of hers into the adornments wherewith she decks its body. We view our servant within fixed limits and our return for his service is likewise limited to a fixed salary. But we view our friend in the unlimited, so ornaments blossom forth in our language and behaviour, in the tone of our voice, our smile, our welcome. In literature we speak of him with decorated words, of which the significance is not in their meaning, but in their feeling the message whereof is brought home by the ring of their melody. The appearances, the thoughts, the dreams which are not made manifest through reasoning—these are of literature.

What in English is called real, is in our language called *sārthaka*.[1] Common truth is one thing, significant truth quite another. Common truth does not admit of selection, it is the

---

1. Significant.

significant that is select Men of every sort come under the head of common truth, the man of significance is hardly to be found in a million. When, on the impulse of his profound pity, Valmiki was stirred to metrical utterance, it was only with the aid of Rishi Narada that he could find a real man, of a significance worthy of his metre.

Not that significantly real things are rare, but anything that is not significant to me is not real for me. Because the world of reality has more extensive boundaries for the poet and the artist, they can bring out the significance of a much larger variety of things. For, in whatsoever we are made aware of some ideal of completeness, that becomes significant to us. A grain of sand is nothing to me, but a lotus flower has for me the full force of certitude. Though at every step the sand may obtrude itself on my attention—grating on my feet, irritating my eye, setting my teeth on edge—nevertheless it has not for me any fulness of truth. The lotus does not have to elbow its way into my notice, rather does my mind of its own accord go out to greet and welcome it.

Let me give an example of the sensitive fastidiousness of the mind when choosing the adornments for the object of its adoration. The flower of the *sajinā* is not lacking in beauty, but the poets, when celebrating the enthronement of the King of Seasons, do not by any chance include its name in their songs of acclamation. It has lost prestige with the poets because it happens to figure as an article of diet. For the same reason the flowers of the brinjal or the pumpkin stand with lowered heads outside the gates of poesy—the kitchen has destroyed their caste. Not alone the poets, but also their sweethearts disdain these flowers as ornaments, though a spray of the delicate *sajinā* flower-clusters in their dark tresses would assuredly not have been ill-becoming. Neither the *kunda* nor *tagar* are gorgeous or scented, yet for them the door to the realm of adornment remains open, for they have not been tainted with the touch of the hunger of the body.

Here pictorial art is at an advantage. The artist's brush need not shrink from painting the superb foliage of the yam whereas to bring that name suggestive of a meal, into the description of any verdant scene would tax all the resources of the poet's pen. The sounds of words, moreover sometimes have undignified associations, by reason of the way they are used in our everyday life, which are liable to give offence in the case of the word picture, for it is not shape or colour, but sound which is of the essence of poetry. I am not usually credited with any squeamish regard for convention, yet have I often to resort to a less usual name, or a round-about phrase, rather than use a word that has a utilitarian significance. I should say here, however, that these considerations do not apply with equal force in the case of the Western poet with whom it is the substance and not the name that dominates.

Be that as it may, it is a common experience that we fail to see in its entirety that which sub serves our use, for it is eclipsed by the shadow of our need. The kitchen and pantry are of everyday necessity to the householder, but these are the rooms he fain would keep out of public view. His reception room, which he for himself can do without, is the one on which he lavishes all furniture and adornment, striving to the best of his means, by carpeting it, hanging it with pictures, stocking it with objects of exotic beauty, to give it a touch of the universal; for he would he known to the larger world outside through this room of his choice, in all the glory of his own personality. In the facts that he eats and stores up food his personality finds no ultimate significance. That he has a special distinction is the tidings which he seeks to communicate through his reception rooms—wherefore they are decorated.

In the realm of biology man and beast are not distinct; as there viewed, self-preservation and race preservation are of equal importance in the nature of both. But man's spirit fails to find in these features the true significance of man. So, however deep-seated or wide-spread man's desire to dine may be, his literature has but scanty recognition of it. Man's eating propensity may be an insistent, but it is not a significant truth; that is why the satisfaction of his hunger is not one of the joys that have found a place in the paradise of his art-world.

The sexual relationship of man and woman stands on a higher plane than man's appetite for food, for it has achieved an intimate connection with the relationship of hearts. The sex instinct which, in a basic view of life, has only a secondary place, has risen, in the sex relations of the larger life of man, to a position transcending even the primary; for love illumines man, within and without, into a supreme intensity of consciousness. That illumination is lacking in the primitive principle of race preservation, which therefore assumes importance only on the plane of science. The union of hearts, as seen by us, is abstracted from the primitive needs of Nature into the glory of its own finality. And hence it has come to occupy so vast a place in literature and the arts.

The supreme significance of the union of the sexes is, for man, not in procreation—*prajanārtham* (for the sake of progeny) as our lawgiver would have it—for in that he is merely animal, but in love wherein he is truly man. I do not use the word animal with any implication of ethical judgement, but from the view-point of the progressive self-realisation of man. Owing to their intimately close contact a natural spirit of rivalry prevails between the animal and the spiritual spheres of man's sex-life in their respective claims for the wreath of victory from art and literature. The psycho-analyst has introduced a further complication by asseverating that the animal sex-instinct is also a deep and potent factor in the mental life of man. But whatever practical utility or intellectual value this dictum of science may have, it can have no place in the realm of literature and art, which is concerned with the valuation of man's feeling of delight according to his standard of the eternal. The same is the case with considerations of social morality. The problems that have arisen with regard to the place of the sex-relation in literature cannot be solved from the scientific or moral stand-point, but from that of aesthetics, which alone can determine which of its two aspects man will adorn and raise on the pedestal of immortality.

We find in every age temporary extraneous circumstances occasionally creating obsessions that penetrate into the field of literature and overshadow for the time its true characteristics. It is not possible, however, for these temporary excitements to find any permanent place in literature, for, being volatile by nature, they soon evaporate. During the great European War, for instance, the war turbulence muddied even the streams of its poetry. When in England the puritanic age was followed by one of license, its exhalations befogged the radiance of its literature, but even while such period lasted, the presence of this cloud testified not to its own significance, but to that of the light which it could not wholly obscure. In the middle ages of Europe the Church attained such power that it tried to throttle science, forgetting that, in its own sphere, science is supreme and owes no allegiance even to religion. Now the opposite phenomenon is at work, and it is science that seeks to establish its sway over every region of man's being: in the pride of its new prestige it has ceased to have misgivings about encroaching beyond its scope.

Science is impersonal. Its very essence is an impartial curiosity about truth. And yet the all-pervading net of this curiosity is gradually enmeshing modern literature within its folds; though of literature, on the contrary, the essence is its partiality—its supreme message is the freedom of choice according to the taste of man. It is this freedom which is being assailed by the invasion of science. The sensualism of which European literature is full today owes its origin to this *curiosity*, as its prototype in the age of the Restoration had its impulse in *lust*. But just as the lust of that age failed to win the laurel which could secure it a permanent place in the Olympus of literature, neither can the scientific curiosity of this age maintain its keenness for ever.

There was a day in our country when a heat wave of licentiousness passed over our society and stimulated our literature into an outburst of carnalism. It was a temporary aberration of which the modern reader refuses to take any serious notice, not by way of moral censure, but because he has ceased to accord it permanent value.

Of late, it is true, we notice the opposite tendency in some of our modern critics who would rank among the eternal verities the intemperance of the flesh that has been imported into our literature from the Western world. But they forget that the eternal cannot wholly contradict the past. The natural delicacy which has always been a feature of man's aesthetic enjoyment, the aristocracy which has always reigned in the realm of art—these are eternal. It is only in the rantings of the science-intoxicated democracy of today that this modesty, this reticence, is dubbed a weakness, and a rude manifestation of physical hunger is proclaimed to constitute the virility of art.

I have seen an example of this begrimed pugilistic modernism in the form that our *holi* play has taken amongst the roughs of Chitpore Road. There is no scattering of red powder, no spraying with rose-coloured perfumes, no laughter, no song. Rolling long pieces of wet cloth in the street mud and therewith bespattering one another and the unfortunate passers-by, to the accompaniment of unearthly yells, is the mad form which this old time spring festival has here assumed. Not to tinge but to taint is the object. I do not say that such propensity is foreign to the mentality of man: the psycho-analyst is therefore welcome to revel in a study thereof. My objection to the importation of this common desire to soil into a festival inspired by man's aesthetic sense is not because it is not true, but because it is not appropriate.

Some of those who seek to defend the bringing in of such muddy carousals into the region of our literary enjoyment do so with the question—But is it not true? That question, as I say, does not arise. When our drug-befuddled Bhojpuri festive party storm the welkin with the unending clang of their intoxicated drums and cymbals, their demoniac shouts of an eternal repetition of the one line of their tuneless song, it is entirely beside the point to ask the suffering neighbours whether or not it is true; the only relevant question can be: How is it music? There is admittedly a kind of self-forgetful joy in inebriation; there is undoubtedly great forcefulness in an unrestrained exercise of lung power; and if the ugliness of incivility has to be taken as a sign of virility, then we must needs admire this athletic intoxication also. But what then? This forcefulness still remains of the slums of Chitpore, it cannot aspire to the Elysium of art.

In conclusion it should be added that, if in the countries ridden by science, an indiscriminate curiosity should, *Duhśāsana*-like seek to strip the goddess of literature of her drapery, they have at least the excuse of science to offer for such conduct. But in our country, where neither within nor without, neither in thought nor in action, has science been permitted an entry, what excuse can serve to cover up the insolence of the spurious, borrowed immodesty that has come to infest its literature? If the question be sent to the other side of the seas: Why this turmoil of the market-crowd in your literature? The answer will come: That is no fault of our literature; the cause lies in the markets that surround us. When that same question is put on this side, the reply will be: True, markets we have none; but the noisomeness of the market-place is all there; that is just the glory of our modernism!

Message to the Parliament
of Religions

After a long spell of scepticism, born of science which is naturally concerned with the process of creation and not with its origin or value, there seems to have set in a favourable reaction in the modern mind towards religion. In consequence of this a large section of men have become ready to surrender themselves, with unreasoning impetuosity, to the rigid grip of creeds that had their genesis in the history of a remote past with its limited range of knowledge. This is having upon other minds the contrary effect of discrediting religion altogether, arousing against it suspicion if not contempt.

We have seen in our own country a recrudescence of the blind faith that makes no discrimination between the spiritual significance of a religion and its outer crust that not only obscures it, but gives it a materialistic grossness of structure. Men who follow the path of indiscriminate acceptance, go to the length of defending their position by a philosophy according to which all conceptions and representations of the infinite have a uniform value, being all equally inadequate or irrelevant. Such sophistry makes it lazily easy for us to confine our devotion within the boundaries of our own sect, and unthinkingly allow our minds to confuse customs that are inert with the wisdom that has eternal dynamic force. It is a symptom of our egotism, this clinging with fanatical fervour to all that is accidental in our religion, making it inhospitable, and a source of endless strife. Such a religious attitude of mind is the greatest calamity, specially in the present age, for the peace and welfare of man.

Sectarianism is materialistic. It ever tries to build its tower of triumph with its numerical strength, temporal power and external observances. It breeds in the minds of its members a jealous sense of separateness that gives rise to conflicts more deadly than conflicts of worldly interests. It is a worse enemy of the truth of religion than atheism, for sectarianism proudly appropriates as its own share the best portion of the homage that we bring to our God.

Today science has offered us facilities that bring the human races outwardly close to one another, yet curiously enough it is our religions that zealously maintain the inner barriers that separate, and often antagonise nations and peoples, their respective votaries not even hesitating blasphemously to take God's own name to humiliate or mortally injure their fellow-beings who happen to belong to a different community. And it is high time for us to know how much more important it is, in the present age, to be able to understand the fundamental truths of all religions and realise their essential unity, thus clearing the way for a world-wide spiritual comradeship, than to preach some special religion of our own with all its historical limitations.

The evils that have followed in the wake of the present meetings of the races—the evils of political and economic exploitation—should not find, in the religious organisations, allies for the creation of dissensions that are truely impious. We must give heed to the call of the present age which urges us to train our mind not merely into a passive tolerance, but into an active understanding of the religions which are not ours, which but diversely emphasise some particular phase of truth, some special process of spiritual realisation.

There are those who have the imperialistic tendency of mind which leads them to believe that their own religion has the sole right to bring the whole human world under its undisputed dominance. They dream of a unity which consists of a grim solitude of *one,* barren and colourless as a desert. But the unity which is at the root of creation, comprehends the countless many, and gives them the rhythm of kinship. Monotony is of death, life is a harmony of varied notes.

The truth which is impersonal is science; the path to approach it is the same for all of us—the sole path of reason that has no individual variedness. The truth which is supremely personal is God, and the paths that lead to Him are not one, but are manifold according to the differences in our personality. The knowledge about this personal truth can never be solely through reason, but must be mostly through sympathy; to know it perfectly is the same as to be intimately related to it.

The personal relationship, in order to be real, has to seek out its own special path and find its idiomatic expression in the medium of its own language. But generally speaking, in the name of religion, our minds are moulded according to the one uniform sectarian standard prevalent in our own community. Therefore, with the exception of those who have rare spiritual gifts, the generality of men, without their knowing it, are godless. They are pious, but not religious; they have not the courage of faith, but the habit of conformity. Such a cult of superficial creeds has, for most of us, brought down our idea of God to the level of the average, the comfortable, the genteel mind, the mind ready to believe that God is on the side of the successful.

Religion is the expression of human aspiration seeking the fundamental unity of truth in the divine person of God. Whereas sectarianism uses religion itself to create disunion among men, sharpening its sword for the killing of brothers as a part of the ritual of the Father's worship. Sectarianism is the dangerous form of worldliness that claims exclusive right to spiritual illumination within its own narrow enclosure, and in the name of God refuses recognition to God himself where He is for all.

The history of man is the history of the building up of a human universe, as has been proved by the fact that everything great in human activity inevitably belongs to all humanity. And we may be sure that all our religious experiences and expressions are building up from the depth of the ages one great continent of religions on which man's soul is to win its prosperity through the universal commerce of spiritual life.

The Philosophy of Leisure

In my country, the cultivation of leisure has been a vital necessity. We may have many other compulsions for work, but hardly one for generating extra heat within our own physical constitution in order to maintain the balance between the outer temperature and the temperature of our body. In consequence, with us, restless activity has not become a pleasure in itself, and our bodily providence has slowed down our physical movements almost below the degree needful for the strenuous purposes of material prosperity.

We should bitterly blame our fate for an utter bankruptcy of civilisation, if this strict economy of life were an absolute miserliness which gives up all prospect of profit to avoid the least risk of loss. Forest land is great, crowded with a furiously competing life; but the seemingly empty prairie land has also its own magnanimity, passively waiting to be wooed yielding inexhaustible wealth which has in it the spirit of cooperation, the deeper strength of meekness. The human world also has its prairie land of fertile leisure and forest land of self-assertive life.

Man has his two phases, the one in which he tries to make indefinite additions to the powers of his senses and limbs from the store-house of cosmic powers; and the other in which he tries to realise, through various stages, his oneness with humanity and thus manifest in himself a truth which reveals him much more intimately than the fact of any extension of power.

Man, along with the animal, is born to this earth where he has the materials of his living; and according to the development of his energy and intelligence which helps him in the acquisition and use of these materials, he becomes powerful and wins in the race of life. In this race, the individual competition for success is the main motive force which man has in common with the animal.

This domain of material progress has for its object success which depends upon quickness in time and bigness in quantity for its achievement.

But man, unlike the animal, is born also to his home, his society and his country. These afford him the background, the perspective needed for the expression of his complete being. They belong to the domain of his civilisation which urges slow centuries to develop creative ideals through cooperation of minds and endeavours, through magnificent hospitality and love's utmost sacrifice.

This is the realm of great leisure in whose bosom appear the revelations of human spirit which work themselves out from the obscure period of the nebula into the constellation of stars.

The complete human truth is comprehended in the mastery of law that gives power and the realisation of harmony which gives perfection, just as in a work of art, the handling of technique and the inspiration of vision are both necessary. Occasionally men lose the sensitiveness of their mind through the rude abrasions of constantly hurried moments. In such a state they become capable only of being aroused by some tortured trick in the technique, by some jerky shock of novelty which is not originality, by even ugliness that coarsely violates our sense of rhythm. These people take pride in proclaiming their disillusionment, after having taken to pieces things that can only have meaning in their wholeness. In this callous world of theirs, Titans have their victory and Gods are defeated.

And have we the time to ask ourselves if some of the sights, that overpower us today with awe, are not the triumphal towers of the Titans, built with the ruins of our paradise?

The spirit of progress is neither moral nor immoral. With equal indifference it uses its efficiency in inflicting as well as in healing wounds, at the same time, in helping us in a perfect system of robbery and in a perfect organisation of charity for those who suffer in consequence. It achieves success through intelligent dealings with Nature's potentialities.

This realm of progress is described in the *Upanishads* as *Anna Brahma*—the infinite in its aspect of utility. It has its urge in man for realising the immeasurable in the domain of quantity through an endlessly progressing process of measurement. Directly we lose our faith in it through lethargy or diffidence, we lapse into an animal state in this material universe, and fall passively under the law of natural selection.

The rule of natural selection finds its full sway in a close system of life with rigidly limited resources and restricted, possibilities. Man broke the prison wall open, declared his sovereignty and refused to be contented with the small allowance originally allotted to him by Nature, just enough to enable him to carry on a perpetual repetition of a narrow programme of life. He mastered his resources and utilises them for his own indomitable purpose. This working out of one's own purpose through the manipulation of Nature's law is great. It carries in it the proclamation of the right to freedom of the human spirit which refuses to acknowledge limits to its power in the very face of powerful contradictions. The present age is resounding with the declaration of independence for man in the world of nature. This independence is not absolute, but it is a sailing upon a perpetually widening current of emancipation. So long as the movement is maintained, it gives us the taste of the infinite at every point, but directly we stop, we become the captive of the finite and lose the dignity of our soul. There are races of men who have allowed themselves to be stranded upon the sterile sand of their past achievement, like a whale on the sea shore, and they remain, to the end of their days, the prey of ravenous evils from all sides. There is a spirit of immortality in the sphere of the material existence which consists in a triumphant movement of realisation. It loses its inspiration and becomes a menace to man when we are meanly overcome by the profit it promises and ignore its great meaning—the expansion of power which gives us the divine right to transform this world into a world for Man.

Truth has its other aspect which is described by the *Upanishad* as *Vijñāna Brahma* or *Ānanda Brahma,* the infinite in its aspect of comprehension, aspect of joy. It is the realm of wisdom and love where mere dimension, number and speed have no meaning, where the value of truth is realised by matured mind through patient devotion, self-control and concentration of faculties. It has its atmosphere of infinity in a width of leisure across which come invisible messengers of life and light, bringing their silent voices of creation.

The process of the packing of fruits gains in merit according to the speed it attains by efficient organisation of work, by economising time through mechanical coordination of movements. But the fruit gains its quality of perfection, its flavour and mellowness, not by any impatient ignoring of time but by surrendering itself to the subtle caresses of a sun-lit leisure. And thus we see that the idea of time finds its meaning not as a mere duration of the world process but as a vehicle of creative energy. In the Hindu Pantheon, the deity of time has its other name as the deity of energy, for we find that time not merely measures but it works. We do not know why a certain period of time is necessary for certain changes to happen, why food should not instantaneously be digested, why the mind should at all depend upon time for the assimilation of thoughts. In fact, we never solve the mystery why there should at all be a process of creation which is a process in time.

It is evident that the modern age is riding on a tornado of rapidity. Quickness of speed in an enormity of material production is jealously competing with its own past every moment. We cannot stop its course, and should not, even if we could. Our only anxiety with regard to it is that we may forget that slow productions of leisure are of immense value to man, for these only can give balance to the reckless rush of ambition, give rhythm to the life that misses its happiness by missing the cadence of chastity in its enjoyment; these only can impart meaning to an accumulation which knows how to grow to a hugeness but not to a majesty of expression. As I have said in the beginning, all civilisations are living wealths that have grown on the deep soil of a rich leisure. They are for conferring honour to our personality and giving it its best worth. The perfection of our personality does not principally consist of qualities that generate cleverness or deftness or even accuracy of observation, or the rationality that analyses and forms generalisations. It depends mostly upon our training in truth and love, upon ideals that go to the root of our being. And these require the ministration of quiet time for their adequate recognition and realisation in life.

A true gentleman is the product of patient centuries of cultivated leisure that has nourished into preciousness a vision of honour whose value is higher than that of life itself. When I first visited Japan I had the opportunity of observing there the two parts of the human sphere strongly contrasted; one, on which grew up the ancient continent of social ideals, standards of beauty, codes of personal behaviour; and on the other part, the fluid element, the perpetual current that carried wealth to its shores from all parts of the world. In half a century's time Japan has been able to make her own the mighty spirit of progress which suddenly burst upon her one morning in a storm of insult and menace. China also has had her rousing when her self-respect was being knocked to pieces through a series of helpless years, and I am sure she also will master before long the instrument which hurt her to the quick. But the ideals that imparted life and body to Japanese civilisation had been nourished in the reverent hopes of countless generations through ages which were not primarily occupied in an incessant hunt for opportunities, which had large tracts of leisure in them necessary for the blossoming of life's beauty and the ripening of her wisdom. These ideals had become one with the nature of the people and therefore these people were often unconscious of their profound value while they were noisily proud of some culture from a foreign market for which they had to pay in cash, because of its utility, and not in sacrifice which is claimed by a truth that has its ultimate value in itself. It is something like being boastful of an expensive pair of high-heeled shoes which has no compunction in insulting the beautiful contour of the living feet that have reached their perfect form in man through ages of evolution.

We have seen the modern factories in Japan, seen numerous mechanical organisations and engines of destruction of the latest type. Along with them we also see some fragile vase, some small pieces of silk, some architecture of sublime simplicity, some perfect lyric of bodily movement. Also we have seen these people's expression of courtesy daily extracting from them a considerable amount of time and trouble, their traditions of behaviours, any deviation from which, however inevitable, so often drove them to suicide. All these have come not from any accurate knowledge of things but from an intense consciousness of the value of reality which takes time for its realisation. What Japan reveals in its skillful manipulation of telegraphic wires and railway lines, of machines for manufacturing things and for killing men, is more or less similar to what we see in other countries which have a similar opportunity for training. But in its art of living, its pictures, its code of conduct, the various forms of beauty which its religious and social ideals assume, Japan reveals its own personality which, in order to be of any worth, must be unique. This national personality acquires its richness from its assimilation of some ideal and not from its possession of some trade secret, some up to date machinery of efficiency.

What gives us cause for anxiety is the fact that the spirit of progress occupies a great deal more of our mind today than the deeper life process of our being which requires depth of leisure for its sustenance. In the present age the larger part of our growth takes place on the outside, and our inner spirit has not the time to accept it and harmonise it into a completeness of creation. In other words, the modern world has not allowed itself time to evolve a religion, a profound principle of reconciliation that can fashion out of all conflicting elements a living work of art—his society. The creative ideals of life, necessary for giving expression to the fulness of humanity, were developed centuries ago. And when today these suffer from some misfit as a result of a constant expansion of knowledge and a variety of new experiences, we fail to adjust them into a more comprehensive synthesis than before, and thus not only lose faith in them but in the fundamental principle that they represent. With strenuous efforts, we make stupendous heaps of materials and when the complaint comes that they miss the character of architecture, we contemptuously say that architecture is a superstition and for a democratic age rude piles are more significant than the rhythmic form of a building. Such remarks are easy to make only because we lack leisure truly to know our minds. We are only familiar with the surface of our life which is constantly being soiled and burdened with the sweepings of an enormous traffic. We grow to be fond of a perpetual shabbiness produced by a miscellany of fragments only because the relegation of these to their proper places requires time. And we say time is money, while we forget to say that leisure is wealth, the wealth which is a creation of human spirit whose material may be money.

Invention, construction and organisation are spreading fast along the high road of our history, but the creative genius of man which acknowledged its mission to express all that has permanent value in his personality is everyday losing its dignity. It accepts cheap payments from the busy multitude, it is engaged in always keeping irreverent minds amused, it makes faces at things men held sacred and tries to prove that the ideals of social life that had given us grace, the majesty of self-mastery and the heroism of voluntary acceptance of suffering were most part unreal, false coins made current by the weak for the pathetic purpose of self-deception. Compressed and crowded time has its use when dealing with material things but living truths must have for their full significance a perspective of wide leisure. The cramped time produces deformities and degeneracy, and the mind constantly pursued by a fury of haste, develops a chronic condition of spiritual dyspepsia. It easily comes to believe that reality is truly represented by nightmare, that nothing but disease is frankly honest in its revelation of the normal, that only the lowest is reliable in its explanation of the highest in a language crudely obscure. Drunkenness may be defined as the habit of enjoyment forced out through a narrowed aperture of sensibility in jets of abnormal sharpness; and all enjoyment takes a drunken character for those who try to snatch it away from fugitive hours that come jumping to them in a *staccato* style. They become hopelessly addicted to undiluted sensationalism for their brief moments or recreations and literature demanded by them grows bewilderingly turbulent with psychological perversity and intellectual somersaults.

Incessantly handling things that have their market price they lose the judgement of the world of values, the self-luminous truth, the kingdom of personality. They claim explanation from every fact for its truth in a universe of reality while they forget that our personality also needs an adequate explanation in a universal truth.

A particle of sand would be nothing if it did not have its background in the whole physical world.

Ideals of Education

The greatest man of modern India, Raja Rammohun Roy was born in Bengal and was the best friend of my grandfather. He had courage to overcome the prohibition against sea voyage which we had in our country at the time; and he crossed the sea, and came into touch with the great western minds.

My father was fortunate in coming under the influence of Rammohun Roy from his early years which helped him to free himself from the sectarian barriers, from traditions of worldly and social ideas that were very rigid, in many aspects very narrow and not altogether beneficial. My father drew from our ancient scriptures, from the *Upanishads*, truths which had universal significance, and not anything that were exclusive to any particular age or any particular people. We were ostracised by society and this liberated us from the responsibility of conforming to all those conventions that had not the value of truth, that were mere irrational habits bred in the inertia of the racial mind. In my boyhood's dreams I claimed such freedom that we had tasted, for all humanity.

Nations are kept apart not merely by international jealousy but also by their own past, handicapped by the burden of the dead and decaying, the breeding ground of diseases that attack the spiritual man. I could not believe that generations of peoples, century after century, must have their birth chamber in a moral and intellectual coffin which has its restricted space-regulation for a body that has lost its movements. Civilisation has its inevitable tendency to accumulate dead materials and to make elaborate adjustments for their accommodation, leaving less and less room for life with its claim to grow in freedom. There are signs of that in India, and I know today that it is more or less true in all races, for our mind has its inclination to grow lazy as it grows old and to shirk its duty to make changes in the rhythm of the changing times. In the very heart of this rigid rule of the dead, I was brought up in an atmosphere of aspiration, aspiration for the expansion of the human spirit. We in our home sought freedom of power in our language, freedom of imagination in our literature, freedom of soul in our religious creeds and that of mind in our social environment. Such an opportunity has given me confidence in the power of education which is one with life and only which can give us real freedom, the highest that is claimed for man, his freedom of moral communion in the human world. The ghosts of ideals which no longer have a living reality have become the obsession of all nations that carry an overwhelming past behind them perpetually overshadowing their future.

The reign of the ghost has strewn the path of our history lessons with mischief, with prejudices that ever obstruct the mutual understanding of nations, that helps in the cultivation of the thorny crop of national vanity and unscrupulousness in international relationship. From our young days our minds are deliberately trained with the aid of untrue words and unholy symbolism in the name of patriotism to a collective moral attitude, which we condemn in individuals.

Persons who have no faith in human nature are apt to think that such conditions are eternal in man—that the moral ideals are only for individuals but the race belongs to that primitive nature which is for the animal. And according to them, in the racial life, it is necessary that the animal should have its full scope of training in the cult of suspicion, jealousy, fierce destructiveness, cruel rapacity. They contemptuously brand optimism as sentimental weakness, and yet in spite of that virulent scepticism an enormous change has worked itself out in course of the growth of civilisation from the darkest abyss of savagery. I refuse to believe that human society has reached its limit of moral possibility. And we must work all our strength for the seemingly impossible, and must believe that there is a constant urging in the depth of human soul for the attainment of the perfect, the urging which secretly helps us in all our endeavour for the good. This faith has been my only asset in the educational mission which I have made my life's work, and almost unaided and alone, I struggle along my path. I try to assert in my words and works that education has its only meaning and object in freedom—freedom from ignorance about the laws of universe, and freedom from passion and prejudice in our communication with the human world. In my institution I have attempted to create an atmosphere of naturalness in our relationship with strangers, and the spirit of hospitality which is the first virtue in men that made civilisation possible.

I invited thinkers and scholars from foreign lands to let our boys know how easy it is to realise our common fellowship, when we deal with those who are great, and that it is the puny who with their petty vanities set up barriers between man and man.

I am glad that I have the opportunity today of letting my friends in Japan know something of my life-long cause and to assure them that it is not special to India but it will ever wait for acceptance by other races.

We in India are unfortunate in not having the chance to give expression to the best in us in creating intimate relations with the powerful peoples of the world. The bond between the nations today is made the links of mutual menace, its strength depending upon the force of panic, and leading to an enormous waste of resources in a competition of browbeating and bluff. Some great voice is waiting to be heard which will usher in the sacred light of truth in the dark region of the nightmare of politics. But we in India have not yet had the chance. Yet we have our own human voice which truth demands. Even in the region where we are not invited to act we have our right to judge and to guide the mind of man to a proper point of view, to the vision of ideality in the heart of the real.

The activity represented in human education is a worldwide one, it is a great movement of universal cooperation interlinked by different ages and countries. And India, though defeated in her political destiny, has her responsibility to hold up the cause of truth, even to cry in the wilderness, and offer her lessons to the world in the best gifts which she could produce. The messengers of truth have ever joined their hands across centuries, across the seas, across historical barriers, and they help to form the great continent of human brotherhood. Education in all its different forms and channels has its ultimate purpose in the evolving of a luminous sphere of human mind from the nebula that has been rushing round ages to find in itself an eternal centre of unity. We individuals, however small may be our power and whatever corner of the world we may belong to, have the claim upon us to add to the light of the consciousness that comprehends all humanity. And for this cause I ask your cooperation, not merely because cooperation gives us strength in our work but because co-operation itself is the best aspect of the truth we represent, it is an end and not merely the means.

My friends, you are new converts to western ideals, in other words, the ideals belonging to the scientific view of life and the world. This is great and it is foolish to belittle its importance by wrongly describing it as materialism. For truth is spiritual in itself, and truly materialistic is the mind of the animal which is unscientific and therefore unable to cross the dark screen of appearance, of accidents, and reach the deeper region of universal laws. Science means intellectual probity in our dealings with the material world. This conscientiousness of mind is spiritual, for it never judges its results from the standard of external profits. But in science the oft-used half truth that honesty is the best policy has proved itself to be completely true. Science being mind's honesty in its relation to the physical universe never fails to bring us the best profit for our living. And mischief finds its entry through this backdoor of utility, and Satan has had his ample chance of making use of the divine fruit of knowledge for bringing shame upon humanity. Science as the best policy is tempting the primitive in man bringing out his evil passions through the respectable cover that it has supplied him. And this is why it is all the more needed today that we should have faith in ideals that have matured in the spiritual field through ages of human endeavour after perfection, the golden crops that have developed in different forms and in different soils but whose food value for man's spirit has the same composition. These are not for the local markets but for the universal hospitality, for sharing life's treasure with each other and realising that human civilisation is a spiritual feast the invitation to which is open to all, it is never for the ravenous orgies of carriage where the food and the feeders are being torn to pieces.

The legends of nearly all human races carry man's faith in a golden age which appeared as the introductory chapter in human civilisation. It shows that man has his instinctive belief in the objectivity of spiritiual ideals though this cannot be proved. It seems to him that they have already been given to him and that this gift has to be proved through his history against obstacles. The idea of millennium so often laughed at by the clever is treasured as the best asset by man in his mythology as complete truth realised for ever in some ageless time. Admitting that it is not a scientific fact we must at the same time know that the instinct cradled and nourished in these primitive stories has its eternal meaning. It is like the instinct of a chick which dimly feels that an infinite world of freedom is already given to it, that it is not a subjective dream but an objective reality, even truer than its life within the egg. If a chick has a rationalistic tendency of mind it ought not to believe in a freedom which is difficult to imagine and contradictory to all its experience, but all the same it cannot help pecking at its shell and ever accepting it as ultimate. The human soul confined in its limitation has also dreamt of a millenium and striven for an emancipation which seems impossible of attainment, and it felt its reverence for some great source of inspiration in which all its experience of the true, good and beautiful finds its reality though it cannot be proved, the reality in which our aspiration for freedom in truth, freedom in love, freedom in the unity of man is ideally realised for ever.

The Educational Mission of the Visva-Bharati

I have been asked to speak this evening to my invisible audience about the educational mission to which I have devoted my life and I am thankful for this opportunity.

I am an artist and not a man of science, and therefore my institution necessarily has assumed the aspect of a work of art and not that of a pedagogical laboratory. And this is the reason why I find it difficult to give you a distinct idea of my work which is continually growing for the last thirty years. With it my own mind has grown, and my own ideal of education found freedom to reach its fulness through a vital process so elusive that the picture of its unity cannot be analysed.

Children's minds are sensitive to the influences of the great world to which they have been born. This delicate receptivity of their passive mind helps them, without their feeling any strain, to master language, that most complex instrument of expression full of ideas that are indefinable and symbols that deal with abstractions. Through their natural gift of guessing, children learn the meaning of the words which we cannot explain.

But it is just at this critical period that the child's life is brought into the education factory, lifeless, colourless, dissociated from the context of the universe, with bare white walls staring like eyeballs of the dead. The children have to sit inert whilst lessons are pelted at them like hailstones on flowers.

I believe that children should be surrounded with the things of nature that have their own educational value. Their minds should be allowed to stumble on and be surprised at everything that happens before them in the life of today. The new tomorrow will stimulate their attention with new facts of life.

The minds of the adults are crowded; the stream of lessons perpetually flowing from the heart of nature does not fully touch them; they choose those that are useful, rejecting the rest as inadmissible. The children have no such distractions. With them every new fact comes to a mind that is always open, with an abundant hospitality. And through this exuberant, indiscriminate acceptance they learn innumerable facts within a short time, amazing compared to our own slowness. These are the most important lessons of life that are thus learnt in the first few years of our career.

Because, when I was young I underwent the mechanical pressure of a teaching process, one of man's most cruel and most wasteful mistakes, I felt it my duty to found a school where the children might be free in spite of the school.

At the age of twelve I was first coerced into learning English. Most of you in this country are blissfully unconscious of the mercilessness of your own language. You will admit, however, that neither its spelling, nor its syntax, is perfectly rational. The penalty for this I had to pay without having done anything to deserve it, with the exception of being born ignorant.

When in the evening my English teacher used to come I was dragged to my daily doom at a most unsympathetic desk and an unprepossessing text-book containing lessons that are followed by rows of separated syllables with accent marks like soldiers' bayonets.

As for that teacher, I can never forgive him. He was so inordinately conscientious! He insisted on coming every single evening—there never seemed to be either illness or death in his family. He was so preposterously punctual too. I remember how the fascination for the frightful attracted me every evening to the terrace facing the road; and just at the right moment, his fateful umbrella—for bad weather never prevented him from coming—would appear at the bend of our lane.

Remembering the experience of my young days, of the school-masters and the class-rooms, also knowing something of the natural school which nature herself supplies to all her creatures, I established my institution in a beautiful spot, far away from the town, where the children had the greatest freedom possible under the shade of ancient trees and the field around open to the verge of horizon.

From the beginning I tried to create an atmosphere which I considered to be more important than the class teaching. The atmosphere of nature's own beauty was there waiting for us from a time immemorial with her varied gifts of colours and dance, flowers and fruits, with the joy of her mornings and the peace of her starry nights, I wrote songs to suit the different seasons, to celebrate the coming of Spring and the resonant season of the rains following the pitiless months of summer. When nature herself sends her message we ought to acknowledge its compelling invitation. While the kiss of rain thrills the heart of the surrounding trees if we pay all our dutiful attention to mathematics we are ostracised by the spirit of universe. Our holidays are unexpected like nature's own. Clouds gather above the rows of the palm trees without any previous notice; we gladly submit to its sudden suggestion and run wildly away from our Sanskrit grammar. To alienate our sympathy from the world of birds and trees is a barbarity which is not allowed in my institution.

I invited renowned artists from the city to live at the school, leaving them free to produce their own work which the boys and girls watch if they feel inclined. It is the same with my own work. I compose my songs and poems, the teachers sit round me and listen. The children are naturally attracted and they peep in and gather, even if they do not fully understand, something fresh from the heart of the composer.

From the commencement of our work we have encouraged our children to be of service to our neighbours from which has grown up a village reconstruction work in our neighbourhood unique in the whole of India. Round our educational work the villages have grouped themselves in which the sympathy for nature and service for man have become one. In such extension of sympathy and service our mind realises its true freedom.

Along with this has grown an aspiration for even a higher freedom, a freedom from all racial and national prejudice. Children's sympathy is often deliberately made narrow and distorted making them incapable of understanding alien peoples with different languages and cultures. This causes us, when our growing souls demand it, to grope after each other in ignorance, to suffer from the blindness of this age. The worst fetters come when children lose their freedom of heart in love.

We are building up our institution upon the ideal of the spiritual unity of all races. I hope it is going to be a great meeting place for individuals from all countries who believe in the divine humanity, and who wish to make atonement for the cruel disloyalty displayed against her by men. Such idealists I have frequently met in my travels in the West, often unknown persons, of no special reputation, who suffer and struggle for a cause generally ignored by the clever and the powerful. These individuals, I am sure, will alter the outlook for the future. By them will be ushered a new sunrise of truth and love, like that great personality, who had only a small number of disciples from among the insignificant, and who at the end of his career presented a pitiful picture of utter failure. He was reviled by those in power, unknown by the larger world, and suffered an inglorious death, and yet through the symbol of this utmost failure he conquers and lives for ever.

For some time past education has lacked idealism in its mere exercise of an intellect which has no depth of sentiment. The one desire produced in the heart of the students has been an ambition to win success in the world, not to reach some inner standard of perfection, not to obtain self-emancipation.

Let me confess this fact that I have my faith in higher ideals. At the same time, I have a great feeling of delicacy in giving utterance to them, because of certain modern obstacles. We have nowadays to be merely commonplace. We have to wait on the reports in the newspapers, representative of the whole machinery which has been growing up all over the world for the making of life superficial. It is difficult to fight through such obstructions and to come to the centre of humanity.

However, I have this one satisfaction that I am at least able to put before you the mission to which these last years of my life have been devoted. As a servant of the great cause I must be frank and strong in urging upon you this mission. I represent in my institution an ideal of brotherhood, where men of different countries and different languages can come together. I believe in the spiritual unity of man, and therefore I ask you to accept this task from me. Unless you come and say, "We also recognise this ideal", I shall know that this mission has failed. Do not merely discuss me as a guest, but as one who has come to ask your love, your sympathy and your faith in the following of a great cause.

2

There is no meaning in such words as spiritualising[1] the machine, we can spiritualise our own being which makes use of the machine, just as there is nothing good or bad in our bodily organs, but the moral qualities are in our mind. When the temptation is small our moral nature easily overcomes it, but when the bribe that is offered to our soul is too big we do not even realise that its dignity is offended. Today the profit that the machine brings to our door is too big and we do not hesitate to scramble for it even at the cost of our humanity. The shrinking of the man in us is concealed by the augmentation of things outside and we lack the time to grieve over the loss. We can only hope that science herself will help us to bring back sanity to the human world by lessening the opportunity to gamble with our fortune. The means of production constructed by science in her attempts to gain access into nature's storehouse are tremendously complex which only proves her own immaturity just as simplicity is wanting in the movements of a swimmer who is inexpert. It is this cumbersome complexity in the machinery which makes it not only unavailable to the majority of mankind but also compels us to centralise it in monster factories, uprooting the workers' life from its natural soil and creating unhappiness. I do not see any other way to extricate us from these tangled evils except to wait for science to simplify our means of production and thus lessen the enormity of individual greed.

I believe that the social unrest prevalent today all over the world is owing to the anarchy of spirit in the modern civilisation.

What is called progress is the progress in the mechanical contrivances; it is in fact an indefinite extension of our physical

---

1. In reply to the question whether machines can be spiritualised.

limbs and organs which, owing to the enormous material advantage that it brings to us, has tempted the modern man away from his inner realm of spiritual values. The attainment of perfection in human relationship through the help of religion, and cultivation of our social qualities occupied the most important place in our civilisation up till now. But today our homes have dissolved into hotels, community life is stifled in the dense and dusty atmosphere of the office, men and women are afraid of love, people clamour for their rights and forget their obligations, and they value comfort more than happiness and the spirit of display more than that of beauty.

Great civilisations in the East as well as in the West, have flourished in the past because they produced food for the spirit of man for all time; they tried to build their life upon the faith in ideals, the faith which is creative. These great civilisations were at last run to death by men of the type of our precocious schoolboys of modern times smart and superficially critical, worshippers of self, shrewd bargainers in the market of profit and power, efficient in their handling of the ephemeral, who presume to buy human souls with their money and throw them into their dustbins when they have been sucked dry, and who eventually, driven by suicidal forces of passion, set their neighbours' houses on fire and are themselves enveloped by the flame.

It is some great ideal which creates great societies of men; it is some blind passion which breaks them to pieces. They thrive so long as they produce food for life; they perish when they burn up life in insatiate self-gratification. We have been taught by our sages that it is Truth and not things which saves man from annihilation.

The reward of truth is peace, the reward of truth is happiness. The people suffer from the upsetting of equilibrium when power is there and no inner truth to which it is related, like a motor car in motion whose driver is absent.

Race Conflict

The problem of race conflict has ever been present in the history of mankind. This conflict has been at the basis of all great civilisations. It is like the clash of elements in the material world giving rise to complex combinations and evolutions of higher growth.

It was the concussion of peoples brought up in different surroundings and with different outlook upon life that started the original energy resulting in complicated social organisations. All civilisations are mixed products. Only barbarism is simple, monadic and unalloyed.

When differences have to be taken into account perforce, when there is no possible escape from them, then men are compelled to find out some central bond which can bring into unity all the diverse elements. This is really the seeking after truth, the search for the one in the many, the universal through the individuals.

Naturally, in the commencement its appearance is simple and crude. Some common visible object of worship is held as a symbol of the oneness of the people. It is very often gross and frightful. For when man has to depend upon external standards of life these have to be made as conspicuous as possible, and nothing is so compelling to primitive imagination as fear.

But, as the community grows larger and, by conquest and other means, peoples of different traditions unite, then fetishes multiply and more gods than one have to be recognized. In that case, these symbols lose their power as common bonds, and they have to be replaced by something whose appeal is not so much to the senses and whose significance is more universal.

Thus, gradually, as the problem grows more and more wide and complex, the solution of it becomes deeper and more far-reaching, and human solidarity seeks for its foundation something which is abiding and comprehensive. This is the purpose of all history, man seeking truth through complexities of experience impelled by the impetus of the immensity of ever-growing life.

There was a time when owing to the restricted means of communication, different races and nations lived in a state of comparative segregation and consequently their social laws and institutions had an intensely local character. They were narrowly racial and aggressively hostile to the aliens. People did not have frequent occasion to learn how to adjust themselves with outsiders. They had to take to violent measures when they collided with alien people. They simplified the problem to its narrowest limits and either absolutely excluded and exterminated all foreign elements or completely amalgamated them.

Men have not yet outgrown this training of racial or national self-sufficiency. They are still burdened with the age-long inheritance of a suspicion of aliens which is the primitive instinct of animals. They still have a lurking ferocity ready to come out at the slightest provocation when in contact with people outside their social boundaries. They have not yet acquired fairness of mind when judging other races and dealing with them. They have not that power of adjusting their mental vision which would enable them to understand the people who are not nearest to them. They strive their utmost to prove the superiority and originality of their own religion and philosophy and they are reluctant to acknowledge that, truth, because it is truth, naturally manifests itself in different countries in different garbs. They are ever prone to put more stress on differences which are external and lose sight of the inner harmony.

This is the result of being brought up in the home training of isolation, which makes one unfit for the citizenship of the world. But this cannot continue for long and with the advent of the new age of science and commerce men have been brought nearer to each other than they ever were before and they are face to face with the highest problem of human history, the problem of race conflict.

This problem has been waiting to be solved by experience, through the expansion of history. It is not a mere matter of sentiment or of intellect. We had prophets who preached equality of man, and philosophy and literature which have us a broader view of reality than is contained in the limits of racial traditions and habits. But this race problem with its vast complexity was never before us—we were not in living contact with it. Humanity, till now, has played with this sentiment of brotherhood of man as a girl does with her doll. It reveals the truth of the feeling which is innate in the heart of man, still it lacks the reality of life. But the playtime is passed and what was only in the sentiment has grown into our life fraught with immense responsibilities.

Of all the ancient civilisations, I think, that of India was compelled to recognise this race problem in all seriousness and for ages she has been engaged in unravelling the most bafflingly complicated tangle of race-differences. Europe was fortunate in having neighbouring races more or less homogeneous, for, most of them were of the same origin. So, though in Europe there were bitter feuds between different peoples, there was not that physical antipathy between them which the difference in colour of skin and in feature tends to produce. In England it did not take long for the Norman and Saxon elements to coalesce and lose their distinctions. Not only in colour and features but in their ideals of life the western peoples are so near each other that practically they are acting as one in building up their civilisation.

But it has been otherwise with India. At the beginning of Indian history the white-skinned Aryans had encounters with the aboriginal people who were dark and who were intellectually inferior to them. Then there were the Dravidians who had their own civilisation and whose gods and modes of worship and social system were totally different from those of the newcomers which must have proved a more active barrier between them than full-fledged barbarism.

In tropical countries life is not so strenuous as it is where the climate is cold. There the necessities of life are comparatively small and nature more prodigal in her bounties; therefore in those countries strifes between contending parties die away for want of incentives. So, in India, after a period of fierce struggles, men of different colours and creeds, different physical features and mental attitudes settled together side by side. As men are not inert matter but living beings, this juxtaposition of different elements became an ever-present problem for India. But with all its disadvantages this it was that stimulated men's minds to find out the essential unity in diversity of forms, to know that, however different be the symbols and rituals, God, whom they try to represent, is one without a second, and to realise him truly is to realise him in the soul of all beings.

When differences are too jarring, man cannot accept them as final; so, either he wipes them out with blood, or coerces them in some kind of superficial homogeneity, or he finds out a deeper unity which he knows is the highest truth.

India chose the last alternative and all through the political vicissitudes that tossed her about for centuries, when her sister civilisations of Greece and Rome exhausted their life force, her spiritual vitality still continued and she still retains her dignity of soul. I do not say for a moment that the difficulties about the race differences have been altogether removed in India. On the contrary, new elements have been added, new complications introduced, and all the great religions of the world have taken their roots in the soil of India. In her attempts at bringing into order this immense mass of heterogeneity India has passed through successive periods of expansion and contraction of her ideals. And her latest has been that of setting up rigid lines of regulations to keep different sections at arm's length to prevent confusion and clash.

But such a negative attitude cannot last long, and mere mechanical contrivances can never work satisfactorily in human society. If, by any chance, men are brought together who are not products of the same history and not moulded in the same traditions, they never can rest till they can find out some broad basis of union which is positive in its nature and which makes for love. And I am sure, in India we have that spiritual ideal, if dormant but still living, which can tolerate all differences in the exterior while recognising the inner unity. I feel sure, in India, we have that golden key forged by ancient wisdom and love which will one day open the barred gates to bring together to the feast of good fellowship men who have lived separated for generations.

From a very remote period of her history till now all the great personalities of India have been working in the same direction. The gospel of universal love that Buddha preached was the outcome of a movement long preceding him, which endeavoured to get at the kernel of spiritual unity, breaking through all divergence of symbols and ceremonies and individual preferences.

With the advent of the Mohammedan power not only a new political situation was created in India but new ideas in religion and social customs were brought before the people with a violent force. Nevertheless, it had not the effect of generating an antagonistic fanatical movement among Hindus. On the contrary, all the great religious geniuses that were born during this period in India sought a reconciliation of the old with the new ideals in a deeper synthesis, which was possible because of the inherited spirit of toleration and accumulated wisdom of ages. In all these movements there was the repeated call to the people to forget all distinctions of castes and creeds and accept the highest privilege of brotherhood of man by uniting in love of God.

The same thing has occurred again when India has been closely brought in contact with the Christian civilisation with the coming of the English. The Brahmo Samaj movement in India is the movement for the spiritual reconciliation of the East and West, the reconciliation resting upon the broad basis of spiritual wisdom laid in the *Upanishads*. There is again the same call to the people to rise above all artificial barriers of caste and recognise the common bond of brotherhood in the name of God.

In no other country in the world is the conflux of races different in every respect so great as in India. Therefore it never could have been possible for her to come to such a simple solution of the difficulty as national unity. The fetish of nationalism is powerless to bring her warring elements into a harmony; she must appeal to the highest power in man, the spiritual power, she must come to her God. There has been going on in India a long continued contention between rigid forms of exclusiveness which is mechanical and a recognition of the unity of mankind which is spiritual. Here, as in every land, the social convention is on the side of the pride of caste, and the higher nature and the deeper wisdom of the people assert in the lives of its greatest personalities the validity of the claims of all men to justice and love. On the one hand there is the regulation which forbids eating and drinking at the same board for men of different castes and on the other hand there comes the voice from the ancient past which preaches that he who realises his own. self in the self of all individuals realises truly. And I have not the least doubt in my mind that it is the urging of this spiritual impulse in man which will win in the end, and will mould all the social forms in such a way that they may not hinder its purpose but become its instrument.

I bring before you this instance of Indian history to show that a problem must be a living one to rouse man's mind for its solution. It has become so in the present age. Races widely separated in their geographical position and historical growth, in their modes of thought and manners of expression have been brought near each other in closer relations. To each man the human world has been enlarged to an extent never dreamt of in former days. That we are not ready for these changed circumstances is becoming painfully evident every day. The caste feeling is running fearfully high. The western people are cultivating an arrogant exclusiveness against all other races. While keeping for themselves their prerogatives of exploiting weaker nations by threat of force they securely bar their own gates against them in a manner cruelly barbarous and inhospitable. Sentiments of humanity are openly discredited and poets of world-wide reputation are exulting in the triumph of brute force. Nations wakened from a lethargy of centuries and bravely struggling for a larger life are held back by others more fortunate, waiting to turn to their own advantage the situation created by the breaking up of old order. Want of consideration for people held to be inferior to themselves, rising into inhuman atrocities where privacy is secured, is not uncommon with the people proud of their colour and the impunity of their position.

Yet, in spite of these untoward aspects of the case I assert strongly that the solution is most assured when difficulties are greatest. It is a matter for congratulation that today the civilised man is seriously confronted with this problem of race conflict. And the greatest thing that this age can be proud of is the birth of Man in the consciousness of men. Its bed has not been provided for, it is born in poverty, its infancy is lying neglected in a wayside stall, spurned by wealth and power. But its day of triumph is approaching. It is waiting for its poets and prophets and host of humble workers and they will not tarry for long. When the call of humanity is poignantly insistent then the higher nature of man cannot but respond. In the darkest periods of his drunken orgies of power and national pride man may flout and jeer at it, daub it as an expression of weakness and sentimentalism, but in that very paroxysm of arrogance, when his attitude is most hostile and his attacks most reckless against it, he is suddenly reminded that it is the direst form of suicide to kill the highest truth that is in him. When organised national selfishness, racial antipathy and commercial self-seeking begin to display their ugly deformities in all their nakedness, then comes the time for man to know that his salvation is not in political organisations and extended trade relations, not in any mechanical rearrangement of social system, but in a deeper transformation of life, in the liberation of consciousness in love, in the realisation of God in man.

THE RELIGION OF MAN

Man's Universe

Light, as the radiant energy of creation, started the ring-dance of atoms in a diminutive sky, and also the dance of the stars in the vast, lonely theatre of time and space. The planets came out of their bath of fire and basked in the sun for ages. They were the thrones of the gigantic Inert, dumb and desolate, which knew not the meaning of its own blind destiny and majestically frowned upon a future when its monarchy would be menaced.

Then came a time when life was brought into the arena in the tiniest little monocycle of a cell. With its gift of growth and power of adaptation it faced the ponderous enormity of things, and contradicted the unmeaningness of their bulk. It was made conscious not of the volume but of the value of existence, which it ever tried to enhance and maintain in many-branched paths of creation, overcoming the obstructive inertia of Nature by obeying Nature's law.

But the miracle of creation did not stop here in this isolated speck of life launched on a lonely voyage to the Unknown. A multitude of cells were bound together into a larger unit, not through aggregation, but through a marvellous quality of complex inter-relationship maintaining a perfect co-ordination of functions. This is the creative principle of unity, the divine mystery of existence, that baffles all analysis. The larger co-operative units could adequately pay for a greater freedom of self-expression, and they began to form and develop in their bodies new organs of power, new instruments of efficiency. This was the march of evolution ever unfolding the potentialities of life.

But this evolution which continues on the physical plane has its limited range. All exaggeration in that direction becomes a burden that breaks the natural rhythm of life, and those creatures that encouraged their ambitious flesh to grow in dimensions have nearly all perished of their cumbrous absurdity.

Before the chapter ended Man appeared and turned the course of this evolution from an indefinite march of physical aggrandizement to a freedom of a more subtle perfection. This has made possible his progress to become unlimited, and has enabled him to realize the boundless in his power.

The fire is lighted, the hammers are working, and for laborious days and nights amidst dirt and discordance the musical instrument is being made. We may accept this as a detached fact and follow its evolution. But when the music is revealed, we know that the whole thing is a part of the manifestation of music in spite of its contradictory character. The process of evolution, which after ages has reached man, must be realized in its unity with him; though in him it assumes a new value and proceeds to a different path. It is a continuous process that finds its meaning in Man; and we must acknowledge that the evolution which Science talks of is that of Man's universe. The leather binding and title-page are parts of the book itself; and this world that we perceive through our senses and mind and life's experience is profoundly one with ourselves.

The divine principle of unity has ever been that of an inner interrelationship. This is revealed in some of its earliest stages in the evolution of multicellular life on this planet. The most perfect inward expression has been attained by man in his own body. But what is most important of all is the fact that man has also attained its realization in a more subtle body outside his physical system. He misses himself when isolated; he finds his own larger and truer self in his wide human relationship. His multicellular body is born and it dies; his multi-personal humanity is immortal. In this ideal of unity he realizes the eternal in his life and the boundless in his love. The unity becomes not a mere subjective idea, but an energizing truth. Whatever name may be given to it, and whatever form it symbolizes, the consciousness of this unity is spiritual, and our effort to be true to it is our religion. It ever waits to be revealed in our history in a more and more perfect illumination.

We have our eyes, which relate to us the vision of the physical universe. We have also an inner faculty of our own which helps us to find our relationship with the supreme self of man, the universe of personality. This faculty is our luminous imagination, which in its higher stage is special to man. It offers us that vision of wholeness which for the biological necessity of physical survival is superfluous; its purpose is to arouse in us the sense of perfection which is our true sense of immortality. For perfection dwells ideally in Man the Eternal, inspiring love for this ideal in the individual, urging him more and more to realize it.

The development of intelligence and physical power is equally necessary in animals and men for their purpose of living; but what is unique in man is the development of his consciousness which gradually deepens and widens the realization of his immortal being, the perfect, the eternal. It inspires those creations of his that reveal the divinity in him—which is his humanity—in the varied manifestations of truth, goodness and beauty, in the freedom of activity which is not for his use but for his ultimate expression. The individual man must exist for Man the great, and must express him in disinterested works, in science and philosophy, in literature and arts, in service and worship. This is his religion, which is working in the heart of all his religions in various names and forms. He knows and uses this world where it is endless and thus attains greatness, but he realizes his own truth where it is perfect and thus finds his fulfilment.

The idea of the humanity of our God, or the divinity of Man the Eternal, is the main subject of this book. This thought of God has not grown in my mind through any process of philosophical reasoning. On the contrary, it has followed the current of my temperament from early days until it suddenly flashed into my consciousness with a direct vision. The experience which I have described in one of the chapters which follow convinced me that on the surface of our being we have the ever-changing phases of the individual self, but in the depth there dwells the Eternal Spirit of human unity beyond our direct knowledge. It very often contradicts the trivialities of our daily life, and upsets the arrangements made for securing our personal exclusiveness behind the walls of individual habits and superficial conventions. It inspires in us works that are the expressions of a Universal Spirit; it invokes unexpectedly in the midst of a self-centred life a supreme sacrifice. At its call, we hasten to dedicate our lives to the cause of truth and beauty, to unrewarded service of others, in spite of our lack of faith in the positive reality of the ideal values.

During the discussion of my own religious experience I have expressed my belief that the first stage of my realization was through my feeling of intimacy with Nature—not that Nature which has its channel of information for our mind and physical relationship with our living body, but that which satisfies our personality with manifestations that make our life rich and stimulate our imagination in their harmony of forms, colours, sounds and movements. It is not that world which vanishes into abstract symbols behind its own testimony to Science, but that which lavishly displays its wealth of reality to our personal self having its own perpetual reaction upon our human nature.

I have mentioned in connection with my personal experience some songs which I had often heard from wandering village singers, belonging to a popular sect of Bengal, called Baüls,[1] who have no images, temples, scriptures, or ceremonials, who declare in their songs the divinity of Man, and express for him an intense feeling of love. Coming from men who are unsophisticated, living a simple life in obscurity, it gives us a clue to the inner meaning of all religions. For it suggests that these religions are never about a God of cosmic force, but rather about the God of human personality.

At the same time it must be admitted that even the impersonal aspect of truth dealt with by Science belongs to the human Universe. But men of Science tell us that truth, unlike beauty and goodness, is independent of our consciousness. They explain to us how the belief that truth is independent of the human mind is a mystical belief, natural to man but at the same time inexplicable. But may not the explanation be this, that ideal truth does not depend upon the individual mind of man, but on the universal mind which comprehends the individual? For to say that truth, as we see it, exists apart from humanity is really to contradict Science itself; because Science can only organize into rational concepts those facts which man can know and understand, and logic is a machinery of thinking created by the mechanic man.

The table that I am using with all its varied meanings appears as a table for man through his special organ of senses and his special organ of thoughts. When scientifically analysed the same table offers an enormously different appearance to him from that given by his senses. The evidence of his physical senses and that of his logic and his scientific instruments are both related to his own power of comprehension; both are

---

1. See Baül Singers of Bengal.

true and true for him. He makes use of the table with full confidence for his physical purposes, and with equal confidence makes intellectual use of it for his scientific knowledge. But the knowledge is his who is a man. If a particular man as an individual did not exist, the table would exist all the same, but still as a thing that is related to the human mind. The contradiction that there is between the table of our sense perception and the table of our scientific knowledge has its common centre of reconciliation in human personality.

The same thing holds true in the realm of idea. In the scientific idea of the world there is no gap in the universal law of causality. Whatever happens could never have happened otherwise. This is a generalization which has been made possible by a quality of logic which is possessed by the human mind. But this very mind of Man has its immediate consciousness of will within him which *is* aware of its freedom and ever struggles for it. Every day in most of our behaviour we acknowledge its truth; in fact, our conduct finds its best value in its relation to its truth. Thus this has its analogy in our daily behaviour with regard to a table. For whatever may be the conclusion that Science has unquestionably proved about the table, we are amply rewarded when we deal with it as a solid fact and never as a crowd of fluid elements that represent a certain kind of energy. We can also utilize this phenomenon of the measurement. The space represented by a needle when magnified by the microscope may cause us no anxiety as to the number of angels who could be accommodated on its point or camels which could walk through its eye. In a cinema-picture our vision of time and space can be expanded or condensed merely according to the different technique of the instrument. A seed carries packed in a minute receptacle a future which is enormous in its contents both in time and space. The truth, which is Man, has not emerged out of nothing at a certain point of time, even though seemingly it might have been manifested then. But the manifestation of Man has no end in itself—not even now. Neither did it have its beginning in any particular time we ascribe to it. The truth of Man is in the heart of eternity, the fact of it being evolved through endless ages. If Man's manifestation has round it a background of millions of light-years, still it is his own background. He includes in himself the time, however long, that carries the process of his becoming, and he is related for the very truth of his existence to all things that surround him.

Relationship is the fundamental truth of this world of appearance. Take, for instance, a piece of coal. When we pursue the fact of it to its ultimate composition, substance which seemingly is the most stable element in it vanishes in centres of revolving forces. These are the units, called the elements of carbon, which can further be analysed into a certain number of protons and electrons. Yet these electrical facts are what they are, not in their detachment, but in their inter-relationship, and though possibly some day they themselves may be further analysed, nevertheless the pervasive truth of inter-relation which is manifested in them will remain.

We do not know how these elements, as carbon, compose a piece of coal; all that we can say is that they build up that appearance through a unity of interrelationship, which unites them not merely in an individual piece of coal, but in a comradeship of creative co-ordination with the entire physical universe.

Creation has been made possible through the continual self-surrender of the unit to the universe. And the spiritual universe of Man is also ever claiming self-renunciation from the individual units. This spiritual process is not so easy as the physical one in the physical world, for the intelligence and will of the units have to be tempered to those of the universal spirit.

It is said in a verse of the Upanishad that this world which is all movement is pervaded by one supreme unity, and therefore true enjoyment can never be had through the satisfaction of greed, but only through the surrender of our individual self to the Universal Self.

There are thinkers who advocate the doctrine of the plurality of worlds, which can only mean that there are worlds that are absolutely unrelated to each other. Even if this were true it could never be proved. For our universe is the sum total of what Man feels, knows, imagines, reasons to be, and of whatever is knowable to him now or in another time. It affects him differently in its different aspects, in its beauty, its inevitable sequence of happenings, its potentiality; and the world proves itself to him only in its varied effects upon his senses, imagination and reasoning mind.

I do not imply that the final nature of the world depends upon the comprehension of the individual person. Its reality is associated with the universal human mind which comprehends all time and all possibilities of realization. And this is why for the accurate knowledge of things we depend upon Science that represents the rational mind of the universal Man, and not upon that of the individual who dwells in a limited range of space and time and the immediate needs of life. And this is why there is such a thing as progress in our civilization; for progress means that there is an ideal perfection which the individual sees to reach by extending his limits in knowledge, power, love, enjoyment, thus approaching the universal. The most distant star, whose faint message touches the threshold of the most powerful telescopic vision, has its sympathy with the understanding mind of man, and therefore we can never cease to believe that we shall probe further and further into the mystery of their nature. As we know the truth of the stars we know the great comprehensive mind of man.

We must realize not only the reasoning mind, but also the creative imagination, the love and wisdom that belong to the Supreme Person, whose Spirit is over us all, love for whom comprehends love for all creatures and exceeds in depth and strength all other loves, leading to difficult endeavours and martyrdoms that have no other gain than the fulfilment of this love itself.

The *Isha* of our Upanishad, the Super Soul, which permeates all moving things, is the God of this human universe whose mind we share in all our true knowledge, love and service, and whom to reveal in ourselves through renunciation of self is the highest end of life.

The Creative Spirit

Once, during the improvisation of a story by a young child, I was coaxed to take my part as the hero. The child imagined that I had been shut in a dark room locked from the outside. She asked me, 'What will you do for your freedom?' and I answered, 'Shout for help'. But, however desirable that might be if it succeeded immediately, it would be unfortunate for the story. And thus she in her imagination had to clear the neighbourhood of all kinds of help that my cries might reach. I was compelled to think of some violent means of kicking through this passive resistance; but for the sake of the story the door had to be made of steel. I found a key, but it would not fit, and the child was delighted at the development of the story jumping over obstructions.

Life's story of evolution, the main subject of which is the opening of the doors of the dark dungeon, seems to develop in the same manner. Difficulties were created, and at each offer of an answer the story had to discover further obstacles in order to carry on the adventure. For to come to an absolutely satisfactory conclusion is to come to the end of all things, and in that case the great child would have nothing else to do but to shut her curtain and go to sleep.

The Spirit of Life began her chapter by introducing a simple living cell against the tremendously powerful challenge of the vast Inert. The triumph was thrillingly great which still refuses to yield its secret. She did not stop there, but defiantly courted difficulties, and in the technique of her art exploited an element which still baffles our logic.

This is the harmony of self-adjusting inter-relationship impossible to analyse. She brought close together numerous cell units and, by grouping them into a self-sustaining sphere of co-operation, elaborated a larger unit. It was not a mere agglomeration. The grouping had its caste system in the division of functions and yet an intimate unity of kinship. The creative life summoned a larger army of cells under her command and imparted into them, let us say, a communal spirit that fought with all its might whenever its integrity was menaced.

This was the tree which has its inner harmony and inner movement of life in its beauty, its strength, its sublime dignity of endurance, its pilgrimage to the Unknown through the tiniest gates of reincarnation. It was a sufficiently marvellous achievement to be a fit termination to the creative venture. But the creative genius cannot stop exhausted; more windows have to be opened; and she went out of her accustomed way and brought another factor into her work, that of locomotion. Risks of living were enhanced, offering opportunities to the daring resourcefulness of the Spirit of Life. For she seems to revel in the daring resourcefulness of the Spirit of Life. For she seems to revel in occasions for a fight against the giant Matter, which has rigidly prohibitory immigration laws against all new-comers from Life's shore. So the fish was furnished with appliances for moving in an element which offered its density for an obstacle. The air offered an even more difficult obstacle in its lightness; but the challenge was accepted, and the bird was gifted with a marvellous pair of wings that negotiated with the subtle laws of the air and found in it a better ally than the reliable soil of the stable earth. The Arctic snow set up is frigid sentinel; the tropical desert uttered in its scorching breath a gigantic 'No' against all life's children. But those peremptory prohibitions were defied, and the frontiers, though guarded by a death penalty, were triumphantly crossed.

This process of conquest could be described as progress for the kingdom of life. It journeyed on through one success to another by dealing with the laws of Nature through the help of the invention of new instruments. This field of life's onward march is a field of ruthless competition. Because the material world is the world of quantity, where resources are limited and victory waits for those who have superior facility in their weapons, therefore success in the path or progress for one group most often runs parallel to defeat in another.

It appears that such scramble and fight for opportunities of living among numerous small combatants suggested at last an imperialism of big bulky flesh—a huge system of muscles and bones, thick and heavy coats of armour and enormous tails. The idea of such indecorous massiveness must-have seemed natural to life's providence; for the victory in the world of quantity might reasonably appear to depend upon the bigness of dimension. But such gigantic paraphernalia of defence and attack resulted in an utter defeat, the records of which every day are being dug up from the desert sands and ancient mud flats. These represent the fragments that strew the forgotten paths of a great retreat in the battle of existence. For the heavy weight which these creatures carried was mainly composed of bones, hides, shells, teeth and claws that were non-living, and therefore imposed its whole huge pressure upon life that needed freedom and growth for the perfect expression of its own vital nature. The resources for living which the earth offered for her children were recklessly spent by these megalomaniac monsters of an immoderate appetite for the sake of maintaining a cumbersome system of dead burdens that thwarted them in their true progress. Such a losing game has now become obsolete. To the few stragglers of that party, like the rhinoceros or the hippopotamus, has been allotted a very small space on this earth, absurdly inadequate to their formidable strength and magnitude of proportions, making them look forlornly pathetic in the sublimity of their incongruousness. These and their extinct forerunners have been the biggest failures in life's experiments. And then, on some obscure dusk of dawn, the experiment entered upon a completely new phase of a disarmament proposal, when little Man made his appearance in the arena, bringing with him expectations and suggestions that are unfathomably great.

We must know that the evolution process of the world has made its progress towards the revelation of its *truth*— that is to say some inner value which is not in the extension in space and duration in time. When life came out it did not bring with it any new materials into existence. Its elements are the same which are the materials for the rocks and minerals. Only it evolved a value in them which cannot be measured and analysed. The same thing is true with regard to mind and the consciousness of self; they are revelations of a great meaning, the self-expression of a truth. In man this truth has made its positive appearance, and is struggling to make its manifestation more and more clear. That which is eternal is realizing itself in history through the obstructions of limits.

The physiological process in the progress of Life's evolution seems to have reached its finality in man. We cannot think of any noticeable addition or modification in our vital instruments which we are likely to allow to persist. If any individual is born, by chance, with an extra pair of eyes or ears, or some unexpected limbs like stowaways without passports, we are sure to do our best to eliminate them from our bodily organization. Any new chance of a too obviously physical variation is certain to meet with a determined disapproval from man, the most powerful veto being expected from his aesthetic nature, which peremptorily refuses to calculate advantage when its majesty is offended by any sudden license of form. We all know that the back of our body has a wide surface practically unguarded. From the strategic point of view this oversight is unfortunate, causing us annoyances and indignities, if nothing worse, through unwelcome intrusions. And this could reasonable justify in our minds regret for retrenchment in the matter of an original tail, whose memorial we are still made to carry in secret. But the least attempt at the rectification of the policy of economy in this direction is indignantly resented. I strongly believe that the idea of ghosts had its best chance with our timid imagination in our sensitive back—a field of dark ignorance; and yet it is too late for me to hint that one of our eyes could profitably have been spared for our burden-carrier back, so unjustly neglected and haunted by undefined fears.

Thus, while all innovation is stubbornly opposed, there is every sign of a comparative carelessness about the physiological efficiency of the human body. Some of our organs are losing their original vigour. The civilized life, within walked enclosures, has naturally caused in man a weakening of his power of sight and hearing along with subtle sense of the distant. Because of our habit of taking cooked food we give less employment to our teeth and a great deal more to the dentist. Spoilt and pampered by clothes, our skin shows lethargy in its function of adjustment to the atmospheric temperature and in its power of quick recovery from hurts.

The adventurous Life appears to have paused at a crossing in her road before Man came. It seems as if she became aware of wastefulness in carrying on her experiments and adding to her inventions purely on the physical plane. It was proved in Life's case that four is not always twice as much as two. In living things it is necessary to keep to the limit of the perfect unit within which the inter-relationship must not be inordinately strained. The ambition that seeks power in the augmentation of dimension is doomed; for that perfection which is in the inner quality of harmony becomes choked when quantity overwhelms it in a fury of extravagance. The combination of an exaggerated nose and arm that an elephant carries hanging down its front has its advantage. This may induce us to imagine that it would double the advantage for the animal if its tail also could grow into an additional trunk. But the progress which greedily allows Life's field to be crowded with an excessive production of instruments becomes a progress towards death. For Life has its own natural rhythm which a multiplication table has not; and proud progress that rides roughshod over Life's cadence kills it at the end with encumbrances that are unrhythmic. As I have already mentioned, such disasters did happen in the history of evolution.

The moral of that tragic chapter is that if the tail does not have the decency to know where to stop, the drag of this dependency becomes fatal to the body's empire.

Moreover, evolutionary progress on the physical plane inevitably tends to train up its subjects into specialists. The camel is a specialist of the desert and is awkward in the swamp. The hippopotamus which specializes in the mudlands of the Nile is helpless in the neighbouring desert. Such one-sided emphasis breeds professionalism in Life's domain, confining special efficiencies in narrow compartments. The expert training in the aerial sphere is left to the bird; that in the marine is particularly monopolized by the fish. The ostrich is an expert in its own region and would look utterly foolish in an eagle's neighbourhood. They have to remain permanently content with advantages that desperately cling to their limits. Such mutilation of the complete ideal of life for the sake of some exclusive privilege of power is inevitable; for that form of progress deals with materials that are physical and therefore necessarily limited.

To rescue her own career from such a multiplying burden of the dead and such constriction of specialization seems to have been the object of the Spirit of Life at one particular stage. For its does not take long to find out that an indefinite pursuit of quantity creates for Life, which is essentially qualitative, complexities that lead to a vicious circle. These primeval animals that produced an enormous volume of flesh had to build a gigantic system of bones to carry the burden. This required in its turn a long and substantial array of tails to give it balance. Thus their bodies, being compelled to occupy a vast area, exposed a very large surface which had to be protected by a strong, heavy and capacious armour. A progress which represented a congress of dead materials required a parallel organization of teeth and claws, or horns and hooves, which also were dead.

In its own manner one mechanical burden links itself to other burdens of machines, and Life grows to be a carrier of the dead, a mere platform for machinery, until it is crushed to death by its interminable paradoxes. We are told that the greater part of a tree is dead matter; the big stem, except for a thin covering, is lifeless. The tree uses it as a prop in its ambition for a high position and the lifeless timber is the slave that carries on its back the magnitude of the tree. But such a dependence upon a dead dependant has been achieved by the tree at the cost of its real freedom. It has to seek the stable alliance of the earth for the sharing of its burden, which it did by the help of secret underground entanglements making itself permanently stationary.

But the form of life that seeks the great privilege of movement must minimize its load of the dead and must realize that life's progress should be a perfect progress of the inner life itself and not of materials and machinery; the non-living must not continue outgrowing the living, the armour deadening the skin, the armament laming the arms.

At last, when the Spirit of Life found her form in Man, the effort she had begun completed its cycle, and the truth of her mission glimmered into suggestions which dimly pointed to some direction of meaning across her own frontier. Before the end of this cycle was reached, all the suggestions had been external. They were concerned with technique, with life's apparatus, with the efficiency of the organs. This might have exaggerated itself into an endless boredom of physical progress. It can be conceded that the eyes of the bee possessing numerous facets may have some uncommon advantage which we cannot even imagine, or the glow-worm that carries an arrangement for producing light in its person may baffle our capacity and comprehension. Very likely there are creatures having certain organs that given them sensibilities which we cannot have the power to guess.

All such enhanced sensory powers merely add to the mileage in life's journey on the same road lengthening an indefinite distance. They never take us over the border or physical existence.

The same thing may be said not only about life's efficiency, but also life's ornaments. The colouring and decorative patterns on the bodies of some of the deep sea creatures make us silent with amazement. The butterfly's wings, the beetle's back, the peacock's plumes, the shells of the crustaceans, the exuberant outbreak of decoration in plant life, have reached a standard of perfection that seems to be final. And yet if it continues in the same physical direction, then, however much variety of surprising excellence it may produce, it leaves out some great element of unuttered meaning. These ornaments are like ornaments lavished upon a captive girl, luxuriously complete within a narrow limit, speaking of a homesickness for a far away horizon of emancipation, for an inner depth that is beyond the ken of the senses. The freedom in the physical realm is like the circumscribed freedom in a cage. It produces a proficiency which is mechanical and a beauty which is of the surface. To whatever degree of improvement bodily strength and skill may be developed they keep life tied to a persistence of habit. It is closed, like a mould, useful though it may be for the sake of safety and precisely standardized productions. For centuries the bee repeats its hive, the weaver-bird its nest, the spider its web; and instincts strongly attach themselves to some invariable tendencies of muscles and nerves never being allowed the privilege of making blunders. The physical functions, in order to be strictly reliable, behave like some model schoolboy, obedient, regular, properly repeating lessons by rote without mischief or mistake in his conduct, but also without spirit and initiative. It is the flawless perfection of rigid limits, a cousin—of the inanimate.

Instead of allowing a full paradise of perfection to continue its tame and timid rule of faultless regularity the Spirit of Life boldly declared for a further freedom and decided to eat of the fruit of the Tree of Knowledge. This time her struggle was not against the Inert, but against the limitation of her own overburdened agents. She fought against the tutelage of her prudent old prime minister, the faithful instinct. She adopted a novel method of experiment, promulgated new laws, and tried her hand at moulding Man through a history which was immensely different from that which went before. She took a bold step in throwing open her gates to a dangerously explosive factor which she had cautiously introduced into her council—the element of Mind. I should not say that it was ever absent, but only that at a certain stage some curtain was removed and its play was made evident, even like the dark heat which in its glowing intensity reveals itself in a contradiction of radiancy.

Essentially qualitative, like life itself, the Mind does not occupy space. For that very reason it has no bounds in its mastery of space. Also, like Life, Mind has its meaning in freedom, which it missed in its earliest dealings with Life's children. In the animal, though the mind is allowed to come out of the immediate limits of livelihood, its range is restricted, like the freedom of a child that might run out of its room but not out of the house; or, rather, like the foreign ships to which only a certain port was opened in Japan in the beginning of her contact with the West in fear of the danger that might befall if the strangers had their uncontrolled opportunity of communication. Mind also is a foreign element for Life; its laws are different, its weapons powerful, its moods and manners most alien.

Like eve of the Semitic mythology, the Spirit of Life risked the happiness of her placid seclusion to win her freedom. She listened to the whisper of a temper who promised her the right to a new region of mystery, and was urged into a permanent alliance with the stranger. Up to this point the interest of life was the sole interest in her own kingdom, but another most powerfully parallel interest was created with the advent of this adventurer Mind from an unknown shore. Their interests clash, and complications of a serious nature arise. I have already referred to some vital organs of Man that are suffering from neglect. The only reason has been the diversion created by the Mind interrupting the sole attention which Life's functions claimed in the halcyon days of her undisputed monarchy. It is no secret that Mind has the habit of asserting its own will for its expression against life's will to live and enforcing sacrifices from her. When lately some adventurers accepted the dangerous enterprise to climb Mount Everest, it was solely through the instigation of the arch-rebel Mind. In this case Mind denied its treaty of cooperation with its partner and ignored Life's claim to help in her living. The immemorial privileges of the ancient sovereignty of Life are too often flouted by the irreverent Mind; in fact, all through the course of this alliance there are constant cases of interference with each other's functions, often because of this antagonism, the new current of Man's evolution is bringing a wealth to his harbour infinitely beyond the dream of the creatures of monstrous flesh.

The manner in which Man appeared in Life's kingdom was in itself a protest and a challenge, the challenge of Jack to the Giant. He carried in his body the declaration of mistrust against the crowding of burdensome implements of physical progress. His Mind spoke to the naked man, 'Fear not'; and he stood alone facing the menace of a heavy brigade of formidable muscles. His own puny muscles cried out in despair, and he had to invent for himself in a novel manner and in a new spirit of evolution. This at once gave him his promotion from the passive destiny of the animal to the aristocracy of Man. He began to create his further body, his outer organs— the workers which served him and yet did not directly claim a share of his life. Some of the earliest in his list were bows and arrows. Had this change been undertaken by the physical process of evolution, modifying his arms in a slow and gradual manner, it might have resulted in burdensome and ungainly apparatus. Possibly, however, I am unfair, and the dexterity and grace which Life's technical instinct possesses might have changed his arm into a shooting medium in a perfect manner and with a beautiful form. In that case our lyrical literature today would have sung in praise of its fascination, not only for a consummate skill in hunting victims, but also for a similar mischief in a metaphorical sense. But even in the service of lyrics it would show some limitation. For instance, the arms that would specialize in shooting would be awkward in wielding a pen or stringing a lute. But the great advantage in the latest method of human evolution lies in the fact that

Man's additional new limbs, like bows and arrows, have become detached. They never tie his arms to any exclusive advantage of efficiency.

The elephant's trunk, the tiger's paws, the claws of the mole, have combined their best expressions in the human arms, which are much weaker in their original capacity than those limbs I have mentioned. It would have been a hugely cumbersome practical joke if the combination of animal limbs had had a simultaneous location in the human organism through some overzeal in biological inventiveness.

The first great economy resulting from the new programme was the relief of the physical burden, which means the maximum efficiency with the minimum pressure of taxation upon the vital resources of the body. Another mission of benefit was this, that it absolved the Spirit of Life in Man's case from the necessity of specialization for the sake of limited success. This has encouraged Man to dream of the possibility of combining in his single person the fish, the bird and the fleet-footed animal that walks on land. Man desired in his completeness to be the one great representative of multiform life, not through wearisome subjection of opportunities with the help of his reasoning mind. It enables the schoolboy who is given a pen-knife on his birthday to have the advantage over the tiger in the fact that it does not take him a million years to obtain its possession, nor another million years for its removal, when the instrument proves unnecessary or dangerous. The human mind has compressed ages into a few years for the acquisition of steel-made claws. The only cause of anxiety is that the instrument and the temperament which uses it may not keep pace in perfect harmony. In the tiger, the claws and the temperament which only a tiger should possess have had a synchronous development, and in no single tiger is any maladjustment possible between its nails and its tigerliness. But the human boy, who grows a claw in the form of a pen-knife, may not at the same time develop the proper temperament necessary for its use which only a man ought to have. The new organs that today are being added as a supplement to Man's original vital stock are too quick and too numerous for his inner nature to develop its own simultaneous concordance with them, and thus we see everywhere innumerable schoolboys in human society playing pranks with their own and other people's lives and welfare by means of newly acquired pen-knives which have not had time to become humanized.

One thing, I am sure, must have been noticed—that the original plot of the drama is changed, and the mother Spirit of Life has retired into the background, giving full prominence, in the third act, to the Spirit of Man—though the dowager queen, from her inner apartment, still renders necessary help. It is the consciousness in Man of his own creative personality which has ushered in this new regime in Life's kingdom. And from now onwards Man's attempts are directed fully to capture the government and make his own Code of Legislation prevail without a break. We have seen in India those who are called mystics, impatient of the continued regency of mother nature in their own body, winning for their will by a concentration of inner forces the vital regions with which our masterful minds have no direct path of communication.

But the most important fact that has come into prominence along with the change of direction in our evolution, is the possession of a Spirit which has its enormous capital with a surplus for in excess of the requirements of the biological animal in Man. Some overflowing influence led us over the strict boundaries of living, and offered to us an open space where Man's thoughts and dreams could have their holidays. Holidays are for gods who have their joy in creation. In Life's primitive paradise, where the mission was merely to live, any luck which came to the creatures entered in from outside by the donations of chance; they lived on perpetual charity, by turns petted and kicked on the back by physical Providence. Beggars never can have harmony among themselves; they are envious of one another, mutually suspicious, like dogs living upon their master's favour, showing their teeth, growling, barking, trying to tear one another. This is what Science describes as the struggle for existence. This beggar's paradise lacked peace; I am sure the suitors for special favour from fate lived in constant preparedness, inventing and multiplying armaments.

But above the din of the clamour and scramble rises the voice of the Angel of Surplus, of leisure, of detachment from the compelling claim of physical need, saying to men, 'Rejoice'. From his original serfdom as a creature Man takes his right seat as a creator. Whereas, before, his incessant appeal has been to get, now at last the call comes to him to give. His God, whose help he was in the habit of asking, now stands Himself at his door and asks for his offerings. As an animal, he is still dependent upon Nature; as a Man, he is a sovereign who builds his world and rules it.

And there, at this point, comes his religion, whereby he realizes himself in the perspective of the infinite. There is a remarkable verse in the Atharva Veda which says: 'Righteousness, truth, great endeavours, empire, religion, enterprise, heroism and prosperity, the past and the future, dwell in the surpassing strength of the surplus.

What is purely physical has its limits like the shell of an egg; the liberation is there in the atmosphere of the infinite, which is indefinable, invisible. Religion can have no meaning in the enclosure of mere physical or material interest; it is in the surplus we carry around our personality—the surplus which is like the atmosphere of the earth, bringing to her a constant circulation of light and life and delightfulness.

I have said in a poem of mine that when the child is detached from its mother's womb it finds its mother in a real relationship whose truth is in freedom. Man in his detachment has realized himself in a wider and deeper relationship with the universe. In his moral life he has the sense of his obligation and his freedom at the same time, and this is goodness. In his spiritual life his sense of the union and the will which is free has its culmination in love. The freedom of opportunity he wins for himself in Nature's region by uniting his power with Nature's forces. The freedom of social relationship he attains through owning responsibility to his community, thus gaining its collective power for his own welfare. In the freedom of consciousness he realizes the sense of his unity with his unity with his larger being, finding fulfilment in the dedicated life of an ever-progressive truth and ever-active love.

The first detachment achieved by Man is physical. It represents his freedom from the necessity of developing the power of his senses and limbs in the limited area of his own physiology, having for itself an unbounded background with an immense result in consequence. Nature's original intention was that Man should have the allowance of his sight-power ample enough for his surroundings and a little over. But to have to develop an astronomical telescope on our skull would cause a worse crisis of bankruptcy than it did to the Mammoth whose densely foolish body indulged in an extravagance of tusks. A snail carries its house on its back and therefore the material, the shape and the weight have to be strictly limited to the capacity of the body. But fortunately Man's house need not grow on the foundation of his bones and occupy his flesh. Owing to this detachment, his ambition knows no check to its daring in the dimension and strength of his dwellings. Since his shelter does not depend upon his body, it survives him. This fact greatly affects the man who builds a house, generating in his mind a sense of the eternal in his creative work. And this background of the boundless surplus of time encourages architecture, which seeks a universal value overcoming each consisting the miserliness of the present need.

I have already mentioned a stage which Life reached when the units of single cells formed themselves into larger units, of a multitude. It was not merely an aggregation, but had a mysterious unity of interrelationship, complex in character, with differences within of forms and function. We can never know concretely what this relation means. There are gaps between the units, but they do not stop the binding force that permeates the whole. There is a future for the whole which is in its growth, but in order to bring this about each unity works and dies to make room for the next worker. While the unit has the right to claim the glory of the whole, yet individually it cannot share the entire wealth that occupies a history yet to be completed.

Of all creatures Man has reached that multicellular character in a perfect manner, not only in his body but in his personality. For centuries his evolution has been the evolution of a consciousness that tries to be liberated from the bonds of individual separateness and to comprehend in its relationship a wholeness which may be named Man. This relationship, which has been dimly instinctive, is ever struggling to be fully aware of itself. Physical evolution sought for efficiency in a perfect communication with the physical world; the evolution of Man's consciousness sought for truth in a perfect harmony with the world of personality.

There are those who will say that the idea of humanity is an abstraction, subjective in character. It must be confessed that the concrete objectiveness of this living truth cannot be proved to its own units. They can never see its entireness from outside; for they are one with it. The individual cells of our body have their separate lives; but they never have the opportunity of observing the body as a whole with its past, present and future. If these cells have the power of reasoning (which they may have for aught we know) they have the right to argue that the idea of the body has no objective foundation in fact, and though there is a mysterious sense of attraction and mutual influence running through them, these are nothing positively real; the sole reality which is provable is in the isolation of these cells made by gaps that can never be crossed or bridged.

We know something about a system of explosive atoms whirling separately in a space which is immense compared to their own dimension. Yet we do not know why they should appear to us a solid piece of radiant mineral. And if there is an onlooker who at one glance can have the view of the immense time and space occupied by innumerable human individuals engaged in evolving a common history, the positive truth of their solidarity will be concretely evident to him and not the negative fact of their separateness.

The reality of a piece of iron is not provable if we take the evidence of the atom; the only proof is that I see it as a bit of iron, and that it has certain reactions upon my consciousness. And being from, say, Orion, who has the sight to see the atoms and not the iron, has the right to say that we human beings suffer from an age-long epidemic of hallucination. We need not quarrel with him but go on using the iron as it appears to us. Seers there have been who have said *Vēdāhamētam*, 'I see', and lived a life according to that vision. And though our own sight may be blind we have ever bowed our head to them in reverence.

However, whatever name our logic may give to the truth of human unity, the fact can never be ignored that we have our greatest delight when we realize ourselves in others, and this is the definition of love. This love gives us the testimony of the great whole, which is the complete and final truth of man. It offers us the immense field where we can have our release from the sole monarchy of hunger, of the growling means, the source of cruel envy and ignoble deception, where the largest wealth of the human soul has been produced though sympathy and co-operation; through disinterested pursuit of knowledge that recognizes no limit and is unafraid of all time-honoured *taboos*; through a strenuous cultivation of intelligence for service that knows no distinction of colour and clime. The Spirit of Love, dwelling in the boundless realm of the surplus, emancipates our consciousness from the illusory bond of the separateness of self; it is ever trying to spread its illumination in the human world. This is the spirit of civilization, which in all its best endeavour invokes our supreme Being for the only bond of unity that leads us to truth, namely, that of righteousness:

Ya ēkō varnō bahudhā saktiyogāt
varnān anēkān nihitārthō dadhāti
vichaitti chānte visvamādau sa dēvah
sa nō budhyā subhayā samyunaktu

He who is one, above all colours, and who with his manifold power supplies the inherent needs of men of all colours, who is in the beginning and in the end of the world, is divine, and may he unite us in a relationship of good will.

Spiritual Union

When Man's preoccupation with the means of livelihood became less insistent he had the leisure to come to the mystery of his own self, and could not help feeling that the truth of his personality had both its relationship and its perfection in an endless world of humanity. His religion, which in the beginning had its cosmic background of power, came to a higher stage when it found its background in the human truth of personality. It must not be thought that in this channel it was narrowing the range of our consciousness of the infinite.

The negative idea of the infinite is merely an indefinite enlargement of the limits of things; in fact, a perpetual postponement of infinitude. I am told that mathematics has come to the conclusion that our world belongs to a space which is limited. It does not make us feel disconsolate. We do not miss very much and need not have a low opinion of space even if a straight line cannot remain straight and has an eternal tendency to come back to the point from which it started. In the Hindu Scripture the universe is described as an egg; that is to say, for the human mind it has its circular shell of limitation. The Hindu Scripture goes still further and says that time also is not continuous and our world repeatedly comes to an end to begin its cycle once again. In other words, in the region of time and space infinity consists of ever-revolving finitude.

But the positive aspect of the infinite is the *advaitam*, in an absolute unity, in which comprehension of the multitude is not as in an outer receptacle but as in an inner perfection that permeates and exceeds its contents, like the beauty in a lotus which is ineffably more than all the constituents of the flower. It is not the magnitude of extension but an intense quality of harmony which evokes in us the positive sense of the infinite in our joy, in our love. For *advaitam* is *anandam*; the infinite One is infinite Love. For those among whom the spiritual sense is dull, the desire for realization is reduced to physical possession, an actual grasping in space. This longing for magnitude becomes not an aspiration towards the great, but a mania for the big. But true spiritual realization is not through augmentation of possession in dimension or number. The truth that is infinite dwells in the ideal of unity which we find in the deeper relatedness. This truth of realization is not in space, it can only by realized in one's own inner spirit.

Ekadhaivanudrashtavyam etat aprameyam dhruvam
This infinite and eternal has to be known as One.

Ākasat aja ātmā—'this birthless spirit is beyond space.' For it is *Purushah*, it is the '*Person*''.

The special mental attitude which India has in her religion is made clear by the word *Yoga*, whose meaning is to effect union. Union has its significance not in the realm of *to have*, but in that of *to be*. To *gain* truth is to admit its separateness, but to *be* true is to become one with truth. Some religions, which deal with our relationship with god, assure us of reward if that relationship be kept true. This reward has an objective value. It gives us some reason outside ourselves for pursuing the prescribed path. We have such religions also in India. But those that have attained a greater height aspire for their fulfilment in union with *Narayana*, the supreme Reality of Man, which is divine.

Our union with this spirit is not to be attained through the mind. For our mind belongs to the department of economy in the human in the human organism. It carefully husbands our consciousness for its own range of reason, within which to permit our relationship with the phenomenal world. But it is the object of *Yoga* to help us to transcend the limits built up by Mind. On the occasions when these are overcome, our inner self is filled with joy, which indicates that through such freedom we come into touch with the reality that is an end in itself and therefore is bliss.

Once man had his vision of the infinite in the universal Light, and he offered his worship to the sun. He also offered his service to the fire with oblations. Then he felt the infinite in Life, which is Time in its creative aspect, and he said, *Yat kincha yadidam sarvam prana ejati nihsritam*, 'all that there is comes out of life and vibrates in it'. He was sure of it, being conscious of Life's mystery immediately in himself as the principle of purpose, as the organized will, the source of all his activities. His interpretation of the ultimate character of truth relied upon the suggestion that Life had brought to him, and not the non-living which is dumb. And then he came deeper into his being and said '*Raso vai sah*', 'the infinite is love itself',—the eternal spirit of joy. His religion, which is in his realization of the infinite, began its journey from the impersonal *dyaus*, 'the sky', wherein light had its manifestation; then came to Life, which represented the force of self-creation in time, and ended in *purushah*, the 'Person', in whom dwells timeless love. It said, *Tam vedyam purusham vedah*, 'Know him the Person who is to be realized', *Yatha ma vo mrityug parivyathah*—'So that death may not cause you sorrow'. For this Person is deathless in whom the individual person has his immortal truth. Of him it is said: *Esha devo visvakarmā mahātmā sadā janānam hridaya sannivishatah*. 'This is the divine being, the world-worker, who is the Great Soul ever dwelling inherent in the hearts of all people.'

Ya etad vidur amritas te bhavanti. 'Those who realize him, transcend the limits of mortality'—not in duration of time, but in perfection of truth.

Our union with a Being whose activity is world-wide and who dwells in the heart of humanity cannot be a passive one. In order to be united with Him we have to divest our work of selfishness and become *visvakarmā* , 'the world-worker', we must work for all. When I use the words 'for all', I do not mean for a countless number of individuals. All work that is good, however small in extent, is universal in character. Such work makes for a realization of *Visvakarmā*, 'the World-Worker' who works for all. In order to be one with this Mahatma, 'the Great Soul', one must cultivate the greatness of soul which identifies itself with the soul of all peoples all not merely with that of one's own. This helps us to understand what Buddha has described as *Brahmavihāra*, 'living in the infinite'. He says:

'Do not' deceive each other, do not despise anybody anywhere, never in anger wish anyone to suffer through your body, words or thoughts. Like a mother maintaining her only son with her own life, keep thy immeasurable loving thought for all creatures.

'Above thee, below thee, on all sides of thee, keep on all the world thy sympathy and immeasurable loving thought which is without obstruction, without any wish to injure, without enmity.

'To be dwelling in such contemplation while standing, walking, sitting or laying down, until sleep overcomes thee, is called living in Brahma'.

This proves that Buddha's idea of the infinite was not the idea of a spirit of an unbounded cosmic activity, but the infinite whose meaning is in the positive ideal of goodness and love, which cannot be otherwise than human. By being charitable, good and loving, you do not realize the infinite, in the stars or rocks, but the infinite revealed in Man. Buddha's teaching speaks of nirvana as the highest end. To understand its real character we have to know the path of its attainment, which is not merely through the negation of evil thoughts and deeds but through the elimination of all limits to love. It must mean the sublimation of self in a truth which is love itself, which unites in its bosom all those to whom we must offer our sympathy and service.

When somebody asked Buddha about the original cause of existence he sternly said that such questioning was futile and irrelevant. Did he not mean that it went beyond the human sphere as our goal—that though such a question might legitimately be asked in the region of cosmic philosophy or science, it had nothing to do with man's *dharma*, man's inner nature, in which love finds its utter fulfilment, in which all his sacrifice ends in an eternal gain, in which the putting out of the lamplight is no loss because there is the all-pervading light of the sun. And did those who listened to the great teacher merely hear his words and understand his doctrines? No, they directly felt in him what he was preaching, in the living language of his own person, the ultimate truth of Man.

It is significant that all great religions have their historic origin in persons who represented in their life a truth which was not cosmic and unmoral, but human and good. They rescued religion from the magic stronghold of demon force and brought it into the inner heart of humanity, into a fulfilment not confined to some exclusive good fortune of the individual but to the welfare of all men. This was not for the spiritual ecstasy of lonely souls, but for the spiritual emancipation of all races. They came as the messengers of Man to men of all countries and spoke of the salvation that could only be reached by the perfecting of our relationship with Man the Eternal,

Man the Divine. Whatever might be their doctrines of God, or some dogmas that they borrowed from their own time and tradition, their life and teaching had the deeper implication of a Being who is the infinite in Man, the Father, the Friend, the Lover, whose service must be realized through serving all mankind. For the God in Man depends upon men's service and men's love for his own love's fulfilment.

The question was once asked in the shade of the ancient forest of India:

Kasmai devāva havishā vidhema?
Who is the God to whom we must bring our oblation?

That question is still ours, and to answer it we must know in the depth of our love and the maturity of our wisdom what man is—know him not only in sympathy but in science, in the joy of creation and in the pain of heroism; *tena tyaktena bhunjitha*, 'enjoy him through sacrifice'—the sacrifice that comes of love; *ma gridhah*, 'covet not'; for greed diverts your mind to that illusion in you which you represent the *parama purushah*, 'the supreme Person'.

Our greed diverts our consciousness to materials away from that supreme value of truth which is the quality of the universal being. The gulf thus created by the receding stream of the soul we try to replenish with a continuous stream of wealth, which may have the power to fill but not the power to unite and recreate. Therefore the gap is dangerously concealed under the glittering quicksand of things, which by their own weight cause a sudden subsidence while we are in the depths of sleep.

The real tragedy, however, does not lie in the risk of our material security but in the obscuration of Man himself in the human world. In the creative activities of his soul Man realizes his surroundings as his larger self, instinct with his own life and love. But in his ambition he deforms and defiles it with the callous handling of his voracity. His world of utility assuming a gigantic proportion, reacts upon his inner nature and hypnotically suggests to him a scheme of the universe which is an abstract system. In such a world there can be no question of *mukti*, the freedom in truth, because it is a solidly solitary fact, a cage with no sky beyond it. In all appearance our world is a closed world of hard facts; it is like a seed with its tough cover. But within this enclosure is working our silent cry of life for *mukti*, even when its possibility is darkly silent. When some huge overgrown temptation tramples into stillness this living aspiration then does civilization die like a seed that has lost its urging for germination. And this *mukti* is in the truth that dwells in the ideal man.

The Vision

I hope that my readers have understood, as they have read these pages, that I am neither a scholar nor a philosopher. They should not expect from me fruits gathered from a wide field of studies or wealth brought by a mind trained in the difficult exploration of knowledge. Fortunately for me the subject of religion gains in interest and value by the experience of the individuals who earnestly believe in its truth. This is my apology for offering a part of the story of my life which has always realized its religion through a process of growth and not by the help of inheritance of importation.

Man has made the entire geography of the earth his own, ignoring the boundaries of climate; for, unlike the lion and the reindeer, he has the power to create his special skin and temperature, including his unscrupulous power of borrowing the skins of the indigenous inhabitants and misappropriating their fats.

His kingdom is also continually extending in time through a great surplus in his power of memory, to which is linked his immense facility of borrowing the treasure of the past from all quarters of the world. He dwells in a universe of history, in an environment of continuous remembrance. The animal occupies time only through the multiplication of its own race, but man through the memorials of his mind, raised along the pilgrimage of progress. The stupendousness of his knowledge and wisdom is due to their roots spreading into and drawing sap from the far-reaching area of history.

Man has his other dwelling place in the realm of inner realization, in the element of an immaterial value. This is a world where from the subterranean soil of his mind his consciousness often, like a seed, unexpectedly sends up sprouts into the heart of a luminous freedom, and the individual is made to realize his truth in the universal Man. I hope it may prove of interest if I give an account of my own personal experience of a sudden spiritual outburst from within me which is like the underground current of a perennial stream unexpectedly welling up on the surface.

I was born in a family which, at that time, was earnestly developing a monotheistic religion based upon the philosophy of the Upanishad. Somehow my mind at first remained coldly aloof, absolutely uninfluenced by any religion whatever. It was through an idiosyncrasy of my temperament that I refused to accept any religious teaching merely because people in my surroundings believed it to be true. I could not persuade myself to imagine that I had a religion because everybody whom I might trust believed in its value.

Thus my mind was brought up in an atmosphere of freedom—freedom from the dominance of any creed that had its sanction in the definite authority of some scripture, or in the teaching of some organized body of worshippers. And, therefore, the man who questions me has ever right to distrust my vision and reject my testimony. In such a case, the authority of some particular book venerated by a large number of men may have greater weight than the assertion of an individual, and therefore I never claim any right to preach.

When I look back upon those days, it seems to me that unconsciously I followed the path of my Vedic ancestors, and was inspired by the tropical sky with its suggestion of an uttermost Beyond. The wonder of the gathering clouds hanging heavy with the unshed rain, of the sudden sweep of storms arousing vehement gestures along the line of coconut trees, the fierce loneliness of the blazing summer noon, the silent sunrise behind the dewy veil of autumn morning, kept my mind with the intimacy of a pervasive companionship.

Then came my initiation ceremony of Brahminhood when the *Gayatri* verse of meditation was given to me, whose meaning, according to the explanation I had, runs as follows:

Let me contemplate the adorable splendour of Him who created the earth, the air and the starry spheres, and sends the power of comprehension with our minds.

This produced a sense of serene exaltation in me, the daily meditation upon the infinite being which unites in one stream of creation my mind and the outer world. Though today I find no difficulty in realizing this being as an infinite personality in whom the subject and object are perfectly reconciled, at that time the idea to me was vague. Therefore the current of feeling that it aroused in my mind was indefinite, like the circulation of air—an atmosphere which needed a definite world to complete itself and satisfy me. For it is evident that my religion is a poet's religion, and neither that of an orthodox man of piety nor that of a theologian. Its touch comes to me through the same unseen and trackless channel as does the inspiration of my songs. My religious life has followed the same mysterious line of growth as has my poetical life. Somehow they are wedded to each other and, though their betrothal had a long period of ceremony, it was kept secret to me.

When I was eighteen, a sudden spring breeze of religious experience for the first time came to my life and passed away leaving in my memory a direct message of spiritual reality. One day while I stood watching at early dawn the sun sending out its rays from behind the trees, I suddenly felt as if some ancient mist had in a moment lifted from my sight, and the morning light on the face of the world revealed an inner radiance of joy. The invisible screen of the commonplace was removed from all things and all men, and their ultimate significance was intensified in my mind; and this is the definition of beauty. That which was memorable in this experience was its human message, the sudden expansion of my consciousness in the super-personal world of man. The poem I wrote on the first day of my surprise was named 'The Awakening of the Waterfall'. The waterfall, whose spirit lay dormant in its ice-bound isolation, was touched by the sun and, bursting in a cataract of freedom, it found its finality in an unending sacrifice, in a continual union with the sea. After four days the vision passed away, and the lid hung down upon my inner sight. In the dark, the world once again put on its disguise of the obscurity of an ordinary fact.

When I grew older and was employed in a responsible work in some villages I took my place in a neighbourhood where the current of time ran slow and joys and sorrows had their simple and elemental shades and lights. The day which had its special significance for me came with all its drifting trivialities of the commonplace life. The ordinary work of my morning had come to its close and before going to take my bath I stood for a moment at my window, overlooking a market place on the bank of a dry river bed, welcoming the first flood of rain along its channel. Suddenly I became conscious of a stirring of soul within me. My world of experience in a moment seemed to become lighted, and facts that were detached and dim found a great unity of meaning. The feeling which I had was like that which a man, groping through a fog without knowing his destination, might feel when he suddenly discovers that he stands before his own house.

I still remember the day in my childhood when I was made to struggle across my lessons in a first primer, strewn with isolated words smothered under the burden of spelling. The morning hour appeared to me like a once-illumined page, grown dusty and faded, discoloured into irrelevant marks, smudges and gaps, wearisome in its moth-eaten meaninglessness. Suddenly I came to a rhymed sentence of combined words, which may be translated thus—'it rains, the leaves tremble'. At once I came to a world wherein I recovered my full meaning. My mind touch the creative realm of expression, and at that moment I was no longer a mere student with his mind muffled by spelling lessons, enclosed by classroom. The rhythmic picture of the tremulous leaves beaten by the rain opened before my mind the world which does not merely carry information, but a harmony with my mind revelled in the unity of a vision. In a similar manner, on that morning in the village, the facts of my life suddenly appeared to me in a luminous unity of truth. All things that had seemed like vagrant waves were revealed to my mind in relation to a boundless sea. I felt sure that some Being who comprehended me and my world was seeking his best expression in all my experiences, uniting them into an ever-widening individuality which is a spiritual work of art.

To this being I was responsible; for the creation in me is his as well as mine. It may be that it was the same creative Mind that is shaping the universe to its eternal idea; but in me as a person it had one of its special centres of a personal relationship growing into a deepening consciousness. I had my sorrows that left their memory in a long burning track across my days, but I felt at that moment that in them I lent myself to a travail of creation that ever exceeded my own personal bounds like stars which in their individual firebursts are lighting the history of the universe. It gave me a great joy to feel in my life detachment at the idea of a mystery of a meeting of the two in a creative comradeship. I felt that I had found my religion at last, the religion of Man, in which the infinite became defined in humanity and came close to me so as to need my love and co-operation.

This idea of mine found at a later date its expression in some of my poems addressed to what I called *Jivan devatā*, the Lord of my life. Fully aware of my awkwardness in dealing with a foreign language, with some hesitation I give a translation, being sure that any evidence revealed through the self-recording instrument of poetry is more authentic than answers extorted through conscious questionings:

> Thou who art the innermost Spirit of my being,
> art thou pleased, Lord of my Life?
> For I gave to thee my cup
> filled with all the pain and delight
> that the crushed grapes of my heart had
> surrendered,
> I wove with the rhythm of colours and songs the
> cover for thy bed,
> and with the molten gold of my desires
> I fashioned playthings for thy passing hours.
>
> I know not why thou chosest me for thy partner,
> Lord of my Life!
> Dist thou store my days and nights,
> my deeds and dreams for the alchemy of thy art,
> and string in the chain of thy music my songs of
> autumn and spring,
> and gather the flowers from my mature moments
> for thy crown?
>
> I see thine eyes gazing at the dark of my heart,
> Lord of my life,
> I wonder if my failures and wrongs are forgiven.
> For many were my days without service
> and nights of forgetfulness;

futile were the flowers that faded in the shade not
offered to thee.
Often the tired strings of my lute
slackened at the strain of thy tunes.
And often at the ruin of wasted hours
my desolate evenings were filled with tears.

But have my days come to their end at last,
Lord of my life,
while my arms round thee grow limp,
my kisses losing their truth?
Then break up the meeting of this languid day.
Renew the old in me in fresh forms of delight;
and let the wedding come once again
in a new ceremony of life.

You will understand from this how unconsciously I had been
travelling towards the realization which I stumbled upon in
an idle moment on a day in July, when morning clouds
thickened on the eastern horizon and a caressing shadow lay
on the tremulous bamboo branches, while an excited group
of village boys was noisily dragging from the bank an old
fishing boat; and I cannot tell how at that moment an
unexpected train of thoughts ran across my mind like a
strange caravan carrying the wealth of an unknown kingdom.

From my infancy I had a keen sensitiveness which kept
my mind tingling with consciousness of the world around me,
natural and human. We had a small garden attached to our
house; it was a fairyland to me, where miracles of beauty were
of everyday occurrence.

Almost every morning in the early hour of the dusk, I
would run out from my bed in a great hurry to greet the first
pink flush of the dawn through the shivering branches of the
palm trees which stood in a line along the garden boundary,
while the grass glistened as the dew-drops caught the earliest

tremor of the morning breeze. The sky seemed to bring to me the call of a personal companionship, and all my heart—my whole body in fact—used to drink in at a draught the overflowing light and peace of those silent hours. I was anxious never to miss a single morning, because each one was precious to me, more precious than gold to the miser. I am certain that I felt a larger meaning of my own self when the barrier vanished between me and what was beyond myself.

I had been blessed with that sense of wonder which gives a child his right of entry into the treasure house of mystery in the depth of existence. My studies in the school I neglected, because they rudely dismembered me from the context of my world and I felt miserable, like a caged rabbit in a biological institute. This, perhaps, will explain the meaning of my religion. This world was living to me, intimately close to my life, permeated by a subtle touch of kinship which enhanced the value of my own being.

It is true that this world also has its impersonal aspect of truth which is pursued by the man of impersonal science. The father has his personal relationship with his son; but as a doctor he may detach the fact of a son from that relationship and let the child become an abstraction to him, only a living body with its physiological functions. It cannot be said that if through the constant pursuit of his vocations he altogether discards the personal element in his relation to his son he reaches a greater truth as a doctor than he does as a father. The scientific knowledge of his son is information about a fact, and not the realization of a truth. In his intimate feeling for his son he touches an ultimate truth—the truth of relationship, the truth of a harmony in the universe, the fundamental principle of creation. It is not merely the number of protons and electrons which represents the truth of an element; it is the mystery of their relationship which cannot be analysed. We are made conscious of this truth of relationship immediately within us in our love, in our joy; and from this experience of ours we have the right to say that the Supreme One, who relates all things, comprehends the universe, is all love—the love that is the highest truth being the most perfect relationship.

I still remember the shock of repulsion I received as a child when some medical student brought to me a piece of a human windpipe and tried to excite my admiration for its structure. He tried to convince me that it was the source of the beautiful human voice. But I could not bear the artisan to occupy the throne that was for the artist who concealed the machinery and revealed the creation in its ineffable unity. God does not care to keep exposed the record of his power written in geological inscriptions, but he is proudly glad of the expression of beauty which he spreads on the green grass, in the flowers, in the play of the colours on the clouds, in the murmuring music of running water.

I had a vague notion as to who or what it was that touched my heart's chords, like the infant which does not know its mother's name, or who or what she is. The feeling which I always had was a deep satisfaction of personality that flowed into my nature through living channels of communication from all sides.

I am afraid that the scientist may remind me that to lose sight of the distinction between life and non-life, the human and the non-human, is a sign of the primitive mind. While admitting it, let me hope that it is not an utter condemnation, but rather the contrary. It may be a true instinct of Science itself, an instinctive logic, which makes the primitive mind think that humanity has become possible as a fact only because of a universal human truth which has harmony with its reason, with its will. In the details of our universe there are some differences that may be described as non-human, but not in their essence. The bones are different from the muscles, but

394   ❖   RABINDRANATH TAGORE SELECTED ESSAYS

they are organically one in the body. Our feeling of joy, our imagination, realizes a profound organic unity with the universe comprehended by the human mind. Without minimizing the differences that are in detailed manifestations, there is nothing wrong in trusting the mind, which is occasionally made intensely conscious of an all-pervading personality answering to the personality of man.

The details of reality must be studied in their differences by Science, but it can never know the character of the grand unity of relationship pervading it, which can only be realized immediately by the human spirit. And therefore it is the primal imagination of man—the imagination which is fresh and immediate in its experiences—that exclaims in a poet's verse:

> Wisdom and spirit of the universe!
> Thou soul, that art the eternity of thought,
> And giv'st to forms and images a breath
> And everlasting motion.

And in another poet's words it speaks of

> That light whose smile kindles the universe,
> That Beauty in which all things work and move.

The theologian may follow the scientist and shake his head and say that all that I have written is pantheism. But let us not indulge in an idolatry of name and dethrone living truth in its favour. When I say that I am a man, it is implied by that word that there is such a thing as a general idea of Man which persistently manifests itself in every particular human being, who is different from all other individuals. If we lazily label such a belief as 'pananthropy' and divert our thoughts from its mysteriousness by such a title it does not help us much. Let me assert my faith by saying that this world, consisting of what we call animate and inanimate things, has found its culmination in man, its best expression. Man, as a creation, represents the Creator, and this is why of all creatures it has been possible for him to comprehend this world in his knowledge and in his feeling and in his imagination, to realize in his individual spirit a union with a Spirit that is everywhere.

There is an illustration that I have made use of in which I supposed that a stranger from some other planet has paid a visit to our earth and happens to hear the sound of a human voice on the gramophone. All that is obvious to him and most seemingly active, is the revolving disc. He is unable to discover the personal truth that lies behind, and so might accept the impersonal scientific fact of the disc as final—the fact that could be touched and measured. He would wonder how it could be possible for a machine to speak to the soul. Then, if in pursuing the mystery, he should suddenly come to the heart of the music through a meeting with the composer, he would at once understand the meaning of that music as a personal communication.

That which merely gives us information can be explained in terms of measurement, but that which gives us joy cannot be explained by the facts of a mere grouping of atoms and molecules. Somewhere in the arrangement of this world there seems to be a great concern about giving us delight, which shows that, in the universe, over and above the meaning of matter and forces, there is a message conveyed through the magic touch of personality. This touch cannot be analysed, it can only be felt. We cannot prove it any more than the man from the other planet could prove to the satisfaction of his fellows the personality which remained invisible, but which, through the machinery, spoke direct to the heart.

Is it merely because the rose is round and pink that it gives me more satisfaction than the gold which could buy me the necessities of life, or any number of slaves? One may, at the outset, deny the truth that a rose gives more delight than a piece of gold. But such an objector must remember that I am not speaking of artificial values. If we had to cross a desert whose sand was made of gold, then the cruel glitter of these dead particles would become a terror for us, and the sight of a rose would bring to us the music of paradise.

The final meaning of the delight which we find in a rose can never be in the roundness of its petals, just as the final meaning of the joy of music cannot be in a gramophone disc. Somehow we feel that through a rose the language of love reached our heart. Do we not carry a rose to our beloved because in it is already embodied a message which, unlike our language of words, cannot be analysed? Through this gift of a rose we utilize a universal language of joy for own purposes of expression.

Fortunately for me a collection of old lyrical poems composed by the poets of the Vaishnava sect came to my hand when I was young. I became aware of some underlying idea deep in the obvious meaning of these love poems. I felt the joy of an explorer who suddenly discovers the key to the language lying hidden in the hieroglyphs which are beautiful in themselves. I was sure that these poets were speaking about the supreme Lover, whose touch we experience in all our relations of love—the love of nature's beauty, of the animal, the child, the comrade, the beloved, the love that illuminates our consciousness of reality. They sang of a love that ever flows through numerous obstacles between men and Man the Divine, the eternal relation which has the relationship of mutual dependence for a fulfilment that needs perfect union of individuals and the Universal.

The Vaishnava poet sings of the Lover who has his flute which, with its different stops, gives out the varied notes of beauty and love that are in Nature and Man. These notes bring to us our message of invitation. They eternally urge us to come out from the seclusion of our self-centred life into the realm of love and truth. Are we deaf by nature, or is it that we have been deafened by the claims of the world, of self-seeking, by the clamorous noise of the market-place? We miss the voice of the Lover, and we fight, we rob, we exploit the weak, we chuckle at our cleverness, when we can appropriate for our use what is due to others; we make our lives a desert by turning away from our world that stream of love which pours down from the blue sky and wells up from the bosom of the earth.

In the region of Nature, by unlocking the secret doors of the workshop department, one may come to that dark hall where dwells that mechanic and help to attain usefulness, but through it one can never attain finality. Here is the storehouse of innumerable facts and, however necessary they may be, they have not the treasure of fulfilment in them. But the hall of union is there, where dwells the Lover in the heart of existence. When a man reaches it he at once realizes that he has come to Truth, to immortality, and he is glad with a gladness which is an end, and yet which has no end.

Mere information about facts, mere discovery of power, belongs to the outside and not to the inner soul of things. Gladness is the one criterion of truth, and we know when we had touched Truth by the music it gives, by the joy of greeting it sends forth to the truth in us. That is the true foundation of all religions. It is not as ether waves that we receive light; the morning does not wait for some scientist for its introduction to us. In the same way we touch the infinite reality immediately within us only when we perceive the pure truth of love or goodness, not through the explanations of theologians, not through the erudite discussion of ethical doctrines.

I have already made the confession that my religion is a poet's religion. All that I feel about it is from vision and not from knowledge. Frankly, I acknowledge that I cannot satisfactorily answer any questions about evil, or about what happens after death. Nevertheless, I am sure that there have come moments in my own experience when my soul has touched the infinite and has become intensely conscious of it through the illumination of joy. It has been said in our Upanishad that our mind and our words come away baffled from the Supreme Truth, but he who knows truth through the immediate joy of his own soul is saved from all doubts and fears.

In the night we stumble over things and become acutely conscious of their individual separateness. But the day reveals the greater unity which embraces them. The man whose inner vision is bathed in an illumination of his consciousness at once realizes the spiritual unity reigning supreme over all differences. His mind no longer awkwardly stumbles over individual facts of separateness in the human world, accepting them as final. He realizes that peace is in the inner harmony which dwells in truth and not in any outer adjustments. He knows that beauty carries an eternal assurance of our spiritual relationship to reality, which waits for its perfection in the response of our love.

The Music Maker

A particle of sand would be nothing if it did not have its background in the whole physical world. This grain of sand is known in its context of the universe where we know all things through the testimony of our senses. When I say the grain of sand *is*, the whole physical world stands guarantee for the truth which is behind the appearance of the sand.

But where is that guarantee of truth for this personality of mine that has the mysterious faculty of knowledge before which the particle of sand offers its credential of identification? It must be acknowledged that this personal self of mine also has for its truth a background of personality where knowledge, unlike that of other things, can only be immediate and self-revealed.

What I mean by personality is a self-conscious principle of transcendental unity within man which comprehends all the details of facts that are individually his in knowledge and feeling, wish and will and work. In its negative aspect it is limited to the individual separateness, while in its positive aspect it ever extends itself in the infinite through the increase of its knowledge, love and activities.

And for this reason the most human of all facts about us is that we *do* dream of the limitless unattained—the dream which gives character to what *is* attained. Of all creatures man lives in an endless future. Our present is only a part of it. The ideas unborn, the unbodied spirits, tease our imagination with an insistence which makes them more real to our mind than things around us. The atmosphere of the future must always surround our present in order to make it life-bearing and suggestive of immortality. For he who has the healthy vigour of humanity in him has a strong instinctive faith that ideally he is limitless. That is why our greatest teachers claim from us a manifestation that touches the infinite. In this they pay homage to the Supreme Man. And our true worship lies in our indomitable courage to be great and thus to represent the human divine and ever to keep open the path of freedom towards the unattained.

We Indians have had the sad experience in our own part of the world how timid orthodoxy, its irrational repressions and its accumulation of dead centuries, dwarfs man through its idolatry of the past. Seated rigid in the centre of stagnation, it firmly ties the human spirit to the revolving wheels of habit till faintness overwhelms her. Like a sluggish stream choked by rotting weeds, it is divided into shallow slimy pools that shroud their dumbness in a narcotic mist of stupor. This mechanical spirit of tradition is essentially materialistic, it is blindly pious but not spiritual, obsessed by phantoms of unreason that haunt feeble minds in the ghastly disguise of religion. For our soul is shrunken when we allow foolish days to weave repeated patterns of unmeaning meshes round all departments of life. It becomes stunted when we have no object of profound interest, no prospect of heightened life, demanding clarity of mind and heroic attention to maintain and mature it. It is destroyed when we make fireworks of our animal passions for the enjoyment of their meteoric sensations, recklessly reducing to ashes all that could have been saved for permanent illumination. This happens not only to mediocre individuals hugging fetters that keep them irresponsible or hungering for lurid unrealities, but to generations of insipid races that have lost all emphasis of significance in themselves, having missed their future.

The continuous future is the domain of our millennium, which is with us more truly than what we see in or history in fragments of the present. It is in our dream. It is in the realm of the faith which creates perfection. We have seen the records of man's dreams of the millennium, the ideal reality cherished by forgotten races in their admiration, hope and love manifested in the dignity of their being through some majesty in ideals and beauty in performance. While these races pass away one after another they leave great accomplishments behind them carrying their claim to recognition as dreamers—not so much as conquerors of earthly kingdoms, but as the designers of paradise. The poet gives us the best definition of man when he says:

> We are the music-makers,
> We are the dreamers of dreams.

Our religions present for us the dreams of the ideal unity which is man himself as he manifests the infinite. We suffer from the sense of sin, which is the sense of discord, when any disruptive passion tears gaps in our vision of the One in man, creating isolation in our self from the universal humanity.

The Upanishad says, *māgridah*, 'covet not'. For coveting diverts attention from the infinite value of our personality to the temptation of materials. Our village poet sings: 'Man will brightly flash into your sight, my heart, if you shut the door of desires.'

We have seen how primitive man was occupied with his physical needs, and thus restricted himself to the present which is the time boundary of the animal; and he missed the urge of his consciousness to seek its emancipation in a world of ultimate human value.

Modern civilization for the same reason seems to turn itself back to that primitive mentality. Our needs have multiplied so furiously fast that we have lost our leisure for the deeper realization of our self and our faith in it. It means that we have lost our religion, the longing for the touch of the divine in man, the builder of the heaven, the music-maker, the dreamer of dreams. This has made it easy to tear into shreds our faith in the perfection of the human ideal, in its wholeness, as the fuller meaning of reality. No doubt it is wonderful that music contains a fact which has been analysed and measured, and which music shares in common with the braying of an ass or of a motor-car horn. But it is still more wonderful that music has a truth, which cannot be analysed into fractions; and there the difference between it and the bellowing impertinence of a motor-car horn is infinite. Men of our own times have analysed the human mind, its dreams, its spiritual aspirations,—most often caught unawares in the shattered state of madness, disease and desultory dreams— and they have found to their satisfaction that these are composed of elemental animalities tangled into various knots. This may be an important discovery; but what is still more important to realize is the fact that by some miracle of creation man infinitely transcends the component parts of his own character.

Suppose that some psychological explorer suspects that man's devotion to his beloved has at bottom our primitive stomach's hankering for human flesh, we need not contradict him; for whatever may be its genealogy, its secret composition, the complete character of our love, in its utter difference from cannibalism. The truth underlying the possibility of such transmutation is the truth of our religion. A lotus has in common with a piece of rotten flesh the elements of carbon and hydrogen. In a state of dissolution there is no difference between them, but in a state of creation the difference is immense; and it is that difference which really matters. We are told that some of our most sacred sentiments hold hidden in them instincts contrary to what these sentiments profess to be. Such disclosures have the effect upon certain persons of the relief of a tension, even like the relaxation in death of the incessant strenuousness of life.

We find in modern literature that something like a chuckle of an exultant disillusionment is becoming contagious, and the knights-errant of the cult of arson are abroad, setting fire to our time-honoured altars of worship, proclaiming that the images enshrined on them, even if beautiful, are made of mud. They say that it has been found out that the appearances in human idealism are deceptive, that the underlying mud is real. From such a point of view, the whole of creation may be said to be a gigantic deception, and the billions of revolving electric specks that have the appearance of 'you' or 'me' should be condemned as bearers of false evidence.

But whom do they seek to delude? If it be beings like ourselves who possess some inborn criterion of the real, then to them these very appearances in their integrity must represent reality, and not their component electric specks. For them the rose must be more satisfactory as an object than its constituent gases, which can be tortured to speak against the evident identity of the rose. The rose, even like the human sentiment of goodness, or ideal of beauty, belongs to the realm of creation, in which all its rebellious elements are reconciled in a perfect harmony. Because these elements in their simplicity yield themselves to our scrutiny, we in our pride are inclined to give them the best prizes as actors in that mystery-play, the rose. Such an analysis is really only giving a prize to our own detective cleverness.

I repeat again that the sentiments and ideals which man in his process of self-creation has built up, should be recognized in their wholeness. In all our faculties or passions there is nothing which is absolutely good or bad; they all are the constituents of the great human personality. They are notes that are wrong when in wrong places; our education is to make them into chords that may harmonize with the grand music of Man. The animal in the savage has been transformed into higher stages in the civilized man—in other words has attained a truer consonance with Man the divine, not through any elimination of the original materials, but through a magical grouping of them, through the severe discipline of art, the discipline of curbing and stressing in proper place, establishing a balance of lights and shadows in the background and foreground, and thus imparting a unique value to our personality in all its completeness.

So long as we have faith in this value, our energy is steadily sustained in its creative activity that reveals the eternal Man. This faith is helped on all sides by literature, arts, legends, symbols, ceremonials, by the remembrance of heroic souls who have personified it in themselves.

Our religion is the inner principle that comprehends these endeavours and expressions and dreams through which we approach Him in whose image we are made. To keep alive our faith in the reality of the ideal perfection is the function of civilization, which is mainly formed of sentiments and the images that represent that ideal. In other words, civilization is a creation of art, created for the objective realization of our vision of the spiritually perfect. It is the product of the art of religion. We stop its course of conquest when we accept the cult of realism and forget that realism is the worst form of untruth, because it contains a minimum of truth. It is like preaching that only in the morgue can we comprehend the reality of the human body—the body which has its perfect revelation when seen in life. All great human facts are surrounded by an immense atmosphere of expectation. They are never complete if we leave out from them what might be, what should be, what is not yet proven but profoundly felt, what points towards the immortal. This dwells in a perpetual surplus in the individual, that transcends all the desultory facts about him.

The realism in Man is the animal in him, whose life is a mere duration of time; the human in him is his reality which has life everlasting for its background. Rocks and crystals being complete definitely in what they are, can keep as 'mute insensate things' a kind of dumb dignity in their stolidly limited realism; while human facts grow unseemly and diseased, breeding germs of death, when divested of their creative ideal—the ideal of Man the divine. The difference between the notes as mere facts of sound and music as a truth of expression is immense. For music though it comprehends a limited number of notes yet represents the infinite. It is for man to produce the music as a truth of expression is immense. For music though it comprehends a limited number of notes yet represents the infinite. It is for man to produce the music of the spirit with all the notes which he has in his psychology and which, through inattention or perversity, can easily be translated into a frightful noise. In music man is revealed and not in a noise.

The Artist

The Fundamental desire of life is the desire to exist. It claims from us a vast amount of training and experience about the necessaries of livelihood. Yet it does not cost me much to confess that the food that I have taken, the dress that I wear, the house where I have my lodging, represent a stupendous knowledge, practice and organization which I helplessly lack; for I find that I am not altogether despised for such ignorance and inefficiency. Those who read me seem fairly satisfied that I am nothing better than a poet or perhaps a philosopher—which latter reputation I do not claim and dare not hold through the precarious help of misinformation.

It is quite evident in spite of my deficiency that in human society I represent a vocation, which though superfluous has yet been held worthy of commendation. In fact, I am encouraged in my rhythmic futility by being offered moral and material incentives for its cultivation. If a foolish blackbird did not know how to seek its food, to build its nest, or to avoid its enemies, but specialized in singing, its fellow creatures, urged by their own science of genetics, would dutifully allow it to starve and perish. That I am not treated in a similar fashion is the evidence of an immense difference between the animal existence and the civilization of man. His great distinction dwells in the indefinite margin of life in him which affords a boundless background for his dreams and creations. And it is in this realm of freedom that he realizes his divine dignity, his great human truth, and is pleased when I as a poet sing victory to him, to Man the self-revealer, who goes on exploring ages of creation to find himself in perfection.

Reality, in all its manifestations, reveals itself in the emotional and imaginative background of our mind. We know it, not because we can think of it, but because we directly feel it. And therefore, even if rejected by the logical mind, it is not banished from our consciousness. As an incident it may be beneficial or injurious, but as a revelation its value lies in the fact that it offers us an experience through emotion or imagination; we feel ourselves in a special field of realization. This feeling itself is delightful when it is not accompanied by any great physical or moral risk, we love to feel even fear or sorrow if it is detached from all practical consequences. This is the reason of our enjoyment of tragic dramas, in which the feeling of pain rouses our consciousness to a white heat of intensity.

The reality of my own self is immediate and indubitable to me. whatever else affects me in a like manner is real for myself, and it inevitably attracts and occupies my attention for its own sake, blends itself with my personality, making it richer and larger and causing it delight. My friend may not be beautiful, useful, rich or great, but he is real to me; in him I feel my own extension and my joy.

The consciousness of the real within me seeks for its own corroboration the touch of the real outside me. When it fails the self in me is depressed. When our surroundings are monotonous and insignificant, having no emotional reaction upon our mind, we become vague to ourselves. For we are like pictures, whose reality is helped by the background if it is sympathetic. The punishment we suffer in solitary confinement consists in the obstruction to the relationship between the world of reality and the real in ourselves, causing the latter to become indistinct in a haze of inactive imagination:

our personality is blurred, we miss the companionship of our own being through the diminution of our self. The world of our knowledge is enlarged for us through the extension of our information; the world of our personality grows in its area with a large and deeper experience of our personal self in our own universe through sympathy and imagination.

At this world, that can be known through knowledge, is limited to us owing to our ignorance, so the world of personality, that can be realized by our own personal self, is also restricted by the limit of our sympathy and imagination. In the dim twilight of insensitiveness a large part of our world remains to us like a procession of nomadic shadows. According to the stages of our consciousness we have more or less been able to identify ourselves with this world, if not as a whole, at least in fragments; and our enjoyment dwells in that wherein we feel ourselves thus united. In art we express the delight of this unity by which this world is realized as humanly significant to us. I have my physical, chemical and biological self; my knowledge of it extends through the extension of my knowledge of the physical, chemical and biological world. I have my personal self, which has its communication with our feelings, sentiments and imaginations, which lends itself to be coloured by our desires and shaped by our imageries.

Science urges us to occupy by our mind the immensity of the knowable world; our spiritual teacher enjoins us to comprehend by our soul the infinite Spirit which is in the depth of the moving and changing facts of the world; the urging of our artistic nature is to realize the manifestation of personality in the world of appearance, the reality of existence which is in harmony with the real within us. Where this harmony is not deeply felt, there we are aliens and perpetually homesick. For man by nature is an artist; he never receives passively and accurately in his mind a physical representation of things around him. There goes on a continual adaptation, a transformation of facts into human imagery, through constant touches of his sentiments and imagination. The animal has the geography of its birthplace; man has his country, the geography of his personal self. The vision of it is not merely physical; it has its artistic unity, it is a perpetual creation. In his country, his consciousness being unobstructed, man extends his relationship, which is of his own creative personality. In order to live efficiently man must know facts and their laws. In order to be happy he must establish harmonious relationship with all things with which he has dealings. Our creation is the modification of relationship.

The great men who appear in our history remain in our mind not as a static fact but as a living historical image. The sublime suggestions of their lives become blended into a noble consistency in legends made living in the life of ages. Those men with whom we live we constantly modify in our minds, making them more real to us than they would be in a bare presentation. Men's ideal of womanhood and women's ideal of manliness are creation by the imagination through a mental grouping of qualities and conducts according to our hopes and desires, and men and women consciously and unconsciously strive towards its attainment. In fact, they reach a degree of reality for each other according to their success in adapting these respective ideals to their own nature. To say that these ideals are imaginary and therefore not true is wrong in man's case. His true life is in his own creation, which represents the infinity of man. He is naturally indifferent to things that merely exist; they must have some ideal value for him, and then only his consciousness fully recognizes them as real. Men are never true in their isolated self, and their imagination is the faculty that brings before their mind the vision of their own greater being.

We can make truth ours by actively modulating its inter-relations. This is the work of art; for reality is not based in the substance of things but in the principal of relationship. Truth is the infinite pursued by metaphysics; fact is the infinite pursued by science, while reality is the definition of the infinite which relates truth to the person. Reality is human; it is what we are conscious of, by which we are affected, that which we express. When we are intensely aware of it, we are aware of ourselves and it gives us delight. We live in it, we always widen its limits. Our arts and literature represent this creative activity which is fundamental in man.

But the mysterious fact about it is that though the individuals are separately seeking their expression, their success is never individualistic in character. Men must find and feel and represent in all their creative works Man the Eternal, the creator. Their civilization is a continual discovery of the transcendental humanity. In whatever it fails it shows the failure of the artist, which is the failure is expression; and the civilization perishes in which the individual thwarts the revelation of the universal. For Reality is the truth of Man, who belongs to all times, and any individualistic madness of men against Man cannot thrive for long.

Man is eager that his feeling for what is real to him must never die; it must find an imperishable form. The consciousness of this self of mine is so intensely evident to me that it assumes the character of immortality. I cannot imagine that it ever has been or can be non-existent. In a similar manner all things that are real to me are for myself eternal, and therefore worthy of a language that has permanent meaning. We know individuals who have the habit of inscribing their names on the walls of some majestic monument of architecture. It is a pathetic way of associating their own names with some works of art which belong to all times and to all men. Our hunger for reputation comes from our desire to make objectively real that which is inwardly real to us. He who is inarticulate is insignificant, like a dark star that cannot prove itself. He ever waits for the artist to give his fullest worth, not for anything specially excellent in him but for the wonderful fact that he is what he certainly is, that he carries in him the eternal mystery of being.

A Chinese friend of mine while travelling with me in the streets of Peking suddenly exclaimed with a vehement enthusiasm: 'Look, here is a donkey!' Surely it was an utterly ordinary donkey, like as indisputable truism, needing no special introduction from him. I was amused; but it made me think. This animal is generally classified as having certain qualities that are not recommendable and then hurriedly dismissed. It was obscured to me by an envelopment of commonplace associations; I was lazily certain that I knew it and therefore I hardly saw it. But my friend, who possessed the artist mind of China, did not treat it with a cheap knowledge but could see it afresh and recognize it as real. When I say real, I mean that it did not remain at the outskirt of his consciousness tied to a narrow definition, but it easily blended in his imagination, produced a vision, a special harmony of lines, colours and life and movement, and became intimately his own. The admission of a donkey into a drawing-room is violently opposed; yet there is no prohibition against its finding a place in a picture which may be admiringly displayed on the drawing-room wall.

The only evidence of truth in art exists when it compels us to say 'I see'. A donkey we may pass by in Nature, but a donkey in art we must acknowledge even if it be a creature that disreputably ignores all its natural history responsibility, even if it resembles a mushroom in its head and a palm-leaf in its tail.

In the Upanishad it is said in a parable that there are two birds sitting on the same bough, one of which feeds and the other looks on. This is an image of the mutual relationship of the infinite being and the finite self. The delight of the bird which looks on is great, for it is a pure and free delight. There are both of these birds in man himself, the objective one with its business of life, the subjective one with its disinterested joy of vision.

A child comes to me and commands me to tell her a story. I tell her of a tiger which is disgusted with the black stripes on its body and comes to my frightened servant demanding a piece of soap. The story gives my little audience immense pleasure, the pleasure of a vision, and her mind cries out, 'It is here, for I see!' She *knows* a tiger in the book of natural history, but she can *see* the tiger in the story of mine.

I am sure that even this child of five knows that it is an impossible tiger that is out on its untigerly quest of an absurd soap. The delightfulness of the tiger for her is not in its beauty, its usefulness, or its probability; but in the undoubted fact that she can see it in her mind with a greater clearness of vision than she can the walls around her—the walls that brutally shout their evidence of certainty which is merely circumstantial. The tiger in the story is inevitable, it has the character of a complete image, which offers its testimonial of truth in itself. The listener's own mind is the eye-witness, whose direct experience could not be contradicted. A tiger must be like every other tiger in order that it may have its place in a book of Science; there it must be a commonplace tiger to be at all tolerated. But in the story it is uncommon, it can never be reduplication. We *know* a thing because it belongs to a class; we *see* a thing because it belongs to itself. The tiger of the story completely detached itself from all others of its kind and easily assumed a distinct individuality in the heart of the listener. The child could vividly see it, because by the help of her imagination it became her own tiger, one with herself, and this union of the subject and object gives us joy. Is it because there is no separation between them in truth, the separation being the *Maya*, which is creation?

There come in our history occasions when the consciousness of a large multitude becomes suddenly illumined with the recognition of a reality which rises far above the dull obviousness of daily happenings. The world becomes vivid: we see, we feel it with all our soul. Such an occasion there was when the voice of Buddha reached distant shores across physical and moral impediments. Then our life and our world found their profound meaning of reality in their relation to the central person who offered us emancipation of love. Men, in order to make this great human experience ever memorable, determined to do the impossible; they made rocks to speak, stones to sing, caves to remember; their cry of joy and hope took immortal forms along the hills and deserts, across barren solitudes and populous cities. A gigantic creative endeavour built up its triumph in stupendous carvings, defying obstacles that were overwhelming. Such heroic activity over the greater part of the Eastern continents clearly answers the question: 'What is Art?' It is the response of man's creative soul to the call of the Real.

Once there came a time, centuries ago in Bengal, when the divine love drama that has made its eternal playground in human souls was vividly revealed by a personality radiating its intimate realization of God. The mind of a whole people was stirred by a vision of the world as an instrument, through which sounded out invitation to the meeting of bliss. The ineffable mystery of God's love-call, taking shape in an endless panorama of colours and forms, inspired activity in music that overflowed the restrictions of classical conventionalism. Our Kirtan music of Bengal came to its being like a star flung up by a burning whirlpool of emotion in the heart of a whole people, and their consciousness was aflame with a sense of reality that must be adequately acknowledged.

The question may be asked as to what place music occupies in my theory that art is for evoking in our mind the deep sense of reality in its richest aspect. Music is the most abstract of all the arts, as mathematics is in the region of science. In fact these two have a deep relationship with each other. Mathematics is the logic of numbers and dimensions. It is therefore employed as the basis of our scientific knowledge. When taken out of its concrete associations and reduced to symbols, it reveals its grand structural majesty, the inevitableness of its own perfect concord. Yet there is not merely a logic but also a magic of mathematics which works at the world of appearance, producing harmony—the cadence of inter-relationship. This rhythm of harmony has been extracted from its usual concrete context, and exhibited through the medium of sound. And thus the pure essence of expressiveness in existence is offered in music. Expressiveness finds the least resistance in sound, having freedom unencumbered by the burden of facts and thoughts. This gives it a power to arouse in us an intimate feeling of reality. In the pictorial, plastic and literary arts, the object and our feelings with regard to it are closely associated, like the rose and its perfumes. In music, the feeling distilled in sound, becoming itself an independent object. It assumes a tune-form which is definite, but a meaning which is undefinable, and yet which grips our mind with a sense of absolute truth.

It is the magic of mathematics, the rhythm which is in the heart of all creation, which moves in the atom and, in its different measures, fashions gold and lead, the rose and the thorn, the sun and the planets. There are the dance-steps of numbers in the arena of time and space, which weave the *maya*, the patterns of appearance, the incessant flow of change, that ever is and is not. It is the rhythm that churns up images from the vague and makes tangible what is elusive. This is *maya*, this is the art in creation, and art in literature, which is the magic of rhythm.

And must we stop here? What we know as intellectual truth, is that also not a rhythm of the relationship of facts, that weaves the pattern of theory, and produces a sense of convincingness to a person who somehow feels sure that he knows the truth? We believe any fact to be true because of a harmony, a rhythm in reason, the process of which is analysable by the logic of mathematics, but not its result in me, just as we can count the notes but cannot account for the music. The mystery is that I am convinced, and this also belongs to the *maya* of creation, whose one important, indispensable factor is this self-conscious personality that I represent.

And the Other? I believe it is also a self-conscious personality, which has its eternal harmony with mine.

The Meeting

Our great prophets in all ages did truly realize in themselves the freedom of the soul in their consciousness of the spiritual kinship of man which is universal. And yet human races, owing to their external geographical condition, developed in their individual isolation a mentality that is obnoxiously selfish. In their instinctive search for truth in religion either they dwarfed and deformed it in the mould of the primitive distortions of their own race-mind, or else they shut their God within temple walls and scriptural texts safely away, especially from those departments of life where his absence gives easy access to devil-worship in various names and forms. They treated their god in the same way as in some forms of government the King is treated, who has traditional honour but no effective authority. The true meaning of God has remained vague in our minds only because our consciousness of the spiritual unity has been thwarted.

One of the potent reasons for this—our geographical separation—has now been nearly removed. Therefore the time has come when we must, for the sake of truth and for the sake of that peace which is the harvest of truth, refuse to allow the idea of our God to remain indistinct behind unrealities of formal rites and theological mistiness.

The creature that lives its life screened and sheltered in a dark cave, finds its safety in the very narrowness of its own environment. The economical providence of Nature curtails and tones down its sensibilities to such a limited necessity. But if these cave-walls were to become suddenly removed by some catastrophe, then either it must accept the doom of extinction, or carry on satisfactory negotiations with its wider surroundings.

The races of mankind will never again be able to go back to their citadels of high-walled exclusiveness. They are today exposed to one another, physically and intellectually. The shells, which have so long given them full security within their individual enclosures have been broken, and by no artificial process can they be mended again. So we have to accept this fact, even though we have not yet fully adapted our minds to this changed environment of publicity, even though through it we may have to run all the risks entailed by the wider expansion of life's freedom.

A large part of our tradition is our code of adjustment which deals with the circumstances special to ourselves. These traditions, no doubt, variegate the several racial personalities with their distinctive colours—colours which have their poetry and also certain protective qualities suitable to each different environment. We may come to acquire a strong love for our own colourful race speciality; but if that gives us fitness only for a very narrow world, then, at the slightest variation in our outward circumstances, we may have to pay for this love with our life itself.

In the animal world there are numerous instances of complete race-suicide overtaking those who fondly clung to some advantage which later on became a hindrance in an altered dispensation. In fact the superiority of man is proved by his adaptability to extreme surprised of chance—neither the torrid nor the frigid zone of his destiny offering him insuperable obstacles.

The vastness of the race problem with which we are faced to day will either compel us to train ourselves to moral fitness in the place of merely external efficiency, or the complications arising out of it will fetter all our movements and drag us to our death.[1]

When our necessity becomes urgently insistent, when the resources that have sustained us so long are exhausted, then our spirit puts forth all its force to discover some other source of sustenance deeper and more permanent. This leads us from the exterior to the interior of our store-house. When muscle does not fully serve us, we come to awaken intellect to ask for its help and are then surprised to find in it a greater source of strength for us than physical power. When, in their turn, our intellectual gifts grow perverse, and only help to render our suicide gorgeous and exhaustive, our soul must seek an alliance with some power which is still deeper, yet further removed from the rude stupidity of muscle.

It is well known that when greed has for its object material gain then it can have no end. It is like the chasing of the horizon by a lunatic. To go on in a competition multiplying millions becomes a steeplechase of insensate futility that has obstacles but no goal. It has for its parallel the fight with material weapons—weapons which must perpetually be multiplied, opening us new vistas of destruction and evoking new forms of insanity in the forging of frightfulness. Thus seems now to have commenced the last fatal adventure of drunken Passion riding on an intellect of prodigious power.

Today, more than ever before in our history, the aid of spiritual power is needed. Therefore, I believe its resources will surely be discovered in the hidden depths of our being. Pioneers will come to take up this adventure and suffer, and through suffering open out a path to that higher elevation of life in which lies our safety.

---

1. See Night and Morning.

Let me, in reference to this, give an instance from the history of Ancient India. There was a noble period in the early days of India when, to a band of dreamers, agriculture appeared as a great idea and not merely useful fact. The heroic personality of Ramachandra, who espoused its cause, was sung in popular ballads, which in a later age forgot their original message and were crystallized into an epic merely extolling some domestic virtues of its hero. It is quite evident, however, from the legendary relics lying entombed in the story, that a new age ushered in by the spread of agriculture came as a divine voice to those who could hear. It lifted up the primeval screen of the wilderness, brought the distant near, and broke down all barricades. Men who had formed separate and antagonistic groups in their sheltered seclusions were called upon to form a united people.

In the Vedic verses, we find constant mention of conflicts between the original inhabitants of Ancient India and the colonists. There we find the expression of a spirit that was one of mutual distrust and a struggle in which was sought either wholesale slavery or extermination for the opponents carried on in the manner of animals who live in the narrow segregation imposed upon them by their limited imagination and imperfect sympathy. This spirit would have continued in all its ferocious vigour of savagery had men failed to find the opportunity for the discovery that man's highest truth was in the union of co-operation and love.

The progress of agriculture was the first external step which led to such a discovery. It not only made a settled life possible for a large number of men living in close proximity, but it claimed for its very purpose a life of peaceful co-operation. The mere fact of such a sudden change from a nomadic to an agricultural condition would not have benefited Man if he had not developed therewith his spiritual condition would not have benefited Man if he had not developed therewith his spiritual sensitiveness to an inner principle of truth. We can realize, from our reading of the Ramayana, the birth of idealism among a section of the Indian colonists of those days, before whose mind's eye was opened a vision of emancipation rich with the responsibility of a higher life. The epic represents in its ideal the change of the people's aspiration from the path of conquest to that of reconciliation.

At the present time, as I have said, the human world has been overtaken by another vast change similar to that which had occurred in the epic age of India. So long men had been cultivating, almost with a religious fervour, that mentality which is the product of racial isolation; poets proclaimed, in a loud pitch of bragging, the exploits of their popular fighters; money-makers felt neither pity nor shame in the unscrupulous dexterity of their pocket-picking; diplomats scattered lies in order to reap concessions from the devastated future of their own victims. Suddenly the walls that separated the different races are seen to have given way, and we find ourselves standing face to face.

This is a great fact of epic significance. Man, suckled at the wolf's breast, sheltered in the brute's den, brought up in the prowling habit of depredation, suddenly discovers that he is Man, and that his true power lies in yielding up his brute power for the freedom of spirit.

The God of humanity has arrived at the gates of the ruined temple of the tribe. Though he has not yet found his altar, I ask the men of simple faith, wherever they may be in the world, to bring their offering of sacrifice to him, and to believe that it is far better to be wise and worshipful than to be clever and supercilious. I ask them to claim the right of manhood to be friends of men, and not the right of a particular proud race or nation which may boast of the fatal quality of being the rulers of men. We should know for certain that such rulers will no longer be tolerated in the new world, as it basks in the open sunlight of mind and breathes life's free air.

In the geological ages of the infant earth the demons of physical force had their full sway. The angry fire, the devouring flood, the fury of the storm, continually kicked the earth into frightful distortions. These titans have at last given way to the reign of life. Had there been spectators in those days who were clever and practical they would have wagered their last penny on these titans and would have waxed hilariously witty at the expense of the helpless living speck taking its stand in the arena of the wrestling giants. Only a dreamer could have then declared with unwavering conviction that those titans were doomed because of their very exaggeration, as are, today, those formidable qualities which, in the parlance of schoolboy science, are termed Nordic.

I ask once again, let us, the dreamers of the East and the West, keep our faith firm in the Life that creates and not in the Machine that constructs—in the power that hides its force and blossoms in beauty, and not in the power that bares its arms and chuckles at its capacity to make itself obnoxious. Let us know that the Machine is good when it helps, but not so when it exploits life; that Science is great when it destroys evil, but not when the two enter into unholy alliance.

The Baül Singers of Bengal

[The following account of the Baüls in Northern India has been given in the Visvabharati Quarterly by my friend and fellow-worker, Professor Kshiti Mohun Sen of Santiniketan, to whom I am grateful for having kindly allowed me to reproduce what he has written in this Appendix.—Editor]

Baül means madcap, from *bayu* (Skt. Vayu) in its sense of nerve current, and has become the appellation of a set of people who do not conform to established social usage. This derivation is supported by the following verse of Narahari:

> That is why, brother, I became a madcap Baül.
> No master I obey, nor injunctions, canons or
> custom.
> Now no men-made distinctions have any hold on
> me,
> And I revel only in the gladness of my own
> welling love.
> In love there's no separation, but commingling
> always.
> So I rejoice in song and dance with each and all.

These lines also introduce us to the main tenets of the cult. The freedom, however, that the Baüls seek form all forms of outward compulsion goes even further, for among such are recognized as well the compulsions exerted by our desires and antipathies. Therefore, according to this cult, in order to gain real freedom, one has first to die to the life of the world whilst still in the flesh—for only then can one be rid of all extraneous claims. Those of the Baüls who have Islamic leanings call such 'death in life' *fana*, a term used by the Sufis to denote union with the Supreme Being. True love, according to the Baüls, is incompatible with any kind of compulsion. Unless the bonds of necessity are overcome, liberation is out of the question. Love represents the wealth of life which is in excess of need From hard, practical politics touching our earth to the nebulous regions of abstract metaphysics, everywhere India expressed the power of her genius equally well....And yet none of these, neither severally nor collectively, constituted her specific genius; none showed the full height to which she could raise herself, none compassed the veritable amplitude of her inner-most reality. It is when we come to the domain of the Spirit, of God-realization, that we find the real nature and stature and genius of the Indian people; it is here that India lives and moves as in her own home of Truth.

The Baüls cult is followed by householders as well as homeless wanderers, neither of whom acknowledge class or caste, special deities, temples or sacred places. Though they congregate on the occasion of religious festivals, mainly of the Vaishnavas, held in special centres, they never enter any temple. They do not set up any images of divinities, or religious symbols, in their own places of worship of mystic realization. True, they sometimes maintain with care and reverence spots sacred to some esteemed master or devotee, but they perform no worship there. Devotees from the lowest strata of the Hindu and Moslem communities are welcomed into their ranks, hence the Baüls are looked down upon by both. It is possible that their own contempt for temples had its origin in the denial of admittance therein to their low class brethren. What need, say they, have we of other temples, is not this body of ours the temple where the Supreme Spirit has His abode? The human body, despised by most other religions, is thus for them the holy of holies, wherein the Divine is intimately enshrined as the Man of the Heart. And in this wise is the dignity of Man upheld by them.

Kabir, Nanak, Ravidas, Dadu and his followers have also called man's body the temple of God—the microcosm in which the cosmic abode of the all-pervading Supreme Being is represented.

Kabir says:

In this body is the Garden of Paradise; herein are comprised the seven seas and the myriad stars; here is the Creator manifest. (I. 101.)

Dadu says:

This body is my scripture; herein the All-Merciful has written for me His message.

Rajjab (Dadu's chief Moslem disciple) says:

Within the devotee is the paper on which the scriptures are written in letters of Life. But few care to read them; they turn a deaf ear to the message of the heart.

Most Indian sects adopt some distinct way of keeping the hair of head and face as a sign of their sect or order. Therefore, so as to avoid being dragged into any such distinctions, the Baüls allow hair and beard and moustache to grow freely. Thus do we remain simple, they say. The similar practice of the Sikhs in this matter is to be noted. Neither do the Baüls believe that lack of clothing or bareness of body conduce to religious merit. According to them the whole body should be kept decently covered. Hence their long robe, for which, if they cannot afford a new piece of cloth, they gather rags and make it of patches. In this they are different from the ascetic *sanyasins*, but resemble rather the Buddhist monks.

The Baüls do not believe in aloofness from, or renunciation of, any person or thing; their central idea is *yoga*, attachment to and communion with the divine and its manifestations, as the means of realization. We fail to recognize the temple of God in the bodily life of man, they explain, because its lamp is not alight. The true vision must be attained in which this temple will become manifest in each and every human body, whereupon mutual communion and worship will spontaneously arise. Truth cannot be communion and worship will spontaneously arise. Truth cannot be communicated to those on whom you look down. You must be able to see the divine light that shines within them, for it is your own lack of vision that makes all seem dark.

Kabir says the same thing:

> In every abode the light doth shine; it is you who are blind that cannot see. When by dint of looking and looking and looking you at length can discern it, the veils of this world will be torn asunder. (II. 33.)

> It is because the devotee is not in communion that he says the goal is far away. (II. 34).

Many such similarities are to be observed between the sayings of the Baüls and those of the Upper Indian devotees of the Middle Ages, but, unlike the case of the followers of the latter, the Baüls did not become crystallized into any particular order or religious organization. So, in the Baüls of Bengal, there is to be found a freedom and independence of mind and spirit that resists all attempt at definition. Their songs are unique in courage and felicity of expression. But under modern conditions they are becoming extinct, or at best holding on to external features bereft of their original speciality. It would be a great pity if no record of their achievements should be kept before their culture is lost to the world.

Though the Baül count amongst their following a variety of sects and castes, both Hindu and Moslem, chiefly coming from the lower social ranks, they refuse to give any other account of themselves to the questioner than that they are Baüls. They acknowledge none of the social or religious formalities, but delight in the ever-changing play of life, which cannot be expressed in mere words but of which something may be captured in song, through the ineffable medium of rhythm and tune.

Their songs are passed on from Master to disciple, the latter when competent adding others of his own, but, as already mentioned, they are never recorded in book form. Their replies to questions are usually given by singing appropriate selections from these songs. If asked the reason why, they say: 'We are like birds. We do not walk on our legs, but fly with our wings.'

There was a Brahmin of Bikrampur, known as Chhaku Thakur, who was the disciple of a Baül of the Namasudra caste (accounted one of the lowest) and hence had lost his place in his own community. When admonished to be careful about what he uttered, so as to avoid popular odium, he answered with the song:

> Let them relieve their minds by saying what they will,
> I pursue my own simple way, fearing none at all.
> The Mango seed will continue to produce Mango trees, no Jambolans.
> This seed of mine will produce the real *me*—all glory to my Master!

Love being the main principle according to the Baüls, a Vaishnava once asked a Baül devotee whether he was aware of the different kinds of love as classified in the Vaishnava scriptures. 'What should an illiterate ignoramus like me know of the scriptures?' was the reply. The Vaishnava then offered to read and explain the text, which he proceeded to do, while the Baül listened with such patience as he could muster. When asked for his opinion, after the reading was over, he sang:

> A goldsmith, methinks, has come into the flower
> garden.
> He would appraise the lotus, forsooth,
> By rubbing it on his touchstone!

Recruits from the higher castes are rare amongst the Baüls. When any such do happen to come, they are reduced to the level of the rest. Are the lower planks of a boat of any lesser importance than the upper? say they.

Once in Vikrampur, I was seated on the river bank by the side of a Baül. 'Father', I asked him, 'why is it that you keep no historical record of yourselves for the use of posterity?' 'We follow the *sahaj* (simple) way', he replied, 'and so leave no trace behind us.' The tide had then ebbed, and there was but little water in the river bed. Only a few boatmen were to be seen pushing their boats along the mud. The Baül continued: 'Do the boats that sail over the flooded river leave any mark? What should these boatmen of the muddy track, urged on by their need, know of the *sahaj* (simple) way? The true endeavour is to keep oneself simple afloat in the stream of devotion that flows through the lives of devotees—to mingle one's own devotion with theirs. There are many classes of men amongst the Baüls, but they are all Baül—they have no other achievement or history. All the streams that fall into the Ganges become the Ganges. So must we lose ourselves in the common stream, else will it cease to be living.'

On another Baül being asked why they did not follow the scriptures, 'Are we dogs', he replied, 'that we should lick up the leavings of others? Brave men rejoice in the output of their own energy, they create their own festivals. These cowards who have not the power to rejoice in themselves have to rely on what others have left. Afraid lest the world should lack festivals in the future, they save up the scraps left over by their predecessors for later use. They are content with glorifying their forefathers because they know not how to create for themselves.'

> If you would know the Man,
> Simple must be your endeavour.
> To the region of the simple must you fare.
> Pursuers of the path of man's own handiwork,
> Who follow the crowd, gleaning their false leavings,
> What news can they get of the Real?

It is hardly to be wondered at that people who think thus should have no use for history!

We have already noticed that, like all the followers of the simple way, the Baül have no faith in specially sacred spots or places of pilgrimage, but that they nevertheless congregate on the occasion of religious festivals. If asked why, the Baül says:

> We would be within hail of the other Boatmen, to hear their calls,
> That we may make sure our boat rightly floats on the *sahaj* stream.

Not what men have said or done in the past, but the living human touch is what they find helpful. Here is a song giving their ideas about pilgrimage:

> I would not go, my heart, to Mecca or Medina,
> For behold, I ever abide by the side of my Friend.
> Mad would I become, had I dwelt afar, not knowing Him.

> There's no worship in Mosque or Temple or special
> holy day.
> At ever step I have my Mecca and Kashi; sacred is
> every moment.

If a Baül is asked the age of his cult—whether it comes before
or after this one or that, he says, 'Only the artificial religions
of the world are limited by time. our *sahaj* (simple, natural)
religion is timeless, it has neither beginning nor end, it is of
all time.' The religion of the Upanishads and Puranas, even
that of the Vedas, is, according to them, artificial.

The followers of the *sahaj* cult believe only in living
religious experience. Truth, according to them, has two aspects,
inert and living. Confined to itself truth has no value for man.
It becomes priceless when embodied in a living personality.
The conversion of the inert into living truth by the devotee
they compare to the conversion into milk by the cow of its
fodder, or the conversion by the tree of dead matter into fruit.
He who has this power of making truth living, is the Guru
or Master. Such Gurus they hold in special reverence, for the
eternal and all-pervading truth can only be brought to man's
door by passing through his life.

The Baül say that emptiness of time and space is required
for a playground. That is why god has preserved an emptiness
in the heart of man, for the sake of His own play of Love.
Our wise and learned ones were content with finding in
Brahma the *tat* (lit. '*tat*'—the ultimate substance). The Baül,
not being Pandits, do not profess to understand all this fuss
about *tat* they want a Person. So their god is the Man of
the Heart (*maner manush*) sometimes simply the Man
(*purush*). Whilst He is revealed within, no worldly pleasures
can give satisfaction. Their sole anxiety is the finding of this
Man.

The Baül sings:

> Ah, where am I to find Him, the Man of my Heart?
> Alas, since I lost Him, I wander in search of Him,
> Thro' lands near and far.

The agony of separation from Him cannot be mitigated for them by learning or philosophy:

> Oh, these words and words, my mind would none of them,
> The Supreme Man it must and shall discover.
> So long as Him I do not see, these mists slake not my thirst.
> Mad am I; for lack of that Man I madly run about;
> For his sake the world I've felt; for Bisha naught else will serve.

This Bisha was a *bhuin-mali*, by caste, disciple of Bala, the Kaivarta.

This cult of the Supreme Man is only to be found in the Vedas hidden away in the Purushasukta (A.V. 19.6). It is more freely expressed by the Upper Indian devotees of the Middle Ages. It is all in all with the Baüls. The God whom these illiterate outcastes seek so simply and naturally in their lives is obscured by the accredited religious leaders in philosophical systems and terminology, in priestcraft and ceremonial, in institutions and temples.

Not satisfied with the *avatars* (incarnations of God) mentioned in the scriptures, the Baül sings:

> As we look on ever creature, we find each to be His *avatar*. What can you teach us of His ways? In ever-new play He wondrously revels.

And Kabir also tells us:

> All see the Eternal One, but only the devotee, in his solitude, recognizes him.

A friend of mine was once much impressed by the reply of a Baül who was asked why his robe was not tinted with ascetic ochre:

> Can the colour show outside, unless the inside is first tinctured? Can the fruit attain ripe sweetness by the painting of its skin?

This aversion of the Baül from outward marks of distinction is also shared by the Upper Indian devotees, as I have elsewhere noticed.

The age-long controversy regarding *dvaita* (dualism) and *advaita* (monism) is readily solved by these wayfarers on the path of Love. Love is the simple striving, love the natural communion, so believe the Baüls. 'Ever two and ever one, of this the name of Love', say they. In love, oneness is achieved without any loss of respective self-hood.

The same need exists for the reconcilement of the antagonism between the outer all of the material world and the inner call of the spiritual world, as for the realization of the mutual love of the individual and Supreme Self. The god who is Love, say the Baül, can alone serve to turn the currents of the within and the without in one and the same direction.

Kabir says:

> If we say He is only within then the whole
> Universe is shamed.
> If we say he is only without, then that is false.
> He, whose feet rest alike on the sentient and on
> the inert,
> fills the gap between the inner and the outer
> world.

The inter-relations of man's body and the Universe have to be realized by spiritual endeavour. Such endeavour is called *Kaya Sadhan* (Realization through the body).

One process in this *Kaya Sadhan* of Baül is known as *Urdha-srota* (the elevation of the current). Waters flow downwards according to the ordinary physical law. But with the advent of Life the process is reversed. When the living seed sprouts the juices are drawn upwards, and on the elevation that such flow can attain depends the height of the tree. It is the same in the life of man. His desires ordinarily flow downward towards animality. The endeavour of the expanding spirit is to turn their current upwards towards the light. The currents of *Shiva* (animal life) must be converted into the current of *Shiva* (God life). They form a centre round the ego; they must be raised by the force of love.

Says Dadu's daughter, Nanimata:

My life is the lamp afloat on the stream.
To what bourne shall it take me?
How is the divine to conquer the carnal,
The downward current to be upward turned?
As when the wick is lighted the oil doth upward flow,
So simply is destroyed the thirst of the body.

The *Yoga* Vasistha tells us:

Uncleansed desires bind to the world, purified desires give liberation.

References to this reversal of current are also to be found in the Atharva Veda (X. 2.9; 2.34). This reversal is otherwise considered by Indian devotees as the conversion of the *sthula* (gross) in the sukshma (fine).

The Baül sings:

Love is my golden touch—it turn desire into service:
Earth seeks to become Heaven, man to become god.

Another aspect of the idea of reversal has been put thus by Rabindranath Tagore in the *Broken Ties*:

> If I keep going in the same direction along which He comes to me, then I shall be going further and further away from Him. If I proceed in the opposite direction, then only can we meet. He loves form, so He is continually descending towards form. We cannot live by form alone, so we must ascend towards His formlessness. He is free, so His play is within bonds. We are bound, so we find our joy in freedom. All our sorrow is because we cannot understand this. He who sings, proceeds from his joy to the tune; he who hears, from the tune to joy. one comes from freedom into bondage, the other goes from bondage into freedom; only thus can they have their communion. He sings and we hear. He ties the bonds as He sings to us, we untie them as we listen to Him.

This idea also occurs in our devotees of the Middle Ages. The 'sahaj' folk endeavour to seek the bliss of divine union only for its own sake. Mundane desires are therefore accounted the chief obstacles in the way. But for getting rid of them, the wise Guru, according to the Baül, does not advise renunciation of the good things of the world, but the opening of the door to the higher self. Thus guided, says Kabir,

> I close not my eyes, stop not my ears, nor
> torment my body.
> But ever path I then traverse becomes a path of
> pilgrimage, whatever work I engage in becomes
> service.
> This simple consummation is the best.

The simple way has led its votaries easily and naturally to their living conception of Humanity.

Rajjab says:

> All the world is the Veda, all creations the Koran.
> Why read paper scriptures, O Rajjab.
> Gather ever fresh wisdom from the Universe.
>
> The eternal wisdom shines within the concourse of
> the millions of Humanity.

The Baül sings:

> The simple has its thirty million strings whose
> mingled symphony ever sounds.
> Take all the creatures of the World into yourself.
> Drown yourself in that eternal music.

I conclude with a few more examples of Baül songs, esoteric and otherwise, from amongst many others of equal interest.

> By Gangaram, the Namasudra:
> Realize how finite and unbounded are One,
> As you breathe in and out.
> Of all ages, then you will count the moments,
> In every moment find the ages,
> The drop in the ocean, the ocean in the drop.
> If your endeavour be but *sahaj*, beyond argument and
> cogitation,
> You will taste the precious quintessence.
> Blinded are you by over-much journeying from bourne
> to bourne,
> O Gangaram, by simple! Then alone will vanish all
> your doubts.

By Bisha, the disciple of Bala:

> The Simple Man was in the Paradise of my heart,
> Alas, how and when did I lose Him,

That now no peace I know, at home or abroad?
By meditation and telling of beads, in worship and
travail,
The quest goes on for ever;
But unless the Simple Man comes of Himself,
Fruitless is it all;
For he yields not to forgetfulness of striving.
Bisha's heart has understood right well,
That by His own simple way alone is its door
unlocked.

'Listen, O brother man', declares Chandidas, 'the Truth
of Man is the highest of truths; there is no other truth
above it.'

Night and Morning

[*An address in the Chapel of Manchester College, Oxford, on Sunday, May 25, 1930, by Rabindranath Tagore.*]

In his early youth, stricken with a great sorrow at the death of his grandmother, my father painfully groped for truth when his world had darkened, and his life lost its meaning. At this moment of despair a torn page of a manuscript carried by a casual wind was brought to his notice. The text it contained was the first verse of the Ishopanishad:

> *Īśāvāsyam idam sarvam*
> *Yat Kincha jagatyām jagat.*
> *tēna tyaktena bhunjīthā*
> *Mā gṛdhah Kasyasvitdhanam.*

It may be thus translated:

> Thou must know that whatever moves in this moving world is enveloped by god. And therefore find thy enjoyment in renunciation, never coveting what belongs to others.

In this we are enjoined to realize that all facts that move and change have their significance in their relation to one everlasting truth. For then we can be rid of the greed of acquisition, gladly dedicating everything we have to that Supreme Truth. The change in our mind is immense in its generosity of expression when an utter sense of vanity and vacancy is relieved at the consciousness of a pervading reality.

I remember once while on a boat trip in a strange neighbourhood I found myself unexpectedly at the confluence of three great rivers as the daylight faded and the night darkened over a desolation dumb and inhospitable. A sense of dread possessed the crew and an oppressive anxiety burdened my thoughts, with its unreasonable exaggeration all through the dark hours. The morning came and at once the brooding obsession vanished. Everything remained the same only the sky was filled with light.

The night had brought her peace, the peace of a black ultimatum in which all hope ceased in an abyss of nothingness, but the peace of the morning appeared like that of a mother's smile, which in its serene silence utters, 'I am here'. I realized why birds break out singing in the morning, and felt that their songs are their own glad answers to the emphatic assurance of a Yes in the morning light in which they find a luminous harmony of their own existence. Darkness drives our being into an isolation of insignificance and we are frightened because in the dark the sense of our own truth dwindles into a minimum. Within us we carry a positive truth, the consciousness of our personality, which naturally seeks from our surroundings its response in a truth which is positive, and then in this harmony we find our wealth or reality and are gladly ready to sacrifice. That which distinguishes man from the animal is the fact that he expresses himself not in his claims, in his needs, but in his sacrifice, which has the creative energy that builds his home, his society, his civilization. It proves that his instinct acknowledges the inexhaustible wealth of a positive truth which gives highest value to existence. In whatever we are mean, greedy and unscrupulous, there are the dark bands in the spectrum of our consciousness; they prove chasms of bankruptcy in our realization of the truth that the world moves, not in a blank sky of negation, but in the bosom of an ideal spirit of fulfilment.

Most often crimes are committed when it is night. it must not be thought that the only reason for this is that in the dark they are likely to remain undetected. But the deeper reason is that in the dark the negative aspect of time weakness the positive sense of our own humanity. Our victims, as well as we ourselves, are less real to us in the night, and that which we miss within we desperately seek outside us. Wherever in the human world the individual self forgets its isolation, the light that unifies is revealed the light of the Everlasting Yes, whose sound-symbol in India is 'OM'. Then it becomes easy for man to be good not because his badness is restrained, but because of his joy in the positive background of his own reality, because his mind no longer dwells in a fathomless night of an anarchical world of denial.

Man finds an instance of this in the idea of his own country, which reveals to him a positive truth, the idea that has not the darkness of negation which is sinister, which generates suspicion, exaggerates fear, encourages uncontrolled greed; for his own country is an indubitable reality to him which delights his soul. in such intense consciousness of reality we discover our own greater self that spreads beyond our physical life and immediate present, and offers us generous opportunities of enjoyment in renunciation.

In the introductory chapter of our civilization individuals by some chance found themselves together within a geographic enclosure. But a mere crowd without an inner meaning of inter-relation is negative, and therefore it can easily be hurtful. The individual who is a mere component part of an unneighbourly crowd, who in his exclusiveness represents only himself, is apt to be suspicious of others, with no inner control in hating and hitting his fellow-beings at the very first sight. This savage mentality is the product of the barren spirit of negation that dwells in the spiritual night. but when the morning of mutual recognition broke out, the morning of co-operative life, that divine mystery which is the creative spirit of unity, imparted meaning to individuals in a larger truth named 'people'. These individuals gladly surrendered themselves to the realization of their true humanity, the humanity of a great wholeness composed of generations of men consciously and unconsciously building up a perfect future. They realized peace according to the degree of unity which they attained in their mutual relationship, and within that limit they found the one sublime truth which pervades time that moves, the things that change, the life that grows, the thoughts that flow onwards. They united with themselves the surrounding physical nature in her hills and rivers, in the dance of rhythm in all her forms and colours, in the blue of her sky, the tender green of her corn shoots.

In gradual degrees men became aware that the subtle intricacies of human existence find their perfection in the harmony of interdependence, never in the vigorous exercise of elbows by a mutually pushing multitude, in the arrogant assertion of independence which fitly belongs to the barren rocks and deserts grey with the pallor of death.

For rampant individualism is against what is truly human— that is to say spiritual—it belongs to the primitive poverty of the animal life, it is the confinement of a cramped spirit, of restricted consciousness.

The limited boundaries of a race or a country within which the supreme truth of humanity has been more or less realized in the past are crossed today from the outside. The countries are physically brought closer to each other by science. But science has not brought with it the light that helps understanding. On the contrary science on its practical side has raised obstacles among them against the development of a sympathetic knowledge.

But I am not foolish enough to condemn science as materialistic. No truth can be that. Science means intellectual probity in our knowledge and dealings with the physical world and such conscientiousness has a spiritual quality that encourages sacrifice and martyrdom. But in science the oft-used half-truth that honesty is the best policy is completely made true and our mind's honesty in this field never fails to bring us the best profit for our living. Mischief finds its entry through this back-door of utility, tempting the primitive in man, arousing his evil passions. And through this the great meeting of races has been obscured of its great meaning. When I view it in my mind I am reminded of the fearful immensity of the meeting of the three mighty rivers where I found myself unprepared in a blackness of universal menace. Over the vast gathering of peoples the insensitive night darkly broods, the night of unreality. The primitive barbarity of limitless suspicion and mutual jealousy fills the world's atmosphere today—the barbarity of the aggressive individualism of nations, pitiless in its greed, unashamed of its boastful brutality.

Those that have come out for depredation in this universal night have the indecent audacity to say that such conditions are eternal in man, that the moral ideals are only for individuals but that the race belongs to the primitive nature of the animal.

But when we see that in the range of physical power man acknowledges no limits in his dreams, and is not even laughed at when he hopes to visit the neighbouring planet; must he insult his humanity by proclaiming that human nature has reached its limit of moral possibility? We must work with all our strength for the seemingly impossible; we must be sure that faith in the perfect builds the path for the perfect—that the external fact of unity which has surprised us must be sublimated in an internal truth of unity which would light up the Truth of Man the Eternal.

Nations are kept apart not merely by international jealousy, but also by their *Karma*, their own past, handicapped by the burden of the dead. They find it hard to think that the mentality which they fondly cultivated within the limits of a narrow past has no continuance in a wider future, they are never tired of uttering the blasphemy that warfare is eternal, that physical might has its inevitable right of moral cannibalism where the flesh is weak. The wrong that has been done in the past seeks to justify itself by its very perpetuation, like a disease by its chronic malignity, and it sneers and growls at the least proposal of its termination. Such an evil ghost of a persistent past, the dead that would cling to life, haunts the night today over mutually alienated countries, and men that are gathered together in the dark cannot see each other's faces and features.

We in India are unfortunate in not having the chance to give expression to the best in us in creating intimate relations with the powerful nations, whose preparations are all leading to an enormous waste of resources in a competition of brow-beating and bluff. Some great voice is waiting to be heard which will usher in the sacred light of truth in the dark hours of the nightmare of politics, the voice which will proclaim that 'God is over all', and exhort us never to covet, to be great in renunciation that gives us the wealth of spirit, strength of truth, leads us from the illusion of power to the fullness of perfection, to the *Sāntam*, who is peace eternal, to the *Advaitam* who is the infinite One in the heart of the manifold. But we in India have not yet had the chance. Yet we have our own human voice which truth demands. The messengers of truth have ever joined hands across centuries, across the seas, across historical barriers, and they help to raise up the great continent of human brotherhood from *avidyā*, from the slimy bottom of spiritual apathy. We individuals, however small may be our power and whatever corner of the consciousness that comprehends all humanity. And for this cause I ask your co-operation, not only because co-operation gives us strength in our work, but because co-operation itself is the best aspect of the truth we represent; it is an end and not merely the means.

Let us keep our faith firm in the objectivity of the source of our spiritual ideal of unity, though it cannot be proved by any mathematical logic. Let us proclaim in our conduct that it has already been given to us to be realized, like a song which has only to be mastered and sung, like the morning which has only to be welcomed by raising the screens, opening the doors.

The idea of a millennium is treasured in our ancient legends. The instinct cradled and nourished in them has profound meaning. It is like the instinct of a chick which dimly feels that an infinite world of freedom *is* already given to it, truer than the narrow fact of its immediate life within the egg. An agnostic chick has the rational right to doubt it, but at the same time it cannot help pecking at its shell. The human soul, confined in its limitation, has also dreamt of millennium, and striven for a spiritual emancipation which seems impossible of attainment, and yet it feels its reverence for some ever-present source of inspiration in which all its experience of the true, the good and beautiful finds its reality.

And therefore it has been said by the Upanishad: 'Thou must know that God pervades all things that move and change in this moving world; find thy enjoyment in renunciation, covet not what belongs to others.'

Ya ēkō varnō bahudhā ṣaktiyogāt
Varṇān anēkān nihitārthō dadhāti.
Vichaiti chāntē viṣvamādau sa dēvaḥ
Sa nō buddhyā ṣubhayā samyunaktu

He who is one, and who dispenses the inherent needs of all peoples and all times, who is in the beginning and the end of all things, may he unite us with the bond of truth, of common fellowship, of righteousness.

GREATER INDIA

East and West in Greater India

Date of Original 1909–10

The History of India—of whom is it the history? This history began with the day when the white-skinned Aryans, overcoming all obstacles, natural as well as human, made their entry into India. Sweeping aside the vast enveloping curtain of forest, which stretched across her from East to West, they brought on the scene sunny fields adorned with corn and fruit, and their toil and skill thus laid the foundation. And yet they could not say that this India was exclusively their India.

The non-Aryans became fused with the Aryans. Even in the first blush of the latter's victorious supremacy, they used to take to themselves non-Aryan girls in marriage. And in the Buddhist age such intermingling became freer. When, thereafter, the Brahminic Samaj set to work to repair its barriers and make its encircling walls impregnable, they found some parts of the country come to such a pass that brahmins of sufficiently pure stock could not be found to conduct the vedic ceremonies, and these either had to be imported, or new creations made by investiture with the sacred thread. The white skin, on the colour of which the difference between Brahmin and Sudra had originally been founded, had meanwhile tarnished into brown. The sudras, with their different manners and ideals, gods and rituals, had been taken into the social polity. And a larger Indian, or Hindu, Samaj had been evolved which not only was not one with the Aryan Samaj of the vedic times, but in many respects even antagonistic.

But was India able to draw the line of her history there? Did Providence allow her to make the assertion that the History of India was the history of the Hindus? No. For, while in Hindu India the Rajputs were busy fighting each other in the vanity of a suicidal competition of bravery, the Mussalmans swept in through the breaches created by their dissensions, and scattering themselves all over the country they also made it their own by living and dying on its soil.

If now we try to draw the line here crying: "Stop! Enough! Let us make the History of India a history of Hindu and Muslim!" will the Great Architect, who is broadening out the history of humanity in ever-increasing circles, modify his plan simply to gratify our pride?

Whether India is to be yours or mine, whether it is to belong more to the Hindu, or to the Muslim, or whether some other race is to assert a greater supremacy than either,—that is not the problem with which Providence is exercised. It is not as if, at the bar of the judgment seat of the Almighty, different advocates are engaged in pleading the rival causes of Hindu, Muslim or Westerner, and that the party which wins the decree shall finally plant the standard of permanent possession. It is our vanity which makes us think that it is a battle between contending rights,—the only battle is the eternal one between Truth and untruth.

The Ultimate, the Perfect, is concerned with the All, and is evolving itself through every kind of obstacle and opposing force. Only to the extent that our efforts assist in the progress of this evolution can they be successful. Attempts to push on oneself alone, whether made by individuals or nations, have no importance in the processes of Providence. That Alexander did not succeed in bringing the whole earth under the flag of Greece was merely a case of unsatisfied ambition which has long ceased to be of concern to the world. The preparation of Rome for a world-empire was shattered to pieces by the Barbarians, but this fall of Rome's pride is not bewailed by the world to day. Greece and Rome shipped their golden harvests on the bark of time,—their failure to get a passage on it, for themselves as well, proved no loss, but rather lightened its burden.

So, in the evolving History of India, the principle at work is not the ultimate glorification of the Hindu, or any other race. In India, the history of humanity is seeking to elaborate a specific ideal, to give to general perfection a special form which shall be for the gain of all humanity;—nothing less than this is its end and aim. And in the creation of this ideal type, if Hindu, Muslim or Christian should have to submerge the aggressive part of their individuality, that may hurt their sectarian pride, but will not be accounted a loss by the standard of Truth and Right.

We are all here to co-operate in the making of Greater India. If any one factor should become rebellious and arrogate to itself an undue predominance, that will only interfere with the general progress. The section which is unable or unwilling to adapt itself to the entire scheme, but struggles to keep up a separate existence, will have to drop out and be lost, sooner or later. And the component which, realising its dedication to the ultimate ideal, acknowledges its own individual unimportance, will lose only its pettiness and find permanence for its greatness in that of the whole.

So, for ourselves, we must bear in mind that India is not engaged in recording solely our story, but that it is we who are called upon to take our place in the great Drama, which has India for its stage. If we do not fit ourselves to play our part, it is we who shall have to go. If we stand aloof from the rest, in the pride of past achievement, content with heaping up obstacles around ourselves, God will punish us, either by afflicting us with sorrow unceasing till He has brought us to a level with the rest, or by casting us aside as mere impediments. If we insist on segregating ourselves in our pride of exclusiveness, fondly clinging to the belief that Providence is specially concerned in our own particular development; if we persist in regarding our *dharma* as ours alone, our institutions as specially fit only for ourselves, our places of worship as requiring to be carefully guarded against all incomers, our wisdom as dependent for its safety on being locked up in our strong rooms; then we shall simply await, in the prison of our own contriving, for the execution of the death sentence which in that case the world of humanity will surely pronounce against us.

Of late the British have come in and occupied an important place in India's history. This was not an uncalled for, accidental intrusion. If India had been deprived of touch with the West, she would have lacked an element essential for her attainment of perfection. Europe now has her lamp ablaze. We must light our torches at its wick and make a fresh start on the highway of time. That our forefathers, three thousand years ago, had finished extracting all that was of value from the universe, is not a worthy thought. We are not so unfortunate, nor the universe, so poor. Had it been true that all that is to be done has been done in the past, once for all, then our continued existence could only be a burden to the earth, and so would not be possible.

With what present duty, in what future hope, can they live who imagine that they have attained completeness in their great grandfathers—whose sole idea is to shield themselves against the influence of the Modern behind the barriers of antiquated belief and custom?

The Englishman has come through the breach in our crumbling walls, as the messenger of the Lord of the world-festival, to tell us that the world has need of us; not where we are petty, but where we can help with the force of our Life, to rouse the World in wisdom, love and work, in the expansion of insight, knowledge and mutuality. Unless we can justify the mission on which the Englishman has been sent, until we can set out with him to honour the invitation of which he is the bearer, he cannot but remain with us as our tormentor, the disturber of our quietism. So long as we fail to make good the arrival of the Englishman, it shall not be within our power to get rid of him.

The India to which the Englishman has come with his message, is the India which is shooting up towards the future from within the bursting seed of the past. This new India belongs to humanity. What right have *we* to say who shall and who shall not find a place therein. Who is this "We"? Bengali, Marathi or Panjabi, Hindu or Mussalman? Only the larger "We" in whom all these,—Hindu, Muslim and Englishman, and whosoever else there be,—may eventually unite shall have the right to dictate who is to remain and who is to leave.

On us to-day is thrown the responsibility of building up this greater India, and for that purpose our immediate duty is to justify our meeting with the Englishman. It shall not be permitted to us to say that we would rather remain aloof, inactive, irresponsive, unwilling to give and to take, and thus to make poorer the India that is to be.

So the greatest men of modern India have all made it their life's work to bring about an approachment with the West. The chief example is Rammohan Roy. He stood alone in his day for the union of India with the world on the broad base of humanity. No blind belief, no ancestral habit was allowed to obscure his vision. With a wonderful breadth of heart and intellect he accepted the West without betraying the East. He, alone, laid the foundation of new Bengal.

Rammohan Roy cheerfully put up with persecution in order to extend the field of our knowledge and work, right across from East to West, to gain for us the eternal rights of man in the pursuit of Truth, to enable us to realise that we too had inherited the earth. It was he who first felt and declared that for us Buddha, Christ and Mohammed have spent their lives; that for each one of us has been stored up the fruits of the discipline of our Rishis; that in whatsoever part of the world whosoever has removed obstacles in the path of wisdom or, breaking the bondage of dead matter, has given freedom to man's true *shakti*, he is our very own, and through him is each one of us glorified.

Rammohan Roy did not assist India to repair her barriers, or to keep cowering behind them,—he led her out into the freedom of Space and Time, and built for her a bridge between the East and West. That is why his spirit still lives with us, his power of stimulating India's creative energies is not yet exhausted. No blind habit of mind, no pettiness of racial pride, were able to make him commit the folly of rebellion against the manifest purpose of time. That grand purpose which could not have found its fulfilment in the past, but is ever marching onwards to the future, found in him a gallant, unflinching standard bearer.

In the Deccan, Ranade spent his life in the making of this same bridge between East and West. In his very nature there was that creative faculty of synthesis which brings men together, builds up the *samaj*, does away with discord and inequity and circumvents all obstacles in the way of knowledge, love and will-power. And so, he rose superior to all the petty or unworthy considerations prevalent in his time, in spite of all the various conflicts of ideas and interests between the Indian and the Englishman. His largeness of heart and breadth of mind impelled him to make a life-long endeavour to clear the way for an acceptance of whatever elements in the British are of value for the true History of India, and to strive for the removal of whatever obstructions stand in the way of India's attainment of perfection.

And the *mahatma* who passed away from us only the other day—Swami Vivekananda—he likewise took his stand in the middle, with the East on his right, the West on his left. His message was not to keep India bound in her latter-day narrowness by ignoring in her history the advent of the West. His genius was for assimilation, for harmony, for creation. He dedicated his life to opening up the high road by which the thought-treasure of the East may pass to the West, and of the West to the East.

Then there was the day when Bankimchandra invited both East and West to a veritable festival of union in the pages of his *Bangadarshan*. From that day the literature of Bengal felt the call of time, responded to it, and having thus justified herself, took her place on the road to immortality. Bengali literature has made such wonderful progress because she cut through all the artificial bonds which would have hampered her communion with the World literature, and regulated her growth in such wise as to be enabled to make her own, naturally and with ease, the science and ideals of the West. Bankim is great, not merely by what he wrote, but because his genius helped to pave the way for such growth.

Thus, from whatever view-point we take a survey, we see that the epoch-makers of modern India, in whom the greatness of man becomes manifest, are gifted, as the very essence of their nature, with that breadth of understanding in which the differences of East and West do not hurt, or conflict with, one another, but where both find their ultimate harmony.

Many of us who belong to the educated class, think that these attempts at union of the different races belonging to India are for the purpose of gaining political strength. Thus, as in so many other cases, do we view the Great as subservient to the Small. That we in India should attain unity, is a much greater thing than any particular purpose which our union may serve,—for it is a function of our humanity itself. That we are not succeeding in becoming united is due to some basic defect in our manhood, which also is the reason why on every side we perceive our lack of *shakti*. It is our own sin that destroys our *dharma*, which again makes for the destruction of everything else.

Our attempts at Union can only become successful when they are made from the stand-point of Righteousness, which cannot be brought within the confines of any petty pride or narrow expediency. And if Righteousness be our guiding principle these efforts will not remain restricted to the different classes of Indians alone, but the Englishman also needs must join hands in the good work.

What then are we to make of the antagonism which has arisen of late between the Englishman and the Indian, educated as well as uneducated? Is there nothing real in this? Is it only the machination of a few conspirators? Is this antagonism essentially different in purpose from the constant action and reaction of making and breaking which are at work in the making of Indian History? It is very necessary for us to come to a true understanding of its meaning.

In our religious literature, opposition is reckoned as one of the means of union. Ravana, for instance, is said to have gained his salvation because of the valiant fight that he fought. The meaning is simply this, that to have to own defeat after a manful contest with the truth is to gain it all the more completely. To accept with a too ready acquiescence is not a full acceptance at all. This is why all science is based on a severe scepticism.

We began with a blind, foolish, insensate begging at the door of Europe, with our critical sense entirely benumbed. That was not the way to make any real gain. Whether it be wisdom, or political rights, they have to be earned, that is to say to be attained by one's own *shakti*, after a successful struggle against obstructing forces. If they be put into our hands by others, by way of alms, they do not become ours at all. To take in a form which is derogatory can only lead to loss. Hence our reaction against the culture of Europe and its ideals. A feeling of wounded self-respect is prompting us to return upon ourselves.

This revulsion was necessary for the purpose of the History which, as I say, Time is evolving in this land of India. Of what we were receiving weakly, unquestioningly, in sheer poverty of spirit, it was not possible for us to appraise the value: therefore we were unable to appropriate it at its worth, and so to put it to use. It remained with us merely as an ornamental incubus. And when we realised this, our desire to get away from it was only natural.

Rammohan Roy was able to assimilate the ideals of Europe so completely because he was not overwhelmed by them: there was no poverty or weakness on his side. He had ground of his own on which he could take his stand and where he could secure his acquisitions. The true wealth of India was not hidden from him, for this he had already made his own. Consequently he had with him the touchstone by which he could test the wealth of others. He did not sell himself by holding out a beggar's palms, but assessed the true value of whatever he took.

This *shakti* which was natural to our first great leader, is steadily developing itself amongst us through constantly conflicting stresses and strains, actions and reactions. Pendulum-wise do our movements touch now this extreme, now the other. An undue eagerness of acceptance and an undue timidity of rejection assail us by turns. Nevertheless are we being carried forward to our goal?

Our soul which was overburdened with uncritically accumulated foreign ideas has now swung to the opposite extreme of wholesale rejection. But the cause of the present tension of feelings is not this alone.

The West has come as India's guest; we cannot send away the visitor while the object of his visit remains unfulfilled; he must be properly accommodated. But, whatever be the reason,—whether it be some defect in our power of recognition, or the miserliness of the West in revealing itself in its truth,— if the flow of this great purpose of Time should receive a check, there is bound to be a disastrous irruption.

If we do not come into touch with what is true, what is best, in the Englishman; if we find in him merely a merchant, or a military man, or a bureaucrat; if he will not come down to the plane in which man may commune with man and take him into confidence;—if, in fine, the Indian and the Englishman needs must remain apart, then will they be to each other a perennial source of unhappiness. In such case the party which is in power will try to make powerless the dissatisfaction of the weaker by repressive legislation, but will not be able to allay it. Nor will the former find any satisfaction in the situation; and feeling the Indian only to be a source of trouble the Englishman will more and more try to ignore his very existence.

There was a time when high-souled Englishmen like David Hare came very near to us and held up before our hearts the greatness of the English character. The students of that day truly and freely surrendered their hearts to the British connexion. The English professor of to-day not only does not succeed in exhibiting the best that is in his race to his pupils, but he lowers the English ideal in their eyes. As the result, the students cannot enter into the spirit of English literature as they used to do. They gulp it down but do not relish it, and we see no longer the same enthusiastic revelling in the delights of Shakespeare or Byron. The approachment which might have resulted from a genuine appreciation of the same literature has thus received a set-back.

This is not only the case the sphere of education. In no capacity, be it as magistrate, merchant, or policeman, does the Englishman present to us the highest that his racial culture has attained, and so is India deprived of the greatest gain that might have been hers by reason of his arrival; on the contrary, her self-respect is wounded and her powers deprived on every side of their natural development.

All the trouble that we see now-a-days is caused by this failure of East and West to come together. Bound to be near each other, and yet unable to be friends, is an intolerable situation between man and man, and hurtful withal. Therefore, the desire to put an end to it must become overwhelming sooner or later. Such a rebellion, being a rebellion of the heart, will not take account of material gains or losses; it will even risk death.

And yet it is also true that such rebelliousness can only be a temporary phase. In spite of all retarding factors our impact with the West must be made good,—there can be no escape for India until she has made her own whatever there may be worth the taking from the West. Until the fruit is ripe it does not get released from the stem, nor can it ripen at all if it insists on untimely release.

Before concluding I must say one word more. It is we who are responsible for the failure of the Englishman to give us of his best. If we remove our own poverty we can make him overcome his miserliness. We must exert our powers in every direction before the Englishman shall be able to give what he has been sent here to give. If we are content to stand at his door empty-handed we shall only be turned away, again and again.

The best that is in the Englishman is not a thing that may be acquired by us in slothful ease; it must be strenuously won. If the Englishman should be moved to pity that would be the worst thing for us. It is our manhood which must awaken his.

We should remember that the Englishman himself has had to realise his best through supreme toil and suffering. We must cultivate the like power within ourselves. There is no easier way of gaining the best.

Those of us who go to the Englishman's durbar with bowed heads and folded hands, seeking emoluments of office or badges of honour,—we only attract his pettiness and help to distort his true manifestation in India. Those, again, who in a blind fury of passion would violently assail him, succeed in evoking only the sinful side of the Englishman's nature. If, then, it be true that it is our frailty which excites his insolence, his greed, his cowardice or his cruelty, why blame him? Rather should we take the blame on ourselves.

In his own country the Englishman's lower nature is kept under control and his higher nature roused to its fullest capacity by the social forces around him. The social conscience there, being awake, compels each individual, with all its force, to take his stand on a high level and maintain his place there with unceasing effort. In this country, his society is unable to perform the same function. Anglo-Indian society is not concerned with the whole Englishman. It is either a society of civilians, or of merchants, or of soldiers. Each of these are limited by their own business, and become encased in a hard crust of prejudice and superstition. So they develop into thorough-going civilians, or mere merchants, or blatant soldiers. We cannot find the man in them. When the civilian occupies the High-Court bench we are in despair, for whenever there is a conflict between the Right and the civilians' gods, the latter are sure to prevail,—but these gods are inimical to India, nor are they worshipped by the Englishman at his best.

On the other hand, the decay and weakness of the Indian *Samaj* itself is also a bar to the rousing of the true British spirit, wherefore both are losers. It is our own fault, I repeat, that we meet only *Burra Sahebs* and not great Englishmen.

And to this we owe all the sufferings and insults with which we have to put up. We have no remedy but to acknowledge our sin and get rid of it.

Nayamatma balahinena labhyah

Self-realisation is not for the weak—nor the highest truth.

Neither tall talk nor violence, but only sacrifice and service are true tests of strength. Until the Indian can give up his fear, his self-interest, his luxury, in his quest for the best and the highest, in his service of the Motherland, our demanding from the Government will but be empty begging and will aggravate both our incapacity and our humiliation. When we shall have made our country our own by sacrifice and established our claim to it by applying our own powers for its reclamation, then we shall not need to stand abjectly at the Englishman's door. And if we are not abject, the Englishman need not lower himself. Then may we become colleagues and enter into mutual arrangements.

Until we can cast off our individual or *Samajic* folly; as long as we remain unable to grant to our own countrymen the full rights of man; as long as our *zamindars* continue to look on their tenantry as part of their property, our men in power glory in keeping their subordinates under their heels, our higher castes think nothing of looking down on the lowest castes as worse than beasts; so long shall we not have the right or power to demand from the Englishman proper behaviour towards ourselves.

At every turn,—in her religion, in her *samaj*, in her daily practice—does the India of to-day fail to do justice to herself. She does not purify her soul by sacrifice, and so on every side she suffers futility. She cannot meet the outsider on equal terms and so receives nothing of value from him. No cleverness or violence can deliver her from the sufferings and insults of which the Englishman is but the instrument. Only when she can meet him as his equal, will all reason for antagonism, and with it all conflict, disappear. Then will East and West unite in India,—country with country, race with race, knowledge with knowledge, endeavour with endeavour. Then will the History of India come to an end, merged in the History of the World which will begin.